FEDERAL GOVERNMENT AND CRIMINAL JUSTICE

Federal Government and Criminal Justice

Nancy E. Marion

palgrave
macmillan

FEDERAL GOVERNMENT AND CRIMINAL JUSTICE
Copyright © Nancy E. Marion, 2011.

First published in 2011 by PALGRAVE MACMILLAN® in the United States—a division of St. Martin's Press LLC, 175 Fifth Avenue, New York, NY 10010.

Where this book is distributed in the UK, Europe, and the rest of the world, this is by Palgrave Macmillan, a division of Macmillan Publishers Limited, registered in England, company number 785998, of Houndmills, Basingstoke, Hampshire RG21 6XS.

Palgrave Macmillan is the global academic imprint of the above companies and has companies and representatives throughout the world.

Palgrave® and Macmillan® are registered trademarks in the United States, the United Kingdom, Europe and other countries.

ISBN: 978-0-230-11015-1

Library of Congress Cataloging-in-Publication Data

Marion, Nancy E.
    Federal government and criminal justice / Nancy E. Marion.
    p. cm.
    1. Crime—Government policy—United States. I. Title.

HV6789.M345 2011
364.973—dc22   2011008868

A catalogue record of the book is available from the British Library.

Design by Scribe Inc.

First Edition: September 2011

10 9 8 7 6 5 4 3 2 1

Printed in the United States of America.

CONTENTS

1	Introduction	1
I	**Criminal Justice System**	**7**
2	Law Enforcement	9
3	Courts	17
4	Prisons and the Death Penalty	37
II	**Federal Antidrug Policies**	**55**
5	Drugs	57
6	Driving Under the Influence	81
III	**Violent Personal Crimes**	**85**
7	Domestic Violence	87
8	Hate Crimes	95
9	Victims	101
IV	**Minors as Victims and Offenders**	**111**
10	Juvenile Offenders	113
11	Crimes against Children	127
V	**Weapons**	**141**
12	Handguns	143
VI	**Organized Crime**	**161**
13	Underworld Crime	163
14	Pornography and Obscenity	177
15	Wiretaps	183
VII	**Regulatory Offenses**	**189**
16	Internet	191
17	Conclusion	199
	Appendix: Laws Passed	201
	Notes	213
	Index	243

CHAPTER 1

INTRODUCTION

IN 1992 A RELATIVE NEWCOMER TO THE national political scene, William Jefferson Clinton, received the Democratic nomination for the presidency and proceeded to run a successful campaign for the office of the president of the United States. Along the way he made many promises about his plans to reduce crime, one of which was an idea to put 100,000 new police officers on the streets of American cities who would focus on community-oriented policing techniques. This policing style was based on the idea that if police officers spent more time with citizens, then they would get to know them and their businesses, making the police not only more likely to notice irregularities but also able to build more trusting relationships within the community. This meant that when a crime occurred, the police would be more likely to notice it. Further, the citizens would be more willing to approach the police to report the incident and to provide evidence. In the long run Clinton hoped that his program would reduce crime and violence in the streets.

His ideas were passed into law by Congress in the Violent Crime Control and Law Enforcement Act of 1994, which not only created a federal grant program to state and local police to enable them to hire more officers to focus on community polic- ing but also provided money for technology to support community policing such as bikes and radios. Clinton went so far as to create an Office of Community Oriented Policing Services (COPS) within the Department of Justice that would be responsible for administering the community-policing grants. Although some would argue that Clinton's program never reached the ultimate goal of hiring 100,000 new police, the program nonetheless added new officers in many cities and changed the way policing was carried out.

After two terms as president, Clinton left office and was replaced with another relatively new political actor, Republican Governor George W. Bush from Texas. His ideas for reducing crime were much different from Clinton's. Bush wanted to replace the community-policing idea with faith-based reintegration programs that would help inmates turn away from crime and reintegrate into society much more smoothly and in the long run reduce recidivism among ex-offenders.

Looking at the bigger picture, it is clear that when Clinton was in office, the community-policing style was made popular and credited for reducing crime. Many departments were able to hire new officers who were active in the community. How- ever, that policy changed when Bush took office. Local communities were no longer encouraged to support community-policing practices, and funds for community- policing officers were slashed, leaving many local police departments short on funds.

Many departments that expanded their personnel under Clinton's COPS program were forced to cut back. Those departments that had modified how they patrolled their communities returned to their old ways of policing, or the traditional methods of policing, returning officers to their cars for a faster response time. Other departments were forced to fire their community-policing officers altogether because of a lack of funds.

In recent months, the American voters chose yet another relative newcomer to serve as president, Democratic Senator Barack Obama from Illinois. As a senator and presidential candidate, Obama supported reinstating the community-policing program and increasing funding for the "cops on the beat" program initiated under Clinton.[1] As president, Obama has promised to return to the community-oriented police approach by increasing funding to local departments for that purpose. Once again, departments may be able to hire more officers to work in the community with citizens.

From this example it is obvious that local police were impacted by the policies made at the federal level. But it was not only the police who were impacted by the changes in policies of the two administrations. Businesses and communities were impacted as well. When Bush decreased funding for the COPS program, there may have been fewer officers entering stores and businesses to make pleasant conversation with the employees and keep an eye on activities. Communities no longer saw police walking the streets as often and as consistently. Schools may have lost safety officers and Drug Abuse Resistance Education (DARE) officers who were assigned to work the schools. Thus, there were many people impacted by decisions made by the president.

This example demonstrates the role that politics plays in creating public policy about crime and how the federal political system (i.e., the president and Congress) can have serious implications on how state and local officials function on a day-to-day basis. In other words, the decisions made by the elected officials in the federal government about crime can have a substantial impact on how local police departments and communities function. It is clear that the political system helps shape and form the public policy of crime, even at the local level.[2] It is also clear that there are multiple ways to solve or address problems in the criminal justice system, and the chosen method has both long-term and short-term impacts on many agencies and people across the nation.

THE FEDERALIZATION OF CRIME

Until the 1960s, crime control, for the most part, was a state concern. The federal government (i.e., president and Congress) took a hands-off approach and let states decide their crime policies. However, that changed, and through a process called the federalization of crime, policies aimed at limiting criminal behavior were increasingly created by the federal government. Today, crime control is a legitimate policy concern for Congress and the president. The federal government has passed an increasing number of laws and carried out policies to limit criminal behavior.

The federalization of crime refers to the increased activity of the federal government in passing crime control legislation. The federal government has also provided financial assistance to states to help fund crime programs on the local level. More directly, the federal government has widened federal criminal jurisdiction and engaged federal law enforcement agencies in different operational roles that deal directly with violent street crime.[3] In short, the government has defined two roles for themselves in crime control: (1) direct operations and (2) financial assistance.[4]

Presidents and Congress have increased their activity in crime control for many reasons. Some point to the federal government's role in creating and maintaining a society that is crime free and where citizens are safe. In part, elected officials may also be using the issue to increase their support in the public and with voters. When they pass laws to fight crime, politicians appear concerned about the public's safety and can then appeal to the fears that voters may have about becoming a victim of crime. At the same time, politicians may be using the crime issue to send a message to the voters that they are concerned about citizen safety and that they are trying to protect them.

Another reason for increased federal involvement in crime control is that some state criminal justice systems are substantially ineffective, as compared to the potential of the federal government, in the detection, prosecution, or punishment of a particular behavior.[5] In some cases the national government has a distinct advantage, as compared to state criminal justice systems, in controlling some criminal actions such as drug trafficking. These offenses are outside the ability of state law enforcement because of a lack of funds and expertise. It is necessary for the federal government to get involved in these cases.

Yet another reason for more federal involvement in crime was the realization that organized crime groups were active in most major cities across the nation. When the Senate Special Committee to Investigate Crime in Interstate Commerce, or the Kefauver Committee, traveled across the nation to investigate the activities of organized criminal groups during the early 1950s, the nation began to understand the true impact of underground criminal groups. Hundreds of people testified, including top mobsters, law enforcement agents, and politicians about the actions of organized crime. The hearings demonstrated the violence involved in organized crime and the extent of political corruption. Because the hearings were televised, the American public saw these once-mythical figures as real people who committed serious crime and violence. When it was over, many citizens called on Congress for action to punish the members and abolish it. They realized that states were not capable of an attack on organized crime by themselves, as organized crime did not respect state boundaries. Furthermore, states simply did not have the resources. Instead, federal involvement was needed.

A reported increase in drug use during the 1960s was another reason for the increase in federal activity in crime control. Drugs were being used openly by young, middle-class Caucasians. Many people saw the dangers of illicit drug use and blamed the influx of drugs from other nations. Again, this was not a problem that states could fight on their own. Drug traffickers and users did not respect state boundaries, and states simply did not have the resources to implement an effective fight against major international drug traffickers. Thus there was a need for federal involvement.

Not only was drug use increasing but so was crime. The FBI's Uniform Crime Reports indicated that crime and violence were increasing. Violent crime rates reached a peak in the late 1960s and early 1970s.[6] At the same time, there was violence and social unrest due to the Vietnam War protests and civil rights movement.[7] Much of that violence was, for the first time, brought into people's homes through television. This made them fearful of becoming a victim, even if crime in their hometown was minimal. Not only was crime increasing but so was the perception of an increase in crime.

The increased mobility and wider communications that enabled criminal offenders to easily escape the boundaries of local jurisdictions led to more federal action in crime control. In the past bank robbers and bootleggers could escape capture by crossing state lines.[8] Horse racing results could be transmitted easily through telegraph wires before betting was closed, enabling some to place guaranteed bets. Local law enforcement was finding it difficult to enforce some statutes under these circumstances.

As a result political candidates began to recognize the importance of crime for their campaigns. For the first time they began to successfully use the issues related to crime to help reach out to the public for support. Presidential candidates used the issues in their campaigns surrounding violence as a way to get votes and get elected to office.

Republican presidential candidate Barry Goldwater was one of the first to do this. In the 1964 campaign between him and Democratic candidate Lyndon Johnson, crime became an important issue. Goldwater blamed the increase in crime on the liberal Democratic policies that were soft on crime. He argued that his Conservative approach to crime, which included more immediate and harsher punishments, would be more effective in reducing crime in our country than the policies supported by the Democratic candidates. Even though Johnson won the election that year, it made people aware of the problem. Goldwater successfully raised the issue of crime to a national campaign concern. The issues of crime and violence have become a staple for presidential candidates since that campaign. In every campaign since 1964, crime has been discussed by candidates to some extent.

That campaign not only made crime a political issue for candidates but for the first time also made it a presidential concern. When Johnson's crime policies were attacked in the campaign, he made promises about what he would do to fight crime if elected president. When he was elected, Johnson had to follow through with his promises during his presidency. He created the President's Commission on Law Enforcement and Administration of Justice in 1967 to study crime in the United States. The commission's final report was called *The Challenge of Crime in a Free Society*. The committee members found that crime and criminals do not respect state boundaries and that many states were unable to fight crime by themselves. They also discovered that many communities were not able to keep their law enforcement technologically current and needed federal assistance to provide better technology. Based on that finding, Johnson created a grant program called the Law Enforcement Assistance Administration (LEAA) to give federal assistance to states to help them develop their criminal justice systems.[9] With all these actions on crime, Johnson was defining the issue as a legitimate presidential concern. Since then every president has addressed crime issues, though in different ways and to different extents. Crime is now a legitimate policy issue for candidates and presidents alike.

IMPLICATIONS OF FEDERALIZATION

In more recent years Congress has been very active in passing anticrime legislation. In some cases Congress is able to raise a typical criminal act from a state to a federal offense by including the provision of crossing state lines as a necessary factor or showing that something affects interstate commerce. For example, kidnapping remains a state offense until the offender takes the victim across state lines or otherwise travels from one state to another to commit the offense.

There are many examples of congressional action into what many would assume to be traditionally state offenses. For example, in 1984, Congress attached some anticrime proposals to the Fiscal 1985 Continuing Appropriations Resolution that made murder for hire a federal crime when interstate commerce was involved. The new law also made violent crimes such as murder, kidnapping, and assaults federal offenses if they were associated with racketeering activities. The law prohibited "solicitation" to commit a crime of violence, meaning that if a person tried to persuade another to commit a crime of violence, it would be a federal crime (PL 98-473).[10]

In most cases drunk driving is a crime that would be punishable under state law. However, in 1985, the Senate passed S. 850 that made it a federal crime for anyone to operate a train, plane, bus, or ship while under the influence of drugs or alcohol. The attached penalty for violating the proposed law would be a fine of up to $10,000, imprisonment of up to five years, or both. The Senate argued that law was needed because even though there were state laws prohibiting drunk driving and operating a vehicle while under the influence of drugs, there was no federal law covering this area.[11]

In 1992 after a rash of carjackings across the country, the Congress passed a law (H.R. 4542/PL 102-519) that made carjacking, a typical state offense, a new federal offense. The bill also required that major car parts be marked with identification numbers to be registered with the FBI. If the carjacking resulted in a death, the offender could be given a life sentence in prison.

In that same congressional session, members considered many bills that would impose stricter penalties on noncustodial parents who failed to pay their child support obligations. The bill that eventually passed, S. 1002 (PL 102-521), made it a federal crime for parents who lived in another state to avoid paying child support. It limited criminal liability to those who willfully avoided payments. Those parents who could not afford child support payments were not covered by the bill. According to the new law, parents who intentionally avoided making child support payments for six months and owed at least $2,500 could face up to six months in jail and a fine of up to $5,000. Repeat offenders could be sentenced to up to two years in prison and fined as much as $250,000.[12]

In 1994 the Congress passed a major crime bill, part of which included a section on motor vehicle theft, a typical state crime. In the crime bill the Justice Department was given six months to establish a voluntary car theft prevention program. Under the program car owners could agree to use a decal indicating how they used their car—for instance, only for daytime commuting. The police would be authorized to stop the car if it was being used in a matter inconsistent with the decal, on the presumption that it had been stolen. The law also made it a federal crime to alter or remove motor vehicle identification numbers or the new decals. Offenders were subject to fines and up to five years in jail.[13]

Motor vehicle theft was again the topic of new federal legislation in 1996, when Congress cleared legislation directing the Justice Department to set up an electronic information system to allow state motor vehicle departments to check instantly whether a vehicle had been stolen before issuing a title for it (H.R. 2803/PL 104-152). Supporters of the proposal said 140,000 cars were stolen each year in one state and issued titles in another. The new law transferred responsibility for establishing the data base to the Justice Department. The 1992 Anti–Car Theft Act had directed the Transportation Department to set up the system, but the department had failed to meet the deadline specified under the act. The new bill gave the Justice Department until October 1, 1997, to set up the titling database.

This book will present the policy choices made by the presidents and Congress when it comes to solving crime-related problems in the United States. Each chapter will examine different approaches supported by presidents and Congresses to solve a specific crime-related problem. It will show the policies that were only debated by Congress, as well as those that had enough support to be passed and signed into law by the president. Of course the president and Congress are not the only actors in the policy process, and the other actors will be included as well. In Part I, the focus is on elements of the criminal justice system and the policies the presidents and Congress have made concerning police, courts, and prisons. The focus of Part II is federal policies toward drug offenses and drinking and driving. Violent personal crimes, including domestic violence, hate crimes, and victims, are the topics of the chapters in Part III. Federal legislation concerning juveniles, both as offenders and as victims, is the focus of Part IV. Part V examines presidential and congressional activities to reduce gun violence across the nation. Another policy concern to presidents and Congress is organized crime, including pornography and wiretaps, and Part VI comprises this topic. Finally, the last unit of the book, Part VII, examines regulatory policies made by Congress and the president concerning crimes committed with the use of the Internet. Overall, the book presents an analysis of federal action regarding crime issues to determine the role of the federal government in making crime policy.

The information in the following chapters was collected from a variety of sources, most prominently from *Public Papers of the Presidents of the United States, Congressional Quarterly Weekly Reports*, and *Congressional Quarterly Almanacs*. The topics for each chapter more or less came naturally as the bills and laws were organized into categories. Thus it became clear that Congress has either considered or passed laws on a wide variety of crime topics—but with some consistency over the years. Congressional action on terrorism and homeland security were not included in the text as they are not the typical street crimes that one immediately conjures up when thinking of crime. Instead the focus is on criminal offenses domestically that occur with frequency across the nation.

It is clear that Congress and the president have acted to pass many crime-related bills. In the early years of the study, the 1940s and the 1950s, and even through the 1960s, the number of crime bills was more limited, and a description of them was manageable. However, in the more recent decades, the number of crime bills introduced into the House and Senate has become almost overwhelming. It is virtually impossible to list and describe each one in a text such as this. Because of that, not all bills related to the different crimes are included. Instead, particularly in the later years, a sample of the bills is described to give the reader an idea of the types of bill that were introduced and their outcomes. Overall, the chapters provide a comprehensive analysis of what Congress and the president have done to reduce crime and violence in the United States.

Part I

Criminal Justice System

The criminal justice system, comprised of law enforcement, courts, and correctional systems, have each been the topic of federal activity. In Chapter 4, presidential and Congressional responses to issues affecting the police are presented. This includes things like the relationship between the federal, state, and local police, police brutality, and different methods of policing (i.e., traditional policing versus community policing). Each president had a different approach to increasing the effectiveness of the police, and Congress has supported those ideas to different degrees.

The second component of the criminal justice system, the courts, has also seen Congressional and presidential action. Policies have been made regarding equal access to the courts, overcrowding, and court efficiency. Presidents have proposed many policies, and Congress has debated them as well. These actions are the subject of Chapter 5.

The final chapter in this part, Chapter 6, focuses on prisons. This involves federal legislation on the quality of the institutions and how prison inmates are treated. Federal policy has also been made on capital punishment, and this is also described in this chapter.

CHAPTER 2

LAW ENFORCEMENT

OVER THE YEARS PRESIDENTS AND CONGRESS HAVE passed legislation concerning law enforcement issues and have assisted state and local law enforcement in many ways. The assistance has grown over time, which clearly demonstrates the federalization of crime—the federal government getting involved in a typically state issue. These policy debates are discussed in the following sections.

PRESIDENT TRUMAN

In 1945, Harry Truman vetoed H.R. 2856, which was intended to "provide for better enforcement of law within the District of Columbia" because it transferred jurisdiction over felonies committed within the park areas in the District of Columbia from the US Park Police to the Metropolitan Police of the District of Columbia. Truman believed the policy would impair rather than improve law enforcement in these park areas.[1]

PRESIDENT JOHNSON

Lyndon Johnson wanted to improve the quality of local law enforcement throughout the country because police are the frontline in the war on crime. He stated that all Americans wanted and deserved better law enforcement, and he intended to give it to them.[2] One way he saw to do that was to provide higher police salaries since many police departments had been encountering "great difficulties" in recruiting qualified candidates.[3] Thus, in March 1996, he recommended "a substantial increase in police salaries to attract and retain the best qualified officers in the District of Columbia."[4]

Another way Johnson attempted to improve the quality of law enforcement was to provide money for training and education. In 1965 President Johnson proposed and the Congress enacted the Law Enforcement Assistance Act, a grant program for the states to help professionalize police to increase training and technology to fight crime. Johnson hoped that under that program, federal, state, local, and private institutions would work together to improve training of law enforcement personnel.[5] Later he asked Congress "to increase appropriations for the Law Enforcement Assistance Act from $7.2 to $13.7 million."[6] When he signed the Safe Streets Act, Johnson said it established "a pioneering aid-to-education program of forgivable college loans and tuition grants to attract better law enforcement officers and give them better education and preparation."[7] It also provided "greatly expanded training for State and local police officers at the National Academy of the FBI."[8]

In addition, he told the attorney general to make grants available to states, cities, colleges, and university police to intensify their training and effectiveness. He said, "I recommend legislation to establish a program to send selected police officers to approved colleges and universities for a year of intensive professional study. I recommend a loan forgiveness program under the National Defense Education Act for students who wish to enter the law enforcement profession."[9]

President Johnson tried to help the police in other ways. He recommended legislation to extend the authority of police to arrest without a warrant in certain serious offenses, such as assault, unlawful entry, and attempted housebreaking.[10] In the District of Columbia, Johnson wanted to increase the number of civilian employees, expand the Police Cadet Corps, and create a force of seven hundred reserve police officers, to whom he wanted to give certain crime-fighting tools.[11] He wanted the police to have better information and deeper and broader research into the causes, prevention, and control of crime.[12]

1965–66: 89TH CONGRESS

In response to President Johnson's requests, the Congress in 1965 passed H.R. 8027 (PL 89-197), the Law Enforcement Assistance Act (LEAA). This new law provided federal assistance for states to upgrade the quality of local law enforcement. Previously, federal assistance to local law enforcement officers was largely limited to training sessions sponsored by the Federal Bureau of Investigation (FBI). Under the new law, the attorney general was authorized to make grants for studies of new police procedures and for demonstration projects of such new techniques. The aim was to determine the efficacy of new methods of crime control and to make those methods available to local law officers.[13]

1967–68: 90TH CONGRESS

This session, Congress did not pass H.R. 11816 or S. 798, which were bills to provide disability and death benefits for state and local police officers injured or killed while enforcing federal laws.

PRESIDENT NIXON

Richard Nixon did not like cases of police brutality and asked the attorney general to make all appropriate investigative resources available to work jointly with state or local police in any case involving an assault upon a police officer.[14] Instead, he wanted to focus on strengthening local law enforcement through the special revenue sharing fund.[15] Nixon wanted to expand the massive funding for local law enforcement assistance and wanted to have law enforcement special revenue sharing.[16] He sent Congress a proposal for special revenue sharing in the field of law enforcement assistance for $500 million.[17] In the following year, he wanted to increase assistance to local law enforcement to over $1.2 million.[18]

1969–70: 91ST CONGRESS

During this session, Congress acted on Nixon's proposals for funding of state law enforcement and authorized an increase in federal aid to state and local agencies. The bill (H.R. 17825/PL 91-644) authorized $3.55 billion for the LEAA, which would channel funds to such agencies.[19]

In addition, the Senate Judiciary Subcommittee on Internal Security held hearings on bills dealing with assaults on police, but no final action was taken on them. The bills included the following:

1. S. 4325: to enable the FBI to join the search for killers of a policeman or fireman within 24 hours of the crime. If an offender crossed state lines to avoid prosecution for such a crime, it would be a federal offense. If no one was apprehended for the crime within 24 hours, it would be assumed that the suspect had fled across state lines.
2. S. 4348: to make it a federal crime to assault, injure, or kill a state or local law enforcement officer, judge, or fireman because of his position.
3. S. 4403 (the Urban Terrorism Prevention Act): to ban the advocacy of urban terrorism, to license all manufacturers and distributors of explosives, and to provide greatly increased penalties for terrorist activities.[20]

1975–76: 94TH CONGRESS

Congress passed H.R. 366 (PL 94-430), a measure to provide federal death benefits to the families of public safety officers killed in the line of duty. The bill authorized federal payments of $50,000 to the survivors of fire fighters, police, and other law enforcement officers killed performing their jobs. The eligibility standards allowed for both accidental and criminal causes of death. Similar proposals failed during the 92nd and 93rd Congresses.[21]

PRESIDENT REAGAN

Ronald Reagan wanted to increase resources to federal law enforcement agencies for apprehension, conviction, and incarceration purposes.[22] In 1984, he introduced legislation to ban the manufacture and importation of bullets designed to penetrate the soft-body armor worn by law enforcement officers, called "cop-killer" bullets.[23] He signed a bill to regulate armor-piercing ammunition (H.R. 3132) that would ban the production or importation of these bullets.[24]

1989–90: 101ST CONGRESS

An omnibus crime bill was passed (S. 1970, H.R. 5269; S. 3266; PL 101-647) that, among other things, included provisions relating to police. The law authorized up to $900 in new federal aid for local law enforcement and called for an increase in federal agents, including 1,000 new agents for the Drug Enforcement Agency (DEA) agents.[25]

1991–92: 102ND CONGRESS

After the televised beating of Rodney King, the House proposed and passed, as part of the crime bill (H.R. 3371), provisions of another measure (H.R. 2972) that would have given the attorney general additional authority to sue a police department in an effort to stop practices of police misconduct. The intent was to give the Justice Department much greater latitude in the war against police brutality. The bill would have also required the Justice Department to collect and publish statistical information on the use of excessive force by police. But the crime bill was stalled and neither chamber took up H.R. 2972 as a freestanding bill.[26]

PRESIDENT CLINTON

As a candidate for president, William Clinton promised to provide funding to allow local departments to hire add an additional 100,000 officers that would focus on community policing.[27] He argued that this style of policing helped prevent crime and lower the crime rate, as well as establish better relationships between law enforcement and the citizens in the community. Furthermore, he argued that community policing reduces the chances of abusive action by police officers and increases the chances of harmony and safe streets.[28] In 1993, he proposed a crime initiative to help meet that goal, including grants to states and localities to recruit officers and a police corps program to provide assistance for education in exchange for a commitment to work as a police officer.[29] In 1998, he reported that the Department of Justice would fund over seven hundred new community police officers who would be on the beat specifically to fight crime in troubled areas, including Chicago, Baltimore, and Miami.[30]

In 1995, Clinton announced support for legislation to ban armor-piercing bullets. He said that "if a bullet can rip through a bullet-proof vest like a knife through hot butter, then it ought to be history. We should ban it."[31] He also provided grants to provide bulletproof vests to police.[32]

CONGRESS

1993–94: 103RD CONGRESS

In H.R. 3398, restrictions of a particularly dangerous new bullet, known as "Black Talon" bullets, passed the Judiciary Crime Subcommittee. The bullets opened on impact to reveal spikes that tore flesh.[33] Congress did not pass this bill.

A major crime bill (H.R. 3355/H.R. 4092/S. 1607; PL 103-322) was passed in 1994, which included many new provisions concerning law enforcement. One proposed program was called "Cops on the Beat," a new grant program intended to boost community policing. The aim was to send more police into neighborhoods where they would be more visible and could develop closer ties to the community. When passed, the law provided $8.8 billion to help communities hire 100,000 new community policing officers.[34] If a local government received the money, a portion of the grant money could be used for training or equipment to enhance community policing programs, but the bulk of the money had to be used to put more officers on the street.

Additionally, the bill created a police corps program, administered by the Justice Department, to grant college or graduate scholarships for students who agreed to serve as state or local police officers for at least four years. Participants who did not honor their commitments to serve as police officers had to repay the scholarships plus 10 percent interest.

The bill also supported recruitment of new police officers. The bill authorized $24 million a year for grants to help recruit and train police officers from minority neighborhoods and other areas that were underrepresented on the police force.

The families of law enforcement were not forgotten in the bill. The Congress authorized $25 million for grants to help state and local law enforcement agencies develop family-friendly policies for their officers. This could include offering family counseling, 24-hour child-care services and stress-reduction programs.

The bill had provisions on police misconduct. The new law allowed the attorney general to sue for civil relief to prohibit law enforcement officials or government authorities from engaging in a pattern of behavior that denied the civil rights of individuals. The measure required the attorney general to collect annual data on the use of excessive force by law enforcement officers.[35]

Other provisions of the bill authorized grant money for different purposes. For example, $245 million was authorized to be used to help enforce antidrug laws in rural areas. Additional funds, specifically $40 million, were reserved to help state officials develop and use DNA tests. The FBI would help states establish minimum state and federal standards regarding the quality of DNA tests and confidentiality of the results. The Congress authorized $130 million in federal assistance to state, local, and tribal criminal justice agencies to improve their training and technological capabilities. Other funds were made available to help improve computer capabilities such as automated fingerprint identification. Training programs, pilot programs for gathering and analyzing information to solve violent serial crimes, and upgrading facilities at the FBI's training center were provided funds.

In another bill (H.R. 4922), telecommunications companies would be required to ensure that their networks and services could be wiretapped. Those opposed to the bill are concerned about privacy issues, but those in support of the bill argue it is necessary to keep up with today's technological advances.

1995–96: 104TH CONGRESS

In 1995, the Republicans wanted to replace Clinton's police hiring program with flexible anticrime block grants. They attempted to change the appropriations bill for the Departments of Commerce, Justice, State, and the Judiciary (H.R. 2076). Clinton vetoed this measure, citing this change as a major reason for his opposition.[36] A similar bill, H.R. 728, would create a $10 billion block grant program for crime reduction that would replace the grant programs established in the 1994 crime bill. The money could be used for crime prevention programs, such as hiring additional officers or purchasing school security equipment.

In 1996, the parties continued discussing the police hiring program. During passage of the fiscal year (FY) 1996 Omnibus Appropriations Bill, congressional members had discussions about the "cops-on-the-beat" grant programs. Republicans criticized the program as heavy-handed intrusion into local crime fighting and proposed to replace it with a flexible anticrime block grant that communities could use as they saw fit. But police groups and others defended the program. Republicans ultimately agreed to provide $1.4 billion for the program—compared with the $1.9 billion requested by the president. Clinton had threatened to veto any legislation that sought to dismantle the police hiring programs.

1997–98: 105TH CONGRESS

H.R. 4112, the Fiscal 1999 appropriations bill, included significant increases for the Capitol police after two officers died in a shootout in the Capitol. The officers would receive a 12 percent increase, with overtime pay for those officers who work nights, holidays, and Sundays. The bill became law (PL 105-275).

1999–2000: 106TH CONGRESS

The House passed H.R. 4999, the Local Government Law Enforcement Block Grants Act, that would authorize $2 billion annually for the following five years for block grants for local law enforcement agencies. The money could be used for activities such as buying equipment, hiring officers, or paying for security measures in and around schools or government buildings. This bill did not pass during this session.

PRESIDENT BUSH

Most of George W. Bush's proposals for law enforcement related to terrorism. He asked Congress for the tools and resources necessary to disrupt, weaken, and defeat terrorists. He was pleased when Congress agreed to legislation that gave these tools to law enforcement officials.[37]

2001–2: 107TH CONGRESS

The USA Patriot Act (H.R. 3162) was passed by Congress after the terrorist attacks of September 11, 2001, gave law enforcement greater authority to conduct searches of property and removed the statute of limitations on some crimes related to terrorism. Further, information received during grand jury proceedings could then be provided to law enforcement. Law enforcement could seize voice mail messages, get subpoenas to obtain credit card and bank account numbers, and use "sneak and peek" searches, which involved searching suspects' property without notifying them if it is believed that notice of a search would have an "adverse effect."[38] This bill was passed by the Congress and signed by the president (PL 107-56).

In S. 2720, the Legislative Branch Appropriations Bill, Senate members included an amendment that provided a 5 percent pay raise to Capitol police officers and a 4.1 percent cost of living increase. The reason for the pay raise was the number of Capitol police leaving the force and better-paying jobs on other police forces. This was enacted into law (PL 107-209). Another appropriations bill, H.R. 2647, would give the Capitol police an 18 percent raise and allow for 79 new officers. The raises would bring the pay scale to equal the pay of other federal law enforcement officers. This proposal became law (PL 107-68).

In H.R. 965, House members considered but did not pass a proposal titled the Racial Profiling Prohibition Act. If passed the law would have the Secretary of Transportation withhold transportation funds from those states that did not choose to adopt and enforce specific policies that prohibited the use of racial profiling when policing the roads and highways. In a similar Senate proposal (S. 989), if it can be proven that an agency used racial profiling, a civil suit could be brought. Neither of these proposals passed.

In S. 924 and H.R. 2009, the Community Oriented Policing Services (COPS) Program would be reauthorized. This bill was titled the Protection Act from "Providing Reliable Officers, Technology, Education, Community Prosecutors, and Training in Our Neighborhoods Act." It would provide money to increase prosecutor presence, enhance new technologies for law enforcement, and provide for more training for law enforcement personnel. The bill did not pass.

2005–6: 109TH CONGRESS

During this session, the Congress considered legislation (S. 1145/H.R. 2662) called the Local Law Enforcement Enhancement Act of 2005. This bill, which did not pass, was intended to provide federal assistance to state and local police agencies in successful prosecution of hate crimes. It authorized the attorney general to provide technical, forensic, and prosecutorial assistance to local law enforcement if it was considered to be an offense committed because of race, color, religion, gender, or sexual orientation against the victim.

2007–8: 110TH CONGRESS

The Library of Congress police would become Capitol police under a reorganizational bill proposed in the House (H.R. 3690). The merger was proposed as a way to streamline security in the two complexes. This proposal was signed by the president and became law (PL 110-178).

Lawmakers in the House passed H.R. 1700 to increase the authorization for the COPS program to $1.15 billion. The law would help state and local law enforcement agencies hire more police officers to focus on some aspect of community policing. The bill also included increased funding to support a recruiting program to hire military veterans who were interested in pursuing a career in law enforcement. The proposal was not signed into law.

The Campus Law Enforcement Emergency Response Act of 2007 (S. 1228) was considered in the Senate. This proposal would amend the Higher Education Act of 1965 regarding law enforcement emergencies. If passed, colleges and universities would be required to provide information concerning its law enforcement emergency response program and the number of law enforcement emergencies to prospective students and employees. This proposal did not make it to the president's desk for his approval.

Another bill considered in the Senate but not passed was S. 2956, titled the Incorporation Transparency and Law Enforcement Assistance Act. This was a proposal to assist law enforcement in detecting, preventing, and punishing terrorism, money laundering, and other offenses that involved US corporations. One provision would require additional identification requirements for owners of corporations, and another would require ownership disclosure information for those who are not citizens of the United States.

PRESIDENT OBAMA

Barack Obama supported law enforcement. He honored the work of police in his remarks at the national Peace Officers' Memorial on May 15, 2010.[39] He called Arizona's immigration law "misguided"; the law allowed for local and state law enforcement officials to determine an individual's immigration status whenever there is reasonable suspicion exists that an individual is in the country illegal.[40]

2009–10: 11TH CONGRESS

A bill to provide police officers and criminal investigators with the authority to execute warrants, make arrests, and carry firearms was proposed in the House during this session of Congress. Under the bill, H.R. 675, officers could make an arrest without a warrant for any offense committed in their presence or for a felony offense when the officer has probable cause to believe that person committed the offense. This bill was not sent to the president for his approval.

The Law Enforcement Officer's Procedural Bill of Rights Act of 2009 was a bill in the House (H.R. 1972) that did not become law. Under the proposal, the due process rights would be granted to a law enforcement officer who was the subject of an investigation or disciplinary hearing. Procedural protection would be granted to the officer before and during any investigation that could result in disciplinary action. These protections include the right to effective counsel, the right to be interrogated at a reasonable hour, and written notice of the findings of the investigation.

The Enhanced Violent Crime Community Policing Act of 2009 was a proposal in the House (H.R. 3154/S. 1424). The proposal would allow for grants that could be used to hire and train new law enforcement officers who would be assigned to communities with high violent crime rates. The proposal did not pass.

Another House proposal that did not pass was H.R. 3752, the Law Enforcement Officers Safety Improvements Act. This proposal would allow for an expanded definition of "law enforcement officer" to include retired law enforcement officers and Amtrak police agents. If passed, these officers could legally carry concealed weapons.

CONCLUSION

Today's executive and legislative branches are actively creating new ways to help police function more effectively to keep communities (and people) safe. This is one area where the federalization of crime is apparent. Congress and the president have proposed many different policies to provide funding for education and training of law enforcement, for hiring of new officers, and for equipment. Showing support for law enforcement is a popular topic for politicians. It is a subject that can be used to show their concern for the safety of citizens and one where they can easily reach out to voters.

CHAPTER 3

COURTS

THE UNITED STATES HAS A DUAL COURT system, meaning that there are courts on the federal, state, and local levels, each with a different jurisdiction or type of case it can hear. Each of these courts, regardless of their jurisdiction, faces problems such as overcrowding, backlogs, and sentencing disparities. The solutions to the problems are not always popular, and there are debates about how to deal with the issues. Over the years, presidents and Congress alike have proposed, debated, and even passed new policies to help the courts be more efficient and provide justice more fairly.

PRESIDENT TRUMAN

In a letter to the vice-president, Harry Truman expressed concern over a bill in the Senate concerning pay raises for federal executives, including judges. He said that judicial salaries were inadequate, so it had become increasingly difficult to get and keep qualified employees. Calling the then current salaries "ridiculously low," Truman argued that the passage of the legislation then pending in the Senate would help the situation tremendously, and he urged the Senate to act favorably on the bill.[1]

1949–50: 81ST CONGRESS

In 1949, the Congress passed H.R. 4963 (PL 81-205) that created 6 new circuit judgeships, 21 new district judgeships, and authorized the appointment of 27 additional federal judges to fill them.[2] Another bill, H.R. 6454 (PL 81-691), created two additional federal judgeships for the Illinois northern district (Chicago).[3]

In 1950, Congress focused on judicial oversight. Senator William Knowland (R-CA) said that the federal judiciary was getting top-heavy with Democrats and recommended that more Republicans be named to the posts by the president. The ratio of judges at the time was 224 Democrats to 84 Republicans. Concurrently, the Senate Judiciary Committee voted to have a five-man subcommittee watch over the federal bench to look for judicial competence, fitness, and the legal qualifications of all federal judges.[4]

1951–52: 82ND CONGRESS

The Senate passed S. 1203 to create 19 new permanent federal district and circuit judgeships, but the measure failed.[5]

PRESIDENT EISENHOWER

In 1953, Dwight Eisenhower created a conference composed of representatives of different departments, the judiciary, and the bar to study problems in the courts such as unnecessary delay, expense, and volume of records in some adjudicatory and rule-making proceedings in the Executive Departments and Administrative Agencies.[6] In 1960, Eisenhower recommended that the Congress create additional federal judgeships to help alleviate some of those problems. The original recommendation was made by the Judicial Conference, which recommended 40 new judges.[7] The recommendation for more judges was supported by virtually every professional organization concerned with the administration of the courts. The president said there was an urgent need for more judges in the federal courts to hear the greatly increased number of cases being filed each year, and he urged swift action on the pending measure.[8]

When asked if he was glad that Congress decided to raise the pay of judges, he agreed and said that he had spoken to many young men who had to decline judicial appointments because they needed money to live. Eisenhower noted that in the past, judges had been badly underpaid, and they should be paid better.[9]

CONGRESS

1953–54: 83RD CONGRESS

Early on, the House and Senate could not agree on the number of new federal judgeships needed. The Senate called for creation of 39 new seats on the federal bench, whereas the House version would have added only 26 new posts.[10] The House and Senate eventually agreed to a compromise measure, creating 30 new federal judgeships in S. 15 (PL 83-294).[11]

Salary increases for federal judiciary were recommended by the Commission on Judicial and congressional salaries, but Congress took no action.[12]

1957–58: 85TH CONGRESS

The president and chief justice both supported legislation that created new judicial positions in this session. The Congress considered 20 bills that would create 26 additional judgeships, but only 1 of these received both House and Senate approval (S. 2413/PL 85-310). The new law provided an additional South Dakota district court judge.

Two additional measures that promised to afford some relief for the overburdened judiciary were considered by Congress as well. One raised the amount that must be in controversy in civil actions between citizens of different states before the cases could be taken before the federal courts. The amount was raised from $3,000 to $10,000. The other bill provided that the administrative duties of chief judges would be transferred when they reached the age of 70 to the next ranking judge.[13]

Another measure (H.R. 110/PL 85-261) permitted appointment of an additional judge to a federal court from which an incumbent judge, though found physically or mentally disabled by the Judicial Council of the circuit, declined to retire. This bill was requested by the Judicial Conference.[14]

1959–60: 86TH CONGRESS

Once again, Congress attempted to alleviate the overburdened federal court system by proposing more judgeships. The Senate Judiciary Committee reported a bill (S. 890) to create 25 new federal judgeships, but the bill never reached the floor.[15] The House members debated H.R. 6159—also a bill to create new judgeships. In the end, even though bills were introduced into both chambers, no final action was taken in either house.[16]

PRESIDENT KENNEDY

John Kennedy requested the attorney general submit legislation to the Congress that would create 59 additional judgeships to relieve serious congestion and delays in many federal Courts.[17] In another action, he signed legislation that authorized 73 new judicial positions in the district courts and in the courts of appeals.[18]

In 1963, Kennedy sent Congress a proposal that would diminish the role that poverty played in the federal system of criminal justice. The proposal would assure effective legal representation for every person whose limited means would otherwise deprive him or her of an adequate defense against criminal charges.[19]

PRESIDENT JOHNSON

Lyndon Johnson asked Congress to pass legislation to reform the bail system by passing the Federal Bail Reform Act. As a result of the new law, the right to bail was no longer dependent on a person's income.[20] He believed the act would be a model for those states and communities that had not already undertaken bail reform.[21] When he signed the bill, he recognized that it was the nation's first real reform of the bail system since 1789. Johnson also sought legislation from Congress that would establish a Federal Judicial Center in the Administrative Office of the U.S. Courts. As he explained it, the center would provide better judicial administration to reduce court delays. It would enable the courts to begin a review of their operations and conduct research and planning that would be necessary for a more effective judicial system and for "better justice in America."[22] He said that the Federal Judicial Center would create a more modern federal court system.

Johnson recommended some reforms to the trial system. One change was to require counsel for those defendants who planned to plead insanity to give advance notice to the prosecution.[23] Along those lines, Johnson supported legislation to permit the government to appeal a pretrial court order granting a motion to suppress evidence.[24]

Jurors were also a concern for Johnson. He wanted to combat discrimination in jury selection,[25] so he proposed legislation to make it unlawful to discriminate on the basis of race, color, religion, sex, national origin, or economic status in either qualifying or selecting jurors in any state court.[26]

Legislation that would compel people to give testimony concerning activities linked with organized crime, also called "immunity legislation," was on the top of Johnson's agenda.[27] He wanted to be able to punish those who used violence and intimidation to prevent others from testifying.[28]

In 1968, Johnson asked Congress to provide funds to allow adding 100 additional assistant US attorneys around the country. He also requested more funds for more than 100 additional agents for the Federal Bureau of Investigation (FBI) and for a substantial increase in the number of lawyers for the Criminal Division of the Justice Department.[29] He supported congressional legislation to increase the number of judges on the court from 12 to 16 and to increase the compensation of the chief judge of the court from $24,000 a year to $28,000 and that each associate judge received an increased compensation from $23,500 to $27,500.[30]

A proposal to create a unified local court system in the District of Columbia received support from the president. He asked the mayor to study the proposal and to develop legislation that would create a unified local court system of the highest excellence for the nation's capital.[31]

Johnson signed a law to replace US Commissioners with the Office of United States Magistrates. He believed that the new policy would bring new standards of professionalism and a higher quality of justice to the judiciary. He explained that commissioners perform such responsibilities as issuing search and arrest warrants, holding arraignments and preliminary hearings, setting bail, and sometimes conducting trials of minor criminal offenses. But though these functions involved complicated legal issues, many of the commissioners were not lawyers. This new act required that magistrates be lawyers.[32]

Overall, President Johnson made many recommendations for improving the federal and state court systems. Many of his ideas were new, and many were consistent with his liberal ideas about society and the criminal justice system.

CONGRESS

1965–66: 89TH CONGRESS

In this session, there were two changes made to increase the efficiency of the courts. Congress passed S. 1666 (PL 89-372), which created 45 new federal judgeships, 10 at the circuit court of appeals level and 35 at the district court level.[33] The purpose of the law was to reverse the growing backlog of cases on the dockets of many federal courts.

Congress passed another law (S. 1357/PL 89-465), the Bail Reform Act of 1966, that set up new procedures for the release of federal prisoners who were charged with noncapital offenses. The bill was aimed at removing inequities in detaining accused persons who were too poor to raise bail. The act represented the first significant reform in federal bail legislation since the basic federal law on bail was passed in 1789. The new law provided for the release of persons charged with noncapital federal offenses unless it appeared that they were unlikely to return for trial. Federal district judges were given discretion to impose a number of conditions on release, including release in custody of another person, restrictions on travel or association, cash deposit toward bond, full bail bond, or any other condition deemed reasonably necessary to assure the person's appearance as required. The act provided for the release of persons charged with a capital crime or convicted of a crime unless there was a danger to the community. The act also provided for giving credit toward sentence for any time served in jail awaiting trial. Penalties for failing to appear as required were included in the new law.[34]

1967–68: 90TH CONGRESS

Congress enacted H.R. 6111 (PL 90-219) to establish a Federal Judicial Center in the Administrative Office of the United States Courts. The center would undertake analysis, research, and planning to improve the efficiency of the federal court system in order to improve the operations of the federal judiciary.[35]

Members of Congress also considered H.R. 8654, a proposal to provide defendants with the right to appeal decisions to suppress evidence. In other words, it allowed the government to obtain an appellate court ruling on the admissibility of evidence before a trial begins. The bill had the support of the American Bar Association (ABA) and the Justice Department but did not pass.[36]

A bill that did pass was S. 676/S. 2188 (PL 90-123), which made it a federal crime to obstruct federal criminal investigations. The president requested the bill early in 1967. The law extended existing law that protected federal witnesses so that it also included potential witnesses, including informants.

PRESIDENT NIXON

Like Johnson, Richard Nixon was very active in attempts to improve the courts. To begin, he asked Congress to provide ten more judges for the courts of the District of Columbia.[37] In 1970, Nixon signed S. 952 (PL 91-272), which provided for the appointment of additional district judges to help reduce the tremendous backlogs of cases that now clog the calendars of federal courts.[38]

He also wanted to provide for a reorganization and restructuring of the court system. He wanted modern computer and management techniques and additional courthouse personnel.[39] In that regard, Nixon signed the District of Columbia Court Reform and Criminal Procedure Act of 1970 (S. 2601/PL 91-358).[40]

Nixon wanted to expand a pilot program for a public defender system in the District of Columbia, the Legal Aid Agency. The pilot project was successful elsewhere, and he wanted to convert this project into a full-fledged public defender program.[41] In 1971, he proposed creating a separate, nonprofit Legal Services Corporation (LSC). The lawyers in the program would have the freedom to protect the best interest of their clients in keeping with the Canons of Ethics and the high standards of the legal profession. He stressed that the nation should continue to give the program the support it needed in order to become a permanent and vital part of the American system of justice.[42] In another attempt to provide legal assistance to indigent offenders, Nixon asked the Congress to pass the Criminal Justice Act Amendments, which would institute fundamental and urgently needed reforms in the provision of legal defenders for poor persons. He explained that vigorous and competent legal defense is fundamental, and it results in justice for not only the accused but also the accuser.[43]

Nixon asked the Congress to pass the Bail Reform Act Amendments. He stated that the proposal to reform the bail system would authorize a judge, after a hearing, to detain a person charged with certain categories of federal crimes, if it was discovered that he or she posed a danger to another person or to the community if released.[44]

He wanted to appoint judges to the court who would strictly construe the Constitution and particularly whose record was strong whenever the question came up of coming down hard on the side of the peace forces as opposed to the criminal forces in the country.[45] He promised to appoint judges who would help to strengthen law enforcement who were fighting against criminals and who would oppose the permissive trend toward light or suspended sentences for convicted drug pushers.[46]

In 1971, Nixon endorsed the National Center for the State Courts, also endorsed by Supreme Court Chief Justice Warren E. Burger. The center would help states conduct research into problems of procedure, administration, and training for state and local judges and other administrative personnel. It would also be a clearinghouse for the exchange of information about state or local court problems and reforms.[47]

CONGRESS

1969–70: 91ST CONGRESS

Congress approved a bill (S. 952/PL 91-272) that provided for the appointment of a court executive for each judicial circuit. This executive would handle administrative problems that were often handled by the chief judge of each circuit.[48] The executive would be appointed by the judicial council of each circuit, which would also determine the administrative duties it considered to be suitable for the court executive. The executive would be certified for the appointment by a board of certification. The salary for the court executive would be determined by the Judicial Conference of the United States.

A federal and community defender system was created by Congress when they cleared a bill (S. 1461/PL 91-447) that expanded coverage of the Criminal Justice Act of 1964.[49] The law authorized the appointment and compensation of counsel for people charged with a crime (including juveniles) but who were financially unable to secure legal counsel. Appointed counsel would be available in all proceedings related to the actual trial procedures. The hourly rate of payment for the court-appointed counsel was increased to $30 for in-court hours and $20 for out-of-court hours and raised the maximum payment for each attorney in a case.

The new law provided that any district or part of a district in which there were at least 200 people each year who required court-appointed counsel could choose to establish a federal public defender organization or a community defender organization. A federal public defender organization would consist of salaried federal attorneys who operated under the supervision of a federal public defender who was appointed by the circuit's judicial council. A community defender organization, or a nonprofit defense counsel service administered by an authorized organization, could initially be funded by a federal grant and could receive periodic sustaining federal grants.[50]

1971–72: 92ND CONGRESS

The Senate Judiciary Committee on Constitutional Rights held five days of hearings on a proposed bill, S. 895, called the Speedy Trial Act of 1971. The proposal mandated guaranteed trials within 60 days of indictment and trials in federal criminal cases within 60 days of indictment or dismissal of the charge.[51] The proposal did not pass.

A Senate Judiciary Subcommittee held hearings on a bill (S. 3309) that would provide for a community-centered rehabilitation program for those people who were accused of nonviolent federal crimes. However, the proposal went nowhere.

Hearings were also held on a bill (H.R. 11441) that would limit habeas corpus relief to people being held in state prisons. But this bill did not pass either.

1973–74: 93RD CONGRESS

The Senate passed S. 271, which eliminated the requirement for three-judge district courts in cases involving attacks on the constitutionality of federal or state laws. The bill eliminated the requirement that suits attacking federal or state laws as unconstitutional and asking that the court order these laws not be enforced be heard by a panel of three federal district judges, instead of only one judge. Appeals of the decisions from these panels would be taken directly to the Supreme Court, instead of moving first to the circuit court of appeals. This shortcut would be eliminated by S. 271. Additionally, under provisions of the bill, three judge panels would still be convened when specifically required by an act of Congress or in any case involving congressional reapportionment or the reapportionment of any statewide legislative body. There was no House action on the bill.[52]

Congress failed to complete action on S. 798, designed to set up a system of pretrial diversion and community supervision and services for selected criminal defendants.[53]

In this session, Congress failed to complete action on a bill (S. 1064) that was designed to bring the statute concerning judicial disqualification from a case in line with the newly adopted code of judicial ethics. The new code broadened the circumstances under which judges should excuse themselves from hearing a case to include all cases in which their impartiality might reasonably be questioned.[54]

PRESIDENT FORD

Gerald Ford believed in a more conservative approach to crime control. He thought it was essential that there be less delay in bringing arrested people to trial, less plea bargaining, and more courtroom determination of guilt or innocence. He also wanted to see that all, or practically all, of the people convicted of predatory crimes would be sent to prison.[55]

Ford supported mandatory sentences. He believed that the sentencing provisions of the then-proposed federal code should be modified to provide judges with standards concerning which prison sentences should be imposed on conviction.[56] He also proposed that the Congress enact mandatory prison sentences for those who committed federal offenses with firearms or other dangerous weapons and for airplane hijackers, kidnappers, traffickers in hard drugs, and repeated federal offenders who commit crimes of violence. Mandatory sentences for crimes that show a potential or actual cause of physical injury were needed, according to Ford. He believed that state and local authorities could take similar steps in this area.[57]

The president proposed changes in the courts, too. He requested a comprehensive review of administration efforts on judicial improvements and an examination of the problems facing the judiciary.[58] Citing a recommendation from the Judicial Conference for the creation of 51 additional federal district court judgeships, Ford called for increasing the number of judges, a recommendation he strongly supported.[59] He promised to work to convince Congress that such action was required.[60]

CONGRESS

1975–76: 94TH CONGRESS

In 1975, the Congress worked on different bills to reduce court congestion. Since the number of judgeships was last increased in 1970, the Senate passed a bill (S. 286) to authorize seven additional judgeships for the US Court of Appeals, but the House took no action on it. Another bill (S. 287) authorized 45 additional district court judgeships in 28 states and Puerto Rico. It was reported by the Judiciary Committee but never reached the Senate floor, nor did the House take any action.[61]

In another attempt to reduce overcrowding of the federal courts, Congress passed S. 537 (PL 94-381), which eliminated the need for three-judge courts in certain situations. The new law eliminated the requirement that three-judge courts be convened whenever an injunction was requested against the enforcement of state or federal laws on grounds of unconstitutionality. The bill did not affect the convening of three-judge courts in cases of congressional or state legislative apportionment, or in cases specifically mandated by Congress. Those supporting the bill said the situations that existed that gave rise to three-judge courts to avoid the arbitrary actions of single judges were no longer applicable.[62]

An idea for a new court, a National Court of Appeals, was presented in S. 2762. The court would hear cases that involved important and controversial issues of federal law that the Supreme Court had not considered. Opponents to the idea argued that it would create an unnecessary layer of judicial review and dilute the influence of the Supreme Court.[63]

A major crime bill, S. 1, which passed in the Judiciary Subcommittee, included a section on the insanity defense. Under the law at the time, insanity had been court defined and therefore variable throughout the United States. Under the existing law, an accused person who carried out a crime while mentally ill should be acquitted if, as a result of the mental illness, he or she was unable to refrain from offending. The new bill would allow insanity as a criminal defense only if the insanity caused a lack of the state of mind required as an element of the offense charged. Mental disease or defect would not otherwise constitute a criminal defense.[64]

A bill that made significant changes to the rules of criminal procedure was passed in this session. H.R. 6799 (PL 94-64) made changes to pretrial discovery, defense of alibis, plea bargaining, summonses and arrest warrants, and the insanity defense. Many of the changes were proposed by the Supreme Court and the US Judicial Conference.[65]

PRESIDENT CARTER

Jimmy Carter supported many changes for court reform, such as merit selection of judges. He said that the proposed Omnibus Judgeship Act, then pending in Congress, would provide a test for the concept of merit selection. The proposed law would also create 152 federal judgeships and expand the functions and the jurisdiction of federal magistrates to reduce the burden on federal judges.[66]

In 1978, Carter announced a program to reform the federal civil justice system.[67] Carter's program consisted of two parts. First, he wanted to develop new ways to handle disputes that did not necessarily require full court resolution. Second, he wanted to provide the courts with sufficient resources and improved procedures so they could function fairly and effectively in those cases brought before them.[68]

Carter presented a bill to Congress that would enlarge the civil and criminal jurisdiction of federal magistrates so they could decide less serious criminal matters so that the capacity of the federal courts would be substantially increased. He also suggested a bill that would improve the means available to the people for resolving everyday disputes, such as complaints by neighbors, customers, tenants, and family members.[69]

CONGRESS

1977–78: 95TH CONGRESS

The LSC was reauthorized for three years this legislative session in H.R. 6666 (PL 95-222). The corporation was originally created by Congress in 1974 to provide lawyers for indigent defendants through grants to locally based programs. The original law creating the LSC included many restrictions on the types of cases that legal services lawyers could handle, because those opposed to the program argued that legal service lawyers were too inclined to engage in social activism while representing their clients. The new bill increased the authorization levels for the program and removed or modified many of the restrictions included in the original bill. The House and the Senate debated a provision to prohibit attorneys from working on school desegregation cases. The prohibition was retained by the conferees.[70]

Then attorney general Griffin Bell supported legislation to broaden or expand the jurisdiction of US magistrates in federal civil and criminal court proceedings and to improve the caliber of magistrates. The bill gave magistrates the authority to conduct trials, empanel juries, find facts, and enter judgments in certain cases. This was an effort to relieve case load burdens on judges. The House and Senate passed different versions of the bill (S. 1613).[71] The House bill required the consent of defendants in order for a magistrate to oversee a criminal trial, while the Senate bill provided mandatory magistrate jurisdiction over minor criminal offenses.[72] There was not enough support for the measure, and it did not pass.

The role of magistrates was also included in a reform of the federal criminal code passed by the Senate. In the proposed revised code, the jurisdiction of US magistrates was expanded to cover all misdemeanors. Magistrates were also permitted to oversee the trial of minor offenses carrying six-month sentences or less. A defendant's right in such cases to elect a trial by jury in a district court was eliminated.[73]

Included in the Senate version of the code reform was an amendment that expanded the list of violent crimes for which a judge may deny pretrial release. The amendment denied release for serious crimes including murder, rape, armed robbery, and hostage situations where a person is seized to negotiate the release of an accused. The bill also lowered the length of time a person may be subjected to a psychiatric examination to determine if they are competent to stand trial from 45 to 15 days. The amendment also allowed a defendant to refuse such an examination if it were requested by the government.[74]

In S. 11, the Senate tried to create the largest single expansion of the federal judiciary in the nation's history. Many thought the bill was essential to relieve massive backlogs in the federal courts.[75] The bill attempted to create 148 new federal judgeships, including 113 district and 35 circuit or appeals court judgeships. The bill was easily passed by the Senate but not in the House. In the House, a judiciary subcommittee proposed H.R. 7843, which recommended the creation of 117 district and 35 circuit judgeships. This cleared Congress and became law (PL 95-486). The bill also included a weak merit selection provision requiring the president to create standards and guidelines for the selection of judges to fill the positions created by the bill. In doing so, the president was given the authority to decide the future role of the Senate in selecting judges. The Senate traditionally had made the key decisions in the selection process.[76]

There were proposals to revise the grand jury system this session. Some members thought there were too many opportunities for prosecutorial abuses and wanted to eliminate it. The House subcommittee members considered H.R. 94, and the Senate considered S. 1449, among other proposals. Despite support from the ABA, representing lawyers, the bill died.[77]

The Senate passed S. 1423 to establish an alternative mechanism for removing federal judges from office. The House Judiciary Committee held no hearings, and the proposal died.[78]

1979–80: 96TH CONGRESS

During this congressional session, members made many proposals and changes to the court system. To begin, Congress cleared legislation (S. 237/PL 96-82) that would expand the authority of federal magistrates. The law allowed magistrates to hold jury and nonjury trials in both civil matters and criminal misdemeanor cases when the parties consented. The bill also provided merit selection to appoint magistrates and allowed part-time magistrates to preside over certain cases.[79] The magistrates could also conduct pretrial hearings in certain civil and criminal matters and make recommendations for disposition of the questions presented to district court judges.

The Senate passed legislation (S. 1477) that would create a new federal appeals court for patent cases and a new trial level court that would hear suits involving claims against the government. The bill also contained a controversial amendment that would make it easier to challenge federal regulations in court. The bill was sent to the House but was not acted on.[80]

The Congress cleared S. 1873 (PL 96-458) to provide procedures for disciplining judges but not actually removing them from office through impeachment. The proposal would allow the chief judges and the judicial councils of the 11 federal circuits to investigate and rule on any complaints made against a judge and impose a sanction. A council could order temporarily suspending the judge or magistrate from handling cases or other punishment considered appropriate under the circumstances. Depending on the evidence, the council could request a judge's voluntary retirement or take other disciplinary action if it found the judge unable to perform his or her duties. A council's decision could be appealed to a new Court of Judicial Conduct and Disability, which would be composed of five federal judges who were appointed by the US Chief Justice.[81]

The Senate passed S. 450, which would give the Supreme Court almost complete discretion to determine the cases it could hear. The bill would eliminate mandatory jurisdiction in virtually all cases that the court is now required to consider. The bill was not considered in House.[82]

The House and Senate passed different versions of a bill (S. 423) that was designed to help citizens resolve minor legal disputes, such as consumer complaints, without going to court. Both versions created a Dispute Resolution Resource Center to exchange information among state and local government about dispute resolution methods within the Justice Department, and both authorized a federal grant program to provide states with funds to develop new dispute resolution systems and to strengthen any existing programs.[83] After a compromise version was agreed to, the proposal became law (PL 96-190).

The Senate approved a bill that would create procedures for diverting some federal offenders from prosecution to education and counseling programs, but it was not acted on by the House. S. 702, also called the Federal Diversion Act of 1979, stated that at the time of arrest, persons would be screened by federal authorities to determine if they were eligible for the diversion program. The guidelines for determining eligibility would be established by the attorney general. Once in the program, the local agency that was responsible for administering the diversion program would supervise the offender's performance. If the program was successfully completed, the original indictment, information, or complaint would be dismissed. However, the US attorney could resume prosecution if an offender failed to complete the plan, voluntarily withdrew from it, or if the US attorney found any new information suggesting the offender should not be in the program.[84]

The House and Senate both passed criminal code revision bills. The House bill created a special committee within the US Judicial Conference, the policy-making arm of the federal judiciary, to develop sentencing guidelines. The Senate created a US Sentencing Commission to develop the guidelines.[85]

The Senate passed legislation to reauthorize the controversial LSC, which was created in 1974 to provide legal assistance for the nation's poor. The agency was controversial for many years, with critics charging that legal services lawyers were more interested in social activism than in helping poor people with routine legal problems like landlord-tenant disputes and divorces. The bill was reported by the House committee, but Congress did not clear a final bill.[86]

The Senate passed and sent the House S. 2483, authorizing the chief justice of the United States to address Congress annually on the state of the federal judiciary. No further action was taken on it.[87]

S. 2705 was proposed to expand federal demonstration programs designed to help federal judges make pretrial bail decisions. Under the program, pretrial service officers would gather pertinent information about a defendant before a bail decision. That information would be provided to the judge. If bail was granted, the pretrial service officers would oversee those persons but would also be required to notify the judge of any violation of pretrial release conditions and recommend modifications of pretrial release condition, if needed. The bill was passed in the Senate, but a similar bill (H.R. 7084) failed to win House passage.[88]

PRESIDENT REAGAN

Ronald Reagan supported many changes to the criminal justice system that reflected his more conservative views about crime. In 1982 and 1983, Reagan sent Congress a package of major anticrime measures that incorporated many of his ideas. The bill was called the Comprehensive Crime Control Act of 1983.

One change concerned bail reform, which would permit judges, under certain conditions, to keep some defendants from using bail to return to the streets.[89] Reagan wanted to make it much more difficult for a defendant who was likely to be a threat to the community to be released on bail pending trial.[90] He wanted to permit judges to deny bail and lock up defendants who were shown to be a grave danger to their communities.[91]

President Reagan also suggested revisions of the exclusionary rule. He wanted a policy such that if evidence in a criminal case were improperly seized, it would be admissible in court upon showing that the officer making the seizure acted in a reasonable good faith. He wanted to stop evidence from being thrown out on the basis of a small technicality.[92]

Revisions of the insanity defense were part of the anticrime package Reagan sent to Congress.[93] The bill would replace the federal insanity defense with a more narrow defense applicable only to those defendants who were unable to appreciate the nature or wrongfulness of their acts.[94] Reagan's intent was to cut back on the misuse of insanity as a criminal defense.[95]

In addition to all of these changes, Reagan also wanted to modify procedures for habeas corpus appeals. His proposals would give greater finality to state court criminal judgments and reduce the sometimes unending chain of appeals and reappeals.[96]

Changes in sentencing were part of Reagan's plans to ensure that sentences meted out by judges would be determinate and consistent throughout the federal system, with no parole possible. He said the policy would make sentencing more uniform and certain because the sentence imposed should be the sentence served.[97] He supported changes in sentencing for those who carried a gun while committing a felony. In those cases, Reagan supported mandatory prison terms.[98]

Criminal forfeiture of property gained because of illegal activity was part of Reagan's plans. His proposals would strengthen the ability of federal prosecutors to confiscate the assets and profits of criminal enterprises.

In addition to all of these changes, Reagan also wanted to see new laws to strengthen child pornography laws and provide greater financial assistance to state and local law enforcement programs.[99]

Reagan asked Congress to disallow LSC funds for political think tanks or national or state support centers. He believed that all LSC funds should be used directly to assist the poor in need of legal help.[100] Reagan later proposed abolishing the LSC and allowing states to provide legal aid to the poor through social service block grants.[101]

Reagan signed the Sentencing Act of 1987, which amended the Sentencing Reform Act of 1984 to reduce unwarranted sentencing disparity and to bring about certainty and fairness in sentencing.[102] He subsequently signed H.R. 4801 (PL 99-363), the Sentencing Guideline Act of 1986, saying that the purpose of the Sentencing Reform Act was to establish a determinate sentencing system with narrow-sentences ranges for criminal offenses. Although he did not like all the provisions of the bill, he signed it nonetheless.[103]

In 1987, Reagan again proposed many of his ideas for changes for the courts, this time in the Criminal Justice Reform Act. In this proposal, he stressed the need to modify the exclusionary rule to allow the good-faith rule when a police officer collects evidence in reasonably good faith. Second, Reagan wanted to modify the rules for habeas corpus appeals because the habeas corpus doctrine was misused by federal courts as a way to oversee state criminal convictions. Finally, Reagan wanted to restore the death penalty. He claimed that there were no adequate procedures on the federal death penalty, and so it was not used in cases where federal statutes provide for capital punishment. He proposed to establish such adequate procedures so that the death penalty provisions already on the books could be used in cases of espionage, treason, and aggravated murder.[104]

CONGRESS

1981–82: 97TH CONGRESS

A continuing appropriations resolution was passed (H.J. Res. 631/PL 97-377) to keep the LSC alive, despite being slated for extinction by the Reagan administration.

The bill measure included $241 million for the corporation for FY 1983. Only 9 of the 11 individuals named by Reagan to the LSC Board of Directors were officially nominated, and none was confirmed.

The Congress passed S. 923 (PL 97-267) to expand nationwide ten federal demonstration pretrial services programs that were aimed at helping judges to make pretrial bail decisions. The demonstration programs were created in 1974 as part of the Speedy Trial Act, which set deadlines for trying those charged with crimes. The bill would require pretrial services programs in all 95 judicial districts within 18 months of the date of enactment. Under the bill, pretrial services officers collected information about a defendant and gave it to a judge prior to a bail decision. If bail was granted, the officers supervised released defendants, notified the judge about any violation of bail conditions and recommended changes in release conditions. A similar House bill (H.R. 3481) was reported by the Judiciary Committee.[105]

The Senate Judiciary Committee approved S. 1554 to allow federal judges to jail criminal defendants before trial if they believed the defendants were dangerous. Under the law at the time, a judge could detain a defendant only after determining there was a real likelihood of the defendant would flee before trial. The American Civil Liberties Union (ACLU) was opposed to the bill.[106]

A comprehensive anticrime package was passed (H.R. 3963) that authorized judges to order restitution to a victim who sustained personal injury or property loss, made it a felony to harass crime victims and witnesses, and called for revocation of bail for any defendant who tried to intimidate a witness. President Reagan vetoed the bill.[107]

After John Hinckley was found not guilty by reason of insanity for his assassination attempt on President Reagan, there were many proposals made to change the law. One of those, S. 2572 (part of an omnibus crime bill), would have replaced the current insanity defense with a new verdict of "not guilty only by reason of insanity."[108] Under this proposal, a defendant would have to prove that he or she did not have the requisite state of mind because of a mental disease or defect. Another proposal, S. 2658, required the defendant to prove by clear and convincing evidence that he or she was insane at the time of the crime. No action was taken on either the bill.[109]

1983–84: 98TH CONGRESS

In 1983, chief justice of the Supreme Court, Warren E. Burger, called on Congress to create a temporary new appeals court to help ease the Court's growing caseload. He said Congress should create a new court to resolve disputes between federal appeals courts in the existing 13 circuits. He wanted the new court to operate for six months to a year while a study commission sought long-range solutions to the Supreme Court's overload. Despite his plea, lawmakers did not act on his request. S. 645, which incorporated Burger's suggestion, was approved by the Senate Judiciary Courts Subcommittee, but it went no further.[110]

More work was done in Congress to revise the insanity defense. A bill overhauling the federal insanity defense, H.R. 3336, required a defendant who was seeking acquittal on grounds of insanity to prove "by a preponderance of the evidence" that he or she met the legal test for insanity. Under existing law, a prosecutor had to prove "beyond a reasonable doubt" that the defendant was sane when he or she committed a crime. The bill also changed the federal legal test for insanity. Supporters claimed the new definition was more precise than the current one, while opponents contended it would wreak havoc on the legal system by casting doubt on case law developed under the existing test. The bill was approved by the House Judiciary Committee, but it did not reach the House floor.[111]

In a bill to reform the federal criminal code that was passed in the Senate (S. 1762), there was a provision that allowed a judge to detain before trial a defendant deemed to pose a danger to the community. Under the then-current law, a judge could jail a defendant before trial only after determining there was a real likelihood the person would flee. The proposal was passed in the Senate but went no further.[112] The Criminal Code Revision Act also included provisions on the insanity defense. The provisions limited the insanity defense to those defendants who could prove, by clear and convincing evidence, that they were unable to appreciate the wrongfulness of their acts. The proposal shifted the burden of proof from the prosecutor to the defendant, who would have to prove his or her insanity by clear and convincing evidence. It also barred psychiatric experts from testifying on whether the defendant had a particular mental disease or defect. Finally, the Criminal Code Revision Act included provisions on sentencing reform. The bill created a commission to write sentencing guidelines to be used by federal judges when imposing sentences. It was intended to eliminate the widespread disparity that existed in sentencing for similar crimes.[113] The proposal was passed in the Senate but went no further.

Another bill, S. 1763, set more restrictive federal procedures for looking at state prisoners' claims that they had been imprisoned in violation of their constitutional rights. This was not passed.[114]

An exception to the exclusionary rule was included in another bill, S. 1764. As it stood, evidence obtained illegally could not be introduced into a trial. The Senate bill would allow the use of certain illegally obtained evidence to be admitted into trial, if the officers were acting with a reasonable, good-faith belief that their conduct was legal.[115] However, the bill died in the House.[116]

In 1984, Congress cleared major anticrime legislation as part of the fiscal 1985 continuing appropriations resolution (H.J. Res. 648/PL 98-473). The new law made changes in the bail system. It authorized federal judges to consider whether a defendant posed a danger to the community in deciding whether to release him or her before trial on bail. If there was enough evidence to charge a defendant with a major drug offense or other serious crime, the defendant was not entitled to pretrial release. The law required that a defendant be detained after conviction pending sentencing or appeal, unless a judge found by clear and convincing evidence that the defendant was not likely to flee or pose a danger to the community. The penalties for jumping bail increased from a maximum of five years in prison and a $5,000 fine to ten years in prison and a $25,000 fine and also required revocation of bail of a person arrested for a crime committed while on pretrial or postconviction release.[117]

The bill included many provisions on sentencing. One major change was that federal judges would now be required to follow sentencing guidelines as a way to reduce the disparity in punishments for defendants who commit similar crimes. It created a grading system for crimes, ranking them according to their seriousness. A seven-member commission was established to write the guidelines. Panel members would be appointed by the president and confirmed by the Senate and were required to include three judges. A judge could deviate from them if he stated in writing the mitigating and aggravating factors that led the judge to do so. If a defendant received a sentence that was harsher than the guidelines, the defendant could appeal. Conversely, the government could appeal a sentence more lenient than the guidelines.

The law phased out parole over five years for prisoners incarcerated before the guidelines took effect, under certain circumstances.[118]

Changes in the insanity defense were part of the 1984 bill. The new law restricted the use of the insanity defense and made it more difficult for criminal suspects to use the defense successfully.[119] It modified the definition of "insanity" to require a defendant to prove that he or she was unable to appreciate the nature and wrongfulness of his or her act as a result of a severe mental disease or defect. In short, the law shifted the burden of proof for establishing insanity to the defendant, who had to show by clear and convincing evidence that he or she met the legal test. A defendant who was found not guilty by reason of insanity could be committed to a mental hospital or other suitable facility until a court determined that the person had recovered sufficiently so that his or her release would not endanger other people.[120]

1987–88: 100TH CONGRESS

Legislation to improve the operations of the federal courts was sent to the president for his signature (H.R. 4807/PL 100-702). The new law streamlined the proceedings in the federal judicial system. One part of the bill created a Federal Courts Study Committee that was a temporary commission to study federal court operations and to recommend improvements. There would also be restrictions on the types of minor disputes involving state laws that could be heard in federal court. Nineteen federal judicial districts were authorized to set up experimental arbitration programs as an alternative to formal civil trials. Finally, the State Justice Institute, a research organization, was reauthorized for two years, and the Federal Judicial Center, which conducted a variety of federal court programs, was granted permission to create a foundation for receiving gifts. The law expanded the court interpreters' program to cover grand jury proceedings and allowed the regional federal appeals court to determine what language services they needed.[121]

PRESIDENT BUSH

Like Reagan, George H. W. Bush proposed changes to the criminal justice system, one of which was to establish a general "good faith" exception to the exclusionary rule to permit evidence to be admitted if the officers carrying out a search or seizure acted with a reasonable belief that they were following the law.[122] In 1991, Bush proposed new legislation that included reform of the exclusionary rule to "limit the release of violent criminals due to legal evidence that has been seized by Federal or State law enforcement officials acting in 'good faith' or a firearm seized from dangerous criminals by a Federal law enforcement officer."[123]

He also wanted habeas corpus reform. He proposed a new policy to establish a one-year time limit on federal applications by state prisoners and to limit the ability of federal and state prisoners to file repetitive habeas corpus petitions.[124] In his proposal, he wanted to stop frivolous and repetitive appeals that, he said, "clogged the courts, and in many cases nullify State death penalties."[125]

CONGRESS

1989–90: 101ST CONGRESS

In this session, Congress cleared legislation (H.R. 5316, S. 2648/PL 101-650), called the Judicial Improvements Act of 1990, that gave President Bush 85 new federal judgeships to fill, which was the first increase in the federal judiciary since 1984. This included 74 district court judgeships and 11 appellate posts.[126] Attached to the bill was a mandate for judges to adopt special plans to speed up civil litigation. The directive left the details of the plans up to federal judges in most districts. Bush also asked Congress for 1,600 new prosecutors and staff to help the courts function more effectively.[127]

1991–92: 102ND CONGRESS

The House approved H.R. 3371/S. 1241 to limit appeals by death row prisoners. This was part of a larger bill, but Bush insisted the bill did not go far enough to restrict appeals by convicted criminals and relax evidentiary rules, and so consequently, the Senate blocked it.[128] Congress failed to break an 11-year impasse over the reauthorization of the LSC, as legislation (H.R. 2039). The bill asked for a five-year reauthorization of the corporation, which provided federal funds for legal aid for the poor.[129] Bush had promised to veto the bill unless it contained provisions prohibiting LSC attorneys from taking abortion cases. The Senate version (S. 2870) authorized the corporation for six years, one year longer than its companion in the House. Both bills would have expanded restrictions on the cases LSC lawyers could have handled, including lobbying. The bill advanced no further than the Judiciary Committee in the House.[130]

The Senate approved S. 646 to authorize the appointment of 32 new federal bankruptcy judges in districts that had seen a significant increase in bankruptcy filings.[131] The House did not act on the bill in this session.

PRESIDENT CLINTON

William Clinton believed that a small number of people commit a significant number of violent crimes, and those people are highly likely to be repeat offenders. He wanted tougher sentencing, including a "three-strikes" provision. He reported that if the law was written properly, it would affect only a small percentage of the prison population at the federal level and a somewhat larger percentage at the state level. But the law would keep people in prison who would be likely to commit a serious violent crime if they were released.[132]

Clinton also wanted reform of habeas corpus, particularly in death penalty cases, where it took an average of eight years to exhaust the appeals process. He said that it was necessary to cut the time delay on the appeals dramatically.[133]

In 1996, Clinton signed the Witness Retaliation, Witness Tampering, and Jury Tampering bills. H.R. 3120 (PL 104-214) dramatically increased the punishment for those who would influence, tamper with, or retaliate against witnesses, jurors, and court officers in federal criminal cases.[134]

CONGRESS

1993–94: 103RD CONGRESS

Supporters of the LSC wanted to reauthorize the program again this session since it had not received formal operating authority since 1980. A proposal that aimed to set clear guidelines for legal services attorneys was approved by a House Judiciary Subcommittee. The bill would have set strict new accounting requirements for groups that received corporation money.[135] No action was taken on the bill.

A major crime bill passed in 1994 (H.R. 3355; H.R. 4092/S. 1607/PL 103-322) that provided a potential waiver from existing federal mandatory minimum sentences for certain first-time, nonviolent drug offenders who exhibited good behavior while in prison.[136] In some cases, judges would be given the authority to relax the mandatory sentences after determining that the defendant met certain criteria, among them that the defendant had provided all the info he or she had regarding the crime to law enforcement authorities.[137]

Another part of the bill required life imprisonment for someone convicted of a third violent felony, known as the "three strikes and you're out" provision. A "strike" consisted of a serious state or federal violent felony conviction, generally defined as those with a potential sentence of ten years or more. The first two felonies could be state offenses, while the last had to be a federal violent felony charge. A serious drug offense could constitute one of the first two "strikes," but not the third. At least two of the three felony convictions had to stem from different incidents.

1995–96: 104TH CONGRESS

H.R. 666 would have allowed federal prosecutors to use evidence obtained improperly, such as through a search conducted without a warrant, provided that police had reason to believe the search was legal. The proposal was known as the "good faith" exception to the exclusionary rule, which generally prohibited the use of evidence obtained in violation of constitutional guarantees against unreasonable searches.[138] Supporters of the bill said it would help prevent criminals from going free because of technical legal problems surrounding the evidence collected. Under the exclusionary rule, prosecutors generally could not use evidence obtained in violation of Fourth Amendment guarantees against unreasonable searches and seizures. The GOP-sponsored bill sought to write the good faith exception into the law and extend it to searches conducted without a warrant, so long as police had good reason to think the search was legal.[139] There was not enough support for the proposal, and it went no further.

The House cleared a bill that retained more stringent sentencing guidelines for money laundering offenses and offenses relating to crack cocaine, despite the advice of the US Sentencing Commission. The commission had recommended a sentence of 21 to 27 months in prison for anyone convicted of laundering more than $100,000. Existing guidelines provided for sentences of 37 to 46 months in prison. The commission also recommended a reduction in mandatory penalties for the distribution and possession of crack cocaine. The guidelines at the time required federal judges to give out a five-year mandatory minimum sentence for offenses involving five or more grams of crack. The commission recommended imposing the mandatory sentence only when at least five hundred grams were involved. That would have put crack on a par with powder cocaine. Despite the disagreement, President Clinton signed the bill, and it became law (S. 1254/PL 104-38).

Once again, there was push to eliminate the LSC. The bill, H.R. 2277, supported by Conservatives in the House, would have replaced the LSC with block grants to the states, but the proposal did not advance beyond the House Judiciary Committee.[140]

The House Judiciary Subcommittee on Commercial and Administrative Law approved H.R. 1802 to establish an independent corps of administrative law judges in the executive branch. Under existing law, administrative law judges were paid by specific federal agencies, which provided their offices and staff and determined which cases they would decide. Supporters of the proposal argued that the bill encouraged the judges to favor agencies instead of individuals; opponents contended that the existing system worked well and would be disrupted if judges were removed from the agencies with which they were familiar. The bill went no further.[141]

A House Judiciary Subcommittee approved H.R. 1443 to encourage out-of-court settlements, but it did not pass the entire Congress. The bill proposed that arbitration procedures should be available in all US district courts. Arbitration would be mandatory for litigants in cases with a maximum value of $150,000 and voluntary in cases involving more money. A 1988 law (PL 100-352) authorized 19 federal judicial districts to set up pilot arbitration programs as an alternative to civil trials. This expired in November 1993.[142]

The House Judiciary Committee approved H.R. 1445 to reinstate a requirement for stenographic recordings of depositions. Audio or video recordings could be used in addition to the stenograph if recording only at the request of the litigants or the court. The bill went no further.[143]

The Senate passed a proposal (S. 956) to split the Ninth Circuit Court of Appeals into two separate courts. The ninth circuit was the largest of the nation's 12 appeals courts and had jurisdiction over 9 Western states, Guam, and the Northern Mariana Islands. The bill proposed to create a new twelfth circuit out of Alaska, Arizona, Idaho, Montana, Nevada, Oregon, and Washington, leaving California, Hawaii, and the territories in the ninth circuit.[144] The House never took up the measure.[145]

In 1996, Congress cleared legislation (H.R. 3120/PL 104-214) that had the potential to increase penalties for those who tampered with or harassed juries and witnesses. The measure allowed a judge to impose the maximum federal penalty (at the time, ten years) or the sentence for the crime for which the defendant was being prosecuted, whichever was more severe. The rule did not apply in death penalty cases.[146]

1997–98: 105TH CONGRESS

In 1997, Congress cleared H.R. 2267 (PL105-119) to create a 5-member commission to study the nation's 12 federal judicial circuits, with special attention to the massive ninth circuit, based in San Francisco and also including Oregon, Washington, Montana, Idaho, Nevada, Arizona, Alaska, Hawaii, Guam, and the Northern Mariana Islands, and had 28 appellate judgeships.[147]

1999–2000: 106TH CONGRESS

A bill in the House (H.R. 1752/S. 2915), the Federal Courts Improvement Act, would allow judges to carry concealed weapons, regardless of state laws. It would also allow cameras and recorders in federal courtrooms. The bill was passed in the House but not the Senate and went no further.[148]

PRESIDENT BUSH

In 2001, George W. Bush said that he would appoint judges who "clearly understand the role of a judge is to interpret the law, not to legislate from the bench."[149] He claimed to support the confirmation of judges who strictly and faithfully interpret the law and would not stand for judges who undermine democracy by legislating from the bench and try to remake the culture by court order.

Most of the statements Bush made about the courts had to do with vacancies in judicial positions. He told the American people that he was unable to get judges confirmed by the US Senate, and because of that, there was a vacancy problem in the federal courts. Too many of the benches had vacancies, meaning that people potentially did not have access to the courts, which endangered the American justice system because it leads to crowded court dockets, overworked judges, and longer waits for Americans who want their cases heard.[150] The problem was caused by senators who blocked votes on qualified nominees.

As a result, Bush believed that the federal courts were in crisis and that the judicial confirmation process did not work as it should. He proposed a clean start for the processes of nominating and confirming federal judges that would create an evenhanded, predictable procedure from the day a vacancy is announced to the day a new judge is sworn in and that would return fairness and dignity to the judicial confirmation process.[151]

Bush agreed as president, he had a responsibility to make sure the judicial system ran well, and he met that responsibility by nominating superb men and women for the federal courts. He accused some members of the Senate of trying to keep his nominees off the bench by blocking votes. Every judicial nominee deserved a fair hearing, and it was time for the members of the US Senate to stop playing politics with American justice.[152]

To create a better system, Bush called on federal judges to notify the president of their intention to retire at least a year in advance, whenever possible. Within 180 days of receiving a notification of a federal court vacancy, Bush proposed that a president submit a nomination to the Senate. He called on the Senate Judiciary Committee to commit to holding a hearing within 90 days of receiving a nomination.[153]

Bush wanted to reform the courts in other ways as well. First, he wanted to get rid of frivolous lawsuits that clog the courts and deny people with legitimate claims.[154] He said that frivolous lawsuits can easily ruin honest businesses.[155] Another proposal was to add two hundred new attorneys that were hired to prosecute crimes committed with a gun.[156]

CONGRESS

2003–4: 108TH CONGRESS

In 2004, Congress passed and the president signed H.R. 5107 (PL 108-405), a bill to improve the quality of legal representation for defendants in capital crime cases and guarantee rights of crime victims. The bill also included hundreds of millions of dollars in grants to cities and states, as well as a law enforcement provision backed by the Bush administration.[157] It included $75 million a year over five years for grants to help states improve the quality of the legal counsel they provide to indigent defendants in death penalty cases and to improve the ability of prosecutors to effectively represent the public in such cases.[158]

In S. 151/PL 108-21, the chief judge in each federal district must compile detailed sentencing reports for the US Sentencing Commission, which then uses that information to analyze sentencing patterns for lawmakers. The law also requires the Justice Department to report to Congress when a judge hands down a lesser sentence than recommended in the sentencing guidelines.[159]

If H.R. 2028 passed, the federal courts (including the Supreme Court) would be prohibited from hearing cases that challenged the constitutionality of the Pledge of Allegiance. Another bill, H.R. 3313, would prevent all federal courts from hearing provisions of the 1996 law called the Defense of Marriage Act. This law gave states the option of not recognizing same-sex marriages performed in other states. The third bill (S. 878) would create more federal court judgeships. If passed, the Ninth Circuit Court would be split into three separate appeals courts. All three bills were passed by the House but not the Senate, so no final action was taken.

PRESIDENT OBAMA

Barack Obama suggested in some comments that liberal justices in the past may have erred and overstepped their bounds, but at the same time he criticized recent conservative rulings from the Supreme Court.[160] In his 2010 State of the Union address, Obama criticized the John Roberts Court and other justices for their rulings.[161] He was particularly angry about a decision that struck down a campaign finance reform law. Obama was able to make two appointments to the US Supreme Court in the first two years of his administration. The first was Judge Sonia Sotomayor, and the second was Elena Kagan.

CONCLUSION

The court system in the United States includes courts on the federal, state, and local levels. The president and Congress have both been active in making laws concerning the judiciary, including setting the number of courts and in some cases their jurisdiction. They have often made laws that regulate procedural aspects of the courts. The role of the federal government is obvious when it comes to judicial issues, and there is little doubt that federal action in this area will persist in the future.

CHAPTER 4

PRISONS AND THE DEATH PENALTY

THE FEDERAL GOVERNMENT OVERSEES THE FEDERAL PRISON system, but it also sets standards for correctional facilities in state and local areas. Serious debate and disagreement exists around the issues of prisons and capital punishment, both in the public and in the government. There is disagreement about who to put in prison, for how long, and if there should be rehabilitation programs that deal with improving an inmate's education or treating their drug addiction or if prisons should be places of punishment. There is debate over the conditions of prisons and the level of services provided to inmates, if any. When it comes to capital punishment, we see debate over what offenses should carry the penalty, how it should be carried out, or even if we should have it at all. Presidents have talked about these issues, and Congress has debated them, sometimes passing new laws concerning prison policies and the death penalty. The following information demonstrates this.

PRESIDENT EISENHOWER

In 1957, Dwight Eisenhower proposed the construction of two new prisons to help ease overcrowded conditions in existing penitentiaries. He was also concerned with providing adequate space for youthful offenders and for the custody of the most dangerous and troublesome prisoners.[1]

1957–58: 85TH CONGRESS

In 1957, the Supreme Court decided *Mallory v. United States* (354 US 449), which invalidated the rape conviction of Andrew Mallory on the grounds that his conviction was not validly obtained because the police had held him for seven and a half hours before any attempt was made to arraign him.[2] The Court said there had been illegal, unnecessary delay before Mallory was arraigned. In response, the House debated H.R. 11477, called the Mallory Rule, to prevent federal courts from disqualifying statements and confessions in criminal proceedings solely because of reasonable delay in the arraignment of a suspect. The bill was intended to reverse the Supreme Court decision.[3] It did not pass.

1959–60: 86TH CONGRESS

The House passed H.R. 4957 to reverse the effects of the *Mallory* decision. The bill provided that a confession or other evidence obtained from a suspect in the period between his or her arrest and arraignment could not be barred as federal court evidence in a criminal case solely because there had been delay in arraigning a suspect. It also required police, before questioning suspects, to advise them they need not answer and that what they said might be used against them. The Senate took no action.[4]

The House also passed an amended bill (H.R. 3216) to limit the use in federal courts of habeas corpus writs for review of state court convictions. The chief aim of the bill was to prevent prisoners from making repeated pleas for writs, using the same facts by varying the pleas slightly on each new petition. Under the bill, a federal court would not be permitted to grant habeas corpus to a state prisoner if he or she had previously been refused habeas corpus by any federal court, of if the Supreme Court had adjudicated the prisoner's case under a proceeding not involving habeas corpus. There was no Senate action.[5]

PRESIDENT JOHNSON

Lyndon Johnson established a Commission on Law Enforcement and the Administration of Justice, which was given the responsibility to complete a systematic study of basic problems related to crime. One of the problems revolved around rehabilitation versus punishment and why one-third of parolees reverted back to committing crime.[6] The committee was made up of lawyers, judges, law enforcement officials, educators, social workers, and government officials.[7] Johnson wanted to learn more because "correctional agencies must have better information and deeper and broader research into the causes, and into the prevention and control of crime."[8]

Johnson said that the Prisoner Rehabilitation Act was the most significant legislative reform in modern American penology. Hundreds of prisoners already were working in daytime jobs as they finished their sentences at night. They were learning job skills that would bring dignity to themselves and help to support to their families.[9] According to Johnson, the country needed "better prisoner rehabilitation,"[10] which would include a broader and more profound range of treatment.[11] As part of his rehabilitation effort, Johnson recommended that the Federal Prison Industries be authorized to manage and operate the industrial program of the district's correctional institutions.[12]

In 1996, Johnson proposed reorganizing and unifying the federal prison, parole, and probation functions within the Department of Justice as a way to consolidate the fragmented correctional system that existed at the time. To succeed in this venture, Johnson directed the secretary of labor to develop effective ways to provide correctional institutions with job information for "good risk" parolees. He also directed the chairman of the Civil Service Commission to reexamine the policies of all federal departments and agencies regarding the hiring of released "good risk" offenders.[13]

In 1965, as another way to improve the American correctional system, President Johnson signed H.R. 6964 (PL 89-176), which would allow the attorney general to commit or transfer adult prisoners to residential community treatment centers (halfway houses). It would also grant prisoners leave for emergency purposes or to contact prospective employers. Third, the legislation would permit them to go into a neighboring community to work at paid employment or to obtain training. Johnson also signed H.R. 2263 (PL 89-178), the Correctional Rehabilitation Study Act of 1965, to help parolees return to society and to a good and useful life for themselves and their families. To help states pay for the programs, in 1968 Johnson asked the Congress to increase the program funds available to the Bureau of Prisons by $3 million.[14]

Overall, Johnson was interested in learning more about prisons and wanted to improve the correctional system by reorganizing the probation and parole systems and by using community corrections as an alternative to traditional institutions. He focused on rehabilitation of offenders rather than punishment, a traditionally liberal approach.

CONGRESS

1965–66: 89TH CONGRESS

The Congress passed a bill (H.R. 6097/PL 89-141) that provided for new methods of rehabilitating federal prisoners, including the establishment of prerelease treatment centers (halfway houses), emergency leaves, and work-release programs.[15] They also passed H.R. 2263 (PL 89-178), which authorized a three-year study of the manpower and training needs in the field of correctional rehabilitation.[16] The act was known as the Correctional Rehabilitation Study Act of 1965. It amended the Vocational Rehabilitation Act and made grants available for studies of personnel needs in the correctional field, such as probation officers, social workers, and rehabilitation counselors.

A reorganization plan gave the secretary of health, education and welfare (HEW) full authority over the health functions of the Public Health Service (PHS) and the power to reorganize PHS. The secretary of HEW created five new bureaucracies, one of which was the Bureau of Health Services, which was to coordinate direct federal health services such medical care for federal prison inmates.[17]

As part of the amendments to the Manpower Training Act that was passed, the secretary of labor was authorized to conduct an experimental two-year training program in correctional institutions to prepare inmates for productive work on their release.[18]

The Bail Reform Act of 1966 (PL 89-465) established new procedures for the release of federal prisoners charged with noncapital offenses. The purpose of the act was to revise the bail system to assure that all persons, regardless of their financial status, will not be detained pending their appearance, or pending appeal, when detention was not necessary. The act provided for the release of persons charged with noncapital federal offenses unless it appeared they were unlikely to return for trial. It accepted that congressional supporters intended the act to serve as a model for the states, within which the main burden of criminal law enforcement fell. In passing the act, Congress specifically postponed consideration of issues relating to crimes committed by persons released while awaiting trial. The House Judiciary Committee in its report on the bill said a solution to the problem of preventive detention "involves many difficult and complex problems which require deep study and analysis."[19]

1967–68: 90TH CONGRESS

The Senate Judiciary Subcommittee on Criminal Laws and Procedures held hearings on S. 1760 to abolish capital punishment in federal crimes and commuting all pending death sentences to life in prison.[20]

PRESIDENT NIXON

One area where Richard Nixon had great concerns was prisons. He believed that many correctional programs were based on tradition and assumption rather than on theories that had been scientifically tested and that few of our programs had been closely studied to see what results they had. To address that problem, Nixon asked the attorney general to combine resources of the Department of Justice in a major new research effort.[21] Because our understanding of mentally disturbed offenders was inadequate, according to Nixon, he proposed to design and construction a federal psychiatric study and treatment facility for mentally disturbed and violent offenders.[22]

In 1969, Nixon set up a ten-year plan for reforming correctional activities.[23] The program would modernize the entire American correctional system to assist local and state correctional programs and to coordinate all levels of corrections and rehabilitation efforts.[24] Nixon wanted to expand the existing correctional programs and develop more innovative correctional methods in an effort to improve probation, parole, and other community-based services.[25] He thought that halfway houses should be given a high priority, and available funds should be used to encourage these centers.[26] To increase the use of halfway houses, Nixon asked the attorney general to prepare legislation that would expand the halfway house program to include a greater number of convicted offenders, specifically those on parole and probation who usually could not participate in the program. He also ordered the Department of Justice to assist states and localities in establishing new centers and expanding existing halfway house projects.[27]

Additionally, he wanted to replace the traditional local jail concept with a comprehensive, community-oriented facility that would bring together a variety of detention options. These centers would have diagnostic services for both adult and juvenile offenders and treatment programs for those who are incarcerated or on supervisory release. Further, Nixon asked the Department of Justice to expand its existing training programs for those who work in correctional institutions.[28]

Nixon thought that federal grants would help the states and local governments who carry the burden for housing inmates. The federal government could provide both technical and financial aid to states.[29]

Nixon believed that the death penalty was not a deterrent as long as there was doubt as to the crimes for which it could be applied. He proposed that the death penalty be restored for certain federal crimes, such as those murders over which the federal government has jurisdiction, treason, and other war-related crimes.[30]

CONGRESS

1969–70: 91ST CONGRESS

In 1970, Congress held hearings but did not act on administration proposals (S. 2600, H.R. 12806) to authorize federal judges to detain dangerous defendants for up to 60 days before trial to ensure the safety of their community.[31] Congress also failed to complete action on S. 1872, which the Senate had passed in 1969 to repeal the Emergency Detention Act of 1950. That act allowed the president, in certain circumstances, to detain persons who might engage in espionage or sabotage.[32]

1971–72: 92ND CONGRESS

The House passed a bill (H.R. 8389) amending the Omnibus Crime Control and Safe Streets Act of 1968 to provide for drug treatment programs at state jails and prisons. The new bill would require that states requesting Law Enforcement Assistance Administration (LEAA) funds create narcotics treatment programs in the prisons.

The Senate Judiciary Subcommittee on Penitentiaries held hearings on S. 662, a bill that provided for demonstration correctional programs that provided reforms and improvements of prisons. The bill would have created a presidentially appointed commission on penal and postadjudicatory programs composed of 17 persons from the corrections field. It would have authorized the commission to select five state and three federal model correction demonstration plans and grant up to $15 million per year for five years for each plan.[33] One expert who testified at the hearings was James Hoffa, former president of the International Brotherhood of Teamsters Union and former inmate in the Lewisburg Federal Penitentiary. Hoffa presented a list of suggestions for prison improvement, ranging from limits on inmate populations to a loosening of clothing and haircut regulations.[34] The bill did not become law.

The House Judiciary Subcommittee No. 5 held a hearing on H.R. 11441 that would limit federal habeas corpus relief to persons in state prisons. Federal law allowed state prisoners to file habeas corpus petitions in federal district courts to have their convictions reviewed. Many state attorneys general complained that state court review procedures were adequate to protect the defendant's rights, that their staffs were overburdened by such petitions, and that relatively few convictions had been overturned by federal courts.[35] Additionally, the House Judiciary Subcommittee No. 3 held seven days of hearings on federal parole practices and procedures but failed to act on the bill.[36]

The Senate Judiciary Subcommittee on National Penitentiaries held hearings on S. 3309 that would establish a community-centered rehabilitation program for those people accused of nonviolent federal crimes. The bill would provide a variety of rehabilitative services for defendants, whose trials would be postponed if they participated in the program. Some of the services provided to inmates would include job placement, job training, or medical and psychological treatment and counseling. If a person successfully completed the program, the charges against him or her would be dismissed, and a trial would never be held.[37] The bill was not passed.

The House Judiciary Subcommittee held hearings on the death penalty during this session. Four bills before the committee (H.R. 193, 3243, 11797, and 12217) would abolish the death penalty for 13 federal crimes that carried it. Three bills (H.R. 8414, 8483, and 9486) would provide a two-year moratorium on executions in the federal and state systems so that Congress could consider whether to abolish capital punishment.[38] None of the bills received enough support for passage.

Finally, the House Select Committee on Crime held hearings on the prison riots that occurred in facilities in Attica, New York, and Raiford, Florida.

1973–74: 93RD CONGRESS

In the House, a bill was passed (H.R. 7352/PL 93-209) to expand the permissible use of furloughs for inmates of federal prisons.

As part of the proposed revision of the federal criminal code, debates were held on the death penalty. Some members of Congress pointed out that an earlier commission (the Brown Commission) proposed abolishing capital punishment, but other members said that capital punishment should be available for those people convicted of intentional murder or treason. The administration proposal was that if a person was convicted of one of the four crimes for which death could be imposed and if one or more aggravating circumstance and no mitigating circumstance were found, then the judge would be required to sentence that person to death.[39] No final legislative action was taken on the issue.

PRESIDENT FORD

Gerald Ford asked the Department of Justice to undertake something he termed the "Career Criminal Impact Program." It would, with the help of state and local governments, target and keep track of professional criminals. By doing this, career criminals would be brought to justice quicker.[40]

However, Ford also believed that inmates should be treated humanely while in prison. Loss of liberty should be the chief punishment. He believed that improvements in both the treatment of prisoners and the facilities for them were long overdue.[41] One improvement Ford supported was to divert some first offenders into rehabilitation programs before proceeding to trial.[42] Ford acknowledged that while the problem of rehabilitating criminals is difficult, we must not give up on our efforts to achieve it, especially with youthful offenders.[43]

Ford proposed that incarceration be made mandatory for those offenders who commit offenses under federal jurisdiction using a dangerous weapon and for these offenders who commit extraordinarily serious crimes, such as aircraft hijacking, kidnapping, and trafficking of hard drugs. In his opinion, repeat offenders who commit federal crimes, either with or without a weapon, that either cause or have the potential to cause personal injury should also face mandatory incarceration.[44]

Ford supported use of the death penalty in the federal criminal system in accordance with proper constitutional standards. According to President Ford, the death penalty should be imposed on conviction for sabotage, subversion, murder, espionage, treason, and other acts that are against the national security of the United States. He also supported capital punishment for kidnapping.[45]

CONGRESS

1975–76: 94TH CONGRESS

In this session, Congress passed and the president signed H.R. 5727 (PL 94-233). The bill reorganized the US Board of Parole as the US Parole Commission, an independent agency within the Justice Department. The bill also introduced new procedural protections for prisoners into the parole process at initial, appellate, and revocation levels in an attempt to ensure a fair and equitable system.[46]

One senator proposed an amendment to delete $38 million from the appropriation of the Bureau of Prisons for construction of two new prison facilities at Otisville,

New York, and Talladega, Alabama. It was argued that instead of spending around $46,000 per unit for new prisons, the federal government should study how existing prison sites were being used, especially those at military bases. Opponents of the amendment said the prison population was rising and acceptable prison space declining. The amendment was rejected by voice vote.[47]

The Judiciary Subcommittee passed S. 1, part of which included the death penalty. It allowed for capital punishment for certain classes of murder, treason, espionage, and sabotage. The members said they tried to draft the law to follow the guidelines of the 1972 Supreme Court decision in *Furman v. Georgia* (408 US 238 [1972]).[48] The bill did not pass in this session.

PRESIDENT CARTER

In 1980, Jimmy Carter signed the Civil Rights of Institutionalized Persons Act to give the attorney general the authority to initiate lawsuits against any public institution, such as a prison, that violated the rights of the people confined there. Under the new law, the attorney general would be able to seek relief in a federal court if there was evidence of the abuse of rights on a continuing basis.[49]

1977–78: 95TH CONGRESS

The House passed H.R. 9400, allowing the attorney general to sue state nursing homes, mental institutions, prisons, and juvenile facilities where the department found a pattern or practice of violating of constitutional rights. The bill was aimed at protecting a class of uniquely vulnerable persons, such as mental patients and inmates, some of the more helpless segments of society, who might be totally incapable of asserting their rights. The Senate did not act on the bill.[50]

The Senate passed a revision of the federal criminal code, part of which had to do with the system of probation. At the time, the law provided for a term of probation of up to five years without regard to the seriousness of the offense. The newly proposed law provided for differing terms depending on the seriousness of the violation.[51] Additionally, the law at the time required offenders to report regularly to probation officers and adhere to other prescribed probation conditions. The new law required the court provide that the defendant not commit another crime during probation as a condition of the probation.[52]

1979–80: 96TH CONGRESS

A provision of the Labor-HHS-Education budget prohibited the use of funds to pay public service jobs wages to prisoners, unless they were within 12 months of their expected release date.[53]

This session, the House and Senate both passed different criminal code revision bills. The House version retained parole for prisoners, while the Senate version would abolish it over a five-year period.[54] The final version would allow probation except for "Class A" felonies, such as murder. There were three terms of probation: up to five years for a felony, up to two years for a misdemeanor, and up to one year for an infraction. All probationers would be given the condition that they do not commit another crime during their time on probation.[55]

In S. 114, the Senate Judiciary debated a bill that would reestablish the death penalty for federal crimes, such as treason, espionage, and killing the president, but the bill did not have enough support to be passed.[56] The new law would also cover murders occurring on federal property and deaths resulting from the commission of kidnapping. At that time, the only federal crime that carried the death penalty was homicide during an aircraft hijacking. To be in line with the Supreme Court's 1972 ruling, S. 114 would establish a two-stage trial. The first part would determine the defendant's guilt or innocence. If found guilty, the defendant would have a separate hearing on the possible punishment. The full Senate failed to act on the bill.[57] A similar measure made no progress in the House.

In 1980, Congress passed H.R.10 (PL 96-247), allowing the federal government to file suits against states to protect the rights of persons confined in state institutions, such as jails, mental hospitals, and juvenile facilities. Before filing any suit, federal officials would have to notify state officials of the alleged deprivations and possible corrective measures. The attorney general was limited to seeking only equitable relief, such as an injunction, and not monetary damages.[58] The bill authorized the attorney general to sue a state after finding a pattern or practice that deprived institutionalized persons of their rights. The attorney general was required to report to Congress each year the number, variety, and outcome of all lawsuits the government filed under the bill.[59]

PRESIDENT REAGAN

Ronald Reagan told the American public that during his administration, millions of dollars would be allocated for prison and jail facilities so that the mistake of releasing dangerous criminals from overcrowded prisons would not be repeated.[60] He also noted that one of his top priorities would be to increase the construction of new prison space to accommodate the increased number of criminals being removed from our streets.[61]

Reagan promised to pursue legislation to restore constitutional procedures to impose capital punishment for heinous federal crimes, including murder, treason, and espionage.[62] He explained federal statutes currently provide for capital punishment for those offenses, but except in the case of air piracy, the death penalty provisions were not accompanied by appropriate procedures required after the Supreme Court's 1972 decision in *Furman v. Georgia* (408 US 238 [1972]) to prevent disparate application.[63]

CONGRESS

1983–84: 98TH CONGRESS

The Congress passed PL 98-473 (H.J. Res. 648), a fiscal 1985 continuing appropriations resolution, but attached some provisions related to prisons. The bill allowed pretrial detention of defendants considered dangerous to the community.[64]

S. 1763 was a proposal to revise federal court procedures for handling writs of habeas corpus and was designed to relieve some of the growing workload of the federal courts. Although there was support for the proposal, it did not pass.

Again the Senate passed a bill (S. 1765) to establish constitutional procedures as mandated by the Supreme Court for imposing the death penalty in certain homicide, treason, and espionage cases and in cases involving attempts to assassinate the president.[65] The bill also authorized the death penalty for crimes that resulted in the death of another person. The bill called for a death penalty when a person seriously injured or came "dangerously close"[66] to killing the president. The provision grew out of the shooting that wounded Reagan. To comply with the Supreme Court guidelines, there would be a two-stage process.[67] The bill was not passed by the House.

1985–86: 99TH CONGRESS

The House considered an amendment to the fiscal 1986 Commerce, Justice, State Appropriations Bill (H.R. 2965) that would bar federal prisons from providing abortions to pregnant inmates unless the woman's life was in danger. Despite concerns from some members of the Senate that the amendment was unconstitutional, it became law (PL 99-180).[68]

H.R. 365, the Prison Industries Improvement Act, was proposed but not passed in this session. This law, if passed, would have amended the federal criminal code to allow the transportation of some items made in the prison industries program through interstate commerce. It would also establish standards in taxes and wages that prison industries in different states must meet. Under one provision, inmates' wages could be held to pay for the cost of room and board or for reimbursement to crime victims.

1987–88: 100TH CONGRESS

One bill, S. 1757, called for inmates who had been provided counsel at trial and throughout their penalty proceedings to have only one chance to litigate their habeas corpus claims in federal court.[69] A committee led by retired Supreme Court Justice Lewis Powell Jr. recommended that prisoners be given a six-month period in which to file for a writ of habeas corpus, after exhausting their state court appeals. Only one round of federal appeals would be permitted.[70] The bill was not passed.

The House debated a bill (H.R. 5210/PL 100-690) known as the Omnibus Anti-Drug Bill. It included the death penalty for drug traffickers who killed people and for those who killed policemen during drug transactions. Once again, to comply with the previous Supreme Court ruling, there was a two-part proceeding set up in the bill, beginning with a trial before a judge or jury on the charges. If the judge or jury found the defendant guilty, then a separate proceeding would be held before a judge or jury where the judge or jury could decide to impose the death penalty. To do this, they would have to determine that the "aggravating" factors in the case, such as the defendant's prior criminal record or the fact that the crime was committed in a particularly brutal manner, outweighed any mitigating factors, such as whether the defendant was under duress at the time or had diminished mental capacity. The death penalty was barred for mentally retarded individuals.[71]

In the Senate, another proposal (S. 32) would institute the death penalty for more than 20 federal crimes, including the murder of a federal official or the defendant's family. Other crimes for which the death penalty could be applied include espionage, murder for hire, murder in aid of racketeering, hostage taking in which a death results, first-degree murder of a foreign official, kidnapping in which a death results, and assassination or a dangerously close attempt to assassinate the president. The bill called for a two-stage trial. It would bar a death sentence if it furthered a racially discriminatory pattern or if the defendants were under 18 at the time of their offense or were mentally retarded.[72] The Judiciary Committee sent the bill to the floor with no response.[73]

Another bill in the Senate, S. 36, covered fewer offenses but added a death penalty for terrorism-related murders. It also applied to defendants who were at least 18 at the time of the crime, rather than 16 as in S. 32.[74] This was not passed.

PRESIDENT BUSH

In 1989, George H. W. Bush asked Congress to authorize an additional $1 billion, over and above the $500 million already slated for 1990, for federal prison construction. These 24,000 new beds would increase federal prison capacity by nearly 80 percent.[75] He also suggested converting unused federal properties for use as federal prisons or jails.[76]

The president sought a revision in habeas corpus appeals, a process that allowed a condemned prison to spend years on efforts to overturn their sentences.[77] He also wanted legislation to relax the exclusionary rule to permit the use of certain illegally obtained evidence in criminal trials.

One issue that Bush firmly supported was the death penalty. He wanted to have capital punishment as a viable option for federal offenses and have it imposed swiftly, firmly, and fairly.[78] He proposed the Comprehensive Crime Control Act of 1989 in which he wanted to restore an enforceable death penalty for the most aggravated federal crimes. His proposal included adequate standards and constitutionally sound procedures for applying the federal death penalty provisions that were in federal statutes for homicide, espionage, and treason. His proposals would authorize the death penalty for a number of new offenses, such as murder for hire.[79]

Also included in the Comprehensive Crime Control Act was a proposal to establish a nationwide program of mandatory drug testing for defendants on postconviction release, including probation parole or supervised release.[80]

Bush believed that if a criminal carried a gun during a crime and someone died, the offender must pay with their own life. He called on Congress to enact the steps necessary to implement the death penalty and to designate the use of a firearm as an aggravating factor for determining whether the death sentence should be imposed.[81]

In 1991, President Bush again proposed new crime legislation that included restoring of the federal death penalty. The legislation attempted to establish constitutionally sound procedures and adequate standards for imposing the death penalty for federal offenses that are already on the books, including mail bombing and murder of federal officials. It also authorized the death penalty for drug kingpins and for certain heinous acts, such as terrorist murder of American nationals abroad, killing of hostages, and murder for hire.[82]

CONGRESS

1989–90: 101ST CONGRESS

During this session, a major omnibus crime bill was passed (S. 3266/PL 101-647) that included some provisions on prisons. The original omnibus bill was S. 1970 and H.R. 5269. The new law authorized $220 million for states to develop alternatives to incarcerating inmates in already-crowded prison buildings. It also gave the Bureau of Prisons the authority to set up a shock incarceration program (sometimes referred to as "boot camp"). The program would enforce a highly regimented schedule of discipline, physical training, labor, drill, and ceremony characteristics of military basic training. Separately, the act stated that all federal inmates should work, except for security, medical, or disciplinary reasons.[83]

S. 380, the Capital Punishment Procedures Act, was proposed but not passed in the Senate. The bill would, among other things, establish criteria for carrying out the death penalty for federal offenses. The government would be responsible for serving notice upon a defendant, before the trial or a plea, that they are seeking the death penalty. A separate sentencing hearing before a jury would be required. The defendant would be permitted to present any information relevant to the sentencing, regardless of the rules of evidence, that could show mitigating factors. The bill would prohibit anyone under the age of 18 at the time of the offense to receive the death penalty.

1991–92: 102ND CONGRESS

The House approved H.R. 3371/S. 1241 to apply the death penalty to more than 50 federal crimes. The provisions were part of a larger bill, but Bush insisted the bill did not go far enough to restrict appeals by convicted criminals and relax evidentiary rules, so the Senate blocked it.[84]

PRESIDENT CLINTON

When it came to prison life, William Clinton believed that repeat, serious violent offenders should not be paroled.[85] He also believed that there should be more alternatives to imprisonment, like boot camps.[86] But he also believed that there was a need to build more prisons.[87] He said that if the country built more prisons and combined that with tough truth-in-sentencing requirements, it will shut the revolving door on violent criminals.[88]

Clinton wanted to test all parolees for drugs. If they tested positive, the offender would be sent back to jail.[89] He said that our prisons must not be illegal drug markets, and anyone given a chance to go straight and live a better life must be absolutely drug free. He signed a bill requiring states to start drug testing prisoners and parolees in order to get federal funding to build prisons.[90] He also wanted to help states get even tougher on drug trafficking in prisons by enacting stiffer penalties for anyone who smuggled drugs into prison. He also wanted all states to investigate the number of prisoners who were actually using drugs so that every year they could track their progress in keeping drugs out of prisons and away from prisoners.[91]

Clinton supported capital punishment and was in favor of legislation that would limit death-row inmates to a single habeas corpus appeal within a six-month time limit but at the same time guaranteeing inmates a higher standard of legal representation than many have had in the past. He proposed legislation that would provide the death penalty for some federal offenses, including killing a federal law enforcement officer.[92] He believed that if someone killed a law enforcement officer in the line of duty, the penalty ought to be death.[93] He also supported the death penalty for terrorism that led to murder.[94]

CONGRESS

1993–94: 103RD CONGRESS

The House debated three bills this session to improve prisons, none of which passed. One was H.R. 3351, to provide for alternatives to prisons. The second, H.R. 3354, provided for drug treatment for prisoners. It proposed authorizing $300 million over three years to help states provide drug treatment to inmates. The third bill, H.R. 3350, required drug treatment in federal prisons. None of the bills received final action.

In the major anticrime bill that passed Congress this session (H.R. 3355/H.R. 4092/S. 1607/PL 103-322), $7.9 billion in state construction grants for prisons and boot camps was authorized. Of that money, 50 percent was to be distributed to states that adopted tough truth-in-sentencing laws requiring repeat violent offenders to serve at least 85 percent of their sentences. Besides the construction grants, $1.8 billion was to go toward reimbursing states for the costs of incarcerating illegal aliens who committed crime.[95] Life imprisonment was mandated for a third violent felony, otherwise known as the "three strikes and you're out" provision. The bill allowed the release of inmates sentenced under this provision who were over age 70 and had served at least 30 years.[96]

There was also a provision in the new law that reimposed the death penalty for many capital crimes already on the books, such as assassination of the president or other top officials, espionage, and kidnapping that results in death. The law also authorized the death penalty for dozens of new federal crimes.[97] These included the death penalty for treason, genocide, causing a death through a train wreck or mailing explosives, drive-by shootings, civil rights murders, certain major drug felonies committed by drug kingpins, and murders committed with a gun during a federal drug felony or violent felony. These potential death penalties had been unenforceable since 1972, when the US Supreme Court ruled that there were not sufficient safeguards. In the new anticrime law, there were new procedures for death penalty prosecutions.

Another provision in the crime bill required that federal prosecutors notify the court and the defendant a reasonable time before the start of a trial if they planned to seek the death penalty. The law required a two-phase trial, the first to determine guilt and a second to determine whether the death penalty was warranted. Both were to be jury trials unless the defendant requested that a judge determine one or both. The federal government was barred from imposing the death penalty on those who were under the age of 18 at the time of the crime or those who were mentally retarded or lacked the mental capacity to understand the death penalty and why it was imposed on that person. Further, women could not be executed while they were pregnant.

Federal assistance to states was a key part of the new law. Grant money would be provided to states to help build new prisons or provide for alternative incarceration methods, such as boot camps, restitution, community service, weekend incarceration, or electronic monitoring. Money would also be available to help states pay for incarcerating illegal aliens who were convicted of felony offenses.

Other provisions prohibited prison inmates from receiving federal college scholarships, known as Pell Grants. The new law required that a prisoner alleging overcrowding in a prison must prove that he or she was unfairly harmed by the overcrowded conditions. An office was established within the Department of Justice that would promote job training and placement for both prisoners and ex-offenders. Any federal inmate released on probation or parole would be required to be drug tested, and any parolee testing positive could be returned to prison. Finally under the new law, federal prison officials were to notify local law enforcement officials when an inmate who was convicted of a federal violent crime or drug trafficking offense was released into the community.

1995–96: 104TH CONGRESS

In the House, members discussed H.R. 667, which would increase federal grants for state prison construction from $7.9 billion under the 1994 law to $10.5 billion. A portion of money was to go for grants to those states that showed they were increasing prison time for violent offenders. The remaining portion was to be reserved for those states with even stronger truth-in-sentencing policies. As amended, states could use up to 15 percent of their grants for local jail facilities provided they adopted tough pretrial detention and bail policies. Lawmakers also agreed to reserve a portion of the money to reimburse states for the cost of incarcerating illegal aliens. The bill also proposed to restrict inmates' ability to sue over their living conditions and limit the scope of court-ordered settlements in such lawsuits. And it proposed to repeal the $1 billion drug court program authorized in the 1994 crime law, although such programs would be eligible for proposed anticrime block grants.[98] This proposal did not pass.

The House passed H.R. 1533 to double the maximum penalty for jailbreaks from federal prisons. It proposed to double the maximum penalty for escaping from a federal prison from five years to ten. Supporters argued that the increase was needed to help deter inmates with long sentences from attempting to escape.[99] The Senate Judiciary Committee gave approval to the bill, but the bill went no further.[100]

Another bill, H.R. 2650, was intended to prevent the Bureau of Prisons from reducing the sentences of prisoners just because they completed drug-treatment programs. The bill was approved by the House, but the measure went no further. In 1984, Congress eliminated parole in federal prisons. As a result, the only way for federal prisoners to reduce their time in jail was by gaining credit for good behavior. For drug-addicted inmates, existing law allowed the bureau to reward a prisoner with up to a one-year reduction in sentence for completing a drug-treatment program. The bill sought to eliminate that one-year reduction and require such prisoners to complete a drug-treatment program before they could earn any credits for good behavior. The bill would have retained other incentives for completing drug-treatment programs, including preferred housing and job assignments. It sought to limit participation in drug-treatment programs to those who were within two years of completing their sentence.[101]

The House passed H.R. 4039 to eliminate Social Security benefits for prisoners. The bill sought to bar criminals from receiving the benefits while in prison. At the same time, prisoners incarcerated for less than one year could receive the benefits; the bill also proposed to give states and localities $400 for the name of each prisoner they reported to the Social Security Administration within certain time limits. The bill went no further.

Another bill that did not pass was H.R. 663, the No Frills Prison Act. Prison officials would need to show that living conditions within the prison are not luxurious. This can include unmonitored phone calls, in-cell televisions, possession of pornographic material, instruction or training on equipment for any martial arts or bodybuilding, or dress other than a uniform.

Republicans in the Senate wanted to restrict death row appeals known as habeas corpus. Originally, they added it to a separate antiterrorism bill (S. 735), and it passed (PL 104-132).[102] The House attached an amendment to restrict death row appeals to H.R. 2703, an antiterrorism bill. But the bill did not go any further.[103] Another bill proposed in the House, H.R. 729, would also restrict the opportunities for an inmate to file habeas corpus petitions. The bill proposed time limits of one year for state inmates and two years for federal. There would be shorter deadlines in those states that provided competent lawyers for death penalty appeals. It did not pass.[104]

Finally, a bill to restrict death penalty appeals was passed in the House (H.R. 729). Specifically, provisions in the bill would limit the opportunities for prisoners on death row to challenge their state convictions in federal court through habeas corpus petitions. Prisoners in state cases would have only one year to file their petitions; those convicted of federal offenses would have two years.

PRESIDENT BUSH

George W. Bush believed in many cases, the old way for punishing offenders had not worked, and the prison system needed a new approach. He said sometimes probation offices, which he agreed did "fine work" in our communities, needed a little boost, needed a little help in their mission, and needed a different curriculum for drug and alcohol programs. And for that he relied on faith-based programs.[105]

Bush believed that the proliferation of prisons, however necessary, is no substitute for hope and order in our souls.[106] Therefore, he welcomed faith-based programs into the prisons to help solve some of the intractable problems of our society.[107] He believed some of the greatest programs had come out of the faith-based programs in churches, synagogues, or mosques. He pointed out there were some fantastic programs that helped drug addicts kick their habits and wanted to focus resources on these programs. He said since the programs were based on the understanding that if you change a person's heart, you change that person's behavior, they were successful. He believed that the government should welcome faith-based programs into our society.[108]

Bush also thought prisoner reentry into society would be made easier with these faith-based programs—where the prisoner is able to be welcomed by a person of faith as a part of the probation experience or parole experience.[109] These programs were also a good basis to help children whose parent may be incarcerated.[110]

Drug testing was a key part to Bush's plan. He stated that those inmates who receive drug treatment are 73 percent less likely to be rearrested and 44 percent less likely to use drugs than those who receive no treatment at all. Therefore, Bush asked the attorney general to come up with a plan to ensure our federal prisons are drug free, to expand drug testing for those offenders who are on probation or parole, and to strengthen our system of drug courts around the nation.[111]

Bush signed S. 1435 (PL 108-79), the Prison Rape Elimination Act of 2003, which provided for the analysis of the incidence and effects of prison rape in federal, state and local institutions and for information, resources, recommendations, and funding to protect individuals from prison rape. The act also created a National Prison Rape Reduction Commission.[112]

Bush supported capital punishment on the federal level and oversaw the execution of Timothy McVeigh for the Oklahoma City bombing.

CONGRESS

2001-2: 107TH CONGRESS

The House considered a bill (H.R. 1577) that would phase out the requirement that federal agencies award large contracts to Federal Prison Industries. Many businesses supported the bill because under a previous law, prison workshops were given the first option for large federal contracts on things like office chairs and uniforms. The bill would phase out the requirement that agencies must do business with the Federal Prison Industries whenever possible.

The Senate considered S. 486, a bill to require DNA testing in federal criminal cases as an attempt to prevent the execution of innocent defendants. Any defendant on death row would also be provided adequate legal representation. The bill would also bar the destruction of biological evidence.

2003-4: 108TH CONGRESS

H.R. 5107 (PL 108-405) was a bill to improve the quality of legal representation for defendants in capital crime cases. The bill also included provisions to make it easier for inmates to get access to postconviction DNA tests that might exonerate them. It was attached to a bill that would guarantee rights of crime victims. The bill also included hundreds of millions of dollars in grants to cities and states, as well as law enforcement provision backed by the Bush administration. The bill established procedures to ensure that federal inmates could apply for DNA tests that could establish their innocence. A court could order testing if an inmate asserted under penalty of perjury that he or she was innocent and if the test results might raise a reasonable probability that the inmate did not commit the offense. The courts could grant new trials or resentencing if the test results and other compelling evidence showed that a new trial was likely to result in an acquittal; it also barred the government from destroying DNA evidence in federal criminal cases while a defendant remained incarcerated.[113]

In H.R. 1707, the nation's prisons would be forced to do better in protecting inmates from sexual assaults. The bill would establish a commission to collect data on the effect of prison policies on rape prevention.

2005-6: 109TH CONGRESS

In H.R. 2965, the federal prison industries program, UNICOR, was again under attack. In the program, federal prisoners supply federal agencies with much of their furniture and office equipment. UNICOR has first option for filling contracts for office such office equipment. But private industries would like to overturn that policy, which was the focus of the House bill.

S. 103 and H.R. 3889 were two bills that were aimed at reducing the production and use of methamphetamine. The proposals would make it more difficult for people to purchase pseudoephedrine, a key ingredient in the production of the drug.

In the renewal of the Anti-Terrorism Act of 2001, provisions would focus on the death penalty for hijacking of airplanes. The Anti-Hijacking Act of 1974 made hijacking a federal crime. Defendants who hijacked planes in between the two decades between the passage of the acts were not subject to a death sentence. If the bill became law, defendants convicted of crimes committed before 1994 could be sentenced to death.

2007–8: 110TH CONGRESS

There was much support in Congress for a new law that would help to equalize the prison terms for possession of crack cocaine and powder cocaine. However, there was disagreement over how much to change the law, so nothing was passed. The bills were S. 1383, S. 1685, S. 1711, H.R. 79, and H.R. 460.

PRESIDENT OBAMA

Barack Obama has stated that the death penalty should only be used serious cases. While serving in the Illinois legislature, he supported reforms to the state's death penalty policy to help prevent innocent people from being executed. Specifically, he supported DNA testing and requiring police to videotape interrogations to prevent coerced confessions. He also opposed a bill to make it easier to give the death penalty to murderers involved in gang violence. He supported the death penalty for heinous crimes, such as the murder of elderly people or the rape of a small child.[114]

2009–10: 111TH CONGRESS

The requirement that the Defense Department and other federal agencies purchase office equipment from federal prison work programs was again under fire. A provision in the Fiscal 2002 Defense Authorization Bill (H.R. 1105) would allow private firms to bid against the Prison Industries.[115] This bill became law (PL 111-8).

House members considered the Federal Prison Bureau Nonviolent Offender Relief Act (H.R. 61), which would amend the federal criminal code so that the Bureau of Prisons would be permitted to release prisoners who served half of their terms of imprisonment if the offender was at least 45 years old, had not been convicted of a violent crime, or had no prison disciplinary infractions. The bill was not passed into law in this session.

Senate members debated the Safe Prisons Communications Act (S. 251). This was a proposal to allow the director of the Federal Bureau of Prisons or the executive of a state to request the Federal Communications Commission to install devices that would prevent, jam, or otherwise interfere with wireless communications within the geographic boundaries of a prison. This also did not become law.

The Death in Custody Reporting Act of 2009 (H.R. 738) was a proposal in the House that would require the states report to the attorney general information about the death of any person who was detained, arrested, en route to incarceration, or incarcerated in a prison. Similarly, law enforcement agencies would also be required to report information regarding the death of any person arrested by that agency, en route to being incarcerated, or incarcerated in a correctional facility. If states did not report the necessary information, the attorney general would be permitted to reduce any criminal justice assistance grants that were provided to those states. On receiving the information, the attorney general would make recommendations as to how to change policy so that future deaths could be prevented. The bill did not have enough support to pass.

In H.R. 1429, the House considered the Stop AIDS in Prison Act, which was a proposal to ask the Bureau of Prisons to develop new policies to provide HIV testing, treatment, and prevention for inmates in federal prison and then on their release into the community. If found to be positive for the virus, inmates would be provided with counseling and medical treatment. Other inmates would be provided with education about the disease. This law did not go to the president.

CONCLUSION

It is obvious that there is still much disagreement over policies directed toward prisons and capital punishment and that debate will continue in the future by both the president and Congress. They will continue to debate and pass laws concerning many prison issues, including solutions to prison overcrowding, treatment versus rehabilitation, and capital punishment. Even though many of these facilities are run by the states, there is a great amount of federal action in this area, too.

PART II

FEDERAL ANTIDRUG POLICIES

THE FEDERAL WAR AGAINST DRUGS HAS BEEN a controversial subject for many years. The United States spends billions of dollars each year to prevent or deter citizens from abusing illicit drugs. The best way to do this has been debated by both presidents and Congress. Chapter 7 includes presidential and congressional action in this area. Chapter 8 focuses on drunk driving, a policy area viewed by most as a state issue. However, in recent years, federal officials have raised the issue to a national issue and have given speeches or passed laws aimed at deterring people from drinking and driving. These actions are all analyzed in this chapter.

CHAPTER 5

DRUGS

THE UNITED STATES HAS SPENT BILLIONS OF dollars in the war against illegal drugs. Our elected officials have adopted various policies that focus on multiple approaches to decrease crime related to drug use. The government has tried increased punishments, international cooperation, alternative sanctions, and education programs to decrease the number of people who use drugs. There have been agencies created to coordinate the antidrug effort, specialized drug courts, and rehabilitation programs for those people addicted to drugs. Despite these varied attempts to reduce the abuse of illegal drugs, the number of people addicted to drugs continues to rise. Today we are still debating the role the government should take in the fight against drugs. Every president has had his own ideas, and Congress has made many laws as well. These are described in the following sections.

PRESIDENT TRUMAN

Harry Truman was disturbed that more narcotics were being brought in illegally from abroad than before and that the number of addicts had increased sharply, mainly among young people under the age of 21. Federal officials who had studied the problem reported that severe prison sentences for the men and women who peddle narcotics were the primary way to stop drug abuse. Truman reported he was informed that one bill, H.R. 3490, which passed in the House of Representatives, would go far toward suppressing the abuse of narcotic drugs and called on the Senate Committee to consider this or a similar bill at the earliest possible time so it could be enacted into law during that session of the Congress.[1]

PRESIDENT EISENHOWER

In 1953, Dwight Eisenhower signed H.R. 3307 (PL 83-76) to provide for the treatment of those who used narcotics in the District of Columbia. This measure, for the first time, made a civil procedure for commitment of narcotic drug users in hospitals for treatment and rehabilitation. Eisenhower believed legislation was the first step toward meeting the problem of drug addiction.[2] But he also understood the country needed more than treatment programs to control drug abuse. In 1955, he talked about the importance of the international control of the traffic in narcotics and cooperation with state and local agencies that would be needed to combat narcotic addiction in our country.[3]

PRESIDENT KENNEDY

John Kennedy decided to learn more about the drug problem before supporting legislation. In 1962, he announced a White House Conference on Narcotics composed of national authorities and leaders, including those in federal, state and local governments, to better understand addiction and formulate a course of action designed to cope with this national problem.[4]

1965–66: 89TH CONGRESS

The Congress in the mid-1960s passed H.R. 9167 (PL 89-793), otherwise known as the Narcotic Addict Rehabilitation Act of 1966. This marked a fundamental change in congressional policy toward the disposition of addicted persons who were charged with narcotic offenses. The change in policy was an effort to combat the steady increase in narcotic addition across the nation at the time.[5] Before the new law, the federal system generally took a punitive approach to those addicted to narcotics, with stiff mandatory minimum sentences for offenses. The new law provided for commitment of addicts to medical institutions instead of prison for long-term treatment. The approach involved treating addicts as persons who were in need of medical attention rather than simply punishing them. There were also provisions for intensive after-care included in the bill to assist former addicts return to normal life without renewing their habit.

PRESIDENT JOHNSON

Lyndon Johnson took a broad approach to drug use. He wanted more attention put on drug rehabilitation, enforcement training, and public education about drugs.[6] He also ordered more research into the problem and possible solutions. Johnson signed the Drug Abuse Control Amendments Bill that was, in his eyes, designed to prevent the misuse and the illicit traffic of potentially dangerous drugs.[7]

In 1965, after the President's Advisory Commission on Narcotic and Drug Abuse made its recommendations for reducing drug abuse, Johnson promised the Justice Department would submit proposals for a federal civil commitment statute to the Congress and for limiting mandatory minimum penalty sentences. The proposals would seek to give offenders a maximum opportunity for return to a normal life.[8] Johnson again asked Congress for legislation to authorize the civil commitment of drug addicts but promised the legislation would retain full criminal sanctions against those who peddle and sell narcotics.[9]

In 1968, Johnson proposed legislation to make the illegal manufacture, sale, and distribution of LSD and other dangerous drugs a felony and possession of those drugs a misdemeanor. He also proposed more than a 30 percent increase in the number of agents enforcing the narcotics and dangerous drug laws. When he signed the bill, it increased the penalty for the sale or manufacture of LSD and imposed a penalty for its possession. Under this bill, the illegal manufacture, sale, or distribution of LSD and similar drugs would become a felony, punishable by five years in prison and a $10,000 fine. The illegal possession of such a drug was made a misdemeanor punishable by up to one year in prison and a $1,000 fine.[10]

Johnson proposed some reorganizational changes to improve the federal response to crime. He suggested providing money to increase the number of federal narcotics agents by more than one-third[11] and to transfer the functions of the Bureau of Narcotics from the Treasury to the Department of Justice and the Bureau of Drug Abuse Control from the Department of Health, Education, and Welfare.[12] He wanted to establish a single Bureau of Narcotics and Dangerous Drugs that would be housed in the Department of Justice to administer those laws and to bring the American people the most efficient and effective federal enforcement machinery possible.[13]

CONGRESS

1967–68: 90TH CONGRESS

The Congress enacted H.R. 14096 (PL 90-639), which set criminal penalties for the illegal possession of stimulant, depressant, or hallucinogenic drugs.[14]

PRESIDENT NIXON

Throughout his term as president, Richard Nixon spoke a great length about how to reduce drug abuse. His policies contained everything from the more liberal rehabilitation programs to a more conservative approach with strict punishments. This was evident in 1972 when Nixon, in proposing an increase in program funding, described his antidrug initiatives as including treatment, rehabilitation, law enforcement, research, education, and prevention.[15] He focused on programs both domestically and internationally. Overall, he discussed the drug problem more than any other president.

When he first became president in 1969, President Nixon recognized a need for a concerted national policy on the federal level to deal with the drug problem, which he called a "growing menace to the general welfare of the US."[16] He considered the drug problem the number one domestic problem that concerned the American people.[17] During a speech in 1971, the American public was told that Nixon was initiating a worldwide escalation in our existing programs for the control of narcotics traffic.[18] He described his three approaches: (1) stop it at the source, (2) provide law enforcement to punish the drug pushers, and (3) allow for treatment of those who become addicted to narcotics.[19]

In 1970, Nixon proposed a large and more vigorous effort to control the traffic in narcotics and dangerous drugs.[20] He went on to announce a greatly expanded federal program to fight this growing problem from the previous administration. The major points included providing $3.5 million to train teachers and other school personnel about drug abuse education; establishing a National Clearinghouse for Drug Abuse Information and Education; providing grant funds for large cities that would fund drug education and law enforcement programs; developing a public service campaign on drug abuse; and increasing funds for research into the effects of marijuana use.[21]

In addition to this expanded federal program, Nixon had many other ideas to attack drug use. One was a program of international cooperation. He planned to reduce illegal drugs by giving more attention to their point of origin, as well as attempting to intercept them at their point of illegal entry into the United States. Nixon proposed additional steps to strike at the supply side of the drug traffic problem by striking at the illegal producers of drugs, those who grow the plants from which drugs are made, and trafficking in these drugs beyond our borders.[22] To do this, he directed the attorney general to create special investigative units within the Bureau of Narcotics and Dangerous Drugs to work in those areas where major criminal enterprises were engaged in the narcotics traffic. He wanted to destroy major criminal systems that imported and distributed narcotics and dangerous drugs.[23]

Nixon frequently talked about cooperation with other countries to control the illicit production and distribution of narcotics. He reported that representatives of his administration talked to Turkey, France, and Mexico to try to stop the production and smuggling of narcotics. He also amended the existing Single Convention on Narcotics Drugs to provide to the International Narcotics Control Board mandatory powers to replace the power to request voluntary compliance.[24] He asked the Congress to amend and approve the International Security Assistance Act of 1971 and the International Development and Humanitarian Assistance Act of 1971 to permit assistance to nations in their efforts to end drug trafficking.[25] He promised he would not hesitate to suspend all military and economic assistance to any county that condones or protects the international drug traffic.[26] To coordinate all of these programs, Nixon created a Cabinet Committee on International Narcotics Control that would formulate and coordinate all policies the federal Government implemented related to curtailing and eliminating the flow of illegal narcotics and dangerous drugs into the United States.[27]

Education was also a key part of Nixon's antidrug program. He asked the Secretary of Health, Education, and Welfare to collect information on the drug problem and to create an educational program geared toward all Americans, and especially young people, about the dangers of drugs.

Along with education, a treatment program was needed because, in Nixon's eyes, "law enforcement alone will not eliminate drug abuse. We must also have a strong program to treat and assist the addict."[28] He instructed the attorney general to identify all federal prisoners who are dependent on drugs be given the most up-to-date treatment available. He also asked the Congress to amend the Narcotic Addict Rehabilitation Act of 1966 to broaden the authority for the use of methadone maintenance programs.[29] He asked Congress for $105 million in funds to be used solely for the treatment and rehabilitation of drug-addicted individuals,[30] and he urged the Congress to appropriate whatever funds were needed for federal drug law enforcement and to build the clinics needed to treat those addicts who seek help.[31]

Nixon's drug plan involved more than just education and treatment. His more conservative side was made apparent when he supported tougher sentences for drug traffickers. He asked the Congress to amend the federal drug statutes so as to require tough, mandatory sentence for heroin traffickers.[32] In 1973, Nixon described his plan to put heroin pushers in prison and keep them there.[33] Nixon supported mandatory criminal penalties with regard to hard drugs.[34] He wanted national laws that would enable judges to take heroin traffickers off the streets, submitting a proposal to provide tough new minimum mandatory prison sentences for heroin traffickers. The proposal would allow a judge to consider the danger to the community before releasing arrested heroin traffickers on bail.[35] At one point, Nixon promised to submit to the Congress legislative proposals that would increase the penalties for those who traffic in narcotics, provide mandatory minimum sentencing of narcotic traffickers for first time offenses, and enable judges to deny bail, under certain conditions, pending trial.[36]

Another part of Nixon's approach to controlling drugs was to provide training to 22,000 state and local officers concerning the rise in the abuse of drugs.[37] He asked Congress to provide an additional $10 million in funds to increase and improve education and training in the field of dangerous drugs.[38] In addition, he requested $1 million to be used by the Bureau of Narcotics and Dangerous Drugs for training of foreign narcotics enforcement officers.[39]

Beyond training, Nixon then asked Congress for a major revision of all federal narcotics laws and requested more men and more money to deal with a problem. He explained that current manpower and resources were at their limits but were inadequate.[40] He thought additional positions were needed within the Bureau of Narcotics and Dangerous Drugs to increase their ability to apprehend those involved in narcotics trafficking and to investigate domestic industrial producers of drugs. He asked Congress to fund 325 additional positions for that purpose.[41] Finally, Nixon asked the Congress to provide an appropriation of $25.6 million for the Treasury Department for drug abuse control.[42]

To further expand the war on drugs, Nixon believed in the need for new laws. He called on Congress to pass the Controlled Dangerous Substances Act that would substantially revise existing drug laws by establishing a new and realistic penalty structure to provide courts with guidance and flexibility in handling offenders. It would also provide more effective enforcement tools for attacking the availability of dangerous drugs.[43] In 1970, Nixon signed the Comprehensive Drug Abuse Prevention and Control Act of 1970 (H.R. 18583/PL 91-513) to provide over 300 new agents, gave the attorney general a larger role over new types of drugs, and provided a forward-looking program in the field of drug addiction.[44]

Nixon believed that a reorganization of agencies would help the battle. He proposed establishing a central authority with overall responsibility for all major federal drug-abuse prevention, education, treatment, rehabilitation, training, and research programs. This agency would be known as the Special Action Office of Drug Abuse Prevention and would be located in the executive office of the president. It would be headed by a director accountable to the president.[45] Nixon signed an executive order to establish a new Office for Drug Abuse Law Enforcement in the Department of Justice. The office was to focus on a concentrated assault on street-level heroin pushers.[46] Finally, he reorganized many of the agencies to create a new agency called the Drug Enforcement Agency that would focus on coordinating the activities of federal drug agencies.[47]

The Special Action Office for Drug Abuse Prevention was created when Nixon signed the Drug Abuse Office and Treatment Act of 1972 (S. 2097/PL 92-255). The office would be responsible for coordinating all federal activities concerned with drug abuse prevention, education, treatment, rehabilitation, training, and research. It would be at the cutting edge of our attack on drug abuse. Besides this, the law created a new formula grant program to assist states in coping with drug abuse. Authorization was provided for $350 million in grants and contracts to be administered by the Department of Health, Education, and Welfare.

Other agencies were created in the bill. One was the National Drug Abuse Training Center, which would develop, conduct, and support a full range of training programs relating to drug abuse prevention functions. Another agency was the National Institute on Drug Abuse, to be housed within the National Institute of Mental Health. The new institute would administer drug abuse programs assigned to the Secretary of Health, Education, and Welfare. Besides these organizations, four advisory bodies would be established to provide counsel and recommendations to the president, the Secretary of Health, Education, and Welfare, and the director of the Special Action Office on means of curbing drug abuse."[48]

In addition to all of this, Nixon had some new, alternative ideas for reducing drug use. He asked the Congress to provide $2 million to the Department of Agriculture for research and development of herbicides that could be used to destroy narcotics plants that did not have adverse ecological effects.[49] Another idea was to designate the week beginning October 3, 1971, as the second annual Drug Abuse Prevention Week. He asked people and businesses to "cooperate in such programs and to seek out new methods by which the risks and dangers of drug experimentation can be communicated to the entire nation."[50]

Overall, Nixon had many proposals to fight drug abuse, and he put drug abuse high on his agenda. His ideas ranged from more liberal to conservative.

CONGRESS

1969–70: 91ST CONGRESS

Congress responded to many of Nixon's requests for action on illicit drugs. In 1969, the Senate reported S. 3246, the Controlled Dangerous Substances Act, which incorporated many of the administration's proposed revisions of drug penalties, including substantial softening of penalties for marijuana violations. The Senate did not act on the bill.[51]

In the second year of the session, Congress passed a new drug control bill that revised and expanded federal policy toward narcotics addiction and drug abuse. The new law, called the Comprehensive Drug Abuse Prevention and Control Act of 1970 (H.R. 18583/PL 91-513), authorized expanded drug abuse education programs and increased rehabilitation and treatment programs for drug addicts and abusers. It also revised the federal laws on narcotics and dangerous drug and the penalties for violations of those laws. It also established new methods for enforcing those laws.[52]

The law reduced the penalty for possessing marijuana from two to ten years in prison and a $20,000 fine for a first offense to a maximum of one year in prison, a $5,000 fine, or both. The law also reduced the offense of distributing a small amount of marijuana from a felony to a misdemeanor punishable by the same penalties as possession. It was hoped that the reduced sentences would serve as a model for the states to follow.

The new law had many other provisions. For example, it provided for a double penalty for someone over the age of 18 who was convicted of providing a controlled dangerous substance to a person under 21. All mandatory minimum sentences for drug offenses would be eliminated, except for professional criminals. Narcotics and dangerous drugs were grouped into five categories, or schedules, based on the type of drug and its effect. Liquid (injectable) methamphetamine (speed), most other amphetamines and barbiturates, and some tranquilizers were placed in the category of controlled substances. Under the new law a law enforcement officer with probable cause to believe a substance might be destroyed or a life endangered if notice of a search were provided could legally enter a residence without notice and search it (known as a "no-knock" search). Finally, the new law tightened controls over the manufacture, importation, and exportation of all controlled substances.

1971–72: 92ND CONGRESS

The House Select Committee on Crime held hearings on heroin addiction in the United States and issued a report calling for a national research program to combat heroin addiction. In the report, committee members reported that heroin addiction had reached epidemic proportions in the United States and asked Congress to provide $50 million from which the federal government could subsidize efforts by pharmaceutical companies to find a drug to combat heroin addiction.[53]

Congress cleared for the president a bill (H.R. 5674/PL 92-13) authorizing additional funds for the Commission on Marijuana and Drug Abuse, which was authorized in the Comprehensive Drug Abuse Prevention and Control Act of 1970. The commission was given $1 million to study the extent and effects of marijuana use in the United States. H.R. 5674 was passed later, increasing the authorization to $4 million.

1973–74: 93RD CONGRESS

The Senate passed S. 1125 to continue existing general alcoholism prevention programs through fiscal 1976. The Nixon administration had proposed phasing out funding for community alcohol treatment programs, starting with fiscal 1974, and had not funded any new projects since June 1972.[54] The law became PL 93-282.

In 1974, Congress cleared S. 3355 (PL 93-481) that repealed laws allowing federal law enforcement agents to conduct no-knock searches. The no-knock provisions stemmed from the Drug Abuse Prevention and Control Act of 1970. The bill struck down one of the most controversial of Nixon's law-and-order measures. Supporters of no-knock authority emphasized the swiftness with which evidence, particularly of narcotics sale or use, could be destroyed if the people engaged in a drug transaction were notified that law enforcement agents were on the scene. Opponents of the no-knock provision argued that it was a violation of the Fourth Amendment guarantee that citizens be protected from unreasonable searches or seizures.

In the final version of the budget, Congress authorized appropriations of almost $400 million for the Drug Enforcement Administration (DEA), the new domestic drug enforcement agency. Further, it made it a federal crime to kill an agent of the DEA.[55]

In one final bill (H.R. 8389) the House debated providing for drug treatment programs at state and local prisons. This did not pass.

PRESIDENT FORD

Gerald Ford promised the American public he would spare no effort to crush the menace of drug abuse.[56] His approach to do that was multifaceted. One part of his approach was to continue providing treatment and rehabilitation programs for the victims of narcotics traffickers.[57] But Ford knew that in most cases, treatment alone was not enough. He said unless something was done to alter the fundamental conditions that led the individual to seek escape through drug use, a relapse was likely.[58]

The Ford administration was committed to maintaining a strong Federal Drug Enforcement Administration to provide leadership in the fight against drugs. At the same time, Ford also wanted to continue cooperation of foreign governments.[59] He consulted with leaders of Mexico, Colombia, and Turkey to urge stronger action by them in cooperation with the United States to control the production and the shipment of hard drugs.[60] He also directed the Domestic Council to undertake a comprehensive review and assessment of the overall federal drug abuse prevention, treatment, and enforcement effort to ensure that our programs, policies, and laws are appropriate and effective.[61]

Ford submitted a proposal to Congress that would require mandatory minimum prison sentences for people convicted of trafficking in heroin and other narcotic drugs. Sentences under the proposed legislation would be at least three years for a first offense and at least six years for subsequent offenses, or for selling drugs to a minor.[62] He also sent to Congress a proposal that would enable judges to deny bail to a defendant arrested for trafficking heroin or other dangerous drugs if the defendant was found (1) to have previously been convicted of a drug felony, (2) to be presently on parole, (3) to be a nonresident alien, (4) to be in possession of a false passport, or (5) to be a fugitive.[63]

Ford sent Congress other proposals as well. In one, he asked Congress to pass legislation requiring the forfeiture of any cash or property in the possession of a narcotics violator if it could be determined that it was used or was intended for use in connection with an illegal drug transaction.[64] He also asked Congress to amend provisions of the law to allow the seizure of vehicles, boats, and aircraft used to smuggle drugs.[65] An increase in federal funds to get drug addicts into treatment and out of crime was recommended by the president.[66] He asked Congress to ratify an existing treaty for the international control of synthetic drugs.[67] And finally, he recommended that the Congress pass legislation that would impose mandatory prison sentences on anyone convicted of trafficking in hard drugs such as heroin and similar narcotics. The sentences would be at least 3 years and would range up to 30 years.[68]

CONGRESS

1975–76: 94TH CONGRESS

There was surprisingly little action by Congress during Ford's administration on drug abuse. Only one bill was proposed. The Congress passed H.R. 13172 (PL 94-303), a supplemental appropriations bill that included a provision that cut off federal funds for the "Study of the Effect of Marijuana on Human Sexual Response" being conducted at Southern Illinois University (SIU). The $111,366 grant was awarded to SIU by the National Institute of Drug Abuse in August 1975.

PRESIDENT CARTER

Jimmy Carter sought to limit the sources of heroin as a way to control drug imports to the United States. As a way to do that, he sought to provide alternative crops for those countries where the sources of heroin were produced. He also approached the United Nations and individual countries to join with the United States in stopping drug traffic.[69]

CONGRESS

1977-78: 95TH CONGRESS

During Carter's administration, Congress passed primarily liberal policies about illicit drug use. Some drugs were reclassified in 1978 when the Senate passed a criminal code revision. The revision included a mandatory minimum sentence of two years for trafficking in an opiate. The possession of less than 150 grams of marijuana was reclassified as a misdemeanor. For the possession of less than 30 grams, no imprisonment could be ordered. The changes in federal marijuana laws were viewed as a significant precedent for state action by the National Organization for the Reform of Marijuana Laws (NORML), a powerful prodrug interest group.[70]

Treatment was the basis of a bill passed in the Senate (S. 2916/PL 95-461) that expanded federal drug abuse prevention and treatment programs. The bill provided for $229 million for the drug abuse programs administered by the National Institute on Drug Abuse (NIDA).[71] The Congress again focused on treatment and rehabilitation programs when it gave final approval to S. 3336 (PL 95-537), which increased the efficiency of federal programs for rehabilitating drug dependent probationers, parolees, and other persons released from prison. Under the bill, the number of supervised "hard" narcotics users and persons dependent on controlled substances such as barbiturates, amphetamines, hallucinogens, and marijuana under supervision would increase. The bill transferred the supervisory function from the Bureau of Prisons to the US Probation Service.

Finally, a two-year reauthorization of the DEA was passed by Congress (H.R. 5742) and signed into law (PL 95-137). The DEA was originally created in 1973 under a reorganization plan and given the primary responsibility for federal drug law enforcement efforts.

1979-80: 96TH CONGRESS

The Congress passed H.R. 2538 (PL 96-350) designed to close a loophole in US drug laws that would make it illegal for anyone to manufacture, distribute, or possess with the intent to manufacture or distribute any controlled substance on the high seas that are under US jurisdiction. Backers of the legislation claimed the loophole had severely hampered US Coast Guard efforts to curb international drug trafficking. Previously, possession of narcotics on the high seas was not prohibited under existing US law.[72]

PRESIDENT REAGAN

Ronald Reagan's approach to drug abuse, like Nixon's, involved many different elements. His strategy focused on international cooperation, education, prevention, detoxification, treatment, and research.[73] One of Reagan's goals was a drug-free workplace for all Americans.[74] He also wanted to create drug-free schools, from grade schools through universities. Reagan wanted to ensure that those involved in drugs found treatment but, at the same time, sought to strengthen law enforcement. Another goal of the Reagan administration was to expand public awareness and prevention.[75] In his last year in office, Reagan described five strategies aimed at reducing the supply of illegal drugs. They included (1) enhanced international cooperation, (2) stepped-up interdiction of drugs coming into the country, (3) improved intelligence on drug activities, (4) stepped-up investigations to eliminate drug trafficking organizations, and (5) targeted prosecution of top drug organizations.[76]

Reagan sought international cooperation to fight importation of drugs. He believed the drug problem was not just an American problem but also an international problem,[77] and he promised to work with other nations to curtail drug production. Throughout his administration, Reagan supported a foreign policy that sought to interdict and eradicate illicit drugs, wherever cultivated, processed, or transported.[78] He worked in cooperation with the governments of those countries that were the source of the drugs, reporting that the other countries were cooperating with us in trying to stop drug traffic.[79] He told the American public that his administration increased efforts overseas to cut drugs off before they left other countries' borders.[80] In 1986, Reagan met with the president of Mexico and said that "both countries were going to work together to eliminate drug crops, to provide heavy patrols on the border, and to step out the prosecution of those who deal in illegal narcotics."[81] He worked to improve US–Mexican cooperation to meet the challenged posed by powerful and wealthy international drug traffickers.[82] He also met with the leaders of Malaysia and Thailand to discuss drug abuse prevention.[83]

He also supported a border policy to improve detection and interception of illegal narcotics imports. He promised to develop better means to stop the flow of drugs over our borders.[84] This involved the use of military resources for detection when necessary.[85] At first, he authorized the use of military radar and intelligence to detect drug traffickers, but when the law was changed, it could no longer be done.[86] Reagan established a Special Council on Narcotics Control to coordinate efforts to stop the drug flow into the United States.[87] Reagan also created the National Narcotics Border Interdiction System (NNBIS) to interdict the flow of narcotics into the United States. It was designed to coordinate the work of the federal agencies that already had responsibilities and capabilities for the interdiction of seaborne, airborne, and cross border importation of narcotics. The NNBIS would complement but not replicate the duties of the regional Drug Enforcement task forces operated by the Department of Justice.[88]

Reagan believed that drug importation and trafficking was related to organized crime. Since drugs were related to an enormous amount of violent crime, drug trafficking and organized crime were among his major targets.[89] In 1984, Reagan proposed a reform to create tougher laws permitting federal prosecutors to seize the profits and assets of organized crime and drug traffickers.[90]

Reagan also supported changes in the criminal justice system as a way to reduce drug use. He asked the Congress for tougher federal penalties for drug trafficking.[91] Reagan wanted to increase the number of judges, prosecutors, and law enforcement people.[92] In 1983, Reagan proposed a new anticrime bill that would substantially increase the penalties for trafficking in drugs and would strengthen the regulatory authority of the DEA to reduce the diversion of legitimate drugs into illegal channels.[93] Reagan created task forces all around the country that were aimed at drug gangs.[94]

Reagan did not believe there was any real way to totally shut off the flow of the drugs themselves. Instead, the best thing that could be done was to take the customers away from the sellers.[95] In other words, Reagan thought the antidrug campaign would be more effective if there were fewer drug users rather than if the government tried to take the drugs away from those who wanted to use them.[96] He said we needed to take the users away from the drugs and reduce the demand side of the drug equation.[97] Education as a way to reduce the demand for drugs was important to Reagan. In 1983, he signed the National Drug Abuse Education Proclamation.[98] He then signed the National Drug Abuse Education and Prevention Week proclamation in 1984 to help teach the drug users and potential drug users to say no to drugs.[99] He proclaimed a "Just Say No to Drugs" week in 1986.[100]

Reagan also wanted treatment programs for those addicted to drugs. He noted that the administration's objective was not to punish users but to help them—not to throw them in jail but to free them from dependency, not to ruin their lives by putting them behind bars but to prevent their lives from being ruined by drugs.[101]

Beyond the traditional methods, Reagan also wanted to seek new approaches to drug abuse. He wanted to get away from the fatalistic attitude of earlier years and assert a positive approach that involved as many elements of this society as possible.[102] He said the efforts to stop drugs from flowing into the country are only one element in an overall solution. Instead, what was important was to develop private sector initiatives, such as community-based solutions to the drug problem.[103] Reagan truly believed that if the battle against drugs was going to be won, "each and every one of us has to take a stand and get involved."[104]

One alternative became law when he signed the Aviation Drug-Trafficking Control Act. Under this law, any individual whose pilot certificate is revoked by the Federal Aviation Administration (FAA) for carrying illegal drugs would have to wait five years, rather than one, before being able to appeal the denial of a new license. For the first time, the FAA would also be able to revoke the registration certificate of an aircraft used in transporting illegal drugs.[105]

Many of Reagan's actions were based on the premise that people were responsible for their own actions. The president thought individual drug users and everyone else understands this in a free society; people are all accountable for their own actions. If the drug problem was to be solved for good, drug users could no longer excuse themselves by blaming society. Nondrug users must be clear that, while we are sympathetic, we will no longer tolerate the use of illegal drugs by anyone.[106]

Reagan signed an executive order that included proposed legislation to combat drug abuse and trafficking. Called the Drug-Free America Act, the law implemented new procedures to ensure a drug-free federal workplace. It addressed the need to get drugs out of the workplace, schools, and our neighborhoods. It helps the states with drug treatment and cracks down on drug traffickers.[107]

Reagan sent a message to Congress about the proposed law. The law included provisions for a drug-free schools and workplace. Part of the proposal included the Substance Abuse Services Amendments of 1986 to provide funds to states for alcohol and drug abuse and mental health programs. There was also a Drug Interdiction and International Cooperation Act of 1986 that emphasized the need for increased international cooperation in the fight against drugs. The Anti-Drug Enforcement Act of 1986, also part of the law, contained several measures that make available the necessary tools to law enforcement and courts to ensure that those convicted of illegal drug offenses are punished. It also substantially increased penalties for drug trafficking. A final part of the bill was the Public Awareness and Private Sector Initiatives Act of 1986, which encouraged increased cooperation between the private sector and the government in educating the public about the hazards of drug abuse.[108] To further aid in the war against drugs, Reagan signed the Anti–Drug Abuse Act of 1986.[109]

In 1987, Reagan put together a National Drug Policy Board that would coordinate the performance of all drug abuse policy functions of the federal government.[110] He then established the White House Conference for a Drug Free America that would bring together knowledgeable individuals from the public and private sector who were concerned with issues relating to drug abuse education, prevention, and treatment and the production, trafficking, and distribution of illicit drugs.[111]

CONGRESS

1981–82: 97TH CONGRESS

There were two bills proposed about drug use this session, neither one of which was passed into law. The first was a comprehensive anticrime package passed in the House (H.R. 3963) that increased fines for trafficking in drugs and gave the government the power to require forfeiture of any property related to an illegal drug enterprise. The bill also created a cabinet-level office to oversee drug enforcement. Another provision in the bill allowed federal officials to drug test all offenders released on parole or given probation. If positive, drug abuse treatment and monitoring was to be provided to help defendants end their drug dependence. The bill substantially increased the penalties for manufacturing, trafficking, and selling illicit drugs. A new, alternative punishment that allowed a judge to fine offenders up to twice their profits or proceeds instead of assessing fixed penalties was established. The bill expanded the authority of US customs officials, in civil proceedings, to dispose of property related to drug operations.[112] In the end, Reagan vetoed the bill.[113]

The second bill (H.R. 2173) was a reauthorization of a program of drug abuse treatment and monitoring for convicted federal offenders released on probation or parole for three years. The program was first authorized by Congress in 1966 and had been extended periodically since then. Participants in the program were drug tested regularly and then monitored to determine if they were using drugs. The bill was not passed by the House.[114]

1983–84: 98TH CONGRESS

The Senate and House both acted on bills (S. 1787/H.R. 4028) to create a central office for drug enforcement, but they were not passed. Both were the drug czar positions that would establish national policies for combating drug abuse. They would have authority to review the annual budgets of the agencies, such as the DEA and the Coast Guard, that were involved in drug control activities. Under the law, the director could make recommendations to the president on the budgets for such agencies before they were submitted to Congress.[115]

Congress cleared major anticrime legislation as part of the fiscal 1985 continuing appropriations resolution (H.J. Res. 648/PL 98-473) that included provisions to increase penalties for drug trafficking and created an interagency council to combat drug trafficking.[116] It also gave federal prosecutors new authority to seize the assets and profits of drug traffickers and organized crime enterprises.[117] Funds in the Justice and Treasury Departments would be used for a variety of purposes, such as maintaining of equipment seized through forfeiture proceedings, payment of rewards for information leading to seizure, the purchase of drugs needed for an undercover operation, and rebuilding seized equipment so it could be used for drug enforcement.[118]

There were many other parts of this bill, some of which focused on penalties. The bill increased the maximum fines for the most serious drug offenses from $25,000 to

$125,000 for individuals. For trafficking in large quantities of drugs such as heroin and cocaine, the maximum fine was set at $250,000 and the maximum prison term at 20 years. A judge would be permitted to fine a drug offender up to twice the gross profits from his or her enterprise, and the first-offense penalty for illegally distributing or making certain drugs was increased from a maximum of 5 years to 15 years. Provisions of the new law increased the penalties for major drug offenses and allowed federal prosecutors the ability to seize the assets and profits of drug traffickers.

New controls were placed on new drugs in the proposed law. The attorney general was given emergency authority to require tighter control of new drugs or chemical substances if he determined such action was necessary to avoid danger to the public. He would be required to give 30 days notice before naming a substance as a "Schedule I" drug. The emergency status would expire after one year, although it could be extended. Any company that manufactured or dispensed a controlled substance would have to obtain a registration from the attorney general, and anyone who dispensed or conduct research with controlled substances would have to meet certain requirements. The attorney general could deny or revoke a registration, if needed, and would also be required to establish programs to help reduce the amount of drugs diverted into the black market.

Finally, the new law established a new agency, the National Drug Enforcement Policy Board, which would be responsible for coordinating federal drug enforcement activities. The attorney general would lead the new agency. Other members included the secretaries of state, treasury, defense, health and human services, the director of the Office of Management and Budget, the director of the CIA, and any other officials the president wanted to appoint.

Reagan signed the Drug Abuse Monitoring Program (H.R. 2173/PL 98-2360), first proposed in the previous congressional session, which reauthorized funding for drug abuse programs for federal offenders. The program reauthorized by the legislation provided drug abuse testing, monitoring, and treatment to convicted federal offenders released on parole or probation. It authorized $16.5 million for the next three years. The drug monitoring program was first authorized by Congress in 1966.

Another bill (S. 1146/PL 98-499) was passed to provide for revocation of the airman and registration certificates of the pilots and owners of aircraft used in drug trafficking. Under the new law, the administrator of the FAA was required to revoke the airman's certificate of any pilot convicted of a state or federal drug-related felony who was flying or was on board an airplane involved in the offense.[119]

1985–86: 99TH CONGRESS

On September 15, Reagan sent the Congress the Drug-Free America Act of 1986, the administration's proposals to address the nation's drug problem. The proposal was eventually passed into law (H.R. 5484/PL 99-570).

The new law provided $889 million for drug enforcement, interdiction, research, prevention, and education for fiscal 1987. The bulk of the money authorized was for law enforcement. This included $500 million in new funds for drug interdiction, $275 million for drug enforcement, and $230 million in grants for state and local law enforcement.

The law increased penalties for narcotics crimes and instituted stricter sanctions for small-scale users. One provision imposed a mandatory $1,000 minimum fine for simple possession of a small amount of illegal drugs.[120] Because it was considered to be more addictive, the penalties for possession of crack cocaine were made more stringent than those for powder cocaine. This became very controversial in later years, with some arguing the provision was penalizing minority drug users who were more likely to be convicted of offenses related to crack cocaine.

Many other provisions had to do with increasing penalties for conviction of a drug-related offense. For example, anyone convicted of the manufacture, distribution, or possession with intent to manufacture or distribute controlled substances could face of fine of up to $4 million as an individual, and for an organization it could be up to $10 million. Mandatory minimum sentences of at least ten years in prison would be required for those convicted of major drug trafficking offense. A mandatory minimum prison term of 20 years to death would be required if serious bodily injury resulted from a drug trafficking offense. For a second conviction of a major drug offense, the fines were set at up to $8 million for an individual and $20 million for an organization and mandatory minimum sentences of 20 years, with mandatory life imprisonment if death or bodily injury resulted. However, if a defendant provided substantial assistance in an investigation or aided in the prosecution of a person accused of a narcotics offense, the courts were authorized to impose less than a minimum mandatory sentence.

Additionally, the new legislation increased criminal penalties under the Controlled Substance Import and Export Act, which prohibits importing controlled substances into the United States and possession of such substances on the high seas with intent to import them. Those who owned or operated a crack house could face penalties of up to 20 years in prison and fines of up to $500,000. The use of minors in drug dealing was also prohibited.

1987–88: 100TH CONGRESS

Drug education programs were extended in an omnibus education bill. It extended the programs through fiscal year 1993 and authorized funding of $250 million in fiscal 1988.[121]

In another funding bill, Congress passed H.R. 5210 (PL 100-690) that authorized $2.7 billion for antidrug activities. It included the death penalty for major drug traffickers, created a cabinet-level "drug czar" to coordinate the nation's fight against drugs, provided additional penalties for both drug dealers and users, and authorized more money for drug-treatment, rehabilitation, and education programs. It authorized more than $2 billion in spending to be split evenly between programs to keep drugs out of the country and programs to treat users. A new death penalty provision targeted major drug traffickers who intentionally killed someone as part of their drug-related transactions. It also included anyone who intentionally killed or caused the killing of a police officer during drug trafficking. There would be increased penalties for drug traffickers, and certain federal benefits (such as contracts) would be denied to repeat drug users. The new law allowed the Justice Department to assess civil penalties of up to $10,000 for possession of a "personal use" amount of illegal drugs but gave offenders the option of a jury trial as opposed to a civil hearing. Convicted drug users, beginning in 1989, could also lose certain federal benefits, such as school and housing loans, but the imposition of such penalties was to be up to the judge's discretion. The law also created new, tough penalties for anyone who either bought or sold child pornography or facilitated the use of a child for the portrayal of explicit sexual acts.[122]

One of the controversial parts of the bill was the creation of a new cabinet-level drug czar position, to which William J. Bennett was appointed. It directed the president to submit a national drug-control strategy to Congress with 180 days of the drug director's confirmation. Thereafter, a drug strategy was to be submitted by February 1 of each year.[123]

In a Defense Department appropriations bill (H.R. 4781/PL 100-463), $300 million was set aside for narcotics-interdiction activities. The bill required at least $40 million to be used for drug-interdiction missions by National Guard and Reserve forces.[124]

PRESIDENT BUSH

Like the presidents before him, George H. W. Bush had many ideas for antidrug programs. One approach taken by Bush was to eliminate drug use through increased education. He believed the answer to the problem of drugs depends more on solving the demand side of the equation than it does on the supply side, the interdiction or sealing the borders. He proposed a major educational effort that involved the private sector and the schools.[125] He reinforced this idea when he said, "but for all we do in law enforcement, in interdiction and treatment, we will never win this war on drugs unless we stop the demand for drugs"[126] That meant Bush wanted to combat drug abuse with education, treatment, enforcement, and interdiction. He also would use our nation's armed services to break the deadly grip of drugs and prevent the drug scourge from taking hold.[127]

Bush wanted to fight drugs on all fronts, not only education, but also treatment, interdiction, and law enforcement.[128] He asked Congress for $1 billion in new outlays for the antidrug program[129] but later asked the Congress for $6 billion for his antidrug program to beef up drug education, rehabilitation, law enforcement, and interdiction.[130]

In his National Drug Control Strategy in 1989, Bush further described his drug policy. In the first part, he wanted to enforce the law as a way to make the streets and neighborhoods safe. Second, he proposed doubling federal assistance to state and local law enforcement. Specifically, he requested an increase of almost $1.5 billion in drug-related federal spending on law enforcement. A third element of Bush's strategy was to look beyond our borders where the cocaine and crack bought on America's streets is grown and processed. He proposed spending more than $1.5 billion on interdiction. That, along with greater interagency cooperation, sophisticated intelligence-gathering, and technology from the Defense Department, will help stop drugs at the borders. The next part of Bush's strategy concerned an expanded drug treatment in order to do a better job of providing services to those who need them. To pay for expanded programs, he proposed an increase of $321 million in federal spending on drug treatment. Along those same lines, Bush proposed a $0.4 billion increase in federal funds for school and community prevention programs to help young people resist trying drugs. He said that every school, college, university, and workplace must adopt tough but fair policies about drug use by students and employees.[131]

For those who were already hooked on drugs, Bush wanted to expand treatment.[132] For those who were convicted of dealing in drugs, Bush asked for tougher penalties, including the death penalty for drug kingpins. He believed it would inhibit the continued flow of drugs into this country.[133]

Bush also appointed Bill Bennett as drug czar to provide more effective education and awareness efforts to decrease the demand for illegal drugs, toughen law enforcement and interdiction to cut off suppliers, and put the dealers behind bars where they belong.[134] Bush created the President's Drug Advisory Council, which was composed of 27 prominent Americans, who would advise Director Bill Bennett and the president on ways to implement the National Drug Control Strategy in the private sector.[135]

Bush supported "'Zero Tolerance," which would enable judges to strictly apply the law on convicted drug offenders and severe sentences for dealers who hire children. He wanted to increase federal drug prosecutions, prison sentences for drug-related crime, and the death penalty for drug kingpins and those who commit these drug-related murders.[136]

Like Reagan, Bush supported drug-free workplaces and schools.[137] To reach the goal of drug-free schools, he asked for funding for urban emergency grants to help the hardest hit school districts rid themselves of drugs and allow the schools to get drugs out of their buildings and get back to basics and let students and teachers learn and educate in an environment where learning can take place.[138]

As part of his comprehensive approach to controlling drugs, Bush supported an international approach. He wanted to put an emphasis on bilateral and UN programs for the conversion of illicit cultivation in the producer countries and support the efforts of producing countries who ask for assistance to counter illegal production or trafficking. To do this, Bush supported strengthening the role of the United Nations in the war against drugs through an increase in its resources.[139] Bush and other country leaders agreed to establish a financial action task force to find new ways to track and prevent the laundering of drug money.[140] He acknowledged that the Colombian government was cooperating with US efforts to combat drugs.[141] He also welcomed the Lao government's agreement to work with us on combating the international scourge of narcotics.[142] Bush discussed the drug problem with the presidents of Argentina[143] and Mexico[144] and with leaders from Spain.[145] He also talked to the leaders of Peru and Bolivia.[146]

Bush asked Congress for legislation to mandate that an individual convicted of a state or federal drug trafficking or possession offense may be denied federal benefits for certain periods of time.[147]

Bush signed multiple laws concerning drug use. He signed the Drug-Free Schools and Communities Act Amendments of 1989 (H.R. 3614/PL 101-226), the International Narcotics Control Act of 1989 (H.R. 3611/PL 101-231), the International Narcotics Control Act (H.R. 5567/PL 101-623), and the Crime Control Act of 1990 (S. 3266/PL 101-647).

Besides these proposals, Bush also proposed a new offensive against drugs. It included $1.6 billion for prison building and support; $409 million for federal courts; $399 million for prevention programs in the Department of Health and Human Services; $685 million for treatment programs to assist those who have become dependent on drugs; $251 million for research on the drug problem; $350 million for law enforcement grants to states and localities; $691 million for the Coast Guard; $471 million for the Customs Service, $313 million for the Department of Defense; and $117 million for the Immigration and Naturalization Service (INS).[148]

1989–90: 101st Congress

To combat drug use, President Bush won some of the antidrug legislation he sought. In H.R. 3611 (PL 101-231), drug-fighting assistance would be given to Colombia, Bolivia, and Peru. It provided for $125 million in US military and law enforcement aid to the Andean nations that were the main source of cocaine in the United States. The money would also provide education and training of law enforcement officials and equipment needed to fight drugs. The president was required to notify Congress of which countries would receive the aid and the type of assistance that would be provided. However, the assistance to Mexico was limited to $15 million. Any country that received the money would need to show that they were providing an appropriate share of the costs.

Further, the law required schools to implement programs aimed at preventing illegal substance abuse by students and employees. Federal money would be provided for those programs, but the amount of funds given to governors was limited to $125 million in fiscal 1990 and $100 million for each year thereafter. Any remaining funds were to be distributed based on a formula so that disadvantaged areas received more. Some money was available for the secretary of education to begin a program for creating drug-free school zones. Local schools would be provided money to implement alternative schools for students with drug problems, and for those juveniles in detention facilities, funds were available to create drug abuse education programs.

Two other bills, H.R. 3630, dealing with alcohol and drug abuse treatment programs, and H.R. 3550, dealing with the use of proceeds from assets seized during drug investigations, did not emerge from committee.[149]

In 1990, a Comprehensive Omnibus Crime Bill was passed (S. 3266/PL 101-647) that included provisions on drugs. The bill was intended to prevent drug activities within schools and their surrounding environments. To do that, the bill allocated $20 million to help police and prosecutors in rural areas investigate illegal drug trafficking. It also had an additional $15 million to train school personnel on drug-use intervention and counseling. The bill provided $1.5 million for a model drug-free school zone project.[150]

1991–92

Legislation known as the Andean initiative was passed by Congress (H.R. 1724/ PL 102-182). It extended duty-free treatment to goods such as leather handbags, luggage, and vegetables exported by Bolivia, Colombia, Ecuador, and Peru. The initiative was intended to provide the Andean nations with greater access to US markets to encourage people in those countries to move from producing coca leaves into legal products to export.[151]

Another drug-related bill was H.R. 3057, intended to extend federal drug-education initiatives for children. The bill authorized funding for the National Diffusion Network, which disseminated information about successful antidrug abuse programs to schools. The bill also provided $1.2 million to support drug-education programs that served rural areas and inner cities. The bill was approved by the House Education and Labor Committee but went no further.[152]

Another bill to focus on the health and safety of children was H.R. 3259 (PL 102-132) in which the Congress authorized drug abuse prevention and education programs for youth gangs and runaways for three years. It authorized $15 million for fiscal 1992, $18 million for fiscal 1993, and $20 million for fiscal 1994 for programs under that section. The second section was aimed at runaway and homeless youths and authorized the same amount for those programs.[153]

In S. 1306 (PL 102-321; companion bill H.R. 3698), known as the Alcohol, Drug Abuse, and Mental Health Reorganization Act, the Alcohol, Drug Abuse and Mental Health Administration was disbanded, and the research branches were put into the National Institutes of Health. The bill also reorganized the way the federal government underwrote mental health and substance abuse research and services.[154] Even though most states had, at that time, laws to prohibit the sale of tobacco products to minors, many were not enforcing them. The new law passed by Congress required states to enforce laws that bar the sale of tobacco products to minors.

PRESIDENT CLINTON

William Clinton followed other presidents in defining his drug agenda very broadly and having a plethora of ideas. Clinton's 1995 drug control strategy involved cutting off drugs at the source, stiffer punishments for drug dealers, more education and prevention, and more treatment. He also focused on boosting efforts to educate young people about the dangers and penalties of drug use.[155]

In 1997, he outlined his five-point antidrug strategy. To begin, it included giving children the straight facts about drugs, because the more children are aware of the dangers of drugs, the more likely they are to avoid them. To that effect, he proposed a media campaign to get out the facts and shape the attitudes of young people. Second, Clinton wanted to reduce drug-related crime and violence. He believed drug trafficking supports gangs and sets off gang warfare. Third, Clinton wanted to work to eliminate the social consequences of illegal drug use, such as AIDS and HIV cases. The fourth thing Clinton proposed was to shield the tons of cargo shipped here every year. Even though a tiny portion of that cargo is illegal drugs, Clinton believed it was still too much. Clinton wanted to bring the violence linked to drugs along our border with Mexico under control. Fifth, Clinton wanted to reduce drug cultivation, production, and trafficking abroad and at home. He supported alternatives to drug crops such as coca cultivation in Peru.

As a last point, Clinton wanted to do more here at home. He promised to host the first White House mayors' conference on drug control that would bring together mayors, police officers, and prosecutors to make sure that every community is doing the best it can. He wanted parents, teachers, law enforcement, and other community leaders to help.[156] He believed in the need to increase the emphasis on education, prevention, and rehabilitation because that is what he believed works. However, he also wanted to adopt law enforcement strategies so that people will take responsibility for themselves and increase the likelihood that they will move off drugs.

One of the elements of Clinton's antidrug program involved a strong education program in the schools. He believed that a strong antidrug message in communities would keep the streets safe and protect the children by giving them something to do. He felt that if kids are told early and clearly by someone they really respect, then the only sensible policy is no use.[157] He said we need to give our children the straight facts about just how dangerous drugs are,[158] and it was necessary to keep them from ever trying drugs in the first place. To do that, he proposed sending prevention educators to 6,500 schools nationwide. He also proposed a National Youth Antidrug Media Campaign to ensure that every time a child turns on the television, listens to the radio, or surfs the Internet, they will get the powerful message that drugs destroy lives.[159]

In 1994, Clinton discussed the need for drug treatment programs and drug courts.[160] He wanted drug treatment on demand.[161] At the same time, he also believed there needed to be a strong enforcement program designed to prevent those people who are bringing drugs into our country in large quantities.[162]

Working with other countries to try to stop drugs from coming into this country was important to Clinton.[163] He wanted to spend more money, resources, and efforts going after the drug dealers and the drug kingpins in their home countries.[164] He wanted to work with foreign governments to cut drugs off at the source.[165] Stopping drugs at their sources was a critical part of his antidrug strategy.[166] Clinton worked with leaders of Mexico,[167] Canada,[168] and Colombia.[169] He promised to hire one thousand more Border Patrol agents and one hundred new DEA agents to work closely with neighboring countries and to use the latest technologies to keep more drugs from coming into America in the first place.[170]

In 1996, Clinton signed the Comprehensive Methamphetamine Control Act of 1996 (S. 1965; PL 104-237). The law increased penalties for trafficking in meth, toughened the penalties for trafficking in those chemicals used to produce meth, and gave the Justice Department the authority to regulate and seize those chemicals.[171]

One of Clinton's concerns revolved around banning advertising for hard liquor. He said, "Liquor has no business with kids, and kids should have no business with liquor. Liquor ads on television would provide a message of encouragement to drink that young people simply don't need. Nothing good can come of it."[172]

He wanted to work on sentencing procedures:

I commend the Sentencing Commission for moving forward with recommendations to Congress for reducing the disparity between crack and powder cocaine penalties. My administration will give them very serious consideration . . . In October 1995, I signed legislation disapproving the Sentencing Commission's recommendation to equalize penalties for crack and powder cocaine distribution by dramatically reducing the penalties for crack. I believe that was the wrong approach then and would be the wrong approach now. Current law creates a substantial disparity between sentences for crack and powder cocaine. This disparity has led to a perception of unfairness and inconsistency in the Federal criminal justice system. The sentencing laws must continue to reflect that crack cocaine is a more harmful form of cocaine. The Sentencing Commission's new recommendations do so . . . I am also pleased that the Sentencing Commission has increased penalties for methamphetamine offenses pursuant to the legislation which I signed into law last year.[173]

CONGRESS

1993–94: 103RD CONGRESS

In this session, Congress considered H.R. 696, the Drug Kingpin Death Penalty Act. Under the law, the death penalty could be imposed on those who committed a federal drug felony as part of a continuing criminal enterprise or who conspired to kill a public official, juror, witness, or family member in an attempt to obstruct the investigation or prosecution of that offense. The bill was not passed into law.

Congress also debated the Federal Drug Treatment Bill (H.R. 3350), but it did not pass. Instead, they focused on passing the major anticrime bill (H.R. 3355; H.R. 4092/S. 1607; PL 103-322). This bill had many sections, one of which provided access to drug treatment for those federal inmates who were addicted to drugs. The Congress authorized $13 million for this treatment. The law also authorized $270 million for grants to help provide drug treatment for drug-addicted inmates in state prisons.

For the first time, nonviolent drug offenders were the focus of some of the bill's provisions. The Congress provided $1 billion to support drug courts for these offenders to provide them with intensive treatment and supervision and to avoid incarceration. Those who violated the terms of the court could face punishments such as community service, electronic monitoring, or boot camp. If the accused continued to offend, he or she could be sent to prison.

Under the law, the US Sentencing Commission would be required to increase the sentencing guidelines related to offenses of manufacturing or dealing drugs in areas previously deemed to be drug-free zones. The commission members were also asked to increase the sentences for those convicted of possessing, smuggling, or distributing illegal narcotics within a federal prison. Prisoners convicted of such crimes would not be eligible for parole.

Another section of the new law allowed the president to designate any place as a "violent crime and drug emergency area," indicating that it had a high rate of violence and drug abuse. If an area was deemed to be such, the president could then provide additional assistance to help state and local law enforcement agencies fight crime.

Finally, the new law required the director of the Office of National Drug Control Policy to submit an evaluation of status of federal drug control efforts every year. This would include an analysis of the availability of different drugs, the amount of drug use, and the status of drug treatment programs.

1995–96: 104TH CONGRESS

Following reports that there was a dramatic increase in teen drug use, the Congress cleared legislation that increased the penalties for the possession and trafficking of methamphetamine, also known as speed. President Clinton signed the measure into law (S. 1965/PL 104-237).

The Congress also passed a new law (H.R. 4137/PL 104-305) that increased the penalties for using the date-rape pill. The bill amended the Controlled Substances Act to require prison terms of up to 20 years and fines up to $2 million for anyone convicted of giving a controlled substance to an individual without that person's knowledge and with intent to commit a violent crime. The bill also increased the penalties for manufacturing, distributing, or possessing with the intent to distribute Rohypnol, the brand name for flunitrazepam. The drugs, called roofies on the street, are inexpensive, colorless, odorless, and tasteless.[174]

In H.R. 3852, penalties for possession and trafficking of methamphetamine (or speed) would be increased to be the same as those for crack cocaine. Possession of 5 grams of methamphetamine would trigger a 5-year mandatory minimum prison sentence, and possession of 50 grams would trigger a 10-year sentence. The bill would also increase the penalties for those who possess and traffic in the drugs used to manufacture methamphetamine and would create an interagency task force that would coordinate government activities geared toward reducing drug use. The Senate passed similar legislation (S. 1965).[175]

H.R. 2259 was a proposal to retain stringent sentencing guidelines for crack cocaine and money laundering offenses, as proposed by the US Sentencing Commission. The bill would reduce the sentences for possession or distribution of crack cocaine in an effort to make them similar to the penalties for possession and distribution of powder cocaine. Additionally, the sentences for money laundering as related to drug offenses would be reduced. The Judiciary Subcommittee voted to approve it.[176]

1997–98: 105TH CONGRESS

The House passed H.R. 2610, providing for a two-year reauthorization of the Office of National Drug Control Policy.[177] This did not go any further.

Clinton certified Mexico as an ally in the war against drugs, but many members of Congress disagreed with Clinton, argued that Mexico was failing in its counternarcotics efforts, and said they had concerns over Mexico's growing conduit for most of the cocaine and marijuana entering the United States. In response to Clinton's designation, the International Relations Committee in the House voted in favor of a resolution (H.J. Res. 8) disapproving the certification.[178] In the end, Congress decided not to overturn Clinton's certification of Mexico as an ally in the fight against narcotics.[179] However, they added more provisions in the 1998 spending package for $870 million to buy more radar surveillance planes, patrol boats, X-ray devices, and other items to detect and prevent narcotics smuggling.[180]

1999–2000: 106TH CONGRESS

The House and Senate passed companion bills (H.R. 1658, S. 1701/PL 106-85) that would make it more difficult for federal agents to seize private property they suspected was linked to a crime. Those who did not support the bill argued it could lead to the abuse of innocent people. The Clinton administration opposed the bill, saying it would hurt crime fighting efforts.[181] However, the law also granted more authority to seize assets once criminal charges have been proven. Under the new law, the government must prove that the property was used in the commission of a crime.[182]

H.R. 2130 was also passed by both chambers and became law (PL 106-172). This bill added the date-rape drugs (GHB or gamma-hydroxybutyric acid) to the list of narcotics subject to federal regulation and criminal prosecution. These drugs are often used with alcohol to make women unconscious and vulnerable to sexual attack. It would add that drug to the roster of Schedule I drugs, or those with no current lawful purpose, making its possession or sale subject to the most stringent federal criminal penalties.[183]

Yet another bill was H.R. 4365/H.R. 2987/S. 486 (PL 106-310), which was an attempt to crack down on the use, production, and sale of methamphetamine (speed). The bill increased the penalties for such offenses.

Congress approved $1.3 billion in emergency spending to fight drug trafficking in South America, mainly in Colombia (H.R. 4811/PL 106-429).[184] In the defense authorization law of 2001 (PL 106-398), the US military would be allowed to assist federal law enforcement in counterterrorism and drug interdiction. Congress then passed the Defense Authorization Law of 2001 (PL 106-259) that allocated $869 million to pay for the plan.

PRESIDENT BUSH

George W. Bush announced an all-out effort to reduce illegal drug use in America. He also said the federal government must do and would do a better job. Bush believed that drug trafficking, drug abuse, and organized crime were major threats to the well-being of society. He wanted to strengthen the law enforcement strategies and institutions, as well as develop more trusting multilateral cooperation. He wanted to reduce the demand for drugs and eliminate narco-trafficking organizations. To this end, he promised to undertake immediate steps to review law enforcement policies and coordination efforts in accordance with each country's national jurisdiction.[185]

Bush said the main reason drugs are shipped through Mexico to the United States was simply because American citizens use drugs. He believed it was important to do a better job of educating our citizenry about the dangers and evils of drug use.[186] He believed the most effective way to reduce the supply of drugs in America was to reduce the demand for drugs. Therefore, the Bush administration decided to focus attention on the demand side of the problem. He recognized that the most important work to reduce drug use would be accomplished in America's living rooms and classrooms; in churches, synagogues, and mosques; in the workplace; and in neighborhoods.[187]

Bush also thought that addicts need to be treated, and that only a small number of people consume most of the drugs. It was vital to find those individuals and help save their lives. When it came to drug treatment, Bush stated that in some cases, a government counselor can make a difference. A lot of times it requires a faith-based program to help break the terrible habit of drug use.[188] He thought that to break the addiction, in some cases, substance abuse programs based on faith could be very effective. But it was also important for Bush to advance the country's basic understanding of drug abuse and addiction, so he planned to increase funding for the National Institute on Drug Abuse and the National Institute on Alcohol Abuse and Alcoholism.[189]

He also wanted to support the benefits of coerced abstinence, and so he supported drug courts and drug testing for prisoners, probationers, and parolees.[190] To provide a supervised treatment alternative to prison sentences for nonviolent drug possession offenders, Bush asked for $50 million for drug courts. This would enable federal assistance to over 120 new or existing drug court programs.[191] Bush also asked for $20 million to assist state and local law enforcement agencies with the costs associated with methamphetamine laboratory clean up.[192]

At the same time, President Bush worked with other countries to stop the flow of drugs into the United States. In October 2007, he announced plans to send $1.4 billion in aid to Mexico to fight illegal drug trafficking.[193] He also certified that Colombia was cooperating with the United States in antidrug efforts.[194]

CONGRESS

2001–2: 107TH CONGRESS

The Congress considered but did not pass the foreign operations spending bills (H.R. 5410; S. 2779). Both bills included funds for US antidrug efforts in Colombia and neighboring countries. The Andean Counterdrug Initiative was launched in 2001 in an attempt to block narcotics shipments to the United States. As part of the fiscal 2002 supplemental spending law, Congress agreed to support a broader campaign aimed at left-wing guerrillas and other paramilitary groups, as well as at drug traffickers.[195]

In an appropriations bill in the House (H.R. 2500), an amendment was offered on medical marijuana. The amendment would have prohibited the Justice Department from prosecuting any state for allowing the distribution of marijuana used for medical purposes. The amendment was withdrawn before being voted on.[196]

2005–6: 109TH CONGRESS

S. 3525 was a proposal to reauthorize the Promoting Safe and Stable Families Program. Called the Child and Family Services and Improvement Act, part of the bill would provide states with $345 million per year in funds for programs that would prevent and address child abuse and neglect. The bill would also reauthorize the Child Welfare Services Program and fund child-protection agencies. The bill was cleared by the House and Senate and became law (PL 109-288).

In S. 103 and H.R. 3889, called the Combat Meth Act of 2005, individual states would have the choice to enact new policies against methamphetamine abuse. It would make it more difficult for those who operate drug labs to purchase the ingredient pseudoephedrine, an ingredient in cold medicine that is used to make the drug. The bill was eventually added to a renewal of the 2001 antiterrorism law (H.R. 3199).[197]

2007–8: 110TH CONGRESS

The Senate debated bills (S. 1711/S. 1383/S. 1685) that would eliminate the difference in triggers for mandatory minimum prison sentences between cocaine and crack. In general, the bills would equalize the sentences for those convicted of cocaine and crack offenses. A similar bill went through the House (H.R. 4545/H.R. 79/H.R. 460/). Despite the variety of bills, they did not pass during this session.

In H.R. 365 and S. 635, passed by both the House and Senate, the Environmental Protection Agency (EPA) would be required to create guidelines for cleaning up illegal methamphetamine labs. The labs typically create waste chemicals such as lye, red phosphorus, hydriodic acid, and iodine, which are toxic to people. The president signed the bill, and it became law (PL 110-8).

PRESIDENT OBAMA

As a candidate for office, Barack Obama promised to help communities fight meth and offer treatment programs to help addicts heal. He often supported treatment over prison for those using drugs. Obama pointed out that the discrepancy between the punishments for crack and powder cocaine was unfair and that African Americans and Hispanics are more than twice as likely as whites to be searched and arrested.[198] His plan for drug use included expanding the use of drug courts, providing ex-offender support to reduce recidivism, and eliminating sentencing disparities.[199]

In April of 2009, the Obama administration and a federal judge urged Congress to pass legislation to equalize prison sentences for those convicted of dealing and using crack versus power cocaine. Instead, they want to focus on punishing drug trafficking networks and those whose crimes involve acts of violence.[200]

Once president, Obama had to deal with a dramatic rise in violence on the border with Mexico. He announced that his administration would cooperate in intelligence-gathering operations with Mexican authorities in an effort to intercept more drugs being brought into the United States. He announced there would be more advanced surveillance techniques used against drug traffickers along the borders.[201] He promised to target transnational gangs, violence, drugs, and organized crime as a way to stem the flow of narcotrafficking.[202]

At the same time, Obama supported programs to stop the use of drugs across America. He proclaimed April 8, 2010, to be National D.A.R.E. Day to help kids choose alternatives to drugs and violence.[203]

2009–10: 11TH CONGRESS

Once again, the Congress considered the problem of discrepancies between powder cocaine and crack. In H.R. 18, the Powder-Crack Cocaine Penalty Equalization Act of 2009, the disparity in sentences for trafficking, possession, importation, and exportation of the drugs, would be changed so that they were more equitable. This bill did not pass. In H.R. 265/S. 1789, the Drug Sentencing Reform and Cocaine Kingpin Trafficking Act, the five-year mandatory minimum prison term for first-time possession of crack would be eliminated—also in an attempt to address the disparity between crack and powder cocaine. This did not become law. In the end, the Congress passed and the president signed S. 1789, the Fair Sentencing Act of 2010 (PL 111-220). This bill would also eliminated the mandatory minim prison term for first-time possession of crack, but it also directed the US Sentencing Commission to review and amend the guidelines to make them more equally.

CONCLUSION

Many proposals to help end drug abuse were made by both presidents and members of Congress. Some proposals focused on international aspects where others focused on domestic concerns. Education, treatment programs, drug testing, drug-free schools, and other proposals were all made. There is no doubt that the debate will continue into the future, and new laws will be passed to stop the harmful effects of drug use. The federal role in the drug war will persist because in the area of fighting drugs, states do not have the money, the technology, or the resources to fight it alone. Instead, they rely on the federal government for help.

CHAPTER 6

DRIVING UNDER THE INFLUENCE

WHEN IT COMES TO DRUNK DRIVING, MOST people would assume it to be a state concern. But in recent years it has been the topic for federal government action. Both presidents and Congress have made it a topic of debate. This is a good example of the federalization of crime, when elected officials have become involved in a traditionally state offense.

PRESIDENT TRUMAN

During the Truman administration our society, in general, did not recognize driving under the influence (DUI) to be as harmful as in today's society. However, in 1955, Harry Truman called on people to drive safely and keep their cars in good operating condition.[1]

PRESIDENT REAGAN

In 1982, Ronald Reagan signed H.R. 6170 (PL 97-364) to establish a new grant program to states to encourage them to establish programs to reduce or eliminate drunk driving.[2] The following year, he signed a proclamation designating a National Drunk and Drugged Driving Awareness Week, intended to begin a national campaign "that will not end until death by drunk and drugged drives is brought under control."[3]

He also created the Presidential Commission on Drunk Driving, which recommended that every state raise its drinking age to 21. Reagan reported that groups such as Mothers Against Drunk Driving (MADD) supported the proposal and that some states had agreed to raise their drinking age. As a result, according to Reagan, arrests and enforcement had been stepped up.[4]

But Reagan was disappointed when less than half the states raised their drinking ages. Because of that, he decided to support federal legislation to withhold 5 percent of a state's highway funds unless it adopted the 21-year-old drinking age.[5] He signed the National Minimum Drinking Age Bill that required states to raise their legal drinking ages to 21.

PRESIDENT BUSH

George H. W. Bush, in 1989, reported that his administration had implemented various policies to reduce drunk driving. He provided technical and financial assistance to launch state-run sobriety checkpoint programs. He also assisted state governments to upgrade their own laws, particularly by working with groups such as Remove Intoxicated Drivers (RID) and MADD who could provide needed training. And the Bush administration also renewed a series of public service ad campaigns to keep this issue high on the national agenda.[6]

PRESIDENT CLINTON

When William Clinton came into office, the issue of safe driving stayed on the agenda. In 1996, Clinton proposed all states make a new law that would make every person wanting a driver's license get a drug test as a way to save lives.[7] He also signed a new law that said every state must pass a law making it illegal for anyone under 21 to drive with alcohol in their blood. If they were caught doing so, their drivers' licenses must be suspended. Under the law, those states that did not choose to implement the law would lose some of their federal highway funds.[8]

Two years later, in 1998, Clinton proposed lowering the legal blood alcohol limit to .08 on all federal property, including national parks and military bases, in an effort to reduce drinking and driving.[9] Clinton wanted to expand the lower blood alcohol limit nationally as well.

Clinton continued to be concerned with drunk driving in 1999. That year, with the help of MADD, the National Drunk Driving Standard legislation (H.R. 4476) passed as part of the Department of Transportation and Related Agencies Appropriations Act of 2001 (PL 106-346).

1993–94: 103RD CONGRESS

In the 1993–94 session, the House passed a bill (H.R. 1385) that would amend the Omnibus Crime Control and Safe Streets Act of 1968 to let states use federal grant money to prosecute drunken drivers.[10] The bill did not pass in the Senate.

Instead, the Senate passed a bill designed to encourage states to adopt tougher laws against unsafe driving by youths and the elderly. The bill (S. 738) sought to reduce highway accidents by encouraging states to enforce laws against high-risk drivers, defined as drivers who were between 16 to 20 years old, elderly drivers over age 75, and repeat offenders. The primary focus of the bill was on teenagers who chose to drink and drive. The legislation offered states incentive grants totaling $100 million over 5 years to encourage them to implement provisional licenses for drivers under age 18. With a provisional license, a young driver would have to maintain a clean record for one year before receiving a full license. Further, states would also have to take steps to improve the driving records of drivers under 21.[11] The bill was not passed in the House.

That same year, Congress passed a major anticrime bill that added a year to a prison sentence given to someone convicted of drunken driving if a child under 18 was in the car and the offense was committed on federal property. The sentence could be increased up to five years if the child was seriously injured and up to ten years if the child was killed.[12]

1995–96: 104TH CONGRESS

In H.R. 558, titled the Marion Malley Walsh Drunk Driving Act, federal highway funds could be withheld from states if they did not meet certain provisions regarding drunk driving. For example, states would be required to have a .08 blood alcohol level for determining drunk driving, which would be .02 for those under the age of 21. States would also need to have an expedited system for revoking or suspending the drivers' licenses of those who were convicted of driving drunk. This was not passed.

1997–98: 105TH CONGRESS

Under the Safe and Sober Streets Act, federal highway funds could be withheld from those states that did not enforce a law that mandated a .08 blood alcohol level when determining if a driver was drunk or impaired. Funds could also be withheld from states under a similar proposal, the Deadly Driver Reduction and Burton H. Greene Memorial Act (H.R. 982). Neither proposal became law.

1999–2000: 106TH CONGRESS

Once again, the Safe and Sober Streets Act was proposed to limit highway funds to states that did not meet provisions concerning drunk driving. The bill did not pass during this session.

2003–4: 108TH CONGRESS

Those states that choose to accept federal highway money had to, among other things, enforce a minimum DUI blood alcohol level of .08 percent and raise its minimum drinking age to 21. In addition, to receive money, a state would have to enforce a higher risk impaired driver law. This would require certain minimum penalties for drunk driving, vehicle impoundment, specified fines, and prison terms for those convicted of drunk driving, among other things. Critics labeled the proposal an unfunded mandate because, in the long run, the enforcement of the DUI-related laws would require extra policing.[13]

H.R. 1745 was a proposal that would make funding available to states that required law enforcement officers to impound the motor vehicles of those who were driving while intoxicated. It did not become law.

2005–6: 109TH CONGRESS

H.R. 473 was a proposal in the House that was intended to reduce alcohol-related traffic accidents. It would have allowed for additional federal grant allocations for those states that adopted a program that entailed impounding vehicles operated by someone who was driving drunk. The bill did not become law.

Another bill proposed in the House and not passed was H.R. 618, a bill to require the National Driver Registry to include information about those convicted of drunk or impaired driving. This means if a prosecutor of district attorney was investigating a traffic-related offense, then his or her past driving records, even in other states, would be made available.

2007–8: 110TH CONGRESS

In this session, the Congress proposed H.R. 2109, the Empowering Our Local Communities Act of 2007. Under this proposal, the federal criminal code would be amended so that a minimum mandatory five-year prison term could be imposed on any illegal alien who was convicted of manslaughter while operating a motor vehicle while drunk. The bill was not passed into law.

2009–10: 111TH CONGRESS

House and Senate members debated H.R. 4890 and S. 3039, the Research of Alcohol Detection Systems for Stopping Alcohol-Related Fatalities Everywhere Act (ROADS SAFE Act). This bill would allow the administrator of the National Highway Traffic Safety Administration to carry out research exploring the feasibility and potential benefits of in-vehicle technology that would prevent people from operating their vehicles if they are impaired. This proposal did not have enough support to pass through the Congress.

The Drunk Driving Repeat Offender Prevention Act was a proposal in the Congress (H.R. 4891/S. 2920) that did not pass. This proposal would allow the secretary of transportation to withhold transportation funds from a state if it did not enact a law that required the installation of ignition interlock devices on those cars operated by an individual who had been convicted of drunk or impaired driving.

CONCLUSION

Although the issue of safe driving is primarily a state concern, presidents and Congress have debated and made policy in this area. The legislation has attempted to make the roadway safer and reduce deaths and injuries resulting from impaired or otherwise unsafe driving. In most years, however, this is not a top agenda item.

VIOLENT PERSONAL CRIMES

THE CHAPTERS IN PART III EACH INVOLVE violent crimes between a victim and offender. The first, in Chapter 7, has to do with domestic violence, or violence in the home. This is a relatively new area of activity for Congress and the president yet one that has garnered much public attention. Another relatively new area of federal activity is hate crimes, or crimes based on a person's race, sexual orientation, religion, or other characteristic. Whether or not crimes based on hate should be prosecuted more severely has been an interesting question for many years, and that issue has been debated in Congress as well. This is described in Chapter 8. In Chapter 9, federal policies designed to stop sex crimes are described. This includes policies such as Megan's law. And finally, services to help those people who have been the victims of violent offenses are described. Over the years, victims have been given more rights in the pretrial process and through to the sentencing process in the courtroom. Some of these federal laws have been used as model laws for states, who have implemented their own victims' rights legislation for victims of state offenses.

CHAPTER 7

DOMESTIC VIOLENCE

TYPICALLY, DOMESTIC VIOLENCE IS AN ISSUE THAT is considered to be under state jurisdiction, and federal involvement to address the problem has been a recent phenomenon. The first president to seriously consider the problem was George H. W. Bush, followed by William Clinton and George W. Bush. They proposed policies such as educating criminal justice personnel and the public about domestic violence, funding for women's shelters, and increasing crimes against offenders. Congress also debated and passed laws on domestic violence. Each of these is detailed in this chapter.

1977–78: 95TH CONGRESS

A new bill (H.R. 4727/PL 95-540) would place limits on the circumstances in which evidence about a rape victim's past sexual conduct would be admissible in a federal rape trial. It also set strict limits on the introduction of evidence in the trial. The intent of the law was to prevent the use of a victim's prior sexual behavior in a trial, since it often is not relevant to the case.

In another bill, the Senate passed a new proposal (S. 2759) to establish a grant program to help fund agencies and shelters for victims of spousal abuse. The House did not support similar legislation in their chamber (H.R. 12299). This did not become law.

PRESIDENT CARTER

Jimmy Carter gave little attention to domestic violence, but at the same time he was the first to do so, adding it to the national agenda. Carter requested $10 million for programs designed to combat domestic violence.[1]

1979–80: 96TH CONGRESS

In 1980, the Congress passed legislation authorizing a new federal program aimed at combating domestic violence. The bill, H.R. 2977, authorized $65 million over three years to aid the victims of physical abuse by family members. Most of the money would have gone to local centers that provided emergency shelter to women who left home because their husbands beat them. The bill was passed by the House easily but ran into trouble in the Senate. Opposition came from conservative "pro-family" groups who said the problem was not a matter for the federal government. Some said centers such as those that would be aided by the bill worked to undermine the traditional family structure, whereas others claimed a number of federally funded programs that already provided assistance to victims of domestic violence. The bill was supported by a coalition of women's, social service, and civil rights organizations for several years. Supporters argued that locally funded domestic violence programs did not have the resources to cope with the problem and that many people who sought to escape dangerous situations at home could not be helped because of lack of space in existing centers. The bill died at the end of the session.[2]

PRESIDENT BUSH

In 1989, George H. W. Bush said it was the responsibility of cities and states to step up their efforts to combat violence against women and to treat victims with compassion and respect. Further, violence against women would not subside unless public attitudes changed. He sought to educate the police, prosecutors, judges, and juries about domestic violence. He also wanted to create a climate where the message our children get from television, schools, and parents was that violence against women is wrong.[3]

CONGRESS

1989–90: 101ST CONGRESS

The Senate Judiciary approved a bill (S. 2745) that was designed to combat violence against women. The bill would have doubled the minimum penalties for rape and aggravated assault, imposed new penalties for repeat offenders, and provided more restitution for victims. It authorized $300 million for new police efforts to identify and combat sex crimes, with the majority of the funds going to the 40 metropolitan areas deemed most dangerous to women by the Bureau of Justice Statistics. Furthermore, the bill tripled funding for shelters for battered women; authorized funds for increased lighting, camera surveillance, and other security measures at public transit facilities; created a National Commission on Violent Crime Against Women; created federal penalties for spouse abuse; and required colleges to provide rape prevention programs.[4]

1991–92: 102ND CONGRESS

The Congress considered a bill (S. 15; H.R. 1502), known as the Violence Against Women Act, which was similar to the bill proposed in the previous session. The intent of the bill was to curb violence against women by stiffening penalties for such crimes and doubling the federal penalty for rape to ten years. Penalties for sex crimes were increased, and restitution for victims was mandated. A Commission on Violent Crime Against Women was created. The law allowed victims of these crimes to bring civil rights suits against the offenders. The bill authorized $300 million for law enforcement efforts to fight sex crimes, with $100 million earmarked for the 40 metropolitan areas most dangerous for women. Another $65 million was authorized for rape prevention and education. Additionally, the measure required states to pay for a medical exam to determine whether a woman had been raped.[5] This proposal did not pass.

In 1992, the Congress passed a new law (H.R. 1252/PL 102-527) that promoted the use of expert witnesses in cases in which battered women assaulted or killed their abusers. The bill authorized $600,000 to the State Justice Institute to provide grants to organizations to collect information on expert testimony about the psychological state of battered women and to help women find expert defense witnesses.[6]

PRESIDENT CLINTON

William Clinton realized that it takes a special effort to prevent crimes of violence against women, who are especially vulnerable to violent crime. He proposed a crime bill that would increase sentences for rape, require rapists to pay damages to victims, protect women against domestic violence, and create training programs to help judges learn more about these crimes, since many judges at that time did not know how to handle these cases effectively.[7]

In 1995, Clinton created the Office of Violence Against Women in the Justice Department.[8] The following year, Clinton launched a 24-hour, 7-day, toll-free hotline so women in trouble could find out about emergency assistance, find shelter, and report abuse to the authorities.[9]

Finally, Clinton signed the Interstate Stalking Punishment and Prevention Act as part of the National Defense Authorization Act for Fiscal Year 1997. The provisions on domestic violence made interstate stalking a federal offense.[10] According to Clinton, if a person stalks and harasses someone, the law will follow. And if a victim of stalking wanted to build a new life somewhere else, they would have the full protection of federal law.[11]

CONGRESS

1993–94: 103RD CONGRESS

Congress passed H.R. 1133, the Crimes Against Women Act, to establish new laws aimed at reducing domestic violence against women. The act contained provisions prodding states to toughen laws against domestic violence. It also provided grants for law enforcement efforts to prosecute and prevent crimes, such as rape, and made interstate stalking and domestic violence federal crimes.[12] This was not passed.

Some attention was paid to domestic violence in the major crime bill passed in 1994 (H.R. 3355; H.R. 4092/S. 1607; PL 103-322). The Congress provided $1.6 billion to implement the Violence Against Women Act, a package of new federal penalties and grant programs designed to reduce domestic violence and other crimes against women.[13]

Many provisions of the new law created or increased penalties for different offenses. For example, new federal penalties were created for interstate stalking and for domestic abuse where the abuser crossed state lines to harass or injure his or her victim or forced the victim to cross a state line. Offenders convicted of these offenses would face 5 to 10 years in prison or 20 years to life if a dangerous weapon was used, if serious physical harm occurred, or if the victim was killed. Penalties were also increased for repeat sexual offenders. Additionally, pretrial detention would be permitted in felony sex offenses or in cases of child pornography. Evidence of prior sexual offenses would now be permitted in trials for those defendants with such backgrounds, but a victim's past sexual behavior would no longer be admissible in federal cases.

Under other provisions, rape victims would be permitted to demand that their assailants be tested for HIV. The results would be disclosed to the defendant, the victim, and in some cases, the victim's parents or guardian. The victim would be allowed to share the results only with a doctor, family members, a counselor, or any sexual partners after the attack.

Other parts of the new law established a civil rights violation for violent crimes that were motivated by gender, which would allow for victims to sue for damages. In another provision, federal money would be provided for states to establish a toll-free hotline for victims of family violence. Domestic victims of battering by immigrant spouses or children could petition for legal residency and obtain a work permit. And finally, the new law required individuals who were convicted of domestic violence crimes in federal courts participate in a rehabilitation program as a condition of probation or supervised release.

1995–96: 104TH CONGRESS

Only one bill was passed in the 1996–97 session of Congress related to domestic violence. In it, laws against stalking were toughened, and the act of stalking someone across state lines or on federal property, such as a military base, was made a federal offense. In the bill, stalking was defined as following any person with the intention of harming or harassing them. The legislation also made restraining orders issued in any state valid in all states. These provisions were attached to the fiscal 1997 Defense Authorization Bill (H.R. 3230/PL 104-201). The 1994 crime bill had made stalking a spouse or former spouse a federal crime in some instances, but it did not address cases in which the victim was not related to the stalker.[14]

1999–2000: 106TH CONGRESS

Congress considered reauthorizing the Violence Against Women Act (S. 2787/H.R. 1248) in this session. The law provides grants to states and private agencies to target crimes against women. The money helps fund programs like those to expand shelter space for victims of abuse.

In 1999, the Supreme Court struck down a provision of the Violence Against Women Act in *United States v. Morrisson* (529 US 598). The Court struck down the civil remedy provision.[15] The following year, a bill (H.R. 3244/PL 106-386) reauthorized the Violence Against Women Act and launched a new effort to combat international slavery and sex trafficking.

There were four other bills incorporated into H.R. 3244. The first was H.R. 1248, the Violence Against Women Act. This bill authorized over $3 billion for grant programs that were designed to address issues of domestic violence, date rape, stalking, and other crimes directed primarily at women. The second bill was H.R. 3244, the Sex Trafficking Act. Under this bill, almost $94.5 million was provided to states to combat human trafficking. The law created a new offense of trafficking in people. It set the punishment for selling a human into slavery at 20 years in prison. It also created a new type of visa (a "T" visa) for victims of trafficking. To receive the special visa, a victim would have to agree to cooperate with law enforcement to provide information and help prosecute offenders. They must also face retribution in their home country if they returned home.

The third bill incorporated into H.R. 1248 was H.R. 894 on sexual predators. This bill included Aimee's Law, which was named after a female student at George Mason University who was raped and murdered in 1996 by a convicted killer who had been released from a prison in Nevada. Under the bill, states had to maintain policies that were geared to ensuring that murderers, rapists, and those convicted of dangerous sexual offenses would serve lengthy sentences. If this was not done, the states could face losing their federal grants for anticrime programs.

The fourth bill incorporated into H.R. 3244 was H.R. 20311, a proposal to place restrictions on the sale of alcohol over the Internet. The intent of this proposal was to assist state officials to more effectively enforce laws that ban the Internet sales and subsequent shipment of alcohol.

PRESIDENT BUSH

George W. Bush believed that domestic violence not only violated the law but also was wrong. He considered it to be a crime that must be confronted by individuals, by communities, and by government. Further, Bush stated that government has a duty to treat domestic violence as a serious crime, which meant there must be serious consequences. He proposed two stages to attack the problem. First, he directed $20 million in 2004 to help communities create family justice centers, where victims of domestic violence could find the services they needed in one place. The second initiative would expand the good work of community and faith-based groups as they provided counseling and mentoring and other services to children who have witnessed domestic violence.[16]

2003–4: 108TH CONGRESS

S. 1019/S. 146 was a proposal titled the Unborn Victims of Violence Act. This law would make it a separate offense to harm a fetus during the commission of a federal crime against a pregnant woman. If a person, while committing a federal crime, intentionally kills or attempts to kill an unborn child, he or she could be punished for intentionally killing or attempting to kill a person. In lieu of this bill, Congress passed H.R. 1997, Laci and Conner's Law. Under this proposal, the prosecution does not need to show that the person committing the offense knew that the victim was pregnant or that the defendant intended to harm the unborn child. This proposal was signed by the president and became law (PL 108-212).

Another bill passed during this session was S. 342, called the Keeping Children and Families Safe Act of 2003 (PL 108-12). The new law renewed the 1996 Child Abuse Prevention and Treatment Act. Title IV of the bill, the Family Violence Prevention and Services Act, would authorize funding to prevent child abuse through local community outreach programs. It also provided grants to programs that provided services for children who witnessed episodes of domestic violence and for training those people who worked with the children.

2005–6: 109TH CONGRESS

A House Committee approved possible legislation (H.R. 2695) that would protect the identity of those victims of domestic violence who were receiving homeless assistance. Under the bill, called the Safe Housing Identity Exception for the Lives of

Domestic Violence Victims Act, the identities of victims of domestic violence would be protected if they received certain housing assistance grants. Because some men's rights groups lobbied to have the language in the law include male victims of domestic violence, it did not have enough support to pass.[17]

S. 1197, the Violence Against Women Act of 2005, was a proposal to reauthorize the Violence Against Women Act of 1994. It would increase penalties for stalking when the offender was subject to a protective order and for repeat offenders. It would also provide grants to states for use in programs designed to combat violent crimes against women. Another provision of the law required the attorney general to develop an educational curriculum for training court personnel who deal with domestic violence issues. The House version of the bill, H.R. 3402, the Violence Against Women and Department of Justice Reauthorization Act, was passed by both chambers and was signed by the president, becoming law (PL 109-162).

2007–8: 110TH CONGRESS

In this session, members of the House proposed H.R. 203, the Domestic Violence Protection Act. This was a proposal requiring states have a policy that law enforcement officers could confiscate weapons in domestic violence cases in order to be eligible for certain federal grants. It would also authorize grants to states that would allow them to hire more personnel who would enter information concerning protection orders into a database. Another provision of the proposed law would authorize grants for training programs and establishment of domestic violence courts. The bill did not move out of the subcommittee.

PRESIDENT OBAMA

In October 2010, Barack Obama announced an effort to combat domestic violence by combining improved legal protections for victims, as well as assistance in housing, health, and financial matters.[18] To bring more attention to domestic violence, Obama declared October 2010, as National Domestic Awareness Month.[19] He also appointed Lynn Rosenthal to serve as the White House adviser on Violence Against Women. She had the task of assisting the president on policy for addressing this concern throughout his administration.[20]

2009–10: 11TH CONGRESS

In a bill designed to protect pregnant women (H.R. 605), grants were authorized to help states provide services to women who were victims of domestic violence, dating violence, or stalking. The bill was called the Pregnant Women Support Act and did not pass. Another bill to provide grants to states for programs directed at helping victims of domestic violence or teen dating was the Teen Dating Violence Prevention Act. This also did not become law.

The Military Domestic and Sexual Violence Response Act was a proposal in the House (H.R. 840) designed to help victims of domestic violence for military families. If passed, the Office of Victims' Advocate would be established to help provide services for victims. It would also require the Department of Defense to provide crisis intervention services for victims of domestic violence, along with training on the prevention of such offenses. This bill was not sent to the president.

CONCLUSION

The crime of domestic violence has received federal attention since the first Bush administration. Since then, both presidents and Congress have debated different proposals to stop it. This is one crime where the federalization of crime is apparent. To be a federal offense, offenders must cross state lines. Many of the bills provided grant money to states to allow them to develop programs for women as they saw necessary.

CHAPTER 8

HATE CRIMES

CRIMES COMMITTED AGAINST OTHERS BECAUSE OF THEIR sexual orientation, race, religion, or any other characteristic have been defined as a hate crime. These offenses became an interest of Congress in 1988, when they approved S. 794 (PL 100-346).[1] Since then, many other proposals have been debated by the federal government to stop hate crimes and help victims of those acts.

PRESIDENT JOHNSON

1967–68: 90TH CONGRESS

A new law passed in this session (PL 90-284) defined hate crimes as those offenses motivated by the race, color, religion, or national origin of the victim. The federal government could intervene and prosecute such crimes if they occurred on federal property or during specific activities such as voting.

1989–90: 101ST CONGRESS

This year, Congress passed H.R. 1048 (PL 101-275) that required the Justice Department to gather and publish hate crime statistics for the next five years. It also required the attorney general to publish an annual summary showing how many crimes each year exhibited evidence of prejudice based on race, religion, sexual orientation, or ethnicity. It was recommended that the crimes included in the report include murder, manslaughter, forcible rape, assault, intimidation, arson, and vandalism.[2]

1991–92: 102ND CONGRESS

The House passed new legislation (H.R. 4797) to strengthen mandatory sentencing guidelines for federal offenses that involved hate crimes. The bill defined a hate crime as one that was motivated by hatred, bias, or prejudice based on race, religion, ethnicity, color, gender, or sexual orientation. If a federal crime was motivated by hatred or prejudice, then the judge would have to sentence the offender to additional time in prison. Prison terms would have been extended by roughly one-third. The Senate failed to act on it.[3]

PRESIDENT CLINTON

In 1997, William Clinton said it was important to make sure our nation's laws fully protect all of its citizens. Even though the current laws already punished some crimes committed against people on the basis of race, religion, or national origin, he believed it was necessary to do more. He wanted to make the current laws tougher and to include all hate crimes that cause physical harm. Further, Clinton wanted to prohibit crimes committed because of a victim's sexual orientation, gender, or disability. He believed that all Americans deserve protection from hate.[4]

CONGRESS

1993–94: 103RD CONGRESS

In this session, the House passed H.R. 1152, which authorized stiffer sentences for crimes motivated by bias. The Senate adopted S. 1522 to enhance the sentences for crimes motivated by prejudice or hatred, but it was not passed into law.

As part of the major 1994 Crime Bill (H.R. 3355; H.R. 4092/S. 1607; PL 103-322), language was included that made a crime motivated by gender a federal civil rights violation. The crime bill directed the US Sentencing Commission to increase sentences for hate crimes.[5]

In another omnibus education bill, the Elementary and Secondary Education Act Reauthorization (H.R. 6), a provision was included to authorize a grant program to local school districts and community-based organizations to assist areas directly affected by hate crimes.[6]

1999–2000: 106TH CONGRESS

In 2000, bills were proposed (S. 2549, H.R. 4205) to expand federal hate crimes to include sexual orientation, gender, and disability. It was attached to the defense authorization bill. It would have expanded both the definition of federal hate crimes and the government's jurisdiction to prosecute them. The bill was signed into law (PL 106-616).[7]

PRESIDENT BUSH

2001–2: 107TH CONGRESS

Legislation to broaden the federal definition of hate crimes failed to get a floor vote in either the House or the Senate. The bill (S. 625/H.R. 1343) would have expanded hate crime laws to cover offenses committed because of a victim's gender, sexual orientation, or disability. Existing law (PL 90-284) enacted in 1968 allowed federal prosecution of crimes based on race, color, religion, or national origin. It could be used only under six specified situations of federal involvement, including crimes committed against victims while they voted or were on federal property.[8]

A bill in the House that did not pass was H.R. 74, the Hate Crimes Prevention Act. The proposal would set penalties for willfully causing bodily injury to any person, or attempting to cause an injury, because of the actual or perceived race, color, religion, national origin, gender, sexual orientation, or disability of any person. Additionally, the proposal would require the US Sentencing Commission to study the issue of adult recruitment of juveniles to commit hate crimes. This bill did not pass.

Another proposal in the House that did not pass was H.R. 682, the Hate Crime Statistics Improvement Act. This proposal would require the attorney general to collect data about crimes based on gender.

2003–4: 108TH CONGRESS

The Hate Crimes Prevention Act (H.R. 80) was similar to a bill proposed in the previous session (H.R. 74), also called the Hate Crimes Prevention Act. The new proposal would, like the previous proposal, set penalties for anyone who willfully caused bodily injury to any person, or attempted to cause an injury to a person, because of their race, color, religion, national origin, gender, sexual orientation, or disability. Again, this bill did not pass.

Also reintroduced this session was the Hate Crimes Statistics Improvement Act. Again, it did not pass.

2005–6: 109TH CONGRESS

Once again, the House proposed the Hate Crimes Prevention Act (H.R. 259). The proposal included the same provision as earlier and again did not pass. The House also reconsidered the Hate Crimes Statistics Improvement Act. And again, it did not have enough support to become law.

H.R. 3132 was passed by the House in response to the abuse and murder of children across the country. The bill, called the Children's Safety Act, focused on increasing the federal registration of sex offenders. However, the bill also included a provision related to hate crimes. Title X of the bill was titled the Local Law Enforcement Hate Crimes Prevention Act. This provision would add a separate federal criminal charge for committing a violent act based on race, color, religion, or national origin. It would also broaden the definition of hate crimes to include sexual orientation, gender, or disability. It would also require the attorney general to publish information about hate crimes.

The Local Law Enforcement Hate Crimes Prevention Act was a proposal (H.R. 2662/S. 1145) that would authorize the attorney general to provide technical, forensic, prosecutorial, or other assistance to local agencies in the investigation and prosecution of hate crimes. But this was not voted on by the entire chamber and did not pass.

2007–8: 110TH CONGRESS

Again, the Local Law Enforcement Hate Crimes Prevention Act was proposed in the House (H.R. 1592) and would require the attorney general to provide technical assistance to states for investigating and prosecuting hate crimes. This law would also expand federal hate crime laws to make them stand-alone crimes. The Senate version was S. 1106, the Matthew Shepard Local Law Enforcement Hate Crimes Prevention Act. This time, George W. Bush threatened to veto the legislation, saying that it is unnecessary to federalize such a large range of violent crimes. The bill did not make it to his desk. Also failing to become law, again, was H.R. 1164, the Hate Crime Statistics Act.

The House also considered H.R. 254, the David Ray Hate Crimes Prevention Act. This proposal would impose penalties for willfully causing harm to any person because of the actual or perceived race, color, religion, national origin, gender, sexual orientation, or disability of any person. The bill was not passed.

Also not passing was H.R. 2217, the Hate Crimes Against the Homeless Enforcement Act. If passed, the definition of hate crime would have included a crime committed against an individual based on their homeless status. A similar bill that did not pass was H.R. 2216, the Hate Crimes against the Homeless Statistics Act of 2007. This bill would require that crimes committed against the homeless be collected by the attorney general.

The David Ray Ritcheson Hate Crime Prevention Act (H.R. 6776) was a proposal to allow victims of hate crimes to claim unemployment insurance for the loss of employment if it resulted directly from the crime. A victim of a hate crime would be allowed to take time off for family and medical leave. It would also prohibit health care insurers from taking into account if a person has been the victim of a hate crime when determining their eligibility for insurance. Further, the head of each federal agency would be required to establish prevention, treatment, and rehabilitation programs and services for their employees who are victims of hate crimes. The proposal was not acted on by the entire House and did not become law.

PRESIDENT OBAMA

As a presidential candidate, Barack Obama promised the gay and lesbian community he would pass new hate crimes legislation that would include violence against gays in federal hate crime laws. As president, Obama issued Proclamation 8387, making June 2009 the Lesbian, Gay, Bisexual, and Transgender Pride Month. In the statement, he said that "LGBT youth should feel safe to learn without the fear of harassment."[9] He also said that he wanted to enhance hate crimes laws.[10] In 2010, Obama again proclaimed June as LGBT Pride Month. In this year, he stressed that his administration supported, and he signed into law, the Matthew Shepard and James Byrd Jr. Hate Crimes Prevention Act to strengthen federal protection against hate crimes.[11]

2009–10: 111TH CONGRESS

Again, the Local Law Enforcement Hate Crimes Prevention Act was proposed in this session (H.R. 1913). The Senate version, S. 909, was titled the Matthew Shepard Hate Crimes Prevention Act. As the earlier proposals, this one would make a hate crime a stand-alone crime and would provide assistance for local law enforcement from the attorney general for the investigation and prosecution of hate crimes. As in the past sessions, the proposal did not become law. The same provisions were included in the David Ray Hate Crimes Prevention Act (H.R. 256), which did not pass.

H.R. 2647 (PL 111-84) was passed to expand the definition of federal hate crimes to cover attacks based on gender, gender identity, sexual orientation, and disability. The measure was attached to the 2010 defense authorization bill. Supporters argued the law was needed to combat attacks on people because of their sexual orientation. As mentioned earlier, the law was called the Matthew Shepard and James Byrd Jr. Hate Crimes Prevention Act. It was named after Matthew Shepard, a gay teenager from Wisconsin who was kidnapped and beaten, and James Byrd Jr., an African American man who was dragged to death in Texas. It would also require the expansion of collecting data and reporting hate crimes by the federal government.

In H.R. 70, the Noose Hate Crime Act of 2009, anyone who displays a noose in public with the intent to harass or intimidate a person because of their race, religion, or national origin could be sent to prison for up to two years or fined. The bill did not leave the subcommittee.

Again this session, members in the House debated the David Ray Ritcheson Hate Crime Prevention Act (H.R. 262). This proposal would allow victims of hate crimes to claim unemployment insurance for the loss of employment if it resulted directly from the crime, among other things. The bill did not pass again. Also reintroduced and failing to pass was H.R. 823, the Hate Crime Statistics Improvement Act.

CONCLUSION

Although limited, there has been some action by Congress and the president to reduce the number of hate crimes that occur in the United States. It is a controversial matter that is often left to states. Many bills are reintroduced each year but fail to receive enough support to become laws.

Chapter 9

Victims

Victims of crime began to receive attention in the 1970s, when people began to recognize the rights of crime victims and their survivors in the criminal process. The federal government's involvement in providing rights to victims began about this same time when the issue was the focus of different proposals. Since then, proposals have centered on victim compensation programs, providing civil remedies, the right to privacy, and many other rights. The changes proposed by the presidents and Congress, for the most part, applied only to the victims of federal offenses. But the laws passed by Congress to help victims often act as models for state legislation. Once the change is made on the federal level, states often follow suit.

President Nixon

1971–72: 92nd Congress

Congress first put the rights of crime victims on its agenda in this session. Congress debated many proposals that provided assistance to victims, but nothing passed. One bill considered by the Senate was S. 750, to compensate innocent victims of crime. Several other bills were considered by the Senate Judiciary Subcommittee on Criminal Laws and Procedures (S. 16, S. 33, S. 750, S. 1081, S. 946, S. 2087, S. 2426, and S. 2748), which would provide compensation to innocent victims of crimes,[1] but these bills went nowhere. The Senate passed a bill that began in the House (H.R. 8389) that included aid to crime victims, but the House did not act on the final action.[2] This bill contained parts of other bills including the following:

1. S. 750: to compensate innocent victims of violent crime, or their survivors, and those who intervened to prevent such crime
2. S. 33: to authorize the US attorney general to provide a group life insurance program for state and local public safety officers
3. S. 2087: to provide cash benefits to survivors of public safety officers killed in the line of duty or to the officer himself if he or she was dismembered
4. S. 16: to strengthen civil remedies for victims of racketeering

1973–74: 93RD CONGRESS

During this session, S. 800 was proposed to provide benefits to public safety officers injured in the line of duty and to survivors of slain public safety officers and innocent victims of crime. This was approved by the Senate, but the House took no action.[3]

PRESIDENT FORD

Gerald Ford wanted to shift attention from the criminal to the victim of crime.[4] He did not want vindictive punishment of criminals but instead the protection of the innocent victim.[5] He thought victims of crime should be the concern of all people who have a role in making or enforcing the criminal law, either at the federal, state, or local level. Additionally, according to Ford, the vast majority of victims of violent crime are poor, old, young, disadvantage minorities, and the most defenseless of our citizens and therefore need extra protection.[6] He said, "A legal system that is exploited by the criminal but ignores his victim is sadly out of balance."[7]

President Ford asked the Congress to pass legislation to meet the uncompensated economic losses of the victims of federal crimes who suffered personal injury as a result of the offense. He suggested the monetary benefits should come from a fund consisting of fines paid by convicted federal offenders.[8]

1977–78: 95TH CONGRESS

Congress agreed with Ford and introduced a bill providing for federal financial assistance to victims of violent crimes advanced in the first session of the 95th Congress. The House passed H.R. 7010, otherwise known as the Victims of Crime Act of 1977, which provided up to 25 percent federal reimbursement to states for funds paid to crime victims under state victim compensation programs. Under the bill, any victims of violent crimes could receive federal funds as compensation for the losses suffered. The bill focused on two issues: (1) the potential cost to the federal government of paying victims of crime for their medical and work-loss expenses and (2) the role of the criminal in compensating his or her victim. Members of the Senate had favored victim compensation legislation in the past. The House version of the bill did not create a direct federal grant program but pledged that up to 25 percent of the money paid out by states with such programs to crime victims would be reimbursed by the federal government.[9] Both the House and Senate passed the legislation, but the House killed the conference report.[10]

Rape victims were the focus of a new law passed this session (H.R. 4727/PL 95-540). The new law would protect the privacy of rape victims in federal trials by limiting the circumstances in which evidence about a rape victim's past sexual conduct would be admissible in a federal rape trial. The law created new rules of evidence that prohibited the use of the victim's reputation or opinions about their past sexual behavior in criminal prosecutions and restricted the use of direct evidence of the victim's past sexual behavior to certain situations.[11]

1979–80: 96TH CONGRESS

In the Senate Judiciary Committee this session, there were discussions about reforming the Federal Criminal Code. One of the revisions gave courts the power to require defendants to give reasonable notice and explanation of the conviction to victims of the offense. The section was intended to help citizens affected by such crimes to bring civil suits to recover damages.[12]

Again, a bill to help compensate the victims of crime was reported by the House Judiciary Committee, but no action was taken on it by the entire body. H.R. 4257 would have provided federal money to states to compensate crime victims. The bill had strong support from many state and local officials and the Senate, which had passed victims' compensation bills in the previous four Congresses.

States were to be reimbursed for 25 percent of the compensation for personal injury or death paid to victims (or their survivors) of crimes specified for coverage in the state programs. One hundred percent reimbursement was provided for victims of crimes subject to exclusive federal jurisdiction.[13] To qualify for money, the state programs would have to meet a number of criteria. One controversial criterion required any person contracting to pay a defendant for any interview or article relating to a crime to place the money in escrow for the benefit of the victim. It was designed to prevent notorious criminals from profiting from books or articles about their crimes before victims were compensated.

A similar bill was S. 190 and was considered in the Senate Judiciary, which did not report the legislation. The bill would have authorized $1.2 billion over three years to states. The maximum reimbursement per victim would have been $35,000.[14]

PRESIDENT REAGAN

Like Ford, Ronald Reagan wanted to focus on the innocent victims of crime. He appointed a Task Force on the Victims of Crime that would be responsible for evaluating the many proposals that were appearing regarding victims and witnesses. He promised to support legislation to permit judges to order offenders to make restitution to their victims, because Reagan believed that victims of crime have needed a voice, and he promised to provide it.[15]

In 1982, Reagan also proclaimed the week beginning April 19, 1982, as Crime Victims Week. By doing so, he wanted all federal, state, and local officials involved in the criminal justice system to devote more attention to the needs of victims of crime and to redouble their efforts to make our system responsive to those needs.[16] In 1983, 1984, and 1985, Reagan again announced a Crime Victims Week.[17]

Reagan signed the Victim and Witness Protection Act of 1982 that would allow a victim to file a victim impact statement with the court. The act also made it a federal offense to intimidate or retaliate against victims or witnesses of federal crimes. Further, it required a federal judge to order restitution when handing down a sentence for a crime involving bodily injury or property loss.[18]

CONGRESS

1981–82: 97TH CONGRESS

Congress passed a new law (S. 2420/PL 97-291) that was designed to make the federal courts more sensitive to crime victims and witnesses. The new law strengthened the law related to the harassment of victims and witnesses and made it a felony offense to intimidate or harass a victim or witness by using or threatening force. If done, an offender could be punished with a fine of up to $250,000 and a prison term of up to ten years, or both. If it was thought a victim or witness could be threatened, a prosecutor could seek a court order to protect the person from such intimidation. The protective order could also apply to other family members as well.

If a defendant attempted to intimidate a victim or witness, any pending bail could be revoked. Further, if that defendant faced sentencing, a victim's impact statement could be introduced that would detail information on the financial, social, psychological, and physical impact of the harassment on the victim. If there was a loss of property or any personal damage, a judge could order restitution to the victim that would cover uninsured medical expenses, property losses, and burial expenses, if appropriate.[19]

1983–84: 98TH CONGRESS

As part of the Omnibus Crime bill passed in this session, there was a section on witness protection. It authorized relocation and protection of federal or certain state witnesses and potential witnesses when the attorney general determined that a crime of violence was likely to be committed against those individuals. In some cases, immediate family members of the witness or another person closely associated with the witness could also be relocated if those individuals might also be in danger. The bill required the attorney general to issue guidelines on the types of cases in which witnesses could be protected and also gave the attorney general the discretion to determine how long to protect a witness. Relocation could include providing the witness with identity documents, housing, transportation to the new home, a payment to meet basic living expenses, and assistance in obtaining a job. Anyone who disclosed information about the identity and location of a protected witness could face a $5,000 fine, a five-year prison term, or both.[20]

The bill also created a Crime Victims Fund in the Treasury Department that would be financed through fines collected from persons convicted of federal offenses plus forfeited bonds and collateral. The bill set a $100 million maximum for the fund and required any excess money to go to the treasury. A portion of the money each year would be available for grants to existing state victim-compensation programs to meet claims and half to states to provide victim assistance programs such as rape counseling.[21]

1985–86: 99TH CONGRESS

The Victims of Handgun Crimes Compensation Tax Act (H.R. 306/H.R. 2862) was proposed but not passed during this session of Congress. If passed, the law would have increased the excise tax on pistols and revolvers from 10 percent to 40 percent. Some of the money from the tax would go toward the Victims of Handgun Crimes Trust Fund. This would be administered through the states to help to compensate victims of handgun crimes.

In H.R. 2198/H.R. 2713, the Restitution Amendments Act, the Federal Criminal Code would be amended so that the ability of the court to order restitution instead of a prison sentence when an offender is convicted of a criminal offense would be eliminated. If a court orders only a partial restitution to a victim, the court must include a statement outlining the reasons for that. The bill was not acted on by the Senate and therefore did not become law.

In 1985, the Victims of Crime Amendments Act was proposed in the House (H.R. 2997) but was not passed. The proposal was an attempt to amend the Federal Criminal Code to require the courts to impose restitution on all people and organizations that were convicted of infractions and misdemeanors.

1987–88: 100TH CONGRESS

Once again, the Victims of Handgun Crimes Compensation Tax Act (H.R. 464) was proposed but not passed. As with the previous proposal, the proposed law would have increased the excise tax on pistols and revolvers, with a portion of the funds going toward the Victims of Handgun Crimes Trust Fund. This would be used to help compensate victims of handgun crimes.

Elderly victims of crime were the topic of H.R. 2018, the Elderly Victims of Crime Act. If passed the law would have required states, in order to receive grants from the Crime Victims' Fund, to show that they provide assistance to elderly crime victims. The bill did not become law.

1989–90: 101ST CONGRESS

H.R. 1402 was a proposal to provide that the excise tax on handguns would be transferred to a trust fund to be used to compensate victims of crime. This did not pass.

PRESIDENT BUSH

George H. W. Bush agreed with Reagan that the victims of crimes should be afforded certain rights. He said, "I happen to believe that it is time to care more about the victims of crime and a little less sympathy for the criminals that are causing the crimes."[22] He acknowledged the plight of crime victims when he announced Crime Victims Week in 1990 [23] and again in 1991.[24] It was a time when government officials could publicize their services for victims. It was also time to make the public aware of some issues that crime victims have and increase their support for victims' programs.

PRESIDENT BUSH

1991–92: 102ND CONGRESS

In this session, the Senate considered S. 1521, the Pornography Victims' Compensation Act. The bill would have given legal recourse to victims of violent sex crimes and the families of those murdered by allowing them to sue the producers and distributors of hard core pornography. The goal was to provide more legal recourse to victims of sex crimes. It was aimed at making those who produced or distributed hard-core pornography liable if victims could prove the material incited the offender to commit the crime. The bill was approved by the Senate Judiciary Committee[25] but not passed into law.

Once again, the House considered but did not pass a proposal to ensure that an excise tax on handguns would be put into a fund from which victims of crime would be compensated (H.R. 750).

PRESIDENT CLINTON

In 1996, William Clinton proposed passing a Victims' Rights Constitutional Amendment because he thought that victims deserved to be heard. In addition, he believed that victims should know when an assailant is released.[26] Because of that, in 1997, Clinton signed into law the Victim Rights Clarification Act of 1997 to ensure that victims of crime and their families would not be prevented from attending criminal trials in federal court simply because they intended to exercise their right to give a statement during a sentencing hearing once guilt had been decided."[27]

CONGRESS

1993–94: 103RD CONGRESS

In the Omnibus 1994 Crime Bill, some attention was given to victims' rights. For example, the bill expanded the right of victims of violent crimes and sexual abuse to be heard at the defendant's sentencing hearing in federal court. In some cases, a parent or legal guardian could give a statement if the victim was younger than 18 or by one or more family members if the victim had died. Existing law gave victims the right to be heard, known as the right of allocution, only in cases where capital punishment was an option. The bill also mandated that the next $10 million deposited in the Crime Victims' Assistance Fund be made available for grants to states for crime victims' assistance. The money was to be divided equally between grants for victims' assistance and grants for victims' compensation, with a small portion going for police training and technical assistance.

Also as part of the major crime bill passed by Congress in 1994, attention was centered on elderly victims of crime. One provision authorized $2.7 million to create an Alzheimer's program, which would create a Missing Alzheimer's Disease Alert Program to locate missing people with Alzheimer's and other related diseases. Another provision directed the US Sentencing Commission to review sentencing guidelines for violent crimes that occur against the elderly population, to determine whether they were tough enough to deter these offenses. The US Sentencing Commission was asked to review sentencing guidelines to ensure that sentences for offenses against the elderly were stiff enough.

Additionally, the bill focused on telemarketing fraud. The bill provided for an additional 5-year sentence for anyone convicted of telemarketing fraud and an additional 10-year sentence if the defendant victimized 10 or more people older than 55 or targeted people over 55. In this case, the courts were required to order convicted defendants to pay full restitution to their victims. The court was prohibited from considering the defendant's economic circumstances when determining the amount of restitution, but the court was allowed to consider such circumstances when determining the payment schedule. Payment of restitution would be a condition for an offender's parole or supervised release. There was $20 million authorized for the Justice Department and the FBI to hire additional staff to investigate and prosecute telemarketing fraud cases and to coordinate with state agencies, if relevant.[28] There were also provisions for granting rewards for anyone who provided information that would lead to prosecution of fraud against senior citizens. The attorney general could pay up to $10,000 for any information.

A key part of the 1994 bill for many people was a provision to expand an existing law (H.R. 1237/PL 103-209) that encouraged states to do background checks on child-care providers to also cover those who provided care to the elderly and disabled.[29]

1995-96: 104TH CONGRESS

The Senate passed a bill (H.R. 665) requiring victim restitution, but full House consideration did not take place.[30] The bill mandated that those convicted of a federal crime provide restitution to their victims. At the time, these orders were optional for federal courts in most cases. The bill also proposed to give federal courts the option of ordering restitution for injured people other than the victim if they could show they were harmed by the crime. It was to apply in federal cases involving drugs, violence, damaged or stolen property, and consumer product tampering. The Senate passed an amended version.[31]

In 1996, the House passed H.R. 2974 to increase penalties for violent crimes against the elderly, children, and the vulnerable, but the Senate did not act on the proposal. The bill would have instructed the US Sentencing Commission to increase the penalties for crimes against those 14 and younger and 65 and older by 50 percent.[32]

In Title III of the Taking Back Our Streets Act (H.R. 3), the court would be required to order restitution to victims of crime when sentencing defendants convicted of certain offenses. The court must also specify the schedule of payments for payment of the restitution. These provisions stood alone in H.R. 665, the Victims Justice Act, which also did not pass.

1997-98: 105TH CONGRESS

In H.R. 924/PL 105-6 the Congress made a new law that expanded the rights of crime victims and their families by allowing certain relatives of the victims of the Oklahoma City bombing to attend the trial of those involved. The bill prevented federal judges from barring people from their courtroom who planned to testify during the penalty in the guilt-or-innocence phase of the trial. Under previous law, witnesses could be barred from hearing courtroom testimony if the judge believed their testimony could be tainted by observing the proceedings. This law was passed in response to a ruling by US District Judge Richard Matsch, the presiding judge in the bombing case. Matsch ruled that victims who planned to make statements at sentencing could not attend other trial proceedings because seeing the defendants in court could influence their testimony.[33]

1999-2000: 106TH CONGRESS

A proposed constitutional amendment (S.J. Res. 3) outlining specific rights for the victims of violent crime was endorsed by the Senate Judiciary Committee, but the House took no action on it. The amendment would give victims nine specific rights, such as the right to be notified of and attend all proceedings related to the case; to speak or submit statements at each public hearing in the case, including parole or other early release hearings; to reasonable notice of those convicted in their cases are released or escape; and to restitution. A new section added would give victims the right to be notified before any state or federal grant of clemency or pardon and to submit a statement about it for the record.[34] The proposal was shelved by the Senate.[35]

A number of bills proposed in the House and Senate (H.R. 3244, S. 2414, S. 2449) were geared toward helping victims of international sex trafficking. The bill would create a special T visa to allow victims who were brought into the United States to stay in the country rather than be deported. Victims would have to show that they were in the country as a direct result of trafficking and that they had a fear of retribution if they were forced to return home. H.R. 3244 was passed by Congress and then signed by the president (PL 106-386).

After President Clinton granted clemency to 16 members of a Puerto Rican terrorist group, the Senate Judiciary Committee approved S. 2042, which would require the pardon attorney in the Justice Department to notify victims when the president considers an executive grant of clemency. Victims could offer their opinions about the cases, which would then be made available to the president. The bill did not have enough support to pass through Congress.

PRESIDENT BUSH

George W. Bush fully supported the victims and families of the 2001 terrorist attacks on Washington, DC and New York. He promised that the full resources of the federal government would be made available to help the victims of the attacks. He requested that Congress provide emergency funding to help the victims.[36]

2001–2: 107TH CONGRESS

The House passed legislation (H.R. 3375) that would make money available to the families of the 12 Americans who were killed and those who were injured in the 1998 terrorist attacks on the US embassies in Tanzania and Kenya. President Bush did not support the bill, arguing that it would create different compensation rates for victims of different attacks. He also said by increasing the number of claimants, it would delay payments.[37] The bill did not pass.

H.R. 2884 was a bill to extend income and estate tax relief to victims of the September 11 terrorist attacks. Under the bill, the estates of those who were killed in the terrorist attacks or the Oklahoma City bombing would not owe any federal income tax in the year the victim died or the preceding year. The bill had significant support in Congress and was signed by the president (PL 107-134).

2003–4: 108TH CONGRESS

In 2004, the House proposed and Congress passed H.R. 5107 (PL 108-405) to guarantee the rights of crime victims. The bill also includes hundreds of millions of dollars in grants to cities and states, as well as law enforcement provisions backed by the Bush administration. With regards to crime victims, it codified eight specific rights for victims of federal crimes, including the right to be reasonably protected from the accused, to be reasonably heard at certain proceedings, to consult with government attorneys on the case, and to receive full and timely restitution. It authorized more than $80 million over five years for victim assistance programs and other support services.[38]

A bill to establish rights for federal crime victims in court proceedings was considered by the Senate (S. 2329). The bill, called the Scott Campbell, Stephanie Roper, Wendy Preston, Louarna Gillis, and Nila Lynn Crime Victims' Rights Act, would guarantee victims of their right to be heard at public court proceedings when a defendant is brought before a judge for sentencing, release, or discussion of a plea bargain. It would also require a judge to take the safety of the victim into account when deciding the fate of a defendant.[39] The bill did not pass.

PRESIDENT OBAMA

Barack Obama supported the victims of crime. To bring attention to the safety of citizens and making neighborhoods safer, the president announced a National Crime Victims Week during April 18 through April 24, 2010.[40] He also declared April 2010 as National Sexual Assault Awareness Month to help lift the veil of secrecy and shame surrounding the crimes of sexual assault.[41]

2009–10: 11TH CONGRESS

House members debated H.R. 448, the Elder Abuse Victims Act of 2009. This was a proposal to require the attorney general to report to the Congress about state laws relating to elderly victims. The attorney general was also authorized to provide victim advocacy grants to states to be used for the study of the special needs of elderly victims. The bill did not have enough support to pass.

CONCLUSION

Only since the 1970s, Congress has debated many proposals for helping victims of crime. Presidents have also felt strongly enough about victims' rights to put the issue on their agendas. The proposals have included compensation, privacy for some victims, retaliation against witnesses and victims, and services such as housing and busing. The Congress has also given certain rights to elderly victims and increased punishments for offenses against the elderly.

MINORS AS VICTIMS AND OFFENDERS

IN PART IV, THE FOCUS IS ON juveniles. Youth under the age of 18 have been involved in the criminal justice system both as offenders and victims. Presidents and Congress have shown concern for both groups and have passed legislation in both areas. Chapter 10 focuses on juvenile offenders and how they should be treated in the criminal justice system. Chapter 11 focuses on juveniles as victims, in crimes such as child abuse, sexual offenses, or even in child pornography.

CHAPTER 10

JUVENILE OFFENDERS

JUVENILE CRIME

JUVENILE CRIME IS ONE AREA WHERE THERE has been consistent federal action beginning in early years. Dealing with juveniles who commit serious crimes is traditionally a state concern, but it is one area where the federal government has consistently passed legislation. The federal government's role in this area is largely limited to providing funds to states and funding research. Nonetheless, presidents and Congress have indicated their concerns with juvenile offenders with many legislative proposals. Their actions are described in this chapter.

PRESIDENT TRUMAN

Harry Truman believed that one aftermath of war was an increase in juvenile delinquency, probably because fathers and mothers who served in the armed forces, business, or war industries were absent from the home. Thus the country was, at that time, paying the social penalties for failing to provide adequate supervision and guidance for many children during their formative years. Instead, the youth at the time needed some moral uplift. He called on parents and churches to help them on the right path.[1]

CONGRESS

1945–46: 79TH CONGRESS

This year, the House passed H.R. 5443, to establish a bureau within the Department of Commerce for Research in Juvenile Delinquency. The bill went unreported by Judiciary Committee.

1953–54: 83RD CONGRESS

In the 1953–54 session, the Senate Judiciary Subcommittee to Investigate Juvenile Delinquency held hearings on problems connected with crimes and misdemeanors committed by young persons.[2] Many experts testified, including the secretary of health, education, and welfare (HEW), attorneys, police chiefs, academics, probation officers, and a representative from the New York City Youth Board. The committee explored the influence of comic books on juvenile delinquents. One person testified that crime on television was "mental poison" to youngsters.[3]

PRESIDENT EISENHOWER

Dwight Eisenhower acknowledged that juvenile delinquency had increased over the past few years, becoming not only a local problem but also a worldwide concern. He also acknowledged that there were many reasons for this, and thus multiple measures were required to fix it. He warned against a tendency to generalize about youth and to blame the failures of the few on all young people.[4] He claimed to hate the term "juvenile delinquency," because he did not believe the country should ever allow conditions to arise and exist that justify the existence of the term. Instead, he wanted to use other, more positive terms, such as "youth training programs."[5]

To help the states do a better job at fighting youth crime, Eisenhower wanted to strengthen the states' resources for preventing and dealing with juvenile delinquency. He planned on proposing legislation to assist the states to promote programs to deal with the problem.[6] He also recommended new grants to states to enable them to strengthen and improve their programs and services for the prevention, diagnosis, and treatment of youth delinquency. The money would be used for planning and coordination of all state and local agencies concerned with juvenile delinquency and for training of personnel and research.[7]

PRESIDENT KENNEDY

John Kennedy was seriously concerned about the increase in juvenile crime. He noted that in the previous decade, juvenile delinquency cases before the courts had more than doubled, and arrests of youth increased 86 percent until they numbered almost one million.[8] He believed that juvenile crime diminished the strength and the vitality of the United States, and it created serious problems for all communities affected, leaving indelible impressions on the people involved.

President Kennedy believed the country needed a better educational and vocational training system to help stop juvenile delinquency.[9] He issued an executive order directing the attorney general, the secretary of HEW, and the secretary of labor to coordinate their efforts to develop a program to assist state and local communities in their efforts to reduce juvenile crime. But that required more money, simply because there was an increase in the youth population.

At that point, Kennedy sent Congress a proposal to enable the federal government to undertake projects designed to demonstrate and evaluate the most effective ways to combat juvenile delinquency within local communities.[10] Kennedy then approved S. 279 (PL 87-274), the Juvenile Delinquency and Youth Offenses Control Act of 1961. The law allowed the federal government to become a partner with state and local communities to prevent and control the spread of delinquency.[11]

In 1963, Kennedy created a Committee on Youth Employment because he believed that youth needed jobs to keep them away from crime. Additionally, the administration's Youth Employment bill was designed to provide useful jobs and training for young persons who need them. He said that a Youth Conservation Corps would be established to put young men to work improving forests and recreation areas. At the same time, it would also provide half the wages and related costs for young people employed on local projects that offer useful work experience in nonprofit community services, such as hospitals, schools, and parks. Kennedy called on Congress to pass it.[12]

CONGRESS

1961–62: 87TH CONGRESS

In 1961, Congress authorized a three-year, $10 million per year program of grants for pilot projects to improve methods for the prevention and control of delinquency.[13]

PRESIDENT JOHNSON

In 1964, Lyndon Johnson created a Committee on Juvenile Delinquency and Youth Crime that proposed a program to attack juvenile delinquency in the District of Columbia. The plan was intended to attack the underlying causes of delinquency and try to improve the methods of dealing with those children who are involved with the justice system. A program was prepared by the citizens of the District and approved by the committee. Johnson promised to give all possible federal aid to the program.[14]

In 1967, Johnson asked Congress to pass the Juvenile Delinquency Prevention Act. According to Johnson, the bill would provide about $25 million in financial assistance to state and local agencies to develop new plans, programs, and special facilities to deal with youthful offenders. There would be 90 percent matching federal grants to assist states and local communities develop plans to improve their juvenile courts and corrections systems. Along with that, the bill would provide 50 percent matching federal grants for the construction of short-term detention and treatment facilities for youthful offenders in or near their communities. Flexible federal matching grants would be available to assist local communities operate diagnostic and treatment programs for juvenile delinquents and potential delinquents. Besides grant allocations, the bill provided for federal support for research and experimental projects concerned with juvenile delinquency.[15] The development of new community correctional programs would be encouraged, as would a greater range of alternatives to jail including halfway houses, youth rehabilitation centers, and family-type group homes.[16]

Johnson signed the act in July of 1968. Upon doing so, he reiterated that the bill was designed to prevent delinquency. It gave funds to states and cities for youth programs and helped local communities train experts on how to combat juvenile crime. Johnson hoped the bill would rehabilitate juveniles. It offered funds for new projects to help young lawbreakers and was intended to help build new facilities to help reclaim the delinquents—not just to punish them. It assisted police and other public agencies to come up with answers to the problems of juvenile crime.[17]

He also recommended legislation to establish a District Youth Services Office that would plan and direct all the services needed to combat juvenile delinquency.[18]

CONGRESS

1963–64: 88TH CONGRESS

In 1964, a bill was passed (S. 1967/PL 88-368) to extend the Juvenile Delinquency and Youth Offenses Control Act of 1961 for two years. It provided for a $5 million demonstration project in Washington, DC.

The Senate Judiciary Juvenile Delinquency Subcommittee began an investigation into the possible connection between the availability of firearms and juvenile crime, arguing that juveniles often get guns through mail order.[19]

1965–66: 89TH CONGRESS

A new grant program (H.R. 8131/PL 89-69) extended the Juvenile Delinquency and Youth Offenses Control Act of 1961 for one year and authorized appropriations of $7.5 million the following two years. The act had been amended in 1964 to run through fiscal 1966, but no funds had been authorized for that year.[20]

1967–68: 90TH CONGRESS

The Juvenile Delinquency Prevention and Control Act of 1967 (H.R. 12120/PL 90-445) was passed to provide $25 million for local juvenile delinquency programs. It was a grants program for states so they could plan and operate projects to prevent juvenile delinquency and to rehabilitate youthful offenders.[21]

PRESIDENT NIXON

Richard Nixon recognized the seriousness of juvenile crime, stating that it was a tragic fact that juveniles composed nearly one-third of all offenders who were receiving correctional treatment and that persons under the age of 25 composed half of that total. He also recognized that the country's treatment facilities were not adequate for those age groups. Because of that, many young offenders were being housed with older criminals. He asked the attorney general to focus on programs for juvenile offenders, such as group homes, modern diagnostic and treatment centers, and new probation services.[22]

He also proposed developing more effective methods for controlling and preventing juvenile crime. He wanted to have a better understanding of criminal behavior, particularly juvenile crime and delinquency.[23]

CONGRESS

1971–72: 92ND CONGRESS

Congress passed a bill (S. 1732/PL 92-31) amending and extending for one year the Juvenile Delinquency Prevention and Control Act of 1968. The bill authorized $75 million to carry out the act. Part of the money would be used by the secretary of HEW to fund up to 75 percent of the cost of rehabilitation programs for juveniles. Any rehabilitation projects run by nonprofit agencies would also be funded through this law. In addition, the law established an Interdepartmental Council on Juvenile Delinquency that would be responsible for the coordination of all federal juvenile delinquency programs. The council would include the attorney general, the secretary of HEW, and representatives of other federal agencies of the president's choosing. The council would be required to meet at least six times a year.

That same year, the House failed to pass a bill (H.R. 45) that would have created an Institute for the Continuing Studies of Juvenile Justice. The institute would have gathered and disseminated information on juvenile justice and trained criminal justice personnel in the area of juvenile crime and delinquency. In addition, the bill would have created an advisory commission to supervise the institute. No final action was taken by Congress.[24]

In 1972, Congress completed action on a bill (H.R. 15635/PL 92-381) amending and extending the Juvenile Delinquency Prevention and Control Act of 1968 for two years. The bill, titled the Juvenile Delinquency Prevention and Control Act Amendments of 1972, authorized $75 million for grants to states and nonprofit groups to help fund youth service programs and other preventive programs. The primary focus of the amendment was to develop community-based preventive services separate from those of law enforcement agencies (police and courts) to aid delinquents, or persons in danger of becoming delinquents, and their families. The services were to be linked to the school system whenever possible. Another requirement was that the funds be given to those areas that were identified as having the highest rates of youth crime, youth unemployment, and school dropouts.

The Senate passed S. 2829, the Runaway Youth Act, which authorized the Department of Health, Education, and Welfare to assist local groups in giving shelter and care to runaway youngsters. The bill would authorize $10 million for each of fiscal 1973–75 and would authorize research into the extent of the problem. It would require that participating shelters provide medical and psychological care and counseling, in addition to living quarters for runaways. The House took no action on the bill.[25]

The Senate Judiciary Subcommittee on National Penitentiaries held hearings on S. 3049 that set minimum standards for federal grants to state and local correctional facilities.[26]

1973–74: 93RD CONGRESS

In 1974, Congress passed S. 821 (PL 93-415) to expand and coordinate federal programs for the prevention and correction of juvenile delinquents. The bill provided a comprehensive response to a juvenile delinquency crisis in which youthful offenders accounted for more than half the crime in the United States. The bill established an office within the Justice Department to administer juvenile delinquency programs that was previously located in the Department of Health, Education, and Welfare. It authorized a three-year, $350 million matching grant program to state and local governments to develop innovative programs for the prevention and treatment of juvenile delinquency. It also authorized a $10.5 million program for runaway youths and provided for basic procedural rights for juveniles in federal courts.[27]

PRESIDENT FORD

In 1974, Gerald Ford signed the Juvenile Justice and Delinquency Prevention Act of 1974. The following year, he reported that he wanted to continue our efforts to rehabilitate young offenders. He did not want to "write off" many young people as "unsalvageable" before they became adults.[28]

CONGRESS

1977–78: 95TH CONGRESS

A three-year renewal of the grant programs created by the 1974 Juvenile Justice and Delinquency Prevention Act was passed into law (H.R. 6111/PL 95-115). The grant programs were intended to aid states in dealing with juvenile crime and younger runaways. The 1977 amendments increased the federal monetary support for the programs, stressed the need to find alternatives to criminal incarceration for juveniles, and expanded the role of advisory groups participating in the administration of the grant program.[29] The legislation provided federal grants to states for two purposes. The first was to improve state juvenile justice systems, with an emphasis on the diversion of juveniles from criminal incarceration to a less severe form of supervision such as halfway houses. The second purpose was to provide assistance to states to provide shelter, counseling, and medical services to runaway children. The 1977 amendments increased the share of federal money to be paid to the states in the formula grant program from 90 percent of approved program costs to 100 percent. H.R. 6111 also increased the minimum state allocation from the formula grant program from $200,000 to $225,000. At the same time, new federal "strings" were attached to the grant money, primarily to limit the portion of the funds that may be expended for administrative and overhead costs rather than "action" programs at the local level.[30]

1979–80: 96TH CONGRESS

Congress cleared a law (S. 2441/PL 96-509) that reauthorized programs to help states combat juvenile delinquency for four years. The authorization was for $225 million annually, with $25 million earmarked for runaway and homeless youth programs. Under the new law, states were required to remove juvenile offenders from adult pretrial detention facilities within five years in order to receive federal funds. Under the bill, a separate office focusing on juvenile justice was formed within the Office of Justice Assistance, Research, and Statistics (OJARS). Juvenile court judges could put "status offenders" into jail if they violated court orders regulating their behavior. One last provision required federal officials to issue regulations allowing juveniles accused of serious crimes to be incarcerated under certain circumstances in adult pretrial facilities if the juveniles were separated by "sight and sound." [31]

1983–84: 98TH CONGRESS

Congress passed a new law (H.J. Res. 648/PL 98-473), the fiscal 1985 continuing appropriations resolution, that included some anticrime provisions. It reauthorized the Office of Juvenile Justice and Delinquency Prevention for fiscal 1985–88 to be funded with such sums as may be necessary for each of the years. The office was to help states develop alternatives to incarceration of juveniles and to develop programs to combat juvenile delinquency.

The bill also reauthorized the Runaway and Homeless Youth Act of 1974 for fiscal 1985–88. This law authorized assistance to state and local facilities that provided emergency shelter care for runaways. It recognized in both the juvenile justice and runaway youth programs that the family of the children involved should be made part of any counseling and treatment program. It continued the two mandates of the original 1974 act. One was the removal of juveniles from adult jails and the creation of institutions, such as group homes, for juveniles who committed no crimes but who were runaways or truants. Second, the bill required for the first time that grants from the administrator's discretionary pool of funds be made on a competitive basis. Previously, there were no statutory requirements for awarding these grants.[32]

PRESIDENT REAGAN

In 1987, Ronald Reagan proposed getting rid of the Office of Juvenile Justice and Delinquency Prevention (OJJDP) but explained there would still be other federal agencies to provide services and programs to benefit juveniles. He reiterated that even though his administration proposed terminating the OJJDP, no one should conclude that his administration's commitment to a strong criminal justice system was less than complete.[33]

CONGRESS

1987–88: 100TH CONGRESS

A bill reauthorizing the Juvenile Justice and Delinquency Prevention Act (PL 93-415) ended up as part of the Omnibus Antidrug Abuse Bill (H.R. 5210/PL 100-690) cleared Congress at the end of the session. The bill reauthorized grants to states to improve their juvenile justice systems, to place runaways and truants in nonsecure facilities rather than in detention, and to remove children from adult jails and lockups. The bill also reauthorized the Runaway and Homeless Youth Act, which provided grants to support shelters for runaways, a national hotline, and the Missing Children's Assistance Act, which authorized a range of activities, including a toll-free telephone system, a national resource center and clearinghouse, and financial aid to missing children centers and research on missing children. The law was last reauthorized in 1984 as part of a major anticrime bill (PL 98-473).[34]

PRESIDENT CLINTON

William Clinton discussed the problem of juvenile delinquency in 1993, explaining that he wanted to give juvenile offenders a second chance. He supported community boot camps for young offenders, because they gave young people discipline, training, and treatment necessary to build a good life.[35]

In 1996, Clinton sent a proposed bill to the Congress that would make it easier to prosecute juveniles who were involved with gangs. He said in his State of the Union address that year that if a teenager commits a crime as an adult, he should be prosecuted as an adult.[36]

To cut off the flow of guns to teens who commit crimes, he asked his Department of the Treasury and Department of Justice to work with local law enforcement in a nationwide initiative that would track guns used in crimes and were then seized by law enforcement. The goal was to use that tracking information to then target the networks that are selling guns to teenagers.[37]

In 1997, Clinton again proposed legislation to Congress to reform the juvenile justice system so that it could handle juvenile offenders better and combat juvenile crime. In this proposal, he wanted to attack youth gangs and punish those juveniles who commit violent crimes with severe punishments. He reiterated the need for 100,000 police on the street. He also provided money to state and local communities to hire more prosecutors to directly deal with violent juveniles and create more special court proceedings for young people that have the flexibility to provide opportunities to those youth who can be saved. At the same time, there should be tougher penalties to punish those who have committed serious offenses. The legislation would also attempt to keep drugs and guns away from children by requiring child safety locks on handguns to prevent unauthorized use. Finally, Clinton said that the real answer to juvenile crime has got to be prevention. To address that issue, Clinton proposed funding 1,000 new after-school initiatives in communities to help keep schools open after school, on the weekends, and in the summer.[38]

Clinton did oppose one bill, H.R. 3, the Juvenile Crime Control Act, because it did not provide a comprehensive plan to crack down on youth and gang violence. He wanted legislation that would declare war on gangs, provide funding for additional local prosecutors to prosecute gang members, extend the Brady law so teen criminals would not have the power to purchase a gun, require federal dealers to sell a child safety lock with every gun, and target resources to keep schools open late, on weekends, and in the summer to keep young people off the street and out of trouble.[39]

Clinton was concerned with excessive violence shown in the media and the impact it had on children. He noted that he was not opposed to all violence in movies and television, but he was concerned with the overall impact of watching several hours a day, every day, and just one violent scene after another being shown to kids. He was concerned that this may make some children more prone to be violent, especially if those children do not have an offsetting influence from their family, school, church, or community.[40] In 1995, Clinton made it clear he did not believe in censorship but reiterated his concern that "excessive exposure to mindnumbing violence or crass abuse of people in sexual and other ways, has a bad impact on young children, especially if they don't have the kind of structure and other leadership in their life that they need."[41] To combat the problem of violence in the media, Clinton suggested parents put a V-chip in the cable television.[42] He also reminded parents that television shows were being rated for content so they could make judgments about whether their small children should watch those shows. He also arranged for three hours of quality children's programming to be aired every week, on every network.[43]

CONGRESS

1991–92: 102ND CONGRESS

A new law passed in the House and signed by the president (H.R. 5194—PL 102-586) was aimed at reducing juvenile violence. It reauthorized the Justice Department's Office of Juvenile Justice and Delinquency Prevention for four years, which was charged with finding ways to prevent children from becoming juvenile delinquents and devising alternatives to detention for juveniles already incarcerated. Also included in the authorization was an increase in funding for state grants to help deter juvenile violence and financial incentives to encourage states to try alternatives to imprisonment for teens convicted of nonviolent offenses.[44]

The Alternative Juvenile Justice Incarceration Act was proposed in the House this session (H.R. 3019). The proposal would authorize the Administrator of the Office of Juvenile Justice and Delinquency Prevention to make grants available to states so that they could implements programs to investigate if incarcerating juveniles in boot camps rehabilitates juvenile offenders effectively. The bill was not passed by the House and went no further.

1993–94: 103RD CONGRESS

Three bills were introduced into the House during this session—none of which passed. First was H.R. 3354, which focused on preventing crime by youth gangs. In the second bill, H.R. 3353, the House authorized $200 million over two years to help states fight juvenile gangs and drug trafficking. The third proposal was H.R. 3351, which intended to provide state grants of up to $200 million a year for three years to develop alternative sentencing for youthful offenders age 22 or younger. One alternative to prison would be boot camp. Youths would not be eligible if convicted of sexual assault, a crime involving a firearm, or any crime punishable by one year or more in prison.[45] None of these bills passed.

In the major 1994 Crime bill (H.R. 3355; H.R. 4092/S. 1607; PL 103-322), a provision allowed juveniles who were 13 years old and older to be tried as adults in the federal court system for certain violent crime and crimes involving a gun.[46] In these cases, both the prosecutor and the presiding judge had to choose an adult trial. However, the law specified that juveniles should not be incarcerated in adult prisons. It authorized sentencing adjustments, including supervised release, for defendants who showed a commitment to avoid further crimes. The law also authorized the federal government to help states develop systems to prosecute more 16- and 17-year-olds as adults for certain violent crimes.

Another provision in the bill focused on gang activity. The law stiffened the sentences for certain federal crimes if they were committed by a repeat offender who was part of a gang. The law added up to ten years to the sentence for certain federal drug and violent felonies.

The bill also provided $50 million over five years for a grant program to help local prosecutors working with police, school officials, and others to identify and prosecute young violent offenders.

1995–96: 104TH CONGRESS

This session, Republicans in the House pushed for action on H.R. 3565, which would have allowed juveniles as young as age 13 to be tried as adults if they were accused of committing violent crimes in federal jurisdictions. It was an attempt to toughen the federal government's response to juvenile crime and encourage states and local governments, which ran overcrowded juvenile courts, to follow suit. But the Democrats attacked it, and it never made it out of the Judiciary Committee. Some experts charged that the local juvenile justice system was not prepared for the strain it might take when the large number of children under age ten reached their teens. Critics also charged that the system treated juveniles with kid gloves and that it was not dealing well with a surge in violent crime and drug use by juveniles.

One provision in the bill would allow federal prosecutors to try juveniles as young as 14 years old as adults if they were accused of committing a violent crime in a federal jurisdiction, such as a national park. In some cases, the attorney general could try juveniles as young as 13 years old as adults. Mandatory minimum sentences for adults or juveniles tried as adults who possessed, brandished, or discharged a firearm in the process of committing a violent crime or drug-trafficking offense were established. Moreover, the proposal would require the attorney general to increase resources for those who prosecuted juvenile offenders. Finally, the Department of Justice's Office of Juvenile Justice and Delinquency Prevention would be abolished and replaced with two grant programs to the states. One of the grants would provide extra money to states and localities that followed the federal examples and set tougher penalties for juvenile criminals. The other was for operating juvenile justice programs.[47]

Another bill passed in 1996 was approved by the Senate Judiciary Committee but was not passed into law. S. 1952 would authorize new research and grant programs for juvenile crime prevention. It would provide $70 million for the National Institute for Juvenile Justice and Delinquency to fund research programs and to evaluate programs designed to combat crimes committed by youth. There would be another $70 million available for states to use for youth crime prevention, drug and alcohol treatment programs, and other activities to curb juvenile offenses. If states did not follow the guidelines, they could be denied up to 50 percent of their funding.[48]

In a bill approved in the House Economic and Educational Opportunities Committee (H.R. 3876), several 1988 amendments to the Juvenile Justice and Delinquency Prevention Act that made it more difficult for juvenile offenders to be detained with adults would be repealed. There would also be an incentive grant program for states that tried juveniles accused of violent crimes as adults and that released juvenile records to law enforcement agencies, courts, and schools.[49] This proposal was not signed into law.

1997–98: 105TH CONGRESS

The House Judiciary worked on H.R. 3 (S. 10), a bill intended to combat juvenile crime by requiring the federal government to try most violent juveniles offenders as adults, and encourage states to do the same. The bill developed punishments for minor crimes and opened juvenile criminal records to police and school authorities. It authorized $1.5 billion over three years for states to fight crime, provided they conform with the requirement of transferring juvenile offenders to adult courts.[50] Although the House passed their version in 1997 and the Senate Judiciary Committee approved their version, floor action in the Senate was delayed. Republicans argued that the current juvenile justice system was not holding juveniles accountable for their wrongdoings, so when they committed serious crimes typically committed by adults, they should be treated as adults. President Clinton's plan combined get-tough policies with money for prevention programs.[51] Both plans would have relaxed restrictions on housing teen offenders and adults together in detention facilities. One interest group, the Gun Owners of America, opposed certain parts of the bill. In the end, the bill was not passed.

H.R. 269 was a proposal to create a Role Models Academy demonstration program. Under the proposal, the secretary of education would implement a four-year, military-style academy for at-risk youth. It would provide secondary school course work (or even precollege courses) and vocational training for the residents. The teachers would be primarily from the armed forces. They would also operate a mentoring program with role models from all sectors of society. The proposal was not passed and did not become law.

The Balanced Juvenile Justice and Crime Prevention Act of 1997 was proposed in the House (H.R. 278) but did not pass. This was a comprehensive proposal to enhance the prosecution of dangerous juvenile offenders. Serious juvenile offenders could be tried as adults in federal court. Money would be available to states to establish juvenile gun courts and drug courts. Funds would also be available for prosecutors to establish community-based juvenile justice programs.

1999–2000: 106TH CONGRESS

House membership considered Aimee's Law (H.R. 894), a bill to stop grants to those states that did not sentence murderers, rapists, and child molesters to long prison terms. As part of the debate in the Senate, members added a provision that would bar juveniles who were convicted of a violent crime from owning a handgun. This did not pass.

Part of H.R. 489/S. 316, the America After School Act, included provisions to establish the After School Crime Prevention Program. Grants would be available to public and private agencies to help fund after-school programs for juveniles in an attempt to reduce or prevent crime. Priority would be given to states that target high-crime neighborhoods or at-risk juveniles and to those programs that were designed to teach juveniles alternatives to crime. The bill did not pass.

H.R. 1501 was a proposal in the House titled the Juvenile Crime Control and Delinquency Prevention Act. Among other things, the proposal included revisions of the Juvenile Delinquency Prevention Block Grant Program to give priority to projects that hold juveniles accountable for their actions, provide treatment to juveniles who are victims of abuse, and include education program and mentoring elements. The proposal would also authorize research and evaluation of programs for juvenile offenders. The proposal was not passed.

A similar bill was H.R. 1498, the Crime Control and Community Protection Act, which would reform existing programs dealing with juveniles. Under this proposal, the administrator of the Office of Juvenile Justice and Delinquency Prevention would be required to collect information on juvenile offender incarceration rates, repeat offenders, weapons used, and juvenile victims of crime. This information could be used to determine grant money. States would have to prove that there was no commingling of adult and juvenile offenders in facilities. The proposal did not have enough support to become law.

In H.R. 2037, the Child Safety and Youth Violence Prevention Act, the proceedings for the transfer of a juvenile to adult court would be amended. It would require that a juvenile be prosecuted as an adult if the juvenile has made that request in writing or if the juvenile is accused of committing the crime after attainting the age of 14, which if committed by an adult, would be a serious violent felony. The bill did not pass.

PRESIDENT BUSH

2001–2: 197TH CONGRESS

Two bills on juvenile crime, H.R. 863 and H.R. 1900, were proposed to deal with juvenile crime. The first bill, H.R. 863, would have authorized $1.5 billion over three years for juvenile justice grants to state and local governments. This was signed into law (PL 107-273). The second bill, H.R. 1900, would consolidate five juvenile justice and delinquency prevention programs into a single block grant to be used by states for activities designed to prevent and reduce juvenile crime.[52] This did not receive enough support to become law.

Another bill, the Faith-Based Charities Bill (H.R. 7) was aimed at making federal money available for nine new categories of faith-based social services and creating tax incentives for private charitable donations. This bill passed the House only. Provisions included a focus on faith-based services. Any religious organizations would be eligible to compete on an equal basis with other groups to provide a greatly expanded list of federally funded social services. Programs would include juvenile delinquency prevention, crime prevention, after-school programs, housing grants, job training, programs for senior citizens under the Older Americans Act, and domestic violence prevention initiatives. This also did not become law.

2003–4: 108TH CONGRESS

Senate members proposed S. 1735, the Gang Prevention and Effective Deterrence Act. This was a bill to increase law enforcement efforts to investigate violent gang-related crime. The bill would criminalize the recruitment of juveniles into gangs. It would also provide $650 million for gang prevention programs. The bill did not become law.

The Project Exile Safe Streets and Neighborhoods Act (H.R. 54) would, among other things, make grants available for supporting the juvenile justice system in states. The bill did not pass. Another bill in the House that did not have support to pass was the juvenile Gun Crime Reporting Act. This would amend the Brady Handgun Violence Prevention Act to prohibit the sale of a firearm to a person who was found guilty of an act committed as a juvenile, which if committed by an adult, would be considered to be an act of violence.

2005–6: 109TH CONGRESS

The Gang Deterrence and Community Protection Act (H.R. 1279) was a proposal to increase funding for programs geared toward fighting gang violence and to apply mandatory minimum sentences to crimes involving gang activity. The intent of the bill was to deter gang violence by applying mandatory minimum sentences to crimes involving organized activity. Under the proposed law, a criminal street gang would be defined as any formal or informal group of three or more people that commits two or more gang crimes, one of which is a crime of violence, in two or more separate criminal episodes. The bill did not become law.

S. 155 was titled the Gang Prevention and Effective Deterrence Act. It was proposed to make it a crime to recruit juveniles into gangs. Authorities would be given new powers that would enable them to prosecute the recruiters similar to organized crime groups. The proposal would also authorize more funding for gang prosecution and prevention. The bill did not make it through the whole Senate.

2007–8: 110TH CONGRESS

H.R. 1592, a bill to help prosecute hate crimes, included money for a study of how juveniles were recruited by adults to commit hate crimes. The bill also included a provision that would provide grants funds to programs designed to combat hate crimes committed by juveniles. This did not pass.

The House also considered but did not pass H.R. 3411, the Juvenile Crime Reduction Act. If passed, the administrator of the Office of Juvenile Justice and Delinquency Prevention would provide grants to states to fund training to those who work with criminal youth. The money could also be used to develop policies for juveniles with mental illness or substance abuse concerns.

H.R. 1806, the Youth Crime Deterrence Act of 2007, set requirements for state policies dealing with juveniles who are truant from detention or other placement, reentry, and aftercare services. The bill would have made grants available for family and community programs that were geared toward preventing and reducing the number of youth in gangs and for treatment programs for juvenile offenders who were victims of child abuse and neglect. Mentoring programs for at-risk juveniles could also be funded. The bill did not have enough support to pass into law.

H.R. 2647, titled the Mental Health and Substance Abuse Juvenile Services Improvement Act of 2007, was a way for the federal government to support programs to promote mental health among children and their families. For those children who needed it, early intervention services would be made available. The proposal never made it out of the subcommittee.

PRESIDENT OBAMA

2009–10: 11TH CONGRESS

In S. 1782, pretrial officers would be allowed to perform various pretrial services for juveniles who were awaiting trial. This was done because many people were concerned that pretrial treatment services were primarily available only for adults. The law made it to the president's desk and was signed by him (PL 111-174).

Once again, members of Congress proposed the Gang Prevention, Intervention, and Suppression Act (H.R. 1022). This bill would prohibit the recruitment of another person to join a criminal street gang. If a murder was committed by a gang in the course of a drug-trafficking offense, then increased criminal penalties could be imposed. Increased penalties could also be imposed for possession of firearms by a juvenile during a violent crime. The attorney general would be required to identify areas with high crime activity and expand programs in those areas to address the problem. The bill did not become law.

CONCLUSION

Over the years, presidents and Congress have proposed many ideas to prevent juvenile crime, passing some of those ideas into law. For the most part, juvenile crime remains a state issue, as the federal government primarily provides financial support for states to fund policies that they feel are successful in their jurisdictions. The federal assistance helps states to develop programs to reduce juvenile crime.

CHAPTER 11

CRIMES AGAINST CHILDREN

FOR MANY YEARS, CRIMES AGAINST CHILDREN HAVE been a concern for both presidents and Congress. This goes back to the 1950s, when the effect of media violence on children was the subject of congressional debate. In 1953, the Congress held hearings on the effect of violence in comic books, radio, and television programs on juvenile delinquency. Tipper Gore, the wife of Senator Al Gore, led a movement against violent lyrics in popular songs of the time. While some wanted to restrict the sale of violent music to children, the music industry felt this was a violation of free speech. In the end, music companies agreed to label those albums that contained graphic lyrics with parental warnings.[1]

In more recent time, the Congress has acted to protect children with regard to the Internet and sex offenders and providing safe schools to children, which became a popular issue after a rash of school shootings in the 1990s. Punishments for those who sexually abuse children have typically been handled by state governments, but beginning with the Reagan administration, it was also a federal issue. This chapter looks at these policy concerns and what solutions the federal government had to solve them.

PRESIDENT NIXON

1973–74: 93RD CONGRESS

The Congress passed a new law (S. 1191/PL 93-247) that would provide federal allocations for the prevention and treatment of child abuse and neglected children. The bill would provide $85 million to help states develop programs dealing with abused and neglected children.[2]

1977–78: 95TH CONGRESS

H.R. 6693 was a proposal that would broaden the federal government's role in treating and preventing child abuse and neglect (PL 95-266). The bill authorized the Child Abuse Prevention and Treatment Act of 1973 (PL 93-247). This act began the federal government's involvement in fighting child abuse.

PRESIDENT REAGAN

Ronald Reagan set the safety and protection of our children as a top priority on the national agenda.[3] In 1982, he signed the Missing Children Act (H.R. 6976/PL 97-292) to help find missing children. The new law mandated a system to allow parents access to a central computer file designed to help trace missing children. The act also helped to identify deceased children to help ease the parents' pain of not knowing the status of their missing child.[4]

In 1984, Reagan then signed the Child Protection Act of 1984 (H.R. 3635/PL 98-292) to toughen the federal laws dealing with the production and distribution of pornographic materials involving children. It strengthened the powers of a prosecuting authority against those who produced and distributed child pornography, and it created stiffer penalties for those offenses.[5]

Reagan proposed further legislation to protect the nation's children in 1987. Called the Child Protection and Obscenity Enforcement Act of 1987, the law made sexual exploitation of children illegal. This would include actions including using computers in child pornography or buying or selling children to produce child pornography. Reagan also wanted to increase the record-keeping requirements for pornography and give more attention to the relationship between child pornography and organized crime. Reagan also wanted to make it illegal to receive or possess obscene matter for sale or distribution, forfeiture of property gained through producing or trafficking in obscenity, the possession and sale of obscene material and child pornography on federal properties, and adding obscenity to the wiretap statute.[6]

He also announced that the attorney general was setting up a new national commission to study the effects of pornography on our society. The commission was to study the dimensions of the problem and what the government's response should be.[7]

In another attempt to keep children safe, President Reagan discussed the issue of school discipline in 1984. He directed the federal government to do all it could to help parents, teachers, and administrators restore order to their classrooms.[8] More specifically, he asked the Department of Justice to establish a National School Safety Center that would publish handbooks informing teachers and other officials of their legal rights in dealing with disruptive students and put together a computerized national clearinghouse for school safety resources.[9]

1981–82: 97TH CONGRESS

The House proposed and the president signed H.R. 6976 (PL 97-292), which was aimed at helping the federal government locate missing children. The bill authorized descriptive data about missing children to be entered into the FBI's central crime computer. If state and local officials would not enter the information, parents or guardians of the missing child could have the FBI do so. The legislation also required a clearinghouse file that would list descriptions of unidentified bodies that had been found anywhere in the country in the FBI computer.

1983–84: 98TH CONGRESS

The issue surrounding missing children was included as part of the omnibus law (H.J. Res. 648/PL 98-473) that made many changes to improve federal action with regards to missing and exploited children. For example, the law required federal assistance in locating missing children. The program required that a national toll-free hotline be established and that members of the public could use it to report information about missing children who were 13 or younger. Technical assistance to the public and to agencies involved in locating missing children would be available, as would assistance to coordinate public and private programs designed to help find missing children. A national clearinghouse to disseminate information about missing children would be created, which could then also conduct periodic studies to determine things, such as how many children were reported missing each year, how many were abducted by strangers, how many were the victims of parental kidnappings, and how many were recovered. Grants to agencies to allow them to conduct research, carry out demonstration projects, or service programs related to missing and sexually exploited children were authorized in the bill. An advisory board was created to make recommendations for federally assisted missing children programs.[10]

In another bill (H.R. 3635/PL 98-292), federal laws against the production and distribution of pornographic materials involving children were strengthened. Congress removed a requirement in the existing law that child pornography be proven obscene before convictions could be obtained. The new bill also raised the age of children protected under the law from 16 to 18. Law enforcement agencies could seize the assets and equipment of pornographers and the profits accumulated from it. For someone convicted for the first time of these charges, the fine was raised from $10,000 to a maximum of $100,000. The fine for a second offense was raised from $15,000 to $200,000. The fine for an organization that was found to have violated the law was set at $250,000. Finally, the law authorized court-approved wiretapping to combat child pornography.[11]

1985–86: 99TH CONGRESS

This session, the Congress passed S. 140 (PL 99-401), aimed at helping states deal with child abuse, especially sexual abuse. The bill established a grant program for states to improve the prosecution, treatment, and prevention of child abuse and to protect the victims. The bill authorized the secretary of health and human services to set up a task force to make recommendations on how to improve the investigation and prosecution of child abuse cases. The task force also would look at ways to reduce emotional damage to victims of abuse. The grants would be financed out of the Crime Victims Fund.[12]

Legislation cleared the Congress (H.J. Res. 738/PL 99-591) that would strengthen federal laws against child pornography by increasing the penalties for repeat offenders and by providing victims an opportunity to get compensation from those who victimized them. The measure raised the penalty for a second child pornography conviction from two to five years. It gave victims who were minors the right to sue anyone who enticed or forced them into helping produce pornographic materials for damages. The child would be entitled to a minimum of $50,000 and attorney's fees. Finally, the bill directed the attorney general to report within a year on courtroom procedures for child witnesses forced to testify against accused pornographers.[13]

1987–88: 100TH CONGRESS

Another new law (H.R. 1900/PL 100-294) reauthorized three programs geared toward preventing and treating child abuse and domestic violence. The bill reauthorized the

1974 Child Abuser Prevention and Treatment Act, the Family Violence Prevention and Services Program, and the Adoption Opportunities Program.

A proposal that did not pass was the Child and Family Development Act (H.R. 95) If passed, the secretary of health and human services would be given the task of carrying out a study of child care needs across the United States that would include day care, education, health, and nutrition needs. Based on that, the secretary would develop a plan to meet the nation's child care needs. This may include additional federal funds to improve child care programs.

H.R. 3889, or the Child Protection and Obscenity Enforcement Act, was a proposal in the House to make it illegal to use a computer to transport child pornography in interstate commerce. There would be penalties for buying, selling, or transferring the custody of a minor knowing that the minor will be used in child pornography. This did not pass.

President Bush

1989–90: 101st Congress

A major omnibus crime bill was passed (S. 3266/PL 101-647) that included provisions on child abuse. The original omnibus bill was S. 1970 and H.R. 5269.[14] In an attempt to prevent child abuse and more effectively investigate and prosecute offenders, the relevant portion provided an option for those children who were witnesses at an abuse trial to testify outside the courtroom through a two-way closed-circuit television. It authorized $10 million toward training for judges, prosecutors, and child advocates on child abuse issues. The law also made possession of child pornography a federal offense and required producers to keep a record of the age of people appearing in hard-core pornography.[15]

H.R. 3/H.R. 30/S. 5, the Act for Better Child Care Services, would make families with a low income eligible for day care services. It would provide federal funds to help pay for the program. The bill was attached to H.R. 5835, the Omnibus Budget Reconciliation Act of 1990, which became law (H.R. 5835/PL 101-508).

In the House, the Child and Family Development Act (H.R. 120) was again proposed and again failed to become law.

H.R. 579, the Child Protection Act, was also not passed. This bill would amend the Racketeer Influenced and Corrupt Organizations (RICO) statute to cover the sexual exploitation of children. It would require a mandatory life sentence in cases involving the sexual exploitation of minors or in kidnapping offenses that included the murder of a minor.

1991–92: 102nd Congress

In S. 838 (PL 102-295), the Congress attempted to help abused children and victims of domestic violence by focusing on improvement of child protective services with up to $100 million in grants to states. The money would allow states to enhance court procedures to include civil and criminal cases, plus cases of child abuse and neglect, not just child sexual abuse. The ultimate aim of the program was to reunite children with their families.[16]

In 1992, Congress cleared H.R. 1253 (PL 102-528), which authorized $600,000 for the State Justice Institute to develop judicial training courses on child custody law to aid courts in identifying those homes at high risk for the abuse of parents or children.[17]

In the Save the Children Act, federal grants would be made available to schools in areas where the dropout rate for high school students was 20 percent or more. If passed, 90 percent of the costs of daily after-school programs for at-risk students in grades four through eight would be available. The law did not have enough support to become law.

Federal funding for child care services would be coordinated by the Administration for Children, Youth and Families (in the Department of Health and Human Services) if H.R. 284 became law. But the proposal did not make it out of the subcommittee. In a related bill, the Quality Child Care Demonstration Act (H.R. 350), federal grants would be made available in rural and urban areas to administer programs that would increase the quality of available child care services. This proposal also did not make it out of the subcommittee.

PRESIDENT CLINTON

During his administration, William Clinton expressed the need to keep the nation's children safe. One of his proposals centered on child support. In 1993, Clinton said he wanted the federal government to set an example for states and pass a tougher child support enforcement program.[18] Two years later, Clinton signed an executive order so that any parent who tried to avoid paying their child support would be tracked down and made to pay. He promised to garnish wages, suspend licenses, track people across state lines, and if necessary, require people to work off what they owed.[19] He also wanted to see employer reporting of newly hired employees to catch deadbeat parents who move from job to job, more uniform interstate child support laws, computerized collection of payments to speed up the process, streamlined efforts to identify the father of every child born, and tough new penalties, like the revocation of drivers' licenses or professional licenses for those people who repeatedly refuse to pay their child support.[20]

Clinton signed two pieces of legislation to protect children. The first was the International Parental Kidnapping Crime Act of 1993 (H.R. 3378) that made international parental kidnappings a federal felony offense.[21] He also signed the National Child Protection Act of 1993 that created a national data base network. The network could be used by child care providers to check the backgrounds of an applicant's to determine if that applicant could be trusted with children and, if not, to prevent that person from ever working with children.[22]

The final part of Clinton's plan to keep children safe was to keep our nation's schools safe. In 1993, as part of an economic program he sent to Congress, Clinton added a "safe schools initiative," which would enable the government to help schools with more security guards, metal detectors, and other equipment that will help to ensure that kids do not come to school with weapons.[23] As Clinton saw it, there are "guns on the playground, guns in the classroom, guns on the bus . . . Guns have no place in our schools and have no place in the hands of our children. If we don't stop this, we can't make the schools safe."[24] To address that problem, Clinton proposed the Gun-Free School Zones Amendments Act of 1995 that would ban guns anywhere near schools.[25] This was necessary, according to Clinton, because, "in the absence of security, not much learning is going to occur."[26] He proposed other ideas to help ensure that children can be drug free, gun free, and violence free,[27] including a school uniform policy.[28]

Clinton supported registration and community notification of sex offenders as a way to warn unsuspecting families of any sexual predators who may be living in their communities.[29] He proposed a three-part plan to stop sexual predators. First, he wanted every state to keep track of sex offenders. Second, he signed Megan's law that mandated states to notify communities when sex offenders move into the neighborhood. The third step was to ask the attorney general to come up with a plan for a national registry of sex offenders.[30]

CONGRESS

1993–94: 103RD CONGRESS

H.R. 324, known as Crimes Against Minors Act,[31] required people convicted of a crime, such as sexual assault against a minor to notify police of their addresses for ten years following their release from prison or their parole. The bill included penalties for states that did not create such registries within three years. The proposal did not become law.

A bill relating to child kidnappings by their parents (H.R. 3378/PL103-173) was passed by Congress and signed by the president. The law made it a federal crime for parents to kidnap their children and take them out of the United States. It also allowed the US government to have the parents extradited to the United States for prosecution.

A new law was passed concerning child care providers (H.R. 1237/PL 103-209). The bill would establish a national system for carrying out criminal background checks on people applying for jobs as child-care providers.

In the major 1994 crime bill (H.R. 3355; H.R. 4092/S. 1607; PL 103-322), the topic of child success was addressed. The new bill supported children through several school programs, including in-school grants for school-based programs that provide academic and other support to youth who were identified as being at risk of becoming involved in crime or drugs. After-school programs were also supported. Grants of up to $567 million were created to help community organizations run after-school, weekend, and summer programs for youth, including tutoring, crafts, and athletics. Finally, a grant program was established for public agencies and nonprofit organizations to help dropouts and other at-risk youth improve their academic or job skills and enhance their self-esteem.

The 1994 crime bill also addressed child pornography. It banned the production of child pornography for import into the United States. The punishment for this would be fines and up to ten years in prison. The law also made it a federal crime to travel overseas and to have sexual relations with a minor, even if doing so was legal in the overseas country.

Other provisions of the crime bill also related to protecting children. For example, the penalties for using children younger than 18 to distribute drugs at or near a drug-free zone, such as a school, playground, or public swimming pool, were increased. The law also strengthened federal criminal penalties against those who assaulted children 16 or younger and directed the US Sentencing Commission to stiffen recommended penalties for those who solicited a minor to commit a crime. Additionally, the law established a federal task force to work cooperatively with the National Center for

Missing and Exploited Children and to use federal resources more effectively to help find missing children.

Finally, the House passed H.R. 2974 to increase penalties for violent crimes against the elderly, children, and other vulnerable populations. The bill would have instructed the US Sentencing Commission to increase the penalties for crimes against those 14 and younger and 65 and older by 50 percent. The Senate did not act on it.[32]

The Congress dealt with the problem of school violence during this session. One bill they considered was H.R. 3375, which would authorize grants to support local school initiatives for preventing crime and violence. The bill was passed by the House committee only. In the Senate, members of the Labor and Human Resources Committee worked on S. 1125, which was aimed at helping local school districts make schools safer. The bill authorized $175 million to provide grants to school districts with a high rate of homicides committed by people under 18, referrals of young people to juvenile court, expulsions and suspensions of students, young people under court supervision, and victimization of young people by violence, crime, or abuse. The grants could be used in several ways, including training school employees to deal with violence, initiating conflict resolution programs, providing alternative after-school programs as safe havens for students, education for students and parents about the dangers of guns and other weapons, or buying and installing metal detectors and hiring security.[33] This bill did not make it to the president's desk. Finally, in an omnibus education bill, the Elementary and Secondary Education Act reauthorization (H.R. 6), a provision that required local districts to develop programs to prevent students and school employers from engaging in violent acts or using illegal drugs, alcohol, or tobacco was included in the bill.[34] This became PL 103-382.

1995–96: 104TH CONGRESS

A bill to crack down on computer-generated pornography was enacted during this session of Congress. The bill expanded the definition of child pornography to cover computer-generated images of minors in sexually explicit activities. In a change from existing law, the images did not have to be made using only minors to qualify as criminal. For example, if someone took a photograph of a child's head and attached it to the body of someone engaged in a sexual activity, it would be considered child pornography. The bill also increased penalties for those convicted of possessing, distributing, or making child pornography. Since the House could not pass the law by itself, it was attached to the fiscal 1997 omnibus appropriations bill (H.R. 3610/PL 104-208).[35]

The Congress cleared a bill to end prison sentences for those convicted of sexually exploiting children. H.R. 1240 was signed by the president (PL 104-71). The new law directed the US Sentencing Commission to increase the recommended penalties for making or trafficking in child pornography, with additional time for offenders who used a computer for distribution or recruiting. It recommended adding six months for a first offense for trafficking in child pornography (for a minimum penalty of 24 to 30 months) and a 12- to 16-month increase for a first-time conviction of making child pornography (for a minimum of 70 to 87 months). Using a computer for these crimes added at least six months to the sentence. The new recommended penalties for federal child prostitution crimes increased months, to 30 to 37 months for a first-time offender. The bill also mandated increased penalties for those who transported a child across state lines to engage in criminal sexual activity.[36]

Attached to a bill about jailbreak penalties was an amendment that required that the FBI and state authorities could collect fees to pay for fingerprinting and checking the backgrounds of volunteers, such as Boy Scout leaders, who worked with children.[37]

Federal child abuse and treatment programs were authorized at $221 million in fiscal 1997 under a bill cleared and signed into law (S. 919/PL 104-235)

A third new law was passed (S. 652/PL 104-104) requiring that new television sets include a V-chip that would allow viewers to block out objectionable programs.

In this session, there was an amendment attached to a bill about jailbreak penalties that required the FBI to establish a database to track the "whereabouts" and "movement" of people convicted of criminal offenses against minors and people convicted of sexually violent offenses.[38]

Congress cleared and the president signed a bill (H.R. 2137/PL 104-145) that required state and local law enforcement agencies to release "relevant information" about those sexual offenders who were required to register under the 1994 crime bill. The bill was named "Megan's law" after 17-year-old Megan Kanka who was raped and murdered by a man who lived across the street from her in New Jersey. The man had been convicted twice of molesting children, but no one in the neighborhood had been informed of his criminal background when he moved there. States that failed to establish proper registration systems by September of 1997 were subject to a 10 percent reduction in federal grants.[39]

Megan's law only applied to states, some of which still had not established registries as mandated under the 1994 crime bill. Some supporters of the law were concerned that there would be a lack of interstate tracking and make the law less effective. To address that concern, Clinton issued an administrative order that required the FBI to keep a national database of sexual offenders registered on state lists. This would make it easier for law enforcement officers to track offenders across state lines. The Congress cleared a bill that accomplished the same thing (S. 1675/H.R. 3456/ PL 104-236). The measure required those convicted of sex offenses to verify their addresses regularly by returning cards with fingerprints to the FBI. If they did not, they could be punished with a $100,000 fine and the possibility of a one-year prison term.[40]

1997–98: 105TH CONGRESS

In response to complaints that the current system of television ratings did not give viewers and parents enough information about the content of the program, the broadcast industry agreed to change the voluntary television ratings system they had put in place at the beginning of the year to include more information about the content of programs. Family advocacy groups supported the new approach.[41]

The House passed H.R. 1683 that was aimed at strengthening state registration programs for convicted sex offenders and closing several loopholes in existing law. Under the proposed bill, sex offenders convicted in military and federal courts would be required to register under existing state programs. The bill would require them to register in the state where they lived and any state where they were employed or enrolled as a student. This would make it easier to track sex offenders across state borders. The Senate did not act on the bill.

Under H.R. 267, states would be required to impose strict penalties on those parents who do not pay child support. If the states fail to do so, the government could revoke funds for state child support enforcement programs. This law did not pass.

1999–2000: 106TH CONGRESS

A bill in the House (H.R. 764) would increase funding for child abuse prevention programs. The money will help state and local government agencies respond more effectively to cases of abused and neglected children. It would also authorize cooperative programs between states and the media to collect and publish information on child abuses. This bill was signed into law (PL 106-177).

S. 876 was a proposal that could lead to a ban on violent television programs in the early evening hours. The Federal Communications Commission (FCC) would be required to assess the effectiveness of policies to require television broadcasters to code programs that could be blocked by parents by a V-chip. The FCC could, if it found necessary, block violent programming during hours when children would be watching. The bill did not pass.

A proposed anticrime bill (H.R. 3244) reauthorized the Violence Against Women Act but also included new provisions to combat international slavery and sex trafficking. The bill created a new crime of trafficking in persons and doubled the punishment for that crime to 20 years in prison. The bill also created a new, nonimmigrant T visa for victims of sex trafficking. The victims who received the new visa must agree to cooperate with law enforcement.[42] This became law (PL 106-386).

H.R. 1356, titled the Freedom from Sexual Trafficking Act, was not passed during this session. The intent of the proposal was to eliminate international sexual trafficking where women and children are taken across international boundaries by means of force and forced into slavery, prostitution, or other offenses. The bill set forth some international standards to eliminate sex trafficking and established an Office for the Protection of Victims of Trafficking.

PRESIDENT BUSH

George W. Bush made many statements about children's safety during his eight years in office. To begin, he promised to help young children whose parents were in prison with a $67 million grant allocation for mentoring programs. He believed there was no better place to mentor a child than in a faith-based program where the word "love" actually rings true.[43]

He promised to increase federal funding to prevent child abuse by 66 percent. He reported to have given $75 million for Project Child Safe, a program that provides gun safety locks for families.[44]

Bush reported that the Justice Department made the prevention and investigation of child abductions a major priority. In addition, the administration was vigorously prosecuting those who preyed on our children, according to Bush.[45] He noted that there were gaps in the AMBER Plan coverage, and he promised to fill them. He wanted to develop more AMBER plans and better coordination among them.[46]

Bush was also concerned with dangers the Internet posed for children because he called it a tool that lures children into real danger. He sought to almost double the funding for the Internet Crimes Against Children Task Forces that was intended to help states and local authorities enforce laws against child pornography and exploitation.[47] Bush also wanted to take several aggressive steps to protect children against pornography. According to Bush, until that time pornography was limited to red-light districts or restricted to adults. But with the Internet, pornography was instantly available to any child who has a computer. Sexual predators use the Internet to distribute child pornography and obscenity. They use the Internet to engage in sexually explicit conversations. They use the Internet to lure children out of the safety of their homes into harm's way . . . involuntarily exposed to pornography. However, Bush reminded people that the chief responsibility to protect America's children lies with their parents.[48]

In 2003, Bush signed S. 151 into law, the Prosecutorial Remedies and Other Tools to End the Exploitation of Children Today Act of 2003, also known as the PROTECT Act. This legislation gave law enforcement authorities new tools to deter, detect, investigate, prosecute, and punish crimes against America's children. In particular, the act expanded and improved the AMBER Alert program to combat child abduction and strengthened laws against child pornography.[49] The law also strengthened federal penalties for child kidnapping. Judges would have the authority to require longer supervision of sex offenders who are released from prison. Finally, the law created important pilot programs to help organizations that deal with children to obtain quick and complete criminal background information on their volunteers.[50]

Another law signed by Bush was the Keeping Children and Families Safe Act of 2003. This legislation required criminal background checks for foster and adoptive parents.[51]

Finally, Bush supported increasing the safety of children in public schools, but he noted that it was a local issue. He reminded people that it was up to state and local authorities to make sure the schools run well, because we do not want the federal government running the public schools in the country. Instead, the federal government's role is only to help.[52]

On the whole, Bush was very active in the race to keep children safe. He often worked with Congress to get new legislation passed that would reduce the potential harm to children.

CONGRESS

2001–2: 107TH CONGRESS

The House passed a bill (H.R. 5422) to combat crimes against children. The bill was an attempt to speed up the development of a federal alert system for abducted children, known as the AMBER Alert plan. The AMBER plan was named after Amber Hagerman, a 9-year-old girl who was abducted and killed in Arlington, Texas in 1996. The plan uses the Emergency Alert System to issue an alert when a child is abducted. The proposed law would provide national coordination and assistance to states and localities that participated in the AMBER plan. Many of the provisions were too sweeping for the Senate, so they did not consider it.[53]

There were also some other bills considered but not acted on during this session. They included the following:

- H.R. 4697: to provide for lifetime supervision of sex offenders who had completed their sentences. This would apply to those convicted of sexual abuse, sexual exploitation and other abuse of children, transportation for illegal sexual activity, and sex trafficking of children by force, fraud, or coercion. It would also apply to those convicted of coercion and enticement, the use of interstate facilities to transmit information about a minor, and kidnapping of a minor under the age of 18.

- H.R. 4477: to provide for new prohibitions on sex tourism. The proposal would make it easier to prosecute those who travel to another country to have sex with a minor, regardless of whether the person originally intended to do so. The bill would make it a crime, punishable by up to 15 years in prison, to travel into the United States for the purpose of engaging in illicit sexual conduct. It would also make it a federal crime for a US citizen or permanent resident traveling abroad to engage or attempt to engage in illicit sexual conduct. Violations would be punishable by fines and up to 15 years in prison.

- H.R. 2146: to provide for a two-strikes-and-you're-out policy for sex offenses against children. This bill would have created a mandatory sentence of life in prison for anyone convicted a second time of a sexual offense against a child.

- H.R. 1877: to authorize the use of wiretaps and other electronic surveillance in investigating crimes of child pornography, the buying and selling of children for sexual exploitation, inducing or coercing someone to cross state lines to engage in illegal sexual activities, and transporting minors for illegal sexual activity.

The House also considered other provisions to increase penalties for sex crimes against children this year. One bill would make murder involving child abuse, child assault, or torture a first-degree murder charge. This included increasing the maximum penalties from 20 to 30 years for sexual exploitation of a child. For anyone with a prior sex offense conviction, the maximum penalty would increase from 30 to 50 years. For those who were convicted of shipping, receiving, or distributing child pornography, including any visual depictions of minors engaged in sexually explicit conduct (including by computer), the punishment was increased from 15 to 20 years. For those with a prior sex offense conviction, the maximum sentence for that offense would increase from 30 to 40 years.[54]

Both chambers passed bills to ban "virtual" child pornography, but they were not able to agree on a final version. The proposal was a response to a Supreme Court ruling that the original 1996 law (S. 2520/PL 104-208) was overly broad and thus unconstitutional. They decided that the law prohibited any image that is, or appears to be, of a minor engaging in sexually explicit conduct. The ban included images that were simulated by computer technology or that used adults who looked like children. The justices decided in *Ashcroft v. The Free Speech Coalition* (535 US 234 [2002]) that extending the reach of child pornography laws to computer-generated and other images involving no real children would also prohibit visual depictions, such as films, art, or medial manuals that had redeeming social value.[55]

2003–4: 108TH CONGRESS

Once again, the Congress passed and the president signed a law (H.R. 1104/S. 151/ PL 108-21) that bolstered the nationwide AMBER child-abduction alert system, outlawed "virtual" child porn, mandated life sentences for twice-convicted child sex offenders, opened the door for electronic surveillance to investigate child porn, dropped the statute of limitations on crimes involving sexual abuse or kidnapping of children, and limited the ability of federal judges to depart from sentencing guidelines.[56]

The Keeping Children and Families Safe Act was a new law (H.R. 14/PL 108-36) that would enhance record collection on child abuse programs. Technical assistance for child abuse cases would be available, as would training resources for law enforcement. Further research into the problem of child abuse, and solutions to it, would be supported.

2005–6: 109TH CONGRESS

H.R. 3132 was passed in the House to strengthen federal registration requirements for convicted sex offenders. If an offender failed to register, it would be a federal crime. The bill was the result of a study that indicated many sex offenders fail to register and cannot be found. A similar bill was introduced in the Senate (S. 1086).

A bill to establish a national sex offender registry was proposed after a young lady, Dru Sjodin, was abducted in North Dakota and murdered by a sex offender. The registry would be searchable by zip code. The bill, S. 792, was passed by the Senate Judiciary Committee. A similar bill was introduced into the House (H.R. 95), but it did not become law.

H.R. 4472 was another proposal intended to improve sex offender registration. Under this proposal, sex crime offenders will face tougher mandatory minimum prison sentences and it will be easier to keep track of them. Sex offenders would be required to provide DNA samples and be subject to frequent in-person verification of the information they provided to the police about their homes and employment. If their workplaces and residences are in different jurisdictions, they must register in both places. An offender who does not register or update registration information could face a ten-year prison term. An offender who commits a violent crime while registered will be subject to a five-year minimum prison term. This bill was signed by President Bush and became law (PL 109-248).

S. 1086/H.R. 2423, the Jacob Wetterling, Megan Kanka, and Pam Lychner Sex Offender Registration and Notification Act was a bill introduced into both the House and Senate to address sex offenders. It required adults and juveniles who were convicted of sexually violent offenses or certain offenses against children to provide information to register with people in their neighborhoods, work, or school states for the rest of their lives. The attorney general would be required to maintain a National Sex Offender Registry that includes information concerning sex offenders. Despite support for the bill, it did not become law.

2007–8: 110TH CONGRESS

The House passed multiple laws aimed at protecting children from predators on the Internet. One of those bills, H.R. 4120, the Effective Child Pornography Prosecution Act, would ensure that federal officials do not have to prove interstate transmission in cases of child pornography. This was in response to a court case in which the court ruled that the government had to prove that interstate transmission had occurred. This bill became law (PL 110-358). Another bill, H.R. 4136, would alter the definition of "possession" of pornography to include "accessing by computer with the intent to view."[57] The bill would also make it easier to prosecute child pornography. It did not pass.

The Congress passed legislation, the Keeping the Internet Devoid of Sexual Predators Act (H.R. 719/S. 431), to require convicted sex offenders to include "online identifiers" such as e-mail addresses and screen names in the sex offender registry. The bill became law (PL 110-400).

A new law would create a special counsel who would focus on child exploitation prevention (H.R. 3845/S. 1738). Called the PROTECT Our Children Act, the bill would create a task force to combat online crimes against children. It established a special counsel for child exploitation prevention and interdiction within the office of the deputy attorney general. It would increase the available resources for regional computer forensic labs and to make other improvements to increase the ability of law enforcement agencies to investigate and prosecute child predators. This proposal was signed by the president (PL 110-401).

Finally, H.R. 4134 was a proposal to provide $5 million for a program called i-SAFE Inc. to conduct Internet crime prevention programs. This would help fund programs to teach parents to recognize and prevent potential criminal activity on the Internet, including sexual or racial harassment, cyberbullying, sexual exploitation, and pornography. This did not become law.

PRESIDENT OBAMA

Barack Obama was concerned about protecting children from crimes. To bring more attention to the issue, he proclaimed April 2009 and April 2010 as National Child Abuse Prevention Month.[58] He also believed that the family can not only prepare children for the future but also act to protect them from crimes. To help demonstrate the importance of the family, he proclaimed September 27, 2010, as family day.[59]

2009–10: 111TH CONGRESS

In an attempt to stop the sex tourism trade, House members made a proposal (H.R. 5138/H.R. 1623) to require convicted sex offenders to report upcoming international travel. Called the International Megan's Law, the bill was an attempt to prevent sexual predators from traveling abroad to abuse children. Convicted sex offenders would be required to report plans to travel internationally at least 30 days before leaving or arriving in the country. The new law, if passed, would also establish a national center to collect the reports and notify officials in foreign countries about future travel. Failure to report upcoming travel would result in a fine, up to ten years in prison, or both. This did not pass.

Another proposal in the House was H.R. 380, called the Infant Abandonment Prevention Act. Under the proposal, the attorney general and the Bureau of Justice Statistics would be responsible for creating the Task Force on Infant Abandonment, which would be responsible for creating and maintaining a database on incidents of where children were abandoned. This would include information on demographics, circumstances outcomes, and trends in child abandonment. The task force would also be responsible for creating and disseminating annual reports and making recommendations to Congress concerning policy toward child abandonment. This bill did not pass during this session.

The House called on the president to hold a Conference on Children and Youth in H.R. 618. The conference would focus on encouraging states to improve the local child welfare services and to develop recommendations for improving children's services in the future. The proposal did not have enough support to pass into law.

CONCLUSION

The federal government has made many policy choices designed to keep our children safe. This is a relatively new policy concern for presidents and Congress but one where they have passed many laws. These have primarily revolved around sex offenders, school safety, and Internet crimes. Since laws geared toward the safety of our children are traditionally considered to be state concerns rather than federal, this is an area where the federalization of crime is obvious.

PART V

WEAPONS

Handguns have always been part of American society. They play such an important role that the founding fathers guaranteed citizens the right to bear arms in the Second Amendment of the US Constitution. That amendment, however, has led to a lot of disagreement and debates among presidents and Congress about who should be able to own a gun and under what circumstances. In Chapter 12, presidential attention to the questions of handgun ownership and violence is described, as is Congressional action.

CHAPTER 12

HANDGUNS

THE FIRST FEDERAL FIREARMS LEGISLATION BECAME EFFECTIVE in 1791 in the Bill of Rights. The Second Amendment to the US Constitution provides that "the right of the people to keep and bear arms shall not be infringed." In 1934, Congress enacted the National Firearms Act, and in 1938 they passed the Federal Firearms Act. Together these acts regulated firearms that were transported in interstate and foreign commerce and aided the states in enforcing firearm regulations. An amendment to the 1938 law was passed in 1961 that prohibited people who had been convicted of a felony (rather than a crime of violence) from having a gun. It also prohibited dealers and gun manufacturers from shipping firearms to people who had a criminal record. This was punishable by a prison term exceeding one year from shipping or receiving firearms in interstate or foreign commerce. Unfortunately, the law did not stop some people with criminal records from obtaining mail-order weapons. They simply lied when asked if they had ever been convicted of a crime.[1]

Since then, gun control has been on both the presidential and Congressional agendas for many years. Certain events have spurred more action, such as the assassination of President John F. Kennedy, the more recent Columbine High School shootings, or the shootings on the campus of Virginia Tech. Politicians debate over whether there should be gun control legislation at all and, if so, what it should entail. Everyone agrees in the need to stop injuries and deaths from firearms, but they disagree as to the best way to do that. For many years, Congress and presidents have suggested and passed many pieces of legislation concerning firearms, beginning with Lyndon Johnson.

PRESIDENT KENNEDY

1961–62: 87TH CONGRESS

To more effectively fight organized crime, Congress passed S. 1750 (PL 87-342) to expand the Federal Firearms Act. The new law prohibited the shipment of firearms to or by any person who had been previously convicted of a felony.

PRESIDENT JOHNSON

In 1965, after the assassination of President Kennedy, President Johnson was very active in his support for gun control. To begin, he proposed legislation that would amend the Federal Firearms Act to prohibit firearms shipments in interstate commerce except among gun importers, manufacturers, and dealers who were licensed by the Treasury Department. Under his proposal, the mail-order sales of weapons would stop.[2] This was a way to limit gun ownership.

The following year, Johnson called for ending the easy availability of weapons to certain populations of people, including dangerous criminals, delinquent youth, those who had been convicted of a violent crime, habitual alcoholics, and those who were "disturbed and deranged."[3] To do that, he recommended a new law that would require every person to obtain a license before they would be allowed to have a gun and also called for the registration of all pistols.[4]

In 1967, Johnson again recommended legislation to the Congress on gun control. This time, his proposal would prohibit certain mail-order sales and shipments of firearms, except between those who held federal licenses. The over-the-counter sales of firearms, other than rifles and shotguns, would be prohibited to any person who did not live in the state in which the federal licensee operated. Federal licensees would be prohibited from selling handguns to anyone under 21 years old and from selling rifles and shotguns to anyone under the age of 18. The imports of surplus military firearms and other firearms not suitable for sporting purposes into the United States would also be curbed in the United States.[5] Further, it would be illegal to carry rifles and shotguns in public, unless unloaded and properly encased. In those cases where a firearm was used in the commission of a robbery, the courts would be authorized to impose increased penalties on the offender.[6] Many times, Johnson called on Congress to pass the law.[7]

Johnson also called on Congress to pass a gun control bill for the District of Columbia, referred to as the D.C. Gun Control Act. The proposed bill would require individuals to obtain a permit to possess or carry a pistol and would limit the sale of pistols to those with valid permits. It would also prohibit possession of pistols by anyone under 21, drug users, alcoholics, or mental incompetents, as well as drug addicts, felons, and other criminals. Under the proposed law, an additional ten years imprisonment would be added to the usual penalty if a firearm was used in a robbery or an attempted robbery. The bill would require all rifles or shotguns to be unloaded and encased while being carried and would require stricter licensing of those who manufacture, sell, or repair firearms. Additionally, records and reports would need to be made concerning the sale and repairs of firearms.[8]

When the Gun Control Act of 1968 was passed by Congress, Johnson signed the bill, saying that the bill would stop murder by mail order. It barred the interstate sale of all guns and the bullets that load them. It stopped the sale of lethal weapons to young people. It also limited cheap foreign "$10 specials" being imported into our country. However, the Congress did not include everything Johnson wanted. The bill did not include a national registration of all guns and the licensing of those who carry guns.[9]

CONGRESS

1963–64: 88TH CONGRESS

During the Johnson administration, Congress held hearings and passed new legislation concerning firearms. In 1964, the Congress debated but did not pass legislation that would curtail the shipment of mail-order firearms in interstate commerce (S. 1975 and S. 2345). The first of those bills, S. 1975, prohibited firearm manufacturers, dealers, and carriers from mailing or delivering a firearm in interstate commerce to anybody who was under 18 years old or to any individual who had been convicted of a crime that was punishable by a sentence of over a year. It also required that anyone who ordered a firearm (other than licensed dealers) in interstate commerce to provide the dealer or manufacturer with a sworn affidavit that he or she was over age 18. The second bill, S. 2345, required that a written certificate be sent by the firearm purchaser to the manufacturer or dealer before the sale of the weapon. The certificate was required to state the purpose for which the weapon was being purchased and that the purchaser criminal record was mentally stable and competent.

1965–66: 89TH CONGRESS

In the 1965–66 congressional session, President Johnson asked Congress to pass amendments to the 1938 Federal Firearms Act that were intended to stop the mail-order deliveries of firearms to individuals, but Congress did not act on the bill (S. 1592).[10]

1967–68: 90TH CONGRESS

During the 1967–68 session, the Congress passed two laws dealing with gun control, including Title Four of the Omnibus Crime and Safe Streets Act and the Gun Control Act of 1968. Together they banned the importation of handguns, banned specified interstate transportation involving guns, refined licensing provisions for businesses and collectors, and set penalties for crimes committed with a gun. However, the laws did not specifically ban the importation of gun parts—a loophole a number of foreign manufacturers discovered almost immediately.[11]

PRESIDENT NIXON

As president, Richard Nixon did not put the issue of firearms or guns high on his agenda. In 1972, he called for controlling the small, cheap guns known as "Saturday Night Specials." He explained that this was a legitimate federal concern because these guns and others could be imported easily from other countries.[12]

CONGRESS

1969–70: 91ST CONGRESS

Despite the lack of presidential support for gun control laws, Congress continued to act on the issue. In 1969, Congress approved an amendment to the Interest Equalization Bill (H.R. 12829/PL 91-128), which repealed provisions of the Gun Control Act of 1968 that required merchants to keep records of their sales of shotgun and rifle ammunition.

The Senate passed and sent to the House S. 849, which authorized additional prison terms for people who used or even carried a gun in committing a federal crime. It amended the penalties set forth in the 1968 Gun Control Act and imposed an additional sentence of 1 to 10 years for an initial conviction and a sentence of 2 to 25 years for subsequent convictions. The House did not act on the measure.[13]

In 1970, the House approved (H.R. 14233) to exempt .22-caliber rimfire ammunition from the record-keeping requirements of the 1968 Gun Control Act (PL 90-618).[14] The Senate did not act on the bill.

1971–72: 92ND CONGRESS

In the 1971–72 session, more than 80 bills were introduced that would repeal the registration requirements under the 1968 Gun Control Act for .22-caliber rimfire ammunition. One of the bills (S. 2057) was a proposal to outlaw the sale of cheap handguns, Saturday Night Specials. The bill also would have weakened the 1968 Gun Control Act by deleting record-keeping requirements for .22-caliber rimfire ammunition and making it easier to transfer long guns interstate. The Senate passed the bill, but the House Judiciary Committee did not pass it.[15]

PRESIDENT FORD

Gerald Ford had many ideas when it came to firearms. He was opposed to federal registration of guns by gun owners, because he did not want to "penalize" legitimate owners.[16] He suggested the Congress pass legislation to provide for more severe and mandatory penalties for people who use a gun in the commission of a crime.[17]

Like Nixon, Ford proposed further restrictions on Saturday Night Specials, as they are involved in a large number of street crimes and did not have a legitimate sporting purpose.[18] In fact, Ford said that these guns "are such a threat to domestic tranquility that we should eliminate their manufacture and sale entirely."[19]

In general, he wanted new federal laws that would limit gun owners and sellers, so that only responsible, bona fide gun dealers would be permitted to obtain federal licenses to sell firearms. This meant that those who violated state laws would not be allowed to sell firearms. According to Ford, there should be more controls over the sale of handguns, including a ban on multiple sales. There should also be a waiting period between the purchase and receipt of a handgun to enable dealers to verify that handguns are not sold to people who should not have them.[20] To ensure that the laws were enforced, Ford ordered the Bureau of Alcohol, Tobacco, Firearms and Explosives (BATF) to hire five hundred additional investigators and to double its investigative efforts in large cities.[21]

CONGRESS

1975–76: 94TH CONGRESS

The Congress during the Ford administration considered one gun bill (H.R. 11193), reported by the House Judiciary Subcommittee on Crime. The bill banned the manufacture, importation, and sale of handguns that did not meet certain requirements. It also required mandatory prison sentences for people who committed crimes with a handgun, waiting periods for handgun purchases, and higher license fees for dealers and manufacturers. The full Judiciary Committee voted on the bill, but it was never brought to the House floor.[22]

PRESIDENT CARTER

1977–78: 95TH CONGRESS

Even though Jimmy Carter did not talk about guns in his speeches, the Congress acted on it. In 1978, the Senate passed a revision of the Federal Criminal Code, part of which had to do with firearms. It provided for mandatory sentences of at least two years for those who commit violent crimes with a firearm.[23]

PRESIDENT REAGAN

Ronald Reagan wanted to remove restrictions on gun owners and sellers that, as he saw it, only served to burden the law abiding. So he willingly signed two amendments to the Gun Control Act of 1968, which removed the record-keeping requirements on sales of .22 rimfire ammunition.[24]

CONGRESS

1981–82: 97TH CONGRESS

During 1981, because of the attempt on Reagan's life, gun control legislation was a major topic in Congress. There were many bills introduced during the session. One of those, S. 904, was a proposal to make it a federal offense to assault or kill presidential or vice-presidential staff members who were on the job. The second, S. 908, was a proposal to require the death penalty for those convicted of a felony committed with a firearm. The last proposal was H.R. 3200/S. 974, which would ban the manufacture, importation, assembly, or sale of Saturday Night Specials. Under this proposal, a waiting period of 21 days would be required for anyone who wanted to purchase a gun. This would allow the FBI and local police to check on the background of the buyer. A person would be prohibited from purchasing more than two guns a year without prior approval from the attorney general, and pawnbrokers would be prohibited from selling handguns. Finally, if this proposal passed, the enforcement of gun control laws would be transferred from the Treasury Department to the Justice Department.

In 1982, a comprehensive anticrime package was passed by Congress. H.R. 3963 authorized federal prosecutions of "career criminals" who repeatedly committed state crimes with a firearm. Reagan vetoed the bill.[25]

In the second year of the session, Congress passed S. 907 (PL 97-285) that made it a federal offense to kill, kidnap, or assault specified US government officials, including Supreme Court justices, senior presidential and vice-presidential aides, cabinet officers and nominees, second-ranking officials in each department, and the director of the CIA. The penalties for committing these offenses ranged from one year in prison, a $5,000 fine, or both for assaults to life imprisonment for murder, manslaughter, kidnapping, and an attempt or conspiracy to harm the listed individuals.[26]

In 1982, the Senate Judiciary Committee approved S. 1030, which made it easier to buy and sell firearms. The proposal revised the 1968 Gun Control Act by lifting most prohibitions on gun sales across state lines. It also permitted sales through the mail between individuals who had previously met face to face, loosened licensing requirements, and required proof of intent to establish any violation of the act, but the bill went no further.[27]

1983–84: 98TH CONGRESS

In 1983, Congress considered S. 1762, which provided for mandatory minimum sentences for using a firearm in the commission of federal crimes. The bill was only passed by Senate.[28]

The following year, Congress attached some gun provisions to the fiscal 1985 continuing appropriations resolution (H.J. Res. 648/PL 98-473). It revised and strengthened existing mandatory minimum sentences for the use of a firearm in the commission of a federal crime. It set a minimum sentence of five years that would be added to the sentence imposed for the underlying crime. The bill also prohibited carrying or using a handgun loaded with armor-piercing ammunition in a violent crime and set a mandatory five-year prison term as the minimum penalty.[29]

1985–86: 99TH CONGRESS

In this session, the Congress passed H.R. 3132/S. 104 (PL 99-408) that barred the manufacture, importation, and sale of armor-piercing bullets that could penetrate protective vests worn by police officers, otherwise known as "cop-killer bullets."[30] Both bills required manufacturers and importers to mark ammunition and label packages of armor-piercing bullets. The bullets could be produced only for use by federal and state government agencies, for export, or for testing or experimentation authorized by the secretary of the treasury. Bullets made for specified sporting purposes and industrial use were exempted from the bill's restrictions. Under the law, the penalty for unlawful manufacture or importation of the bullets would be up to five years in prison and a fine of up to $250,000. Ammunition dealers who willfully violated the law could have their licenses revoked. The bill also provided a prison sentence of five to ten years for anyone convicted of a crime of violence with a firearm who had in his or her possession armor-piercing ammunition "capable of being fired" from the gun used in the crime.[31]

In addition, the Congress passed and President Reagan signed S. 49 (PL 99-308) to relax many provisions of the 1968 Gun Control Act. Most importantly, the bill would allow over-the-counter interstate sales of rifles, shotguns and handguns, as long as the sale was legal in the state of the buyer and seller. The bill allowed gun owners to transport their weapons interstate, as long as the gun was not loaded and not readily accessible. Additionally, it allowed licensed gun dealers to conduct business at gun shows as long as they were maintaining records, but federal agents could inspect those records without a warrant under certain circumstances. The bill limited the number of people who were required to get licenses to sell firearms as gun collectors were no longer required to obtain a dealer's license to sell weapons from their private collections. Those who sold ammunition would be exempt from record-keeping requirements.

The bill also included a mandatory five-year sentence if an offender used a firearm during a federal crime of violence or a drug felony or for carrying a handgun loaded with armor-piercing bullets. If someone used a machine gun or a gun equipped with a silencer during a federal crime of violence, the penalties for that were increased to 10 years for a first offense and 20 for a subsequent offense. It made it illegal for anyone, not just a licensed gun dealer, to sell a firearm to certain groups of people who were prohibited from owning one, such as convicted felons, drug addicts, or anyone who had been committed to a mental institution. The penalty for doing so was set as a fine of up to $5,000 and imprisonment for up to five years.

The bill also banned the importation of barrels, frames, and receivers for Saturday Night Specials, as well as small handguns that were identified as not suitable for sporting purposes. This ban on gun parts was not included in the original 1968 law. The bill was not considered in the House.[32] Law enforcement groups vigorously opposed S. 49, because they believed the bill's provisions would make it more difficult for police to trace guns that were used in crimes. To appease these groups the Congress passed a separate measure revising three sections of S. 49 (S. 2414/PL 99-360).

1987–88: 100TH CONGRESS

In this session, legislators cleared H.R. 4445 (PL 100-649) that banned the manufacture, importation, sale, or delivery of undetectable firearms that are primarily made of plastic. The proposed ban would last for ten years, at which point Congress would be required to reconsider the bill. The bill also banned guns that failed to trigger detection devices in the same manner as a test gun made of 3.7 ounces of stainless steel. Any gun had to be detectable by cabinet X ray systems used in airports around the country. Violators could be fined, imprisoned up to five years, or both.[33]

PRESIDENT BUSH

George H. W. Bush opposed proposals to ban every pistol and rifle, and he opposed banning semiautomatic hunting rifles that could be used by legitimate sportsmen. But after a gunman used an AK-47 to kill 5 schoolchildren and wound 30 others in a shooting at a schoolyard in Stockton, California,[34] he wanted to ban fully automated AK-47s.[35] He ordered the Treasury Department to review the suitability of these weapons for sporting purposes and asked for a temporary suspension of imports of certain semiautomatic weapons. He authorized the secretary of the treasury to expand a temporary suspension on imports to include an additional 24 types of weapons.[36] In the end, the Bush administration permanently barred the imports of more than 40 types of foreign-made semiautomatic assault weapons.[37]

Bush wanted to "go after" criminals who used guns.[38] He asked Congress for legislation that would double the mandatory minimum penalties for those who used semiautomatic weapons in crimes involving violence or drugs. He proposed that anyone who carried or used a semiautomatic weapon to commit a crime would be sentenced to an automatic ten extra years in federal prison, with no chance for probation or parole, "no matter which judge they get."[39]

As another way to limit gun use, Bush proposed the same gun provisions as part of the Comprehensive Crime Control Act of 1989. These included the following:

1. Doubling the mandatory penalty from five to ten years for the use of a semiautomatic firearm during the commission of a violent crime or drug felony
2. Allowing for pretrial preventive detention of defendants accused of certain serious federal firearms and explosive offenses
3. Authorizing criminal penalties and mandatory minimum sentences for those defendants accused of the theft of a firearm
4. Enhancing penalties for smuggling firearms in the United States while engaged in drug trafficking.[40]

In addition, Bush proposed legislation that would ban selling firearms to people convicted of any serious drug offense. These people would also be prohibited from possessing firearms. He also wanted to prohibit the "importation, manufacture, transfer, or sale of gun magazines of over fifteen rounds for use by private citizens."[41]

CONGRESS

1989–90: 101ST CONGRESS

Congress proposed S. 747 that would prohibit future sales of five types of foreign and four types of domestic semiautomatic weapons. It required that those people who already owned the weapons would obtain proof of ownership from a licensed dealer and keep a record if they sold that weapon to anyone else.[42] The bill did not pass, but some of the same provisions were considered in the Senate in S. 1970, a comprehensive anticrime bill. The House Judiciary Committee considered similar provisions in H.R. 4225. The bill would outlaw certain semiautomatic weapons that were not deemed to meet the "sporting purpose" test, but it was never brought to the floor of the House.[43] By the end of the session, Congress passed a major omnibus crime bill (S. 3266/PL 101-647) that included provisions to ban some assault style weapons.[44]

Two other proposals were made in Congress, S. 1236 and H.R. 467, more commonly known as the Brady Handgun Violence Protection Act, or the Brady Bill, named after former White House press secretary James Brady who was wounded in the assassination attempt on President Reagan. The proposed bill called for a seven-day waiting period to enable gun dealers to obtain identification from someone wanting to purchase a handgun and send it to law enforcement authorities, who would then check to see if the buyer was a convicted felon who should be barred from buying that gun.[45] The bill was controversial and did not pass at this time.

1991–92: 102ND CONGRESS

This session, the House approved H.R. 3371/S. 1241 to impose a five-day waiting period for the purchase of a handgun. This time, it was part of a larger bill. The bill was blocked in the Senate when Bush insisted the bill did not go far enough to restrict appeals by convicted criminals and relax evidentiary rules.[46] The Brady Bill was also proposed separately as H.R. 7, but it went nowhere.[47]

Another proposal, H.R. 5633, would have required gun dealers to report the names of people who bought more than one firearm within a 30-day period. The bill passed the House Judiciary Subcommittee on Crime and Criminal Justice, but it stalled because of opposition from the Bush administration.[48]

PRESIDENT CLINTON

William Clinton supported a person's right to own a weapon. This was made clear when he said, "I believe strongly in the right of Americans to own guns."[49] Further, he believed that people who hunt must always be permitted to own guns and protect their homes. Clinton called on those same hunters and sportsmen who lawfully own guns to join in his campaign to reduce gun violence.[50] However, he also said there were certain people should not own guns. "If you're convicted of a felony, you shouldn't have one. If you're a fugitive from the law, you shouldn't have a gun. If you're stalking or harassing women or children, you shouldn't have a gun. And if you commit an act of violence against your spouse or your child, you shouldn't have a gun."[51] During his eight years in office, Clinton had many ideas for stopping gun violence. First, he wanted to pass a law that limited the number of handgun sales to an individual to no more than one a month. Second, he also wanted to pass the Brady Bill, which would require a waiting period before people could buy a handgun to check their criminal history. Once the Brady Bill was passed by Congress, he promised to veto any attempt to repeal it.[52] Third, Clinton wanted to ensure that only legitimate gun dealers were the ones selling guns. To do that, he wanted to review the rules governing gun dealers.[53] He saw the need to regulate gun dealers because some dealers at times put weapons into circulation in ways in which they would end up in the hands of criminals.

Another one of Clinton's ideas to reduce gun violence was to limit semiautomatic assault weapons that had no purpose other than to kill. He promised to enforce the statutory restrictions on the importation of firearms that did not meet the sporting-purposes test.[54] The Treasury Department was prepared to take the necessary action to suspend the importation of foreign-made assault pistols, which had become the weapons of choice for many gangs and drug dealers.[55] Clinton threatened to veto any attempt to repeal the assault weapons ban.[56]

Clinton called on states to review their ownership laws that made it illegal for minors to have guns unless they were in the presence of their parents, either hunting or on a target range. He thought it was imperative to get guns out of the hands of the children. One way to do that was to close the gun show loophole.[57]

CONGRESS

1993–94: 103RD CONGRESS

During the 1993–94 congressional session, members passed legislation that eased gun permit requirements for armored car guards. H.R. 1189 (PL 103-55) was enacted after complaints were made by armored car guards, who said that obtaining gun permits for every state they passed through during delivery or pickups was a bureaucratic hassle that caused delays and increased costs. Under the law, gun permits from the state in which armored car guards were primarily employed were declared valid for other states as well.[58]

Another bill, the Youth Handgun Ban (H.R. 3098), prohibited the sale of handguns or ammunition to minors. Specifically, it made it a federal crime to sell or transfer a handgun to a person under the age of 18 or for the minor to possess the gun. There were some exceptions in the bill, such as allowing minors to use guns under limited circumstances with proper parental supervision. The bill did not go to the president for his signature.

After many years of debate, the Brady Bill finally passed Congress and was signed by Clinton. H.R. 1025 (PL 103-159) required a five-business-day waiting period before purchasing a handgun. This would allow for a cooling-off period and time to check the buyer's background. The bill also raised licensing fees for gun dealers and required that police be notified of any multiple gun purchases. This was the first major gun control legislation to pass through Congress since 1968.[59]

A related bill was also proposed into Congress and was given the name Brady Bill II. This bill, S. 1882, was another attempt to keep handguns away from criminals—this time by establishing new requirements for gun purchasers and dealers. The bill would put a ban on certain firearms and impose licensing and registration requirements on others. Under the proposal, handgun purchasers would have to pass a background check and a firearms safety course. It would also tighten regulation and screening of gun dealers by requiring sellers of used guns to register the transfer with state police. Handgun purchases would be limited to one per person per month. The bill also banned some semiautomatic assault weapons and other weapons that were identified as having no apparent sporting purpose. The bill also required gun manufacturers to install safety devices on handguns to prevent small children from accidentally discharging them.[60] The bill did not have enough support to pass.

In a major crime bill passed by the Congress in this session (H.R. 3355; H.R. 4092/S. 1607; PL 103-322), there were many new restrictions placed on weapons. One provision banned the manufacture, sale, or possession of 19 assault weapons, as well as copycat models and semiautomatic guns with two or more characteristics associated with assault weapons for a ten-year period. The bill specifically exempted more than 670 semiautomatic weapons that were used for sporting purposes and allowed gun owners to keep guns they owned legally before the law was passed. The measure also banned high-capacity ammunition-feeding devices that held more than ten rounds.[61] Anyone violating these provisions could face a fine of $5,000 and five years in prison, or both.

Limits were also place on gun ownership by youth. As part of the bill, the sale or transfer of handguns or ammunition to a juvenile without parental consent would be banned. Juveniles were also prohibited from possessing a handgun or ammunition. Violators were subject to a maximum of one year in jail. Additionally, any adult who sold or transferred a handgun or ammunition to a minor knowing that the minor planned to use it in a violent crime could be imprisoned for up to ten years.

Further, the bill addressed gun violence in domestic situations. The bill prohibited the possession of a firearm by anyone under a restraining order. This was an attempt to prevent that person from harassing, stalking, or interfering with a spouse, partner, or a child. Anyone who knowingly sold, transferred, or obtained a gun in violation of this law could face up to ten years in prison.

The new law increased the federal requirements for obtaining a license to be a firearms dealer. Those people who were interested in doing so were now required to submit their photographs and fingerprints and certify that they would comply with all relevant state and local laws. Firearms dealers were required to report the theft or loss of a gun within two days and to respond to federal tracing requests within 24 hours.

Finally, the new law increased penalties for many federal gun crimes, including using a semiautomatic weapon in a federal violent crime or drug trafficking crime, interstate gun trafficking, or making a false statement when purchasing a gun. The law also made it a penalty to smuggle guns into the country for use in a violent crime or for drug trafficking.

1995–96: 104TH CONGRESS

In this session, Republicans in both the House and Senate pledged to repeal the 1994 assault weapons ban that was included in the 1994 crime bill.[62] Besides repealing the ban, the bill (H.R. 125) proposed to increase minimum mandatory sentences for people convicted of using a firearm during the commission of a violent or drug-related federal crime. Bill supporters said stiffer prison penalties would be a more effective deterrent than a gun ban. The National Rifle Association (NRA) liked the idea of repealing the ban and lobbied actively for it.[63] The House voted to repeal the existing ban, but President Clinton vowed to veto the legislation if it reached his desk. It never reached his desk.

Again, the House passed a bill (H.R. 3431) to allow guards for armored car companies to carry weapons across state lines while on duty, but the Senate did not act on it. Under the bill, a weapons permit issued by a guard's primary state of employment would be valid in other states. The bill would address problems with the 1993 Armored Car Industry Reciprocity Act. Some states had already complied with the law's requirements for reciprocity, which included conducting annual criminal background checks and firearms training. But this did not pass in this session.

1997–98: 105TH CONGRESS

The House Judiciary Committee approved a bill (H.R. 424) that called for tougher sentences for crimes committed with firearms, but the bill went no further. The main purpose of the legislation was to expand a law passed in 1988 that created mandatory penalties for using a gun while committing a crime. The bill was a response to a 1995 Supreme Court decision in *Bailey v. United States* (516 US 137), in which the Court ruled that overt use, not mere possession, of a weapon was necessary for the mandatory sentencing requirement to take effect. It did not have enough support to pass.

Once again, the House passed a bill (H.R. 624) that was intended to make it easier for armored car guards to carry their guns across state lines. This was yet another attempt to amend the 1993 Armored Car Industry Reciprocity Act that was intended to relieve guards of having to obtain a separate permit from each state they entered. It required states to recognize weapons permits issued by another state to armored car guards if the issuing state required annual criminal background checks and firearms training. However, only five states met the law's eligibility requirements for reciprocity. In addition, states would only have to conduct a criminal background check when an individual first applied for a license. This time, it became law (PL 105-287).[64]

H.R. 424/H.R. 2340 was a bill proposed in the House to provide for increased mandatory minimum sentences for criminal offenders who used a gun in a crime of violence or a drug-trafficking crime. The bill would require an additional sentence of 10 years for possessing a firearm, 15 years for brandishing a firearm, and 20 years for discharging a firearm during a crime. For second offenses, the mandatory minimums would range from 20 to 30 years. The bill did not pass.

Another gun-related bill that did not pass during this session was H.R. 788, the Firearms Safety and Violence Prevention Act (H.R. 788). The proposal, among other things, would regulate firearms products (such as ammunition) and prohibit the importation and exportation of uncertified firearms products. The attorney general would be directed to maintain a Firearms Violence Information Clearinghouse for information on the cause and prevention of death and injury associated with firearms.

Another bill that did not pass was H.R. 2721, the Second Amendment Protection Act of 1997. It would repeal the Brady Handgun Violence Prevention Act and restore any provisions the law amended. This new proposal would make it seem as if the Brady Bill had never been enacted.

1999–2000: 196TH CONGRESS

Some members of the Congress believed that the problem of juveniles who used guns as part of their crimes would be addressed by creating five new US District Court judgeships and expanding the cities in which the BATF traced guns used by youth in crimes. The FBI would be authorized to help local police investigate deaths of those younger than 13. The effects of media violence on children would be examined in a federal study, and the entertainment industry would be encouraged to lessen the production of violent acts. Schools and libraries that failed to place an obscenity filtering or blocking device on computer terminals with Internet access would be ineligible to receive federal aid to pay for high-speed access to the Internet.

In 2000, the House debated two bills about juveniles and guns. H.R. 1501 and H.R. 4051 were juvenile justice bills, but Democrats added amendments to tighten gun control after Dylan Klebold and Eric Harris killed 13 schoolmates and a teacher at Columbine High School in Colorado. H.R. 4051 was designed to encourage states to toughen their enforcement of laws for crimes committed with guns. The bill included provisions to increase penalties for teenage criminals who use guns and provide state grants for crime prevention. Life sentences and the death penalty would be allowed for repeat convictions of sex offenses involving children. The bill included Project Exile, which would authorize $100 million in grants to states with tough gun sentencing laws, including a five-year mandatory minimum sentence for using a gun while committing a violent or serious drug-trafficking crime. The bill also authorized $1.5 billion for block grants to state and local governments to enact projects to strengthen their juvenile justice systems. This could include things like graduated sentences, jail construction, youth witness assistance, enhanced records systems for young violent offenders, mental health and drug treatment, or activities to encourage character education and development. The bill was considered in the House but not considered in the Senate and did not pass.[65]

Two bills, H.R. 1342 and S. 735, were designed to prevent criminal activity and accidents involving guns. Gun dealers would be penalized for selling guns to minors or if their guns were used by a minor to commit a crime. The bill would also require a number of safety features on guns, including trigger locks.[66] Neither bill had enough support to become law.

One last bill considered this session was S. 254, which was designed to prevent and punish those juveniles who committed crimes. The proposal went untouched for 18 months, during which time the Columbine shooting occurred, so there was renewed interest in the bill. The bill included many gun control proposals. It provided for $2.7 billion for block grants to states to help them strengthen their juvenile justice systems. The gun-tracing program would be expanded to 250 cities and counties by fiscal year 2004, and the entertainment industry was encouraged to set guidelines to limit violence and other harmful influences on children. The bill would require federal studies of the impact of violent music and video games on children and of practices of marketing violent and sexually explicit materials to minors and would ban unlicensed dealers from using the Internet to advertise guns or explosives for sale to juveniles or others not eligible to own guns or explosives. Internet service providers would be required to offer their customers access to filtering or screening software. Drug testing of students by school officials would be permitted with parental or legal guardian consent. Those juveniles who had been previously tried as adults or those who were 14 years or older when they committed a violent serious drug felony crime could be tried as adults. The trial deadline was 70 days. Officials would be required to keep juveniles away from adults in prison facilities. Juvenile proceedings would be open to the public. Those convicted of recruiting for a criminal street gang would be subject to a term of one to ten years in prison and a minimum of four years if the recruit is a minor. However, the proposal did not pass.

PRESIDENT BUSH

George W. Bush did not talk about firearms to a great extent but acknowledged that gun violence was still a serious problem in the country and said there was a need for a national strategy to ensure that every community was attacking gun violence. He announced such an initiative in 2001, called Project Safe Neighborhoods. The program was intended to establish a network of law enforcement and community initiatives aimed at reducing crimes committed with guns.[67]

In 1989, Bush directed the attorney general to advise America's prosecutors to end plea bargaining for violent federal firearms offenses. He wanted those who use guns to do hard time in prison.[68]

In 2007, a 23-year-old gunman at Virginia Polytechnic Institute had some calling for new gun legislation. One representative, Carolyn McCarthy, introduced legislation that would restrict the ability of people with a history of mental illness to purchase firearms.[69]

CONGRESS

2001–2: 107TH CONGRESS

The House and Senate considered bills (H.R. 4635/S. 2554/H.R. 5005) titled the Arming Pilots Against Terrorism Act. The bill was a proposal to permit pilots to have guns. Under the proposed program, pilots could volunteer to be deputized as federal law enforcement officers and have the power to defend the flight decks against an act of criminal violence or air piracy. The officers would receive training, supervision, and equipment. H.R. 5005 became law in 2002 (PL 107-296).

The Law Enforcement Officers Safety Act (S. 2480) was a proposal to exempt off-duty and retired law enforcement officials from bans on carrying concealed weapons. Retired police officers would be required to have 15 years of experience to carry concealed firearms and would also have to meet the same training and qualification standards required of active duty officers. They would not be able to carry the firearms in places where the state has prohibited them. The law did not pass.

Many other gun-related bills did not pass this session. One was H.R. 278, the Gun Buy Back Partnership Grant Act. This proposal would provide funds to state and local governments to enable them to conduct gun buyback programs. Another bill that failed was the No Guns for Violent Perpetrators Act (H.R. 891). This would prohibit the shipment, transportation, or possession of a firearm or ammunition by a person who committed a violent act as a juvenile that would be considered a violent felony if committed by an adult. The third proposal that did not pass was the Second Amendment Protection Act to in essence repeal the Brady Bill. This was H.R. 1762. Finally, H.R. 3679 was a proposal to prohibit the possession or transfer of Saturday Night Specials.

2003–4: 108TH CONGRESS

In this session, the House passed H.R. 1036, a bill to make it harder to file civil lawsuits against firearms manufacturers and gun dealers. Supporters said the legislation, called the Protection of Lawful Commerce in Arms Act, was needed to protect manufacturers from lawsuits intended to force them into bankruptcy.[70] In the Senate, the companion bills were S. 1805/S. 1806. All bills were defeated.[71]

H.R. 3193 would have repealed the municipal gun control laws of the District of Columbia. It would have lifted a ban on private ownership of handguns and their ammunition, allowed residents to legally own semiautomatic weapons, and allowed them to keep loaded, unlocked guns in their homes and businesses. This was passed in the House, but the Senate took no action.

In H.R. 3348, the Plastic Gun Law would be reauthorized for ten years. This means that guns made of plastic and other materials that cannot be detected in metal detectors would continue to be banned. That meant that it would be illegal to manufacture, import, possess, or transfer a firearm that is not detectable. The bill had the backing of the NRA and became law (PL 108-174).

Again this session, the Second Amendment Protection Act (H.R. 153) was proposed but failed. It was a proposal to repeal the Brady Bill. The House also considered, but did not pass, the Ballistic Imaging Evaluation and Study Act, to allow the attorney general, the National Research Council, and the National Academy of Sciences to study ballistic imaging technology. The Nationwide Gun Buyback Act was proposed but also failed. This was a proposal to make grants available to local government to enable them to implement gun buyback programs. Another bill that did not have the support to pass was H.R. 2946, the Detectives Nemorin and Andrews Anti–Gun Trafficking Act. The bill would prohibit the sale or transfer of two or more guns, at least two of which were handguns, semiautomatic assault weapons, short-barreled shotguns, short-barreled rifles, or machine guns if one of the firearms was stolen or had the manufacturer's serial number removed. The sale of the firearms would also be prohibited if the purchaser was under 18, in a school zone, or resided in another state.

2005–6: 109TH CONGRESS

The Congress passed S. 397 (PL 109-92), which limited the legal liability of firearms makers and dealers. One part of the bill specifically prohibited civil liability actions from being brought in any state or federal court against firearm and ammunition manufacturers, distributors, dealers, or importers. Under the legislation, trade groups were also protected from civil liability, and all pending legal action against gun makers was dismissed. However, anyone who sold or transferred a firearm knowing it was intended to be used for a crime of violence or drug trafficking could be the subject of a lawsuit.[72]

The law required gun importers, manufacturers, and dealers to provide a secure storage or safety device for each handgun sold, delivered, or transferred to any person. Anyone who violated this provision could have their licenses revoked or suspended for up to six months and could also be subject to a $2,500 fine. In situations where the firearm was sold to US agencies, law enforcement officials, and rail police officers, the manufactures would be exempt from the requirement.[73]

One last part of the bill related to armor-piercing bullets. The new law prohibited the manufacture or sale of armor-piercing ammunition. There was an exception if the ammunition was to be used by the federal or state government for export only or had been approved by the Justice Department for testing and experimental uses. The criminal penalties were increased for those individuals who used or carried armor-piercing ammunition in a violent or drug-trafficking crime. Besides the sentence for the crime, there would be a minimum prison sentence of 15 years. If the crime resulted in death, the sentence would be execution or life imprisonment.[74]

In H.R. 5005, the Firearms Corrections and Improvements Act, the BATF would be prohibited from releasing data used to trace guns back to previous owners, sellers, and dealers as a part of lawsuits, and the act would make it harder for lawyers of cities that sue gun dealers to get the kind of information that could prove their links between criminals. The proposal did not pass the subcommittee.

The NICS Improvement Act (H.R. 1415), proposed new federal funding to help states enter their felony criminal convictions, mental disability, and domestic violence records into the FBI's National Instant Criminal Background Check System. The bill died in the full committee.

If passed, H.R. 1384 would allow the interstate sale of handguns, authorize dealers to sell guns at out-of-state gun shows, and permit dealers to transfer firearms in person rather than requiring shipment. The bill, titled the Firearm Commerce Modernization Act, did not pass.

Another bill to modernize part of the system was the Bureau of Alcohol, Tobacco, Firearms, and Explosives Modernization and Reform Act (H.R. 5092). This proposal would alter the federal regulations governing the suspension and revocation of gun sellers' licenses. It would also require that any civil penalties for violations of firearms laws be based on the nature of the violation and the size of the business involved. The attorney general, when the government intended to deny a license to an applicant, would notify applicants in writing. If denied a license, an applicant would have a right to appeal the denial in a hearing. This did not pass.

H.R. 800/S. 397, the Protection of Lawful Commerce in Arms Act, would protect manufacturers, distributors, dealers, and importers of guns or ammunition from liability for harm suffered because of misuse of the weapons. Under the bill, a civil liability suit could not be brought against a gun manufacturer or seller for damages or harm resulting from a crime. This was signed into law by the president (PL 109-92).

2007–8: 110TH CONGRESS

The Second Amendment Enforcement Act (H.R. 6842) included new gun regulations for the District of Columbia. It would allow the District to rewrite its gun control regulations and enact new regulations that complied with a Supreme Court decision, *District of Columbia v. Heller* (554 US 570 [2008]). In this case, the justices decided in a 5-4 decision to overturn the city's ban on possession of handguns, the strongest in the nation. They also overturned a provision that all handguns stored in the home must be either locked up or kept disassembled. The Court declared that the Second Amendment of the Constitution protects an individual's right to bear arms. Similar bills (H.R. 6691 and H.R. 1399) would also restrict the District's ability to regulate firearms ownership. They would repeal the semiautomatic weapons ban, prohibit registration requirements for most guns, and eliminate criminal penalties associated with possessing an unregistered firearm or having a gun in the home. None of the bills passed into law.

The NICS Improvement Act was proposed again during this session in the House. H.R. 297 would provide federal funding to states that submit the information on crimes by people who used a handgun, have mental illness, or committed an act of domestic violence into the FBI's National Instant Criminal Background Check System. This bill passed into law (PL 110-180).

In the Citizen's Self-Defense Act, a person who has not been prohibited from purchasing a firearm will have the right to do so for their own defense, or the defense of their family, against a perceived threat of imminent injury. If any person believed his or her gun rights had been previously violated, the individual could bring an action in the federal courts against the United States for relief. The proposal did not become law.

The Gun Show Loophole Act (H.R. 96) was also not passed in the House. This was a proposal to provide for regulation of firearm sales at gun shows or other events. Additionally, a person could not host a firearms event without first notifying the attorney general. There would be specific responsibilities of the operators, including performing background checks on purchasers, special firearms event license requirements, and penalties if these new rules were violated. The bill did not become law.

PRESIDENT OBAMA

In 2007, when Barack Obama was considering a run for the presidency, he gave a speech in which he challenged the government to do more to stop gun violence.[75] During the 2008 presidential campaign, many alleged that Obama was opposed to gun rights and ownership. Although he stated that individuals had the right to bear arms, he also stated that state and local governments should have the right to constrain that right under certain circumstances.[76] He called for a common sense regulation on guns.

President Obama has stayed away from the subject of firearms. During the first two years of his administration, he did not seek gun legislation. In August of 2010, he signed a law that gave a tax break to manufacturers of firearms and ammunition.[77] He also sought to reinstate the assault weapons ban that expired in 2004.[78]

2009–10: 111TH CONGRESS

S. 160 was a voting rights bill for the District of Columbia, but it also included provisions concerning gun rights. The amendment would bar District officials from prohibiting firearms possession and repeal the city's fun registration laws. Further, officials would be prohibited from repealing the city's policy that firearms in homes had to be stored disassembled or secured with a trigger lock or other locking device. It was similar to legislation the House passed in 2008. The bill did not become law.

There were many gun-related amendments added to other, unrelated bills in this session. H.R. 627 (PL 111-24) was a bill regulating credit cards, but Section 512 was added to the bill to allow visitors to national parks to bring concealed and loaded guns. Under the new law, the secretary of the interior would be prohibited from enforcing any rule that prohibits a visitor from possessing a firearm in the national park if that person is not otherwise prohibited from carrying a weapon.

S. 1390 was a defense authorization bill, but it included an amendment to allow licensed gun owners to carry concealed firearms across state lines if they had valid permits or were legally entitled to do so by their home state. The amendment was rejected in the Senate and did not become law. H.R. 3288, a bill authorizing the Fiscal 2010 Transportation-Housing and Urban Development Appropriations, included an amendment that would allow Amtrak passengers to carry guns in their checked bags. This became law (PL 111-117).

The Citizens' Self-Defense Act was again proposed in the House (H.R. 17) to prohibit a person from obtaining firearms for their safety and the safety of their families. As during the previous Congressional session, this did not become law.

A second proposal in the House that was defeated was H.R. 197, the National Right-to-Carry Reciprocity Act. Under this law, the federal criminal code would be amended to set a national standard for carrying a concealed firearm by nonresidents. That meant that a person who had a permit to carry a concealed weapon in one state could do so in another state. A similar bill was S. 371, the Respecting States Rights and Concealed Carry Reciprocity Act. This also did not pass.

H.R. 623 would allow for greater judicial discretion in sentencing for certain firearms offenses. If passed, this proposal would amend the federal criminal code to allow for exceptions to mandatory minimum prison terms for using a firearm during a violent criminal offense. This proposal was not sent to the president.

CONCLUSION

Gun control is a very controversial issue in the United States, with one side fighting for the right to bear arms and the other advocating for limits on gun ownership. Of course, the concern about guns relates to the amount of gun violence, injuries, and death caused by guns each year. Over the past 50 years, presidents and Congress have debated many different proposals concerning gun ownership and violence, making it a valid issue for federal involvement.

ORGANIZED CRIME

FOR MANY YEARS, ORGANIZED CRIME WAS ALLOWED to develop and thrive under the radar of federal and local law enforcement. However, during the 1960s, the federal government began to recognize the violence caused by organized crime structures and passed more laws giving more powers to law enforcement to attack criminal organizations. Their actions, as well as presidential actions, are described in Chapter 13 of Part VI. One common activity of organized crime is pornography. Congress has passed many laws to halt the traffic in pornography, which is the topic of Chapter 14. The final chapter of Part VI is on wiretaps, which were used by law enforcement to gather strong evidence against crime groups and prosecute them for their crimes.

CHAPTER 13

UNDERWORLD CRIME

ORGANIZED CRIME HAS HELD THE ATTENTION OF presidents and Congress for many years. The issue came to light in the early 1950s after a major meeting of crime bosses in Appalachian, New York, and the Kefauver hearings in Congress where the American public saw and heard testimony from the men involved in a violent underground crime syndicate. After that, our knowledge of organized crime grew, and Congress passed legislation that allowed law enforcement to effectively attack organized crime groups and help put many of the crime family leaders in prison. Beyond organized crime itself, one topic that elected officials discuss is gambling, because it is often linked to organized crime. Today, even though organized crime has changed its focus to become a global problem linked to terrorism, the business of organized crime remains an issue for the federal government.

PRESIDENT TRUMAN

Harry Truman noted that there had been a substantial postwar increase in crime in the United States, particularly in crimes of violence. He also noted that the increase in crime had been accompanied by a resurgence of underworld forces, which thrive on vice and greed. He said that the criminal underworld, which was largely responsible for the general increase in crime, used its resources to corrupt the moral fiber of some citizens and some communities. This problem affected every community in the country, both rural and city, and every level of government. It was important, therefore, that communities work together in combating organized crime, including courts, law enforcement agencies, and the moral forces of our people.[1]

Truman told the public that the Senate Special Crime Investigating Committee was established to study and investigate whether organized crime either used the facilities of interstate commerce or otherwise operated in interstate commerce. He promised to cooperate with the committee to the fullest possible extent and asked all of his departments and agencies to cooperate with the committee as well.[2]

CONGRESS

1951–52: 82ND CONGRESS

In 1950, Senator Estes Kefauver (D-TN) introduced a resolution calling for a nationwide investigation into organized crime, and it was approved by the Senate Judiciary

Committee. The resolution called for an investigation by a subcommittee, which subsequently held extensive, televised hearings in many cities on the extent of an underworld criminal organization. The Special Committee to Investigate Organized Crime in Interstate Commerce held hearings through September 1, 1951. The committee heard testimony in many major cities in the United States from gangsters as well as lawmakers. Some of those testifying included the head of the FBI, J. Edgar Hoover, the Chief of the Bureau of Narcotics, Harry Anslinger, Undersecretary of the Treasury Edward Foley, and federal narcotics agents Charles Siragusa[3] and George Belk.[4]

Kefauver reported organized crime was costing the American public at least $17 billion a year.[5] The committee eventually submitted an interim report that said it had found evidence that a loose interstate crime network possibly existed.[6] The report said organized criminals not only had a strong grip on gambling and related illegal activities but also were moving quickly into legitimate business fields.[7] The committee as a whole made a number of recommendations, including a thorough overhaul of state and local laws to make them more effective in the fight against organized crime. They suggested that a stronger federal attack on the narcotics trade be made that included the cooperation of state and local officials. Further, committee members suggested that a special squad be created within the Federal Narcotics Bureau that would focus on training local police in the techniques of enforcing narcotics laws. To supplement that, the committee recommended doubling the staff of the Narcotics Bureau, more effective use of income tax reports to collecting evidence against criminals, and new federal legislation to permit wiretapping by federal agents.

After the hearings ended, Senator Kefauver proposed federal legislation to ban the interstate shipment of gambling devices, require a five-minute delay in transmission of race results, keep racing wire services out of hoodlums' hands, forbid sending bets through the mail, require more information on money handled by gangsters in income tax returns, prohibit conspiracy to violate state laws through interstate commerce and coordinate investigative and intelligence functions of the post office, Internal Revenue Bureau, and FBI.[8]

1953–54: 83RD CONGRESS

During this session, the Senate passed S. 16 to require witnesses to testify in return for a grant of immunity from prosecution, but there was no action by the House.

PRESIDENT EISENHOWER

Dwight Eisenhower recommended strengthening federal laws against organized crime[9] but provided no further suggestions about how to do that.

CONGRESS

1957–58: 85TH CONGRESS

The Senate Select Committee on Improper Activities in the Labor or Management Field began hearings in 1957 on allegations of labor racketeering and management malpractices. Headed by John McClellan (D-AR), the scope of the hearings was later expanded to cover union violence, corruption, and secondary boycotts.[10] The Select

Committee also held hearings on coin machine and gambling rackets in various areas, including Chicago and New York. The eight-member committee then investigated allegations of violence and corruption in the Teamsters Union.[11] One of the witnesses they questioned was Jimmy Hoffa, head of the Teamsters.

The committee issued its first interim report in March 1958. It found that Hoffa used union funds for his own benefit and for the benefit his friends and that he consistently supported the interests of his racketeer friends. The committee made recommendations for congressional action in the report, including the need for federal regulation and control of pension, health, and welfare funds and federal regulation and control of union funds. The committee recommended periodic elections of officers by use of a secret ballot in elections and other vital union decisions as a way to ensure democratic procedures in the union. The committee further recommended control of "management middlemen" and closing the jurisdictional gap in union-management disputes.[12]

1959–60: 86TH CONGRESS

The McClellan Committee ended its investigations in early 1960. The committee had held 270 days of hearings and heard 1,526 witnesses.[13] After the hearings were complete, the Justice Department reported that it had developed cases against 44 people, businesses, organizations, and unions whose activities had been investigated by the committee, including William Presser, president of the Ohio Conference of Teamsters and Cleveland Local 555 (of contempt), mobster Peter Licavoli (of contempt), Maurice Hutcheson, president of the United Brotherhood of Carpenters and Jointers of America (for contempt), and many others.[14] When the final report was released, the committee members reported local law enforcement was unable to deal with organized crime and proposed a National Crime Commission to keep surveillance on top leaders and disseminate information to law enforcement agencies.[15]

PRESIDENT KENNEDY

John Kennedy had the opportunity to sign three important bills he hoped would aid the government and the people of this country in the fight against organized crime.[16] The bills were S. 1653/PL 87-228, S. 1656/PL 87-216, and S. 1757/PL 87-218, all described in the following sections.

CONGRESS

1961–62: 87TH CONGRESS

The attorney general, Robert Kennedy, called for eight new laws to strengthen federal authority to clamp down on organized crime, some of which became law. One of the laws (S. 1653/PL 87-228) outlawed interstate travel or use of interstate facilities to establish, promote, deliver the proceeds of or commit a violent crime to further illegal gambling, liquor, narcotics, or prostitution businesses. It also outlawed interstate movement to commit extortion or bribery illegal under federal or state law.[17]

Another new law, S. 1656 (PL 87-216), made it a crime for anyone to knowingly use a wire communication facility to transmit any bets or wagers or information to aid the placing of bets or wagers or any communication that helps or entitles the recipient to collect money or credit as a result of the wagers or bets in interstate commerce.[18]

A Senate bill, S. 1657 (PL 87-218), made it a crime to knowingly carry or send in interstate commerce, or to send in the mail within a state, any records, paraphernalia, tickets, slots, tokens, paper, or other devices used or to be used in bookmaking, wagering pools, or numbers games. A House bill also became law. H.R. 468 (PL 87-368) expanded the Fugitive Felon Act, which made it a federal crime to cross state lines to avoid prosecution after committing crimes of violence such as rape or murder. The penalties for flight were set at $5,000, five years in prison, or both.

Congress also passed, and the president signed, a bill (S. 1658/PL 87-840) to broaden the ban on interstate transportation of gambling devices to include shipment to points in the United States through foreign commerce and any machines. In S. 1750 (PL 87-342), Congress and the president agreed to expand the Federal Firearms Act to prohibit the shipment of firearms to or by any person convicted of a felony. The new law gave federal law enforcement groups additional jurisdiction in its fight against organized crime by broadening the groups of people who could be prosecuted.

One proposal that was not acted on was a proposal to give the attorney general the power to compel a witness to testify and prohibited the intimidation of witnesses (S. 1655).[19]

PRESIDENT JOHNSON

Lyndon Johnson was determined to use every resource of the federal government, in cooperation with state and local authorities, to eradicate organized crime in all of its forms, from shakedown racketeers who prey on business and labor to smut peddlers who prey on our youth.[20] He called on each federal department and agency, such as the attorney general, the secretary of the treasury, and the other heads of the federal law enforcement departments, to redouble their efforts against organized crime. He wanted the Department of Justice to submit legislative proposals to the Congress that would strengthen and expand these efforts.[21] Even in 1966, Johnson reiterated his concern to intensify the campaign against organized crime.[22]

Johnson wanted to encourage witnesses to testify against organized crime members but understood that they were often too intimidated to do so. To encourage testimony, he proposed legislation to expand the authority of the Department of Justice to immunize hostile but knowledgeable witnesses against prosecution and thereby enable them to testify without incriminating themselves. The legislation would extend it to such racketeering crimes as bribery, graft, bankruptcy fraud, jury tampering, and other schemes for the obstruction of justice.[23] He also asked that the Congress enact legislation to make it a federal crime to coerce or threaten a person who is willing to give vital information to federal investigators, thus extending additional protection to potential witnesses at the beginning of an organized crime investigation before a grand jury has been convened.[24] Additionally, he recommended that the obstruction of justice statute be extended to cover interference with criminal investigations before charges had been filed.[25] He recommended that the police in the District of Columbia be given the authority to take custody of a material witness when there is reason to believe that he or she will not be available to testify in court.[26]

Johnson supported the newly created task forces located in major cities to attack organized crime. He said in the fight against organized crime, one of the top priorities of the Justice Department and the attorney general was the strike forces in those cities under siege by racketeers.[27]

Johnson linked gambling to organized crime, claiming that gambling was a major source of revenue for organized crime, and in 1968, Johnson recommended that national gambling laws be strengthened. He suggested Congress broaden the current law to make it a federal crime to engage in gambling as a substantial business affecting interstate commerce. Second, Johnson suggested modifying the Federal Wagering Statute to preserve the taxing authority.[28]

CONGRESS

1963–64: 88TH CONGRESS

In 1963, the Senate Investigation of Organized Crime began. This time it was called the Senate Government Operations Permanent Investigations Subcommittee.[29] At one point, the members heard from Joseph Valachi, a low-level soldier in the Gambino crime family from New York. Valachi testified about the organization of the crime families, the people involved, and the crimes they committed. For the first time, Congress and America were learning the truth about crime families from an insider.

1965–66: 89TH CONGRESS

In this session, Congress took no action on a variety of bills aimed at organized crime, including measures outlawing membership in the Mafia and similar secret crime societies (S. 2187), making it a federal crime to bribe federal agents or informants (S. 2188), legalizing certain wiretapping (S. 2189), and permitting compelled testimony and witness immunity in federal prosecutions (S. 2190).[30]

1967–68: 90TH CONGRESS

Congress passed and the president signed S. 676 (PL 90-123) to protect informants and potential witnesses during federal criminal investigations.

PRESIDENT NIXON

Richard Nixon put organized crime high on his presidential agenda. In an effort to intensify the national effort against organized crime, he asked the Congress to increase the fiscal 1970 budget by $25 million, which would roughly double the expenditures for the organized crime effort at the time. Nixon called for a new general witness immunity law to cover all cases involving the violation of a federal statute. Under the proposal, a witness in a federal criminal case could be compelled to testify under threat of a prison sentence for contempt. Further, a witness could not be prosecuted on the basis of anything he or she said while testifying, but the individual would not be immune from prosecution based on other evidence of his or her offense. Once the government had granted the witness immunity, a refusal then to testify would bring a prison sentence for contempt. With this new law, Nixon believed the federal government would be better able to gather evidence to attack the leadership of organized crime and not just the rank-and-file members.

Nixon focused on the gambling activities of organized crime, because organized crime would shrivel up without its gambling operations.[31] He asked for new legislation that would make it a federal crime to engage in an illicit gambling operation from which five or more persons derive income, which had been in operation more than 30 days, or from which the daily "take" exceeded $2000. Nixon called for swift enactment of proposals (S. 1624 and H.R. 322) that were intended to amend the wagering tax laws and enable the IRS to play a more active and effective role in collecting the revenues owed on bets. The proposed bills would also increase the federal operator's tax on gamblers from $50 annually to $1000. He asked the authority for Justice Department agents to enter any community and shut down large-scale gambling operations.

Finally, because illegal gambling on a large scale cannot go on without cooperation of corrupt law enforcement, Nixon asked Congress to make corruption of local authorities who were tied in with such gambling operations a federal crime. He stressed the great urgency of these measures.[32] Nixon called on Congress to pass legislation to make the systematic corruption of community political leadership and law enforcement a federal crime.[33]

Nixon proposed increasing the strike forces against organized crime and continuing the experimentation with strike forces also using state and local enforcement officers.[34] He then established the National Council on Organized Crime to formulate an effective, coordinated national strategy to eliminate organized crime.[35]

The president also asked Congress to pass the Organized Crime Control Act. He told Congress the bill embodied the recommendations of the President's Crime Commission, the National Commission on Reform of Federal Criminal Laws, and other groups and described the law as strengthening existing laws related to the prosecution of organized crime. He believed the law would make large-scale gambling a federal offense and would make it a felony for a large-scale gambler, law enforcement officers, or other public officials to obstruct enforcement of laws against gambling through bribery. He also described the law as replacing many witness-immunity laws scattered throughout the US Code with a single-uniform provision. He proposed increased sentences: up to 30 years for dangerous adult special offenders, including organized crime leaders.[36] In the end, Congress passed the bill, and Nixon signed it into law.

Nixon, in 1970, also focused on modifications to the Wagering Tax Amendment. He asked Congress to modify it in such a way so it would increase the coverage and amount of the taxes, and he authorized a grant of immunity to essential witnesses.[37] In 1971, Nixon again proposed the Wagering Tax Act to broaden the coverage of the wagering tax and increase the level of taxation.[38]

CONGRESS

1969–70: 91ST CONGRESS

In this session, Congress passed the Organized Crime Control Act of 1970 (S. 30/ PL 452) to strengthen the federal attack on large-scale organized crime[39] and other professional criminal organizations.[40] The most effective part of the act was Title IX, the Racketeer Influenced and Corrupt Organizations Act, which became known as RICO. In the end, it became one of the most important and effective bills ever enacted against organized crime.[41] The bill was a top priority in the Nixon administration's war on crime, and he endorsed the bill after suggesting additional provisions.[42]

The bill revised laws governing evidence and evidence gathering, extended federal jurisdiction over gambling operations, and authorized the use of civil antitrust remedies against businesses corrupted by racketeers. Under the new law, both criminal prosecutions for specified activities and civil suits aimed at corrupt business practices would be allowed. To provide a deterrent against illegal activity, triple damages could be awarded to plaintiffs in suits.

The bill authorized special grand juries to investigate organized criminal activities, set a uniform procedure for judicial bodies to grant witnesses immunity from use of their testimony, and provided physical facilities to protect witnesses. If the law passed, there would be limited challenges to evidence obtained by illegal electronic surveillance and limited disclosing any evidence obtained from the surveillance. Civil antitrust remedies could be used against those people who used income from organized crime to acquire or operate a legitimate business. The proposal extended federal jurisdiction over almost every illegal gambling operation of any size and authorized increased sentences of up to 25 years for dangerous adult offenders.[43] It created a new federal crime of falsely testifying under oath.

To attack the business of organized crime groups, Congress defined 32 predicate offenses and made it a crime to use income from those offenses to establish, acquire, or operate legitimate business that was involved in interstate commerce. The predicate offenses included offenses such as kidnapping, drug trafficking, sports bribery, contraband cigarettes, and embezzlement of union funds. One of the predicate offenses had to have been committed within the previous five years, but the second could have been committed within the prior ten years. This new rule essentially gave law enforcement 15 years to prosecute crimes under RICO statutes. Further, an individual member of a group or organization, known as an "enterprise," was guilty of an offense, even if the acts were committed by others in the group. Basically, the RICO statute made membership in an organized crime a legal offense.[44] Violations of the act could be punished by up to a $20,000 fine and 20 years in prison, in addition to the forfeiture of any assets derived from the activity. In the end, law enforcement was able to use the new law to prosecute most of the heads of the large organized crime families and send them to prison for lengthy prison terms.

The Congress established special grand juries that would sit in major cities or other areas as needed to hear charges against those involved in organized criminal behaviors. Those willing to testify for the government (or otherwise forced to do so) could be granted immunity and would be protected by the government. Those who refused to testify could be held without bail until they complied but for no longer than 18 months. If defendants made contradictory statements under oath during the trial process, they could be convicted of perjury. Under the new law, it would be a federal crime to plot to obstruct state law. Punishments were increased for organized crime figures who were convicted of a felony.

1973–74: 93RD CONGRESS

The House proposed, but did not pass, a bill to provide for more training for prosecutors of organized crime (H.R. 771). They would hold an annual conference for federal, state, and local officials to help provide assistance for prosecuting those charged with organized crime.

A bill in the Senate that did not pass was S. 742, the Civil Remedies for Victims of Racketeering Activity and Theft Act. Under this bill, any person could start proceedings for civil relief in federal court as an effort to prevent and restrain racketeering actions.

PRESIDENT FORD

The issue of organized crime was not high on Gerald Ford's presidential agenda during his administration. Ford asked Congress to write into the revised Federal Criminal Code stronger provisions to allow federal action against organized crime.[45]

In 1975, Ford linked gambling with organized crime. He said the leaders of organized crime could only be prosecuted if it could be shown that they participated in a specific offense, such as gambling, loan-sharking, or selling narcotics. He believed a reformed criminal code should strike directly at organized criminal activity by making it a federal crime to operate or control a racketeering syndicate. This revision would make the criminal law apply to organized crime leaders who sought to conceal their roles in the syndicate's criminal activities.[46]

PRESIDENT CARTER

Jimmy Carter acknowledged that organized crime was a very serious problem facing the country. He considered it a problem that ought to be addressed from a national level, but it was also crucial to have local, state, and federal law enforcement agencies cooperate in a more effective manner to exchange ideas and information and in the prosecution of offenders.[47]

CONGRESS

1975–76: 94TH CONGRESS

In 1976, the House passed legislation concerning betting on horse races. The House passed H.R. 14071 that outlawed interstate off-track betting and authorized civil suits between residents of different states for violations of the act. The bill also provided that any person who accepted an interstate off-track wager would be liable for damages to the state in which the race was run, the owners of horses participating in the race, and the host racing association. Those latter groups could institute civil action in either state or US district court against violators of the act.[48] The law did not have enough support to pass.

1977–78: 95TH CONGRESS

In a criminal code revision that was passed in the Senate, there was a section on organized crime. In the new code, Congress created a new crime of laundering racketeering proceeds to prevent mobsters from investing the proceeds from rackets in legitimate businesses. The law also tightened up federal loan-sharking laws and provided tougher penalties for operation of a racketeering syndicate (up to 25 years in prison).[49]

Another bill passed by Congress and signed by the president, S. 1487/PL 95-575, was aimed at controlling illegal interstate traffic in cigarettes. It extended federal anti-racketeering laws to cover cigarette bootlegging and provided penalties of up to five years in prison and $100,000 in fines for violations. Because organized crime was thought to be involved in the illegal sales of cigarettes, federal money was provided to those states with high cigarette taxes that had suffered major revenue losses through sales of contraband cigarettes brought in from low-tax states. It was estimated that the crime families collected $200 million a year from it.

The new law made it illegal for anyone to knowingly ship, transport, receive, possess, sell, distribute, or purchase contraband cigarettes. Moreover, the law made it illegal for anyone to knowingly make any false statement about the information kept in records concerning transactions of quantities of cigarettes in excess of 60,000. "Contraband cigarettes" were defined to mean a quantity in excess of 60,000 cigarettes, which bear no evidence of the payment of applicable state cigarette taxes in the state where cigarettes are found, if that state requires such stamps.

The law provided fines of up to $100,000 and prison terms of up to five years for knowing violations of the section dealing with illegal transactions of contraband cigarettes. Fines were set up to $5,000 and three years in jail for violation of the record-keeping provisions. It also allowed for seizure and forfeiture of contraband cigarettes held in violation of the act.[50]

1979–80: 96TH CONGRESS

In the proposed revision of the Federal Criminal Code (passed only by the Senate Judiciary Committee), a new offense of trafficking in counterfeit sound recordings or motion pictures, a common activity for organized crime at the time, was included.[51] There was also a section on laws concerning racketeering. One law made it a crime to acquire or keep control of any enterprise engaged in or affecting interstate commerce through a pattern of racketeering activity or through collection of an unlawful debt. Another law prohibited an employee or associate of an enterprise engaged in or affecting interstate commerce to conduct the enterprise's affairs through a pattern of racketeering activity. The third new law prohibited interstate travel in aid of racketeering and the commission of acts of violence in aid of racketeering.[52]

In the criminal code revision, a new crime of "operating a racketeering syndicate" was included in the proposal. The new law was intended to facilitate the prosecution of persons who directed large criminal syndicates.[53]

Congress cleared a bill (H.R. 1301/PL 96-90) to permit the overseas shipment of lottery materials. It authorized American manufacturers to ship lottery tickets and other lottery materials to foreign countries where lotteries were permitted.[54]

PRESIDENT REAGAN

Ronald Reagan described organized crime as reaching into every segment of our society. He described organized crime as having millions of dollars of assets in legitimate businesses and controlling union locals. He said organized crime ran burglary rings, fenced stolen goods, and held a virtual monopoly on the heroin trade. It thrived on gambling, pornography, gunrunning, car theft, arson, and a load of other illegal activities.[55] His administration goal was to "break the power of the mob in America and nothing short of it. We mean to end their profits, imprison their members, and cripple their organizations."[56] He also said, "Our goal is a frontal assault on criminal syndicates in America. We mean to cripple the mobsters' organization, dry up their profits, and put their members behind bars where hey belong."[57] He promised to mobilize every government agency and cooperate with local and state police to wipe out all types of organized crime.[58]

Reagan believed organized crime and drugs were intimately related. Therefore, his goal was to crack down not only on the drug trade but on all organized criminal syndicates that had been permitted to exist in America.[59] He promised to bring together all the law enforcement and other agencies of the federal government in a comprehensive attack on drug trafficking and organized crime under a cabinet-level committee chaired by the attorney general. Their job was to review interagency and intergovernmental cooperation in the struggle against organized crime and, when necessary, ring problems in these areas to the president's attention.[60]

To fight organized crime, Reagan asked for revision of the Tax Reform Act to make it easier for federal departments to cooperate in making income tax cases against major organized crime figures and drug dealers.[61] He also pushed for stronger criminal forfeiture laws as a way to take a lot of the profit out of drug pushing and other forms of organized crime.[62]

He promised to establish 12 additional task forces, under the direction of the attorney general, to work closely with state and local law enforcement officials.[63] Further, a panel composed of 15 distinguished Americans from diverse backgrounds and professions with practical experience in criminal justice and combating organized crime was created. The purpose of this commission, which was to last for three years, was to undertake a region-by-region analysis of organized crime's influence and impact on American society, to analyze and debate the data it gathers, and to hold public hearings on the findings. The commission was also to make judicial and legislative recommendations about the most effective way to fight organized crime.[64]

To assist and train local law enforcement agents and officials in combating new kinds of syndicated crime,[65] Reagan established a national center for state and local law enforcement training at the federal facility in Glynco, Georgia.

CONGRESS

1987–88: 100TH CONGRESS

The Senate Judiciary Committee approved legislation to limit the use of RICO to settle private business disputes, since there was a growing perception that RICO suits were often used by businesses to harass competitors. The bill never made it to the floor. The bill was an attempt to make it harder for a private party, particularly a business, to sue another business in order to collect the triple damages that were available under the law. The bill, approved by the Senate Judiciary Committee, would have allowed triple-damage awards only when the defendant had been convicted of a criminal racketeering offense, when suit alleged insider-trading violations, or when a suit was filed either by a consumer or by the federal, state, or local governments.[66]

In the 1980s, American Indian tribes began taking advantage of their status to set up gaming operations as a source of revenue. The gambling operations grew after 1982, when the US Supreme Court left standing a ruling by a lower court that Florida could not regulate bingo on American Indian reservations if the game was legal elsewhere in the state. In 1987 the Court gave the same ruling in *California v. Cabazon Band of Mission Indians*. The federal government feared organized crime figures could corrupt the games. In 1988, a new law was passed (S. 555/PL 100-497) that regulated high-stakes bingo games and other forms of gambling on American Indian reservations. The new law established three classes of gambling, applying different degrees of regulation to each:

Class I: Traditional ceremonial gaming or social games for prizes of limited value, would be under sole control of the tribes

Class II: Bingo, lotto, and certain card games (but not blackjack, chemin de fer, or baccarat) were subject to oversight by a five-member National Indian Gaming Commission appointed by the president and confirmed by the Senate. Three of the commissioners would have to be members of federally recognized American Indian tribes

Class III: Casino gambling, slot machines, horse and dog racing, and jai alai would be prohibited unless they were legal in the state and a tribe entered into a compact with the state for their operation

Another part of the law allowed the continuation of American Indian–sponsored blackjack or other prohibited card games in operation in four states: Michigan, North Dakota, South Dakota, and Washington. The clause did not allow expansion of the existing operations to new sites. New authorizations of $2 million were provided for the first year of operations of the gaming commission, with at least half of the funding to be raised by the tribes from gambling revenues. The commission was given the authority to approve and enforce tribal gaming ordinances, close down games that violated the law, conduct background investigations of the contractors who operated games, collect civil fines, and audit all books and records of gaming operations.[67]

PRESIDENT BUSH

1989–90: 101ST CONGRESS

Two bills, S. 438, H.R. 5111 were debated during this session that were aimed at cutting back private suits under the RICO statute. They won approval from the Senate and House Judiciary Committees in 1990 but were not enacted. Business groups maintained that the RICO Act had been transformed from a weapon against organized crime into a bludgeon against established businesses, accountants, lawyers, and other professionals, and they wanted to limit the provisions for bringing triple-damage suits under the law.[68]

The House introduced a bill to amend the RICO statute, but it was not passed. H.R. 1046 would include additional predicate offenses within the definition of "racketeering activity." These new offenses would include prostitution involving minors, computer fraud, and activities relating to terrorist acts internationally. Another bill to amend the RICO statute was also not passed. This was H.R. 3522, a bill to exclude nonviolent protest from the definition of "racketeering activity." H.R. 5111 would exclude forms of nonviolent public speech from the definition of "racketeering activity," but it also did not pass.

1991–92: 102ND CONGRESS

S. 543 was attached to a broad bank powers bill and was prompted by increased reports about the money-laundering operations of drug traffickers. The goal was to stop what had grown into a $100 billion operation in the United States. The bill was intended to catch the attention of both unscrupulous bank operators who had cooperated in laundering schemes and banks that had shown negligence by not complying with currency transaction laws. This became PL 102-242.

Two bills (H.R. 1717 and S78) were efforts to scale back the civil provisions of RICO. They won approval from the House Judiciary committee in 1991, but the measure did not reach the floor of the House. Business-related groups complained that plaintiffs were tempted by the possibility of collecting triple damages in a successful RICO action, so the law was being misused and resulted in harmful actions against legitimate businesses.[69]

The House also considered H.R. 5534, a money-laundering bill that established increased penalties on banks and bank employees who were found guilty of money laundering. Eventually the provisions were attached to an unrelated housing bill, and it became law (PL 102-550).[70]

In 1992, the Congress passed S. 474 (PL 102-559), which prohibited additional states from sponsoring sports-based lotteries. The law was based on a concern that state-sponsored gambling could undercut the integrity of professional sports. The provisions did not affect betting on horse and dog racing or the numbers games that were the most common type of lottery. Only betting on professional and collegiate sports such as basketball, football, and baseball was prohibited.[71]

PRESIDENT CLINTON

William Clinton continued the federal war against organized crime. He called it a "scourge that has exacted a terrible toll . . . a toll in lives ravaged by narcotics, brutalized by violence, destroyed by murder."[72] Unlike other presidents, Clinton took an international approach to organized crime. He asked the Departments of Justice and the Treasury to do all they could to strengthen the cooperation between American and Italian law enforcement.[73] He also promised to work with our allies to share information on growing crime syndicates to better derail their schemes.[74]

1993-94: 103RD CONGRESS

H.R. 4922 and S. 2375 were proposals to expand the federal wiretapping laws. The new law helped police keep pace with new telephone technology. Law enforcement officials sought the legislation for many years, because technology was advancing so quickly. In response, the new laws gave telephone companies four years to make changes in their services that were necessary to ensure that court-ordered wiretaps would be successful. Specifically, law enforcement wanted to be able to track and record calls made to and from certain phone numbers. President Clinton signed the new law (PL 103-414).[75]

1995-96: 104TH CONGRESS

The Congress approved a bill (H.R. 497/PL 104-169) that authorized a nine-member commission to study the proliferation of legalized gambling in the country. The commission would be called the National Gambling Impact and Policy Commission and would be made up of three members named by the president, three by the House Speaker, and three by the Senate majority leader. The Commission was to have subpoena power and would be required to issue a report to the president and Congress in two years. It was to study the economic impact of legalized gambling and the relationship between gambling and crime.[76]

A portion of the bill focused particularly on gambling on American Indian reservations. Federal oversight of the gaming industry run by American Indians on tribal land was increased by establishing a three-member Federal Indian Gaming Regulatory Commission that would regulate the gaming on reservations, an operation that made $2.6 billion annually. The commission would develop operating standards for American Indian gaming and would be authorized to impose fines of up to $50,000 a day for violations of such standards. The commission would have the power to shut down gaming operations if deemed necessary. The new panel would replace the National Gaming Commission that was created by Congress in 1988, which had limited jurisdiction over gaming activities on tribal lands. Supporters of American Indian gaming said the gambling operations were necessary as a means to raise money because of recent cuts in federal programs for American Indians.[77] Opponents said gaming regulation was the responsibility of state governments.[78]

A proposal was made in the House (H.R. 230) to amend the RICO statute to revise the definition of "pattern of racketeering activity" to require that the activity revolve around seeking a profit. The bill did not pass. Another bill proposed to amend the RICO statute was H.R. 305, the Alien Smuggling Prosecution Act. This would change the federal criminal code to include peonage and slavery offenses as predicate offenses. This also did not pass.

1997–98: 105TH CONGRESS

The Senate Judiciary Committee addressed the problem of unregulated and growing cyberspace gambling operations, some of which were allegedly operated by organized crime. At the time, gambling on the Internet was considered illegal under the 1961 Interstate Wire Act (PL 87-216). It prohibited interstate gambling over the telephone or other wire communications but did not specifically outlaw wagering on the Internet. Additional problems arose because most Internet gambling operations were located outside the United States and outside the jurisdiction of US law enforcement. To address those issues, the Senate Committee approved S. 474, which would prohibit gambling on the Internet. Supporters of the bill said Internet gambling was particularly open to addiction, fraud, and access by minors because it was unregulated and available in the privacy of the user's home.[79] But the bill did not become law.

1999–2000: 106TH CONGRESS

H.R. 5018 was a bill to outline restrictions on law enforcement's use of electronic surveillance. Some members of Congress learned that, unlike in the past, wiretapping techniques can now gather information such as credit card numbers and other private details. The bill would make it more difficult for law enforcement officials to obtain basic information, such as information on outgoing phone calls and email addresses.

PRESIDENT BUSH

2003–4: 108TH CONGRESS

Lawmakers sought once again to attack the Internet gambling industry by blocking Internet wagers as they debated H.R. 2143, H.R. 21, and S. 627. The bills were attempts to prohibit credit card companies from accepting online bets. The bills did not apply to state-regulated gambling interests. Because floor action was not scheduled in the Senate, the bills went nowhere.[80]

S. 1177 was otherwise known as the PACT Act, or Prevent All Cigarette Trafficking Act. This proposal would amend the Jenkins Act (PL 81-363), a 1949 law that requires cigarette vendors to file sales reports with state tax and local officials. The new law would require reports to state officials on smokeless tobacco and include telephone numbers, emails, websites, as well as the name, address, and phone number, for all places of businesses that receive the cigarette shipments. This was not passed.

2005–06:109TH CONGRESS

The Congress finally passed a law (H.R. 4954/PL 109-347) geared toward curbing wagering on the Internet. This time they attached the provisions to the conference report on a port security bill. Supporters agreed that Internet gambling created a host of social ills from addictive behavior to criminal activity, including money laundering, and that minors could too easily gain access to gambling websites, but in the past, restricting the industry had proved difficult.[81]

PRESIDENT OBAMA

2009–10:111TH CONGRESS

The Witness Security and Protection Grant Program Act (H.R. 1741) would provide more federal grant funds for state witness-protection programs. The bill would require the Justice Department to provide grants to state and local governments to establish or maintain witness protection and aid to people in witness-protection programs. In addition, the bill would provide grant funds to protect witnesses in court hearings involving a homicide, a violent felony, or a serious drug offense. The bill did not pass.

Another House bill that did not pass was H.R. 1173, the Organized Retail Crime Act. Under this proposal, the crime of "organized retail theft" would be defined as the stealing, embezzlement, or obtaining by fraud, false pretenses, or other illegal means of retail merchandise in quantities that would not be normally purchased for personal use.

CONCLUSION

The issue of organized crime was one of the first crime issues to become a concern of the federal government. After congressional hearings in the 1950s, the public had a better understanding of the violence and criminal acts that were a normal part of typical crime groups. Both presidents and Congress made new proposals to allow law enforcement to attack crime families. Over the years, the underlying problem of organized crime has changed from a domestic problem to an international one, but the federal government continues to debate and pass legislation in this crime area.

Chapter 14

Pornography and Obscenity

The availability and dangers of pornographic and obscene material has been part of congressional debate for many years. Federal involvement is needed because it involves the mail system, computers, the Internet, or children. These are not circumstances where states can act easily, so it becomes a legitimate area for federal involvement. Sometimes problems surround the definition of pornographic or obscene material and leads to controversy, disagreement, and debate. The policies proposed by the presidents and Congress related to these concerns are included in this chapter.

President Johnson

1953–54: 83rd Congress

As early as 1953, Congress was debating issues surrounding obscenity. This year, the Senate approved two bills (S. 10 and S. 11) dealing with pornography. S. 11 was intended to broaden the definition of "banned material" to include any article, matter, thing, device, or substance. This would then cover items such as phonograph records that were not specifically banned under the law at the time. S. 10 would have banned the interstate shipment of obscene matter by private conveyance, as well as by mail or common carrier, for the purpose of sale or distribution.[1] It also would have increased the penalties for such transmission. The bills were not acted on by the House.[2]

During that session, a Select Committee to Study Current Pornographic Materials reported its findings and warned that pornography is big business and that filth, perversion, and degeneracy in many pocket-sized books were a national disgrace.[3]

President Nixon

The first president to discuss the issues surrounding pornography was Richard Nixon. In 1969 he wanted to stop the mailing of unsolicited sexually oriented materials to families who did not want the material sent to them through the nation's postal system. He was also concerned about children who might see it and the resulting psychological harm. In response, he proposed three legislative proposals to protect American citizens from pornography and asked Congress to pass them.[4] Then in 1970, he asked Congress to pass the Protection of Minors from Obscenity Act and the Prohibition of Transportation of Salacious Advertising Act, which were bills to prohibit the use of the mail to distribute matter harmful to minors or "advertisements explicitly designed and intended to appeal to a prurient interest in sex."[5] They did not pass, and in 1971 Nixon again proposed the same legislation.[6]

1969–70: 91ST CONGRESS

The Congress debated measures to control the flow of unsolicited obscene mail and advertisements into American homes, as Nixon requested.[7] The House approved a bill backed by the administration (H.R. 11032) that would ban the use of interstate facilities, including the mails, to transport unsolicited obscene advertising. The Senate did not act on that bill before the end of the session, but it approved another bill (S. 3220) that required that unsolicited sexually oriented advertising sent through the mails be labeled as such and allowed those who received such mail to return it unopened at the expense of the sender. The House did not act on the Senate bill before the end of the session.[8] Thus, neither bill was passed, despite the president's many requests for it.

However, in this session, the Congress added a provision to the Postal Reorganization Act (PL 91-375) that had been requested by the administration to expand an individual's protection against unsolicited smut advertising.[9]

PRESIDENT CARTER

1977–78: 95TH CONGRESS

The House first expressed its wish to punish pornographers by adding criminal penalties to a child abuse bill (H.R. 6693). When the committee bill (H.R. 8059) came to the floor, it did not contain penalties for distribution of child pornography. In the end, neither bill passed.

In 1978, the Senate passed a reform of the Federal Criminal Code, part of which concerned obscene material. Previously, the Supreme Court ruled that "obscenity" was a matter to be determined by community standards. Conservatives sought to make it easier to prosecute obscenity cases while liberals sought to make it more difficult.[10]

President Jimmy Carter signed S. 1585/PL 95-225, which made it a federal crime to use children for prostitution or the production of pornographic materials or to sexually abuse children under the age of 16. The bill also banned the sale and distribution of obscene materials depicting children in sexually explicit conduct if the materials were mailed or transported in interstate commerce. The Senate added an amendment to the bill that would penalize those who sold or distributed material that depicted children engaged in sexual conduct, whether or not the material met legal definitions of obscenity.[11]

1979–80: 96TH CONGRESS

In the proposed Federal Criminal Code revision, a section was included on obscene material. This clause made it a crime to disseminate obscene material to a minor or, without consent, to any person who was unable to avoid seeing the material. There was also a section on prostitution and the operation of a prostitution business. The law made it a crime to operate directly or indirectly a prostitution business. The offense also covered procuring patrons or prostitutes for the business. It was written to apply either to men or women.[12]

PRESIDENT REAGAN

Ronald Reagan brought up the issue of obscenity in 1984. He supported legislation to tighten the laws against child pornography and was also concerned about the enforcement of all the federal antiobscenity laws.[13]

1983–84: 98TH CONGRESS

Both the House and Senate passed bills to toughen federal child pornography laws, but they could not resolve differences between the two measures before the end of the year. The bill considered by the House, H.R. 3635, was designed to toughen the federal law against the production and distribution of pornographic materials involving children. It raised the fine for a first offense from $10,000 to a maximum of $100,000, while the maximum fine in the Senate's version was $75,000. The House bill prohibited reproduction of child pornography for distribution through the mails or in commerce and authorized the Justice Department to seek court-ordered wiretaps in child pornography cases. Both bills raised the maximum age of children protected from 16 to 18, removed an existing requirement that sexually explicit materials depicting children be "obscene" before they were banned, and prohibited the production of child pornography regardless of whether it was commercially disseminated. The differences in the bills were worked out, and it became law (PL 66-292).[14]

1985–86: 99TH CONGRESS

H.R. 3506 was a bill called the Pornography Forfeiture Proceedings Venue Act. It would require that customs officers, on the discovery or attempted importation into the United States or seizure of obscene material, transmit that information to the US attorney, who should then begin proceedings for the forfeiture, confiscation, and destruction of that material. This was not passed into law.

1987–88: 100TH CONGRESS

H.R. 5, a proposal for improving elementary and secondary schools, included a provision concerning dial-a-porn. The provision would prohibit a service carrier from providing access to pornographic services over a telephone to a subscriber who has not requested access to that communication. This became law (PL 100-297).

Another proposal in the House, H.R. 1213, was the Pornography Victims Protection Act. This proposal would make it a criminal offense for a person to coerce, intimidate, or fraudulently induce a person over 18 to engage in sexually explicit conduct and produce material of the conduct. It did not pass into law.

H.R. 1339 would prohibit the importation of immoral articles and permit customs officials to transmit information on such material to the US attorneys in the district. Forfeiture proceedings for obscene materials would begin within 30 days of seizure. Although this bill did not pass, some of the provisions were incorporated into H.R. 4848, the Omnibus Trade and Competitiveness Act, which became law (PL 100-418). Another version of the Omnibus Trade and Competitiveness Act (H.R. 3) would increase the period for instituting judicial proceedings for the forfeiture of seized pornography imports from 14 to 30 days. This bill failed passage after the Senate failed to override a presidential veto.

PRESIDENT BUSH

1989–90: 101ST CONGRESS

The House members debated a bill called the Dial-a-Porn Prevention and Corrections Act in which making an indecent telephone call to a person under 18 or to any person without their consent would be illegal. For each intentional violation, a person convicted of the offense could be fined $50,000 plus another $50,000 civil fine. The proposal did not become law.

Another House bill (H.R. 3472), the Pornography Victims Protection Act, was reintroduced this session. It did not pass again. Another proposal that failed to pass was H.R. 3785, the Pornography Victims Compensation Act. This bill would create a cause of action against a person who produced, distributed, exhibited, or sold sexually explicit material by a victim of rape, sexual assault, or sexual crime. Damages could be awarded for economic loss, compensation for pain and suffering, attorney's fees, and costs to plaintiffs.

1991–92: 102ND CONGRESS

Again, the Pornography Victims Protection Act was proposed in the House, but it did not pass. The Pornography Victims' Compensation Act was reintroduced (S. 983) but again not passed.

In H.R. Res. 349 and S. Res. 200, the week of October 27–November 2, 1991 would be designated as "National Pornography Victims Awareness Week," but it did not pass. The Senate proposed S. Res. 13, a joint resolution to remove offensive sexual material from television broadcasting. This failed to pass. Another bill that failed passage was S. 192, a proposal to provide criminal penalties for the mailing of unsolicited sexually oriented advertisements.

PRESIDENT CLINTON

1993–94: 103RD CONGRESS

Again, the Pornography Victims Protection Act was proposed and failed passage.

If a person sent material in the mail that included obscene matter on the envelope or outside cover or wrapper, it would be a federal law under H.R. 2316, the Graphic Postcard Act. However, the proposal was not passed.

1995–96: 104TH CONGRESS

H.R. 1540 was a proposal called the Family Viewing Cable Television Act that would impose a fine and up to two years in prison for any person who knowingly disseminates indecent material on a channel provided as part of a basic cable television package. The proposal was not passed.

Television shows would be given a rating under H.R. 1807. That rating would indicate sexual, violent, and indecent television programming that is inappropriate for children. All televisions with screens of 13 inches or larger would be equipped with blocking technology to allow viewers to block programs. The bill did not pass. A similar proposal was made in H.R. 2030, the Parental Choice in Television Act. This also did not pass.

1997–98: 105TH CONGRESS

Once again, the Graphic Postcard Act was introduced but not signed into law. Also reintroduced and not passing was the Family Viewing Cable Television Act (H.R. 2892). H.R. 2648 also did not become law. This was the Abolishing Child Pornography Act, which set penalties for knowingly possessing any material containing child pornography that has been mailed, shipped, or transported, including by computer, in interstate or foreign commerce.

A bill to prohibit unsupervised access to the Internet by state prisoners as a way to stop pornography in prisons did not become law. This was H.R. 3729, the Stop Trafficking of Pornography in Prisons Act.

1999–2000: 106TH CONGRESS

Language was added to a fiscal 2001 spending measure for the Labor, Health and Human Services and Education bill (H.R. 4577) that would force schools and libraries to use "technology protection measures" to block access by children to Internet pornography. This became law (PL 106-554).

PRESIDENT BUSH

2001–2: 107TH CONGRESS

In S. 2520/H.R. 4623, written after the Supreme Court declared a law prohibiting pornographic images that appear to be of children unconstitutional, the Congress rewrote the ban. This law, called the Child Obscenity and Pornography Prevention Act, would prohibit any computer-generated image that is nearly indistinguishable from a minor who is engaging in sexually explicit conduct. The Senate bill would make it a crime to pander, or solicit, child pornography.[15] The bills did not pass.

The Stop Material Unsuitable for Teens Act (H.R. 1523) would increase the age for persons considered to be minors for purposes of prohibiting the transfer of pornographic materials to minors. The age would increase from 16 to 18. The bill did not pass.

2003–4: 108TH CONGRESS

S. 151 was a proposal to address crimes committed against children and at the same time prohibit "virtual" child pornography. The bill mandated life sentences for twice-convicted child sex offenders and would allow federal law enforcement to use wiretaps when investigating allegations of child pornography. It would eliminate the statute of limitations for prosecuting sexual or physical abuse or kidnapping of children and would limit the ability of federal judges to diverge from sentencing guidelines in cases involving crimes against children.[16] The bill was signed into law (PL 108-21).

H.R. 1104, the Child Abduction Prevention Act, was an attempt to bolster the AMBER child-abduction alert system. Title 5 of the law prohibits making a visual depiction that is a digital image, computer-generated image, or one that is indistinguishable from a real image of a minor engaged in sexually explicit conduct. It would also be illegal to provide, sell, receive, or purchase a visual depiction of a minor engaging in such conduct. Increased penalties would be provided for recidivists in child pornography cases. This proposal was tabled.

2005–6: 109TH CONGRESS

H.R. 5319 was a proposal that would require schools and libraries that accept certain federal technology grants to implement procedures to prevent children from accessing obscene material or chat rooms at schools or public libraries.

H.R. 310 provides that if a broadcast station shows obscene, indecent, or profane material, they could be fined no more than $500,000 for each violation. The Senate version of this bill was S. 193, also called the Broadcast Decency Enforcement Act, and became law (PL 109-235).

The Child Pornography Prevention Act (H.R. 3726) was proposed but not passed during this session. The proposal would prohibit producers of visual depictions of sexually explicit behavior from refusing the attorney general access to business records. If material is confiscated, that material must remain in the care and custody of the government or the court and cannot be reproduced. The bill was not passed.

2007–8: 110TH CONGRESS

Under H.R. 4120, the Effective Child Pornography Prosecution Act, the government would not have to prove interstate transmission occurred when prosecuting child pornography cases. The bill was written in response to a decision by the US Court of Appeals in *United States v. Schaefer* (501 F. 3d 1197 [2007]) in which the justices reversed a conviction for the receipt and possession of child pornography. The justices held that the government had to prove that interstate transmission of the material had occurred. The proposed legislation would also change the definition of possession of child pornography to include material that someone "knowingly accesses with intent to view."[17] The bill became law (PL 110-358).

CONCLUSION

It is obvious that presidents and Congress have been concerned about the publication and dissemination of obscene material, especially with regards to children. Federal involvement in matters surrounding pornography and obscenity often revolves around the use of the mails or children. In these cases, the states cannot solve the problem on their own, so the federal government must step in to help. This is an issue that every president or Congress would be opposed, but debate surrounds what method would be the best method to solve the problem. This is where presidents and Congress sometimes disagree. Nonetheless, they have proposed and passed many laws concerning pornographic material. In later years, much of the attention for pornographic material became focused on the Internet and the content and availability of pornography on the Internet. Even though legislation to limit pornography is tricky because of the issues concerning freedom of speech and the press, some legislation has been passed, and this issue will continue to be a concern of the federal government.

CHAPTER 15

WIRETAPS

WIRETAPPING IS WHEN LAW ENFORCEMENT ATTACHES A hidden receiver to a telephone line to intercept a phone conversation. On the other hand, eavesdropping is when law enforcement uses hidden microphones or other sensitive devices that can pick up a voice to overhear conversations within a room.[1] Presidents and Congress disagree over whether or not wiretapping should be allowed and, if so, under what circumstances.

The controversy revolving around the use of wiretaps began in 1928, when the Supreme Course ruled in *Olmstead v. United States* (277 US 438) that the use of wiretap evidence in a federal court did not violate constitutional guarantees in the Fourth and Fifth Amendments against unreasonable search and seizure and self-incrimination. This decision seemed to allow wiretapping by government agents as a way to detect crime. In 1934, Congress passed the Communications Act, which included a section that stated no person should intercept any communication or divulge the contents to anyone else. Upon review by the Supreme Court, the Communications Act seemed to make it illegal for anyone to tap a telephone wire. Further, the Court ruled that evidence obtained by wiretapping could not be used in federal courts.[2]

Since these early decisions and laws, Congress and the presidents have debated the issues surrounding wiretaps and if the evidence obtained from them should be allowed as evidence in a court. The proposals and debates are noted in this chapter.

PRESIDENT TRUMAN

1953–54: 83RD CONGRESS

In 1953, the House Judiciary Subcommittee held three days of hearings on bills to authorize wiretapping in cases involving national security. The House suggested H.R. 408 to allow the FBI and intelligence divisions of the army, air force, and navy, on approval of the US attorney general, to use wiretapped evidence in court cases involving treason, sabotage, and other violations of national security. They also proposed H.R. 477 and H.R. 3552 to authorize the FBI and intelligence divisions of the armed forces, with the approval of the attorney general and a permit from a federal judge, to obtain and use wiretapped evidence in court cases involving national security. Unauthorized wiretapping would be a felony.[3] None of these laws passed.

1961–62: 87TH CONGRESS

Hearings were held by the Senate Judiciary Committee on wiretapping, but no action was taken.[4] One proposal they debated was S. 1086, since it was not a federal crime for state law officials, where state law permitted, to tap telephones and use the evidence in state courts. Before placing a tap, the officials would be required to obtain permission from a state court based on a showing that the tap would probably disclose evidence of a crime. Another bill, S. 1822, was the same as S. 1086 but limited taps to 30 days and to a particular phone to be designated in the court order. A third bill, S. 1221, permitted wiretapping by federal law enforcement officers under a court order and outlawed eavesdropping by any acoustical devices except by federal or state law-enforcement officers operating under a court order. Finally, the Senate considered S. 1495, which permitted the attorney general, without any court order, to authorize federal agents to make wiretaps in cases involving espionage, treason, sabotage, sedition, and kidnapping.[5] None of the bills passed.

PRESIDENT JOHNSON

1963–64: 88TH CONGRESS

Congress took no action on a bill (S. 1308) legalizing wiretapping by authorized personnel in investigating certain serious crimes, outlawing other wiretapping, and granting immunity to witnesses in certain court cases. Attorney General Robert Kennedy wanted it passed.[6]

1967–68: 90TH CONGRESS

No action was taken on H.R. 5386 that would ban all wiretapping and electronic eavesdropping except in national security cases. The administration had sought to prohibit all official and private wiretapping and eavesdropping except by federal agencies in national security cases, but as part of the Safe Streets Act (H.R. 5037) broad wiretapping authority was granted to all levels of government, while banning private wiretapping or electronic eavesdropping. Congress enacted the Senate measures and the Safe Streets Act became law, but the president criticized them when signing the bill.[7] But the Safe Streets Act clearly stated that whoever willfully intercepted wire or oral communications, used wiretapping or electronic bugging devices, or disclosed or used such interception would be fined not more than $10,000 and imprisoned not more than five years.[8]

PRESIDENT NIXON

In 1969, Richard Nixon explained his attitude toward electronic surveillance was that it should be used very sparingly and very carefully, having in mind the rights of those who might be involved but very effectively to protect the internal and external security of the United States.[9]

1971–72: 92ND CONGRESS

The Senate Judiciary Subcommittee on Administrative Practice and Procedure held a hearing on the meaning of the Supreme Court decision that warrantless electronic eavesdropping on citizens was unconstitutional.[10]

1975–76: 94TH CONGRESS

In 1976, two bills were considered (H.R. 12750, S. 3197) that required warrants for domestic wiretaps conducted in the United States for national security reasons and established procedures for obtaining the warrants and protecting the rights of wire-tapped persons. The bills became too controversial to pursue during the session, and they did not pass.[11]

There was a temporary Senate Select Committee on Intelligence Operations. It issued a lengthy report and recommended curbing intelligence activities by federal agencies within the United States. It recommended more stringent control of intrusive investigative techniques such as wiretapping, mail surveillance, and the use of informants. Two days later, the National Wiretap Commission released its final report urging that the use of wiretaps be expanded to aid law enforcement agencies in domestic criminal cases and that regulations for obtaining those wiretaps be eased.[12]

PRESIDENT CARTER

Jimmy Carter supported the commission's proposals recommending that a court order for electronic surveillance expressly authorize entry on a private place or premises to install an eavesdropping device if such entry is necessary to execute the warrant. He also suggested Congress investigate possible encroachments on individual privacy by new forms of the art, such as computer technology.[13]

1977–78: 95TH CONGRESS

In 1978, the Carter administration announced a major new attempt to deal with the controversial practice of electronic surveillance for foreign intelligence or "national security" purposes. The legislation approved by Congress, the Foreign Intelligence Surveillance Act of 1977 (H.R. 7308/S. 1566/PL 95-511), for the first time imposed a judicial warrant requirement on any electronic surveillance conducted by the executive branch for foreign intelligence-gathering purposes. That meant that all intelligence agencies had to obtain a judicial warrant for almost all intelligence surveillance conducted in the United States. Existing law required warrants only for domestic criminal cases. In national security cases, executive officials had been able to use taps and bugs without judicial scrutiny. The legislation also amended the president's claim of an inherent power to order wiretaps that were in the national interest. Critics of the bill argued that the standards judges were to follow in granting warrants for electronic surveillance were so loose that they became a threat to the privacy and civil liberties of US citizens.[14]

The new law was the first significant legislative effort to monitor possible invasions of citizens' privacy rights and violations of free speech by law enforcement by requiring a judicial warrant for most foreign intelligence agency electronic surveillance conducted in the United States.[15] It also provided special protections for US citizens, requiring intelligence agencies to produce evidence that a crime was about to be committed before they could be granted a warrant.

This was the first major law to oversee electronic surveillance conducted in the United States for national security purposes. It required a warrant for all but one category of foreign intelligence surveillance and required evidence of criminal activity before a warrant could be issued for surveillance of a US citizen.[16] The law was a top priority of the Carter administration.

During this session, the Senate passed another bill to reform the federal code, and some of it had to do with wiretaps. There were several changes in federal wiretap laws, including a reduction in the number of investigations in which electronic surveillance could be used. The bill for the first time required a neutral magistrate to find probable cause of a crime before issuing a warrant for electronic surveillance.[17]

PRESIDENT REAGAN

1987–88: 100TH CONGRESS

The House passed a bill (H.R. 1212) to outlaw private employers' use of lie detectors on workers or job applicants. The bill would have banned most private sector polygraph tests as a condition of employment, but they could still be used by government employers and by private companies doing business with the Department of Defense, the FBI, the CIA, or the Department of Energy.[18] Those companies providing certain security services and those that manufacture and sell controlled drugs were exempt from the ban. Polygraph tests were also allowed if an employer had a "reasonable suspicion" that one of his or her workers was involved in a crime causing economic harm to the company, such as embezzlement.[19] Reagan signed the bill in 1988 (PL 100-347).

A provision in the Child Protection and Obscenity Enforcement Act (H.R. 3889/S. 2033) would add obscenity to the list of crimes for which the federal government could obtain a wiretap. However, this bill did not become law. Another bill (H.R. 5210/PL 100-690) adds obscenity offenses to the list of crimes for which the government may obtain wiretaps.

PRESIDENT BUSH

1989–90: 101ST CONGRESS

The Financial Crimes Prosecution and Recovery Act (H.R. 5353) would amend the Federal Criminal Code so that wiretaps could be authorized for bank fraud and related offenses. This did not pass. Another proposal, H.R. 5387, would do the same, but it also did not pass.

S. 1970 was a proposal that involved many aspects of the criminal justice system. One provision in the proposed law set penalties for the disclosure of intercepted wiretaps or oral communications obtained during the course of official duties in connection with a criminal investigation or disclosure of wiretaps to impede an investigation. This bill was not passed. A similar bill, H.R. 5269 contained the same provision as did S. 1972. None of the bills became law.

1993–94: 103RD CONGRESS

The Omnibus 1994 Crime Bill made it a federal crime to disclose the results of an authorized wiretap with the intention of disrupting a criminal investigation.

Wiretaps could be used for investigations of illegal immigrant smuggling under H.R. 3320, but it did not pass. That provision was also included in H.R. 2836, H.R. 3860, S. 580, S. 1333, and H.R. 3363, which also did not become law.

1995–96: 104TH CONGRESS

Many bills were proposed using wiretaps to investigate illegal immigration and alien smuggling. These included H.R. 668, H.R. 756, H.R. 1018, H.R. 1915, H.R. 1219, and H.R. 2768, but none passed. In many other bills proposed in the House, wiretaps could be used for investigating terrorist threats. These included H.R. 1635 and H.R. 1710, but neither became law.

1997–98: 105TH CONGRESS

One provision of the Effective Antiterrorism Tools for Law Enforcement Act would expand law enforcement's authority for multipoint wiretaps. This did not pass.

2003–4: 108TH CONGRESS

The Security and Freedom Ensured Act (SAFE Act) amends provisions of the USA Patriot Act concerning roving wiretaps. The changes would require that for an order approving an electronic surveillance, the identity of the target or the place to be wiretapped must be identified. Further, the surveillance should only be conducted when the suspect is present at the place being wiretapped. This bill (S. 1709/H.R. 3352) did not become law.

2005–6: 109TH CONGRESS

The SAFE Act was again proposed in Congress (S. 737/H.R. 1526) but again did not pass. It included the same provisions on wiretaps as in the 108th Congress. Similar provisions were included in H.R. 3199, the USA Patriot Act Improvement and Reauthorization Act, which became law (PL 109-177). This new law also required law enforcement to report back to a court within 15 days of using the wiretap and required law enforcement to report on the total number of electronic surveillances that have been conducted.

2007–8: 110TH CONGRESS

In the Intercept Child Predators Act of 2007 (H.R. 3811), the offense of child sexual exploitation and child pornography would be added to the list of crimes for which wiretaps could be authorized. Additionally, the offenses of embezzlement or theft of government property would be predicate offenses for wiretaps in S. 1946, the Public Corruption Prosecution Improvements Act. Neither bill passed.

PRESIDENT OBAMA

2009–10: 111TH CONGRESS

H.R. 1467, the Safe and Secure America Act, would amend the USA Patriot Act to extend provisions that authorized the use of roving or multipoint wiretaps for national security purposes. This did not become law.

The offense of government theft and bribery would be included as predicate offenses for racketeering and money laundering cases, as well as for wiretaps if H.R. 2822 and S. 49 passed, but they did not.

CONCLUSION

There is much controversy over collecting criminal evidence through wiretaps or bugs placed by the government. It is sometimes seen as opening up possible violations of citizens' privacy. On the other hand, law enforcement relies on the evidence obtained through these investigative efforts to collect evidence of criminal behavior. Wiretaps and bugs placed for national security are more accepted but still controversial. Presidents and Congress remain divided on whether such techniques should be used and, if so, under what circumstances.

REGULATORY OFFENSES

In Part VII, regulatory policy as it relates to crime is described. Use of the Internet is not a crime in and of itself, but certain uses of the Internet must be regulated to ensure proper behavior and reduce the risk of victimization. Although the Internet is a new phenomenon in our society, it is now a vital part of business, research, and social networks. Unfortunately, many people choose to use it for criminal activity. Congress has passed many laws to deter this behavior, and these are described in Chapter 16.

CHAPTER 16

INTERNET

SINCE ELECTRONIC CRIMES ARE A RELATIVELY NEW offense, presidents have only spoken about the problems and concerns related to computers and technology recently. The exception to that was President Clinton. In 1996 he signed the Economic Espionage Act of 1996 (H.R. 3723) that strengthened our protections against the theft or misuse of proprietary business information. It helped law enforcement crack down on acts like software piracy and copyright infringement that cost American businesses billions of dollars in lost revenues. And it also advanced our national security.[1]

The following year, Clinton spoke about concerns surrounding the safety of our children and the Internet. He was particularly concerned after a Supreme Court ruling that struck down a portion of the Communications Decency Act. At that point, Clinton brought together industry leaders and groups representing teachers, parents, and librarians to discuss how to create a "family friendly" Internet. A three-point plan was devised that included new technologies, enforcement of existing laws, and more active participation of parents. Clinton explained that the computer industry was developing new technologies to do a similar thing for the Internet that the V-chip did for television. However, he also recognized the need for strict enforcement of existing laws, such as the antistalking, child pornography, and obscenity laws as they apply to cyberspace. And finally, he recognized that in the end, the responsibility for our children's safety rests largely with their parents.[2]

CONGRESS

1979–80: 96TH CONGRESS

One of the first bills introduced concerning computer crime was a bill intended to make computer fraud a federal crime. The new proposal, S. 240, would make it a crime to use or attempt to use a computer to carry out a criminal act, obtain property by false pretenses, embezzle, steal or convert another person's property. Possible penalties for such acts included a fine of not more than two times the amount of gain or $50,000 (whichever was higher), five years in prison, or both. The bill also made it a crime to intentionally damage a computer. The penalty for this act was set at up to $50,000, imprisonment for not more than five years, or both. The bill was approved by the Senate Criminal Justice Subcommittee but was not acted on by the full Judiciary Committee.[3]

1983–84: 98TH CONGRESS

In 1984, Congress attached some crime-related provisions to the fiscal 1985 continuing appropriations resolution (H.R. Res. 648/PL 98-473). The provisions prohibited tampering with computers and unauthorized use of credit cards or bank account access numbers.[4] It also made it a felony to gain unauthorized entry into a computer for the purpose of obtaining classified information if the information would be used against the Untied States. Unauthorized use of classified information by someone who had permission to access the computer was also banned. Those who committed the offense would be guilty of a felony, with a maximum penalty on the first offense of $10,000 or twice the value obtained, and a maximum prison term of ten years. A second offense would carry a maximum $100,000 fine or twice the value obtained and a maximum 20-year prison term.[5]

Another bill debated in Congress was H.R. 5831, which was a bill that imposed large fines and jail sentences on computer hackers if they tapped into or changed computerized medical records. It authorized fines of up to $5,000 or prison sentences of up to a year for unauthorized access to computerized medical records. If records were altered, the fine was up to $25,000, the prison term up to five years. The bill passed the House but not the Senate.[6]

An early law concerning copyrights was S. 32, aimed at giving record companies and songwriters a greater share of the profits earned by those retail stores that would rent record albums to their customers. It amended the 1976 Copyright Act by prohibiting retail stores from renting record albums without the permission of those own owned the record copyrights. The proposal became law (PL 98-450).[7]

1987–88: 100TH CONGRESS

The issue of copyrights was again a topic for Congress in 1988. This time, legislation passed that extended the ban on commercial rental of most record albums without the copyright owner's permission for eight years (S. 2201/PL 100-617). Members sought to amend an existing law (PL 98-450) that was enacted in 1984 but expired in 1989. It was aimed at curbing a growing practice in which record stores were renting records for a small fee and then selling blank tapes to customers. The customers taped the records at home and returned the albums to the store thus depriving the copyright holder of any royalty on the sale of the record.[8]

1991–92: 102ND CONGRESS

In 1992, Congress cleared S. 756/PL 102-307 that was designed to improve the nation's copyright system. Under the new law, authors of works copyrighted before January 1, 1978, did not need to formally seek a second term of copyright protection for their work. For works copyrighted in 1978 or later, the law already profited a copyright term of 50 years after the death of the author.[9]

Another new law (H.R. 4412/PL 102-492) allowed writers, scholars, and others to use parts of unpublished copyrighted works. The law upheld the "fair use" principle, which allowed the use of copyrighted works without permission of the author or his or her estate.[10]

1993–94: 103RD CONGRESS

In 1994, a major crime bill passed Congress. Among other things, the bill established federal penalties for sending a computer transmission that caused damage or loss of access to another computer that was involved in interstate commerce. Violators were subject to up to five years in jail and fines of up to $250,000. Victims of such crimes also could sue for civil damages.[11]

1995–96: 104TH CONGRESS

In 1996, Congress passed H.R. 3802 (PL 104-231), which made revisions to the Freedom of Information Act (FOIA). The bill clarified that computer-generated federal records were subject to the FOIA, which required government agencies release certain documents upon a request from a member of the public. Since some agencies had backlogs of months or even years after a FOIA request, the new law was also designed to improve the government's response time on those requests. Further, the bill required agencies to report annually on the number of pending requests and provide an estimate as to how long it would take to respond. The final version of the bill did not define exactly what a "document" was but left this question to agencies and, if necessary, the courts to decide.[12]

Another new law passed by Congress this session (H.R. 3723/PL 104-294) subjected hackers who intentionally caused damage to computers, broke security codes, or committed other computer-related crimes to felony charges. The bill imposed a minimum ten-year prison sentence on anyone who knowingly used a computer to gain access to classified government information that could hinder national security. The aim of the bill was to crack down on cybercrimes by protecting the security of computer systems from unauthorized use. First-time computer thieves who obtained financial information of minimal value or government records that did not impair national security were subject to misdemeanor charges. The crime would become a felony if the information was worth more than $5,000 or was used for commercial purposes or personal financial gain.[13]

Finally, attached to a bill about penalties for escaping from jail was an amendment that made computerized theft of information across state or international lines a federal crime that was punishable by one year in prison or fines. It also called for federal penalties of up to five years in prison for those who transmitted threats across state or international lines. Further, it proposed to make browsing through another person's computer system without permission a crime punishable by up to five years in prison or fines.[14]

Efforts to revise federal copyright law did not pass this session. In the Senate, S. 483 was approved by the Judiciary Committee to extend the duration of copyrights by 20 years, but it went no further. In the House, the extension was part of another larger bill (H.R. 2441) aimed at upgrading copyright law by proposing rules for protecting digitized music, books, videos, and other works posted on the Internet and on-line services. This bill never got out of a House Judiciary subcommittee.

1997–98: 105TH CONGRESS

In this session, the House debated H.R. 2265 (PL 105-147), which criminalized the piracy of copyrighted works on the Internet. It prohibited the unlawful electronic transmission of copyrighted works for commercial advantage or financial gain. The new law made it a crime to steal one or more copies of copyrighted works having a total retail value of $1,000 or to reproduce or distribute ten or more copies of one or more copyrighted works having a total retail value of $2,500 or more. Violators would be subject to up to $250,000 in fines and prison terms of up to six years.[15]

Congress then passed H.R. 4151 (PL 105-318), the Identity Theft and Assumption Deterrence Act, which made it illegal to knowingly transfer or use someone else's personal information, such as a Social Security number, with the intent of committing a crime. The legislation was prompted by the increasing use of the Internet to gain personal information about an individual, which could then be used by a criminal to steal another person's identity to borrow money and purchase items. Under the new law, violators could face penalties of up to 20 years in prison and a fine for using the information in the commission of a violent crime. Other, less serious crimes carried a penalty of up to 15 years. The victims of identity theft are also entitled to restitution for losses and costs they incurred.[16]

H.R. 98 was a proposal to prohibit a computer service from disclosing to a third party any personal information without the third party's consent. This did not pass. Another proposal that did not pass was H.R. 774, the Freedom and Child Protection Act. The proposal would repeal provisions prohibiting the use of a telecommunications device to make obscene communication to a minor. It would also be illegal to use a computer to send or display an image of sexual organs to a minor. In another attempt to protect children from inappropriate material on the Internet, the House proposed H.R. 1180, the Family-Friendly Internet Access Act. This law would require an Internet access provider to offer screening software that was designed to allow a customer to limit online access to that material that may be unacceptable. The bill did not have enough support to pass.

During this session, the Supreme Court struck down provisions of the 1996 Communications Decency Act, a telecommunications law that attempted to bar indecent communications on the Internet and the online communications. The provisions would have banned the dissemination of material that was "indecent" or "patently offensive" to minors.

1999–2000: 106TH CONGRESS

H.R. 4942 and S. 313 were proposed to protect the confidentiality of an individual's personal information from being released on the Internet. But Internet companies supported self-regulation, and the bill was not passed by either chamber. Other bills were also proposed in this session, including H.R. 4049 and S. 2448, but nothing was passed.[17]

The Senate cleared H.R. 3456 (PL 106-160), which addressed the issue of software piracy by increasing statutory damages for copyright infringement. The bill would provide for statutory damages ranging from $750 to $30,000 for copyright infringement. The new penalties were about 50 percent higher than those in current law.[18]

The Congress considered H.R. 543/S. 97, the Children's Internet Protection Act. The bill would make elementary and secondary schools, as well as libraries, ineligible to receive federal funds unless they can prove that they have technology to filter inappropriate material from minors. The bill did not become law.

In H.R. 612, the Protection Against Scams on Seniors Act, the secretary of health and human services would be required to provide information to seniors about the dangers of telemarketing fraud and fraud on the Internet. The bill would also amend the Federal Criminal Code to include criminal fraud protections for transmissions made over the Internet, including the initiation and transmission of unsolicited email. The proposal did not pass.

2001–2: 107TH CONGRESS

A bill (H.R. 1542) was aimed at loosening legal restrictions imposed on the regional Bell phone companies by the 1996 Telecommunications Act. It would have allowed the Bells to transmit high-speed Internet traffic over telephone lines outside their service regions without first having to meet requirements in the 1996 law that they open their local systems to competition. The bill also would have rolled back regulatory requirements that allowed rivals to use Bells' advanced lines and equipment at a discount to provide high-speed Internet services. It went no further.[19]

H.R. 3482, or the Cyber Security Enhancement Act, would amend federal-sentencing guidelines to address computer hacking and would also give Internet service providers the ability to disclose the content of suspicious communications to law enforcement. Law enforcement would have more access to electronic communications to investigate computer hacking crimes. The bill did not pass.

The Online Personal Privacy Act (S. 2201) was a proposal to require companies that collect consumer information online to get a customer's consent before gathering any personal data. The proposal gave consumers who were victimized the right to sue a company for misusing sensitive information, such as Social Security numbers, medical or financial data, or personal information including a person's ethnicity, religion, sexual orientation, or political beliefs. This did not pass.

S. 630, the CAN-SPAM Act (Controlling the Assault of Non-Solicited Pornography and Marketing Act), would crack down on unsolicited email (spam) and give the Federal Trade Commission the ability to punish violators with a fine. Online marketers would be required to provide a return address to which recipients can respond and refuse any more emails. If marketers deliberately disguised their identities through false email headers or false information on a subject lines, they may be subject to federal penalties. This did not pass into law.

In an attempt to curb online gambling, the House proposed H.R. 556, the Leach-LaFalce Internet Gambling Enforcement Act. Under the law, any person who operates a betting business is prohibited from knowingly accepting credit or electronic fund transfers. The proposal did not pass.

2003–4: 108TH CONGRESS

In the Senate, a bill was passed (S. 877/PL 198-187) to crack down on fraudulent, pornographic, and misleading junk email, also called spam. It gave consumers the right to opt out of unsolicited email messages by creating a "do not spam list." It outlawed some of the most common tools used by spammers to reach mass audiences. It also required all commercial email to include a subject line showing that it was a commercial message. As a penalty for committing these acts, the law imposed millions of dollars in fines and up to five years in prison.[20]

Another law was proposed in the House and passed into law (H.R. 1731/S. 153/ PL 108-275) that addressed identity theft, one of the fastest growing crimes in the country. Congress cleared a bill to establish tougher criminal penalties for identity theft and made it easier for prosecutors to charge offenders. The bill focused in particular on those who steal identities to commit terrorist acts and other serious crimes. One provision established new penalties for aggravated identity theft, defined as identity theft committed in relation to a list of other serious crimes, such as mail, bank and wire fraud, posing as a US citizen, and theft or embezzlement from employee benefit plans. It imposed a two-year prison sentence beyond the penalty for the underlying crime but five years if the theft was linked to an act of terrorism.

Another provision on identity theft made it easier to prosecute cases of identity theft by broadening the definition of the offender to include not only someone who transferred or used the stolen information but also someone who possessed it. The prosecutor also was required to prove only that the defendant had used the stolen information in connection with a crime.

Finally, the law increased the maximum penalty for identity theft from three years to five. It also allowed prosecutors to aggregate all individual amounts of federal benefits stolen using fraudulent identities to ensure that such cases qualified for tougher penalties.[21]

During this session of Congress, the entertainment industry asked for help to curb online piracy. This stemmed from a case in 2003, where a federal judge in Los Angeles ruled that two major file-sharing companies—Streamcast Networks Inc. and Grokster—could not be held liable for the songs, movies, and other copyright works swapped online by their users. The entertainment companies said the practice was costing them billions of dollars in lost revenue each year. Congress responded and proposed S. 2560, which would make it illegal for any company to facilitate or intentionally induce infringement by computer users. The bill stalled, but the Senate passed S. 2237, which give prosecutors the right to file civil suits against online pirates. This was then approved by the Judiciary Committee but went no further.

Some other bills were proposed but not passed. One of these, S. 1932, was geared toward cracking down on the distribution of copies of movies or songs before they were officially released or fully marketed, either in physical form or on the Internet.[22] H.R. 2929 and S. 2145 would require software companies to get permission from consumers before installing programs capable of collecting personal information and sending it to third parties. Finally, H.R. 4661 established criminal penalties against individuals convicted of tapping into personal computers with the intent of stealing information or damaging a machine. None of these passed.[23]

2005–6: 109TH CONGRESS

Four bills, H.R. 29, H.R. 744, S. 687, and S. 1004 addressed the issue of spyware, or computer programs that access hard drives to collect personal data for third parties. The first, H.R. 29, required software companies to get the computer user's permission before installing programs that could collect personal information. Some technology companies opposed this bill, arguing that it could restrict legitimate interactive software and result in consumers being deluged with consent notices. The second bill, H.R. 744, called for fines and prison sentences for individuals convicted of tapping into personal computers with the intent of committing fraud or damaging a machine. S. 687 was much like H.R. 29 and required the consumer's permission before companies could install software that could collect sensitive personal information. The last bill, S. 1004, provided for stiffer punishment for those who installed or used spyware. The House passed two bills to limit it, and in the Senate a bill won the committee approval, but none were passed.[24]

Many other bills were proposed that were aimed at protecting US citizens from identity theft and other types of fraud. They were H.R. 3997, H.R. 4127, and H.R. 5318, none of which passed. H.R. 3997, which failed to pass, would require the Federal Trade Commission (FTC) to establish regulations to require that businesses that have personal data on customers have procedures for securing that information. In H.R. 4127, guidelines would be developed to help consumers who feel that a breach of data security has occurred. This did not pass. The last bill, H.R. 5318, would prohibit obtaining personal information from a protected computer. It also expands the crime of computer fraud. This also did not pass.

H.R. 4411 was proposed in the House to prohibit banks and credit card companies from processing payments for online gambling bets. It was intended to stop the flow of money to offshore gaming sites. A similar bill, H.R. 4777, would also prohibit businesses from accepting credit card or electronic transfers for online betting. Neither bill passed.

2007–8: 110TH CONGRESS

H.R. 5938 was a bill that would extend Secret Service Protection to former vice-presidents. But it contained provisions that would make it easier to prosecute identity theft and other cybercrimes by increasing penalties for those who sought to install malicious spyware to collect personal data. This proposal passed and became law (PL 110-696).

The Web Video Violence Act (H.R. 668) was a proposal to reduce funding for those states that do not certify that they have increased penalties for criminal defendants who were convicted of a violent crime and who then upload a video or image of the crime onto the Internet. The bill did not pass.

H.R. 719, or the Keeping the Internet Devoid of Sexual Predators Act, would authorize additional federal funds that could be used to evaluate and purchase Internet filtering programs and to train probation officers how to use the programs to supervise sex offenders. The money could also be used to hire more probation officers to supervise convicted sex offenders more effectively. The Senate version of the bill was S. 431, which became law (PL 110-400).

2009–10: 111TH CONGRESS

The Cybersecurity Act (S. 773) was legislation aimed at addressing the nation's vulnerability to attacks on critical computer infrastructure. It had to do with protecting information and information systems from unauthorized access, use, disclosure, modification, or destruction. The president would be required establish a way to identify any information system that, if disrupted, could have a debilitating impact on national security. The bill was not passed into law.

H.R. 2267, the Internet Gambling Regulation, Consumer Protection, and Enforcement Act, would give the Treasury Department the authority to establish policies regarding the licensing of online gambling organizations. It would effectively repeal an online gambling ban and instead establish rules that would oversee Internet gambling. It would allow financial institutions to process bets for licensed Internet gambling.

S. 3480 was a proposal to create the Office of Cyberspace Policy, a new office in the executive office of the president. The office would develop a national policy for increasing the security of cyberspace and oversee and coordinate all federal policies relating to cyberspace security. The bill was not passed into law.

CONCLUSION

The growth of computers and other electronic devices have given criminals many new opportunities for criminal activities. The federal government has responded with new proposals and laws that attempt to deter criminal activity. This is an area where federal involvement is justified, as it would be difficult for individual states to fight these offenders on their own. Computer criminals do not respect state boundaries, which do not really exist online. The laws on Internet crimes have become more prevalent in recent years, as more people have access to computers and society relies on them more and more. As a result, there are more crimes committed via computers that require federal action. There is no doubt that this crime will continue to flourish as our reliance upon computers continues to grow.

Chapter 17

Conclusion

The federal government's role in crime control began with the Mann Act and has grown tremendously since then. Today, presidents and the Congress make policies on all types of crime issues, from domestic violence and drunk driving to victims and juvenile offenders. The issues are sometimes debated at length, with opposing parties taking different points of view about what the proper course of action should be.

Federal anticrime policies have emerged over time, but they have all had the goal of reducing societal harm in some way. The increased involvement in crime control over the past few years, called the federalization of crime, has meant that presidents and Congress have spent more time debating issues surrounding the safety of communities. Candidates for office have also made crime concerns a viable campaign issue that can help them get elected to office.

Once in office, presidents have put crime on their agendas each year. The extent to which they have discussed crime has varied, and the topics they have chosen to discuss have varied as well. Nonetheless, presidents recognize that voters want them to show some action to reduce crime, and they act accordingly. Presidents get involved in the policy process only by suggesting new legislation and supporting that legislation in Congress. They also have veto power over congressional action, which some presidents have used to prevent some legislation from turning into law.

Elected members of Congress have also discussed crime issues more in recent years. It is sometimes the result of an event or because of increased media attention put on a concern. Like presidents, members of Congress both respond to constituent concerns at crime and, at the same time, use crime to reach out to voters. The congressional role in policy making is much more obvious than the presidential role and includes proposing bills, holding hearings, debating, and voting.

The previous parts have each shown that the presidents and Congress have passed laws concerning many types of crimes, some of which were more established and others relatively new. Some have led to great debate and disagreement, whereas others have seen more agreement. In some cases, political ideology drives the debate but, in other cases, it is disagreement between the president and Congress.

It would be easy to predict that in the future, the federal government's role in crime control will only continue to grow and expand. Not only will they continue to debate the issues listed here, but as new crimes develop, presidential candidates, those elected to serve as president, and members of Congress will choose to debate those issues and make policies to prevent them.

LAWS PASSED

THE FOLLOWING LAWS PASSED ARE LISTED IN the order as discussed in the chapters.

CHAPTER 2

Congressional Session	Bill Number	Result
1965–66	H.R. 8027	PL 89-197
	H.R. 11816/S. 798	Not Passed
1969–70	H.R. 17825	PL 91-644
	S. 4325	Not passed
	S. 4348	Not passed
	S. 4403	Not passed
	H.R. 366	PL 94-430
1989–90	S. 1970/H.R. 5269/S. 3266	PL 101-647
1991–92	H.R. 3371 (H.R. 2972)	Not passed
1993–94	H.R. 3355/H.R. 4092/S. 1607	PL 103-322
	H.R. 3398	Not passed
1995–96	H.R. 2076	Vetoed

CHAPTER 3

Congressional Session	Bill Number	Result
1949–50	H.R. 4963	PL 81-205
	H.R. 6454	PL 81-691
1951–52	S. 1203	Not passed
1953–54	S. 15	PL 83-294
1957–58	S. 2413	PL 85-310
	H.R. 110	PL 85-261
1959–60	S. 890/H.R. 6159	Not passed
1965–66	S. 1666	PL 89-372
	S. 1357	PL 89-465
1967–68	H.R. 6111	PL 90-219

Congressional Session	Bill Number	Result
1969–70	S. 2601	PL 91-358
	S. 952	PL 91-272
	S. 1461	PL 91-447
1971–72	S. 895	Not passed
1973–74	S. 271	Not passed
	S. 798	Not passed
	S. 1064	Not passed
1975–76	S. 286	Not passed
	S. 287	Not passed
	S. 537	PL 94-381
	S. 2762	Not passed
	S. 1	Not passed
1977–78	H.R. 6666	PL 95-222
	S. 1613	Not passed
	S. 11	Not passed
	H.R. 7843	PL 95-486
	H.R. 94/S. 1449	Not passed
	S. 1423	Not passed
1979–80	S. 237	PL 96-82
	S. 1477	Not passed
	S. 1873	PL 96-458
	S. 450	Not passed
	S. 423	PL 96-190
	S. 702	Not passed
	S. 2483	Not passed
	S. 2705/H.R. 7084	Not passed
1981–82	H.R. Res. 631	PL 97-377
	S. 923/H.R. 3481	PL 97-267
	S. 1554	Not passed
	H.R. 3963	Vetoed
	S. 2572	Not passed
	S. 2658	Not passed
1983–84	S. 645	Not passed
	H.R. 3336	Not passed
	S. 1762	Not passed
	S. 1763	Not passed
	S. 1764	Not passed
	H.R. Res. 648	PL 98-473
1985–86	H.R. 4801	PL 99-363
1987–88	H.R. 4807	PL 100-702
1989–90	H.R. 5316/S. 2648	PL 101-650
1991–92	H.R. 3371/S. 1241	Not passed
	H.R. 2039/S. 2870	Not passed
	S. 646	Not passed
1993–94	H.R. 3355/H.R. 4092/S. 1607	PL 103-322

Congressional Session	Bill Number	Result
1995–96	H.R. 3120	PL 104-214
	H.R. 666	Not passed
	S. 1254	PL 104-38
	H.R. 2277	Not passed
	H.R. 1802	Not passed
	H.R. 1443	Not passed
	H.R. 1445	Not passed
	S. 956	Not passed
1997–98	H.R. 2267	PL 105-119
2003–4	H.R. 5107	PL 108-405

CHAPTER 4

Congressional Session	Bill Number	Result
1957–58	H.R. 11477	Not passed
1959–60	H.R. 4957	Not passed
	H.R. 3216	Not passed
1965–66	H.R. 6964	PL 89-176
	H.R. 2263	PL 89-178
	H.R. 6097	PL 89-141
	S. 1357	PL 89-465
1967–68	S. 1760	Not passed
1969–70	H.R. 12806/S. 2600	Not passed
	S. 1872	Not passed
1971–72	H.R. 8389	Not passed
	S. 662	Not passed
	H.R. 11441	Not passed
	S. 3309	Not passed
	H.R. 193	Not passed
	H.R. 3243	Not passed
	H.R. 11797	Not passed
	H.R. 12217	Not passed
	H.R. 8414	Not passed
	H.R. 8483	Not passed
	H.R. 9486	Not passed
1973–74	H.R. 7352	PL 93-209
1975–76	H.R. 5727	PL 94-233
	S. 1	Not passed
1977–78	H.R. 9400	Not passed
1979–80	S. 114	Not passed
	H.R. 10	PL 96-247
1984–83	H.R. Res. 648	PL 98-473
	S. 1765	Not passed
	S. 1763	Not passed
1985–86	H.R. 2965	PL 99-180

Congressional Session	Bill Number	Result
1987–88	S. 1757	Not passed
	H.R. 5210	PL 100-690
	S. 32	Not passed
	S. 36	Not passed
1989–90	S. 3266	PL 101-647
1991–92	H.R. 3371/S. 1241	Not passed
1993–94	H.R. 3351	Not passed
	H.R. 3354	Not passed
	H.R. 3350	Not passed
	H.R. 3355/H.R. 4092/S. 1607	PL 103-322
1995–96	H.R. 667	Not passed
	H.R. 1533	Not passed
	H.R. 2650	Not passed
	H.R. 4039	Not passed
	S. 735	PL 104-132
	H.R. 2703	Not passed
	H.R. 729	Not passed
2003–4	H.R. 5107	PL 108-405
	S. 1435	PL 108-79

CHAPTER 5

Congressional Session	Bill Number	Result
1953–54	H.R. 3307	PL 83-76
1965–66	H.R. 9167	PL 89-793
1967–68	H.R. 14096	PL 90-639
1969–70	H.R. 18583	PL 91-513
	S. 3246	Not passed
1971–72	S. 2097	PL 92-255
	H.R. 5674	PL 92-13
1973–74	S. 1125	PL 93-282
	S. 3355	PL 93-481
	H.R. 8389	Not passed
1975–76	H.R. 13172	PL 94-303
1977–78	S. 2916	PL 95-461
	S. 3336	PL 95-537
	H.R. 5742	PL 95-137
1979–80	H.R. 2538	PL 96-350
1981–82	H.R. 3963	Vetoed
	H.R. 2173	Not passed
1983–84	S. 1787/H.R. 4028	Not passed
	H.J. Res. 648	PL 98-473
	H.R. 2173	PL 98-2360
	S. 1146	PL 98-499

Congressional Session	Bill Number	Result
1985–86	H.R. 5484	PL 99-570
1987–88	H.R. 5210	PL 100-690
	H.R. 781	PL 100-463
1989–90	H.R. 3614	PL 101-226
	H.R. 5567	PL 101-623
	H.R. 3611	PL 101-231
	S. 3266	PL 101-647
	H.R. 3630	Not passed
	H.R. 3550	Not passed
1991–92	H.R. 1724	PL 102-182
	H.R. 3057	Not passed
	H.R. 3259	PL 102-132
	S. 1306/H.R. 3698	PL 102-321
1993–94	H.R. 3350	Not passed
	H.R. 3355/H.R. 4092/S. 1607	PL 103-322
1995–96	S. 1965	PL 104-237
	H.R. 4137	PL 104-305
1997–98	H.R. 2610	Not passed
1999–2000	H.R. 1658/S. 1701	PL 106-185
	H.R. 2130	PL 106-172
	H.R. 4365	PL 106-310
	H.R. 4811	PL 106-429
2001–2	H.R. 5410/S. 2779	Not passed

CHAPTER 6

Congressional Session	Bill Number	Result
1981–82	H.R. 6170	PL 97-364
1993–94	H.R. 1385	Not passed
	S. 738	Not passed
2001–2	H.R. 4476	PL 106-346

CHAPTER 7

Congressional Session	Bill Number	Result
1979–80	H.R. 2977	Not passed
1989–90	S. 2745	Not passed
1991–92	S. 15/H.R. 1502	Not passed
	H.R. 1252	PL 102-527
1993–94	H.R. 1133	Not passed
	H.R. 3355/H.R. 4092/S. 1607	PL 103-322
1996–97	H.R. 3230	PL 104-201
1999–2000	H.R. 3244	PL 106-386

CHAPTER 8

Congressional Session	Bill Number	Result
1987–88	S. 794	PL 100-346
1989–90	H.R. 1048	PL 101-275
1991–92	H.R. 4797	Not passed
1993–94	H.R. 1152/S. 1522	Not passed
	H.R. 3355/H.R. 4092/S. 1607	PL 103-322
1999–2000	S. 2549/H.R. 4205	PL 106-616

CHAPTER 9

Congressional Session	Bill Number	Result
1971–72	S. 16	Not passed
	S. 33	Not passed
	S. 750	Not passed
	S. 1081	Not passed
	S. 946	Not passed
	S. 2087	Not passed
	S. 2426	Not passed
	S. 2748	Not passed
	H.R. 8389	Not passed
1973–74	S. 800	Not passed
1977–78	H.R. 7010	Not passed
	H.R. 4727	PL 95-540
1979–80	H.R. 4257	Not passed
	S. 190	Not passed
1981–82	S. 2420	PL 97-291
1991–92	H.R. 2092	PL 102-256
	S. 1521	Not passed
1993–94	H.R. 1237	PL 103-209
1995–96	H.R. 665	Not passed
	H.R. 2974	Not passed
1997–98	H.R. 924	PL 105-6
1999–2000	S. Res. 3	Not passed
2003–4	H.R. 5107	PL 108-405
	S.J. Res. 1	Not passed

CHAPTER 10

Congressional Session	Bill Number	Result
1945–46	H.R. 5443	Not passed
1961–62	S. 279	PL 87-274
1963–64	S. 1967	PL 88-368

Congressional Session	Bill Number	Result
1965–66	H.R. 8131	PL 89-69
1967–68	H.R. 12120	90-445
1971–72	S. 1732	PL 92-31
	H.R. 45	Not passed
	H.R. 15635	PL 92-381
	S. 2829	Not passed
	S. 3049	Not passed
1973–74	S. 821	PL 93-415
1977–78	H.R. 6111	PL 95-115
1979–80	S. 2441	PL 96-509
1983–84	H.R. Res. 648	PL 98-473
1987–88	H.R. 5210	PL 100-690
1991–92	H.R. 5194	PL 102-586
1993–94	H.R. 3354	Not passed
	H.R. 3353	Not passed
	H.R. 3351	Not passed
	H.R. 3355/H.R. 4092/S. 1607	PL 103-322
1995–96	H.R. 3565	Not passed
	S. 1952	Not passed
	H.R. 3876	Not passed
1997–98	H.R. 3/S. 10	Not passed
2001–2	H.R. 863	PL 107-273
	H.R. 1900	Not passed
	H.R. 7	Not passed

CHAPTER 11

Congressional Session	Bill Number	Result
1981–82	H.R. 6976	PL 97-292
1983–84	H.R. 3635	PL 98-292
	H.R. Res. 648	PL 98-473
1985–86	S. 140	PL 99-401
	H.R. Res. 738	PL 99-591
1989–90	S. 3266	PL 101-647
1991–92	S. 838	PL 102-295
	H.R. 1253	PL 102-528
1993–94	H.R. 324	Not passed
	H.R. 3378	PL 103-173
	H.R. 1237	PL 103-209
	H.R. 3355/H.R. 4092/S. 1607	PL 103-322
	H.R. 2974	Not passed
	H.R. 3375	Not passed
	S. 1125	Not passed
	H.R. 6	PL 103-382

Congressional Session	Bill Number	Result
1995–96	H.R. 1240	PL 104-71
	S. 919	PL 104-235
	S. 652	PL 104-104
	H.R. 2137	PL 104-145
	S. 1675/H.R. 3456	PL 104-236
1997–98	H.R. 1683	Not passed
2001–2	H.R. 5422	Not passed
	H.R. 4697	Not passed
	H.R. 4477	Not passed
	H.R. 2146	Not passed
	H.R. 1877	Not passed
2003–4	S. 151	PL 108-21

CHAPTER 12

Congressional Session	Bill Number	Result
1961–62	S. 1750	PL 87-368
1963–64	S. 1975	Not passed
	S. 2345	Not passed
1965–66	S. 1592	Not passed
1967–68	H.R. 5037	PL 90-351
	H.R. 17735	PL 90-618
1969–70	H.R. 12829	PL 91-128
	S. 849	Not passed
	H.R. 14233	Not passed
1971–72	S. 2057	Not passed
1975–76	H.R. 11193	Not passed
1981–82	S. 904	Not passed
	S. 908	Not passed
	S. 909	Not passed
	H.R. 3200	Not passed
	S. 974	Not passed
	H.R. 3963	Vetoed
	S. 907	PL 97-285
	S. 1030	Not passed
1983–84	S. 1762	Not passed
	H.R. Res. 648	PL 98-473
1985–86	H.R. 3132/S. 104	PL 99-408
	S. 49	PL 99-308
	S. 2414	PL 99-360
1987–88	H.R. 4445	PL 100-649

Congressional Session	Bill Number	Result
1989–90	S. 747	Not passed
	S. 1970	Not passed
	H.R. 4225	Not passed
	S. 3266	PL 101-647
	S. 1236	Not passed
	H.R. 467	Not passed
1991–92	H.R. 3371/S. 1241	Not passed
	H.R. 5633	Not passed
	H.R. 7	Not passed
1993–94	H.R. 1189	PL 103-55
	H.R. 3098	Not passed
	H.R. 1025	PL 103-159
	S. 1882	Not passed
	H.R. 3355/H.R. 4092/S. 1607	PL 103-322
1995–96	H.R. 125	Not passed
	H.R. 3431	Not passed
1997–98	H.R. 424	Not passed
	H.R. 624	PL 105-287
1999–2000	H.R. 1501	Not passed
	H.R. 4051	Not passed
	H.R. 1342	Not passed
	S. 735	Not passed
	S. 254	Not passed
2003–4	H.R. 1036	Not passed
	S. 1805	Not passed
2005–6	S. 397	PL 109-92

CHAPTER 13

Congressional Session	Bill Number	Result
1953–54	S. 16	Not passed
1961–62	S. 1653	PL 87-228
	S. 1656	PL 87-216
	S. 1657	PL 87-218
	H.R. 468	PL 87-368
	S. 1658	PL 87-840
	S. 1750	PL 87-342
	S. 1655	Not passed
1965–66	S. 2187	Not passed
	S. 2188	Not passed
	S. 2189	Not passed
	S. 2190	Not passed
1967–68	S. 676	PL 90-123
1969–70	S. 30	PL 91-452
1975–76	H.R. 14071	Not passed

Congressional Session	Bill Number	Result
1977–78	S. 1487	PL 95-575
1979–80	H.R. 1301	PL 96-90
1987–88	S. 555	PLL 100-497
1989–90	S. 438/H.R. 5111	Not passed
1991–92	S. 543	PL 102-242
	H.R. 1717/S. 78	Not passed
	H.R. 5334	PL 102-550
	S. 474	PL 102-559
1995–96	H.R. 497	PL 104-169
1997–98	S. 474	Not passed
2003–4	H.R. 2143/S. 627/H.R. 21	Not passed
2005–6	H.R. 4954	PL 109-347

CHAPTER 14

Congressional Session	Bill Number	Result
1953–54	S. 10	Not passed
	S. 11	Not passed
1969–70	H.R. 11032	Not passed
	S. 3220	PL 91-375
1977–78	H.R. 6693	Not passed
	H.R. 8059	Not passed
	S. 1585	PL 95-225
1983–84	H.R. 3635	PL 96-292

CHAPTER 15

Congressional Session	Bill Number	Result
1953–54	H.R. 408	Not passed
	H.R. 477	Not passed
	H.R. 3552	Not passed
1961–62	S. 1086	Not passed
	S. 1822	Not passed
	S. 1221	Not passed
	S. 1495	Not passed
1963–64	S. 1308	Not passed
1967–68	H.R. 5386	Not passed
1975–76	H.R. 12750/S. 3197	Not passed
1977–78	S. 1566/H.R. 7308	PL 95-511
1987–88	H.R. 1212	PL 100-347

CHAPTER 16

Congressional Session	Bill Number	Result
1979–80	S. 240	Not passed
1983–84	H.R. Res. 648	PL 98-473
	H.R. 5831	Not passed
	S. 32	PL 98-450
1987–88	S. 2201	PL 100-617
1991–92	S. 756	PL 102-307
	H.R. 4412	PL 102-492
1995–96	H.R. 3802	PL 104-231
	H.R. 3723	PL 104-294
	S. 483	Not passed
	H.R. 2441	Not passed
1997–98	H.R. 2265	PL 105-147
	H.R. 4151	PL 105-318
1999–2000	H.R. 4942	Not passed
	H.R. 4049	Not passed
	S. 2448	Not passed
	H.R. 3456	PL 106-160
2001–2	H.R. 1542	Not passed
2003–4	S. 877	PL 198-187
	H.R. 1731	PL 108-275
	S. 2560	Not passed
	S. 2237	Not passed
	S. 1932	Not passed
	H.R. 2929	Not passed
	S. 2145	Not passed
	H.R. 4661	Not passed
2005–6	H.R. 29	Not passed
	H.R. 744	Not passed
	S. 687	Not passed
	S. 1004	Not passed
	H.R. 3997	Not passed
	H.R. 4127	Not passed
	H.R. 5318	Not passed
	S. 3421/H.R. 5815	PL 109-461

NOTES

CHAPTER 1

1. "Barack Obama on Crime," On the Issues, accessed November 24, 2008, http://www.ontheissues.org/2008/Barack_Obama_Crime.htm.
2. Nancy E. Marion and Willard M. Oliver, *The Public Policy of Crime and Criminal Justice* (Upper Saddle River, NJ: Pearson Prentice Hall, 2006).
3. Philip B. Heymann and Mark H. Moore, "The Federal Role in Dealing with Violent Street Crime: Principles, Questions and Cautions," *Annals of the American Academy of Political and Social Science* 543 (1996, 103–15): 104. *Annals of the American Academy of Political and Social Science* is hereafter shortened to as *Annals AAPSS.*
4. Ibid., 103.
5. Franklin E. Zimring and Gordon Hawkins, "Toward a Principled Basis for Federal Criminal Legislation," *Annals AAPSS* 543 (January 1996, 15–26): 23.
6. Heymann and Moore, "Federal Role," 106.
7. Ibid.
8. Kathleen F. Brickey, "The Commerce Clause and Federalized Crime: A Tale of Two Thieves," *Annals AAPSS* 543 (1996).
9. Heymann and Moore, "Federal Role," 106.
10. PL stands for "Public Law." This is the sequential number given to all bills signed into law by a president. "Major Crime Package Cleared by Congress," *Congressional Quarterly Almanac* 40 (1984, 215–24): 218. *Congressional Quarterly Almanac* is hereafter shortened to *CQA.*
11. "Drunk Driving," *CQA* 41 (1985): 243.
12. "Hill Gets Tougher with Deadbeat Parents," *CQA* 48 (1992): 474.
13. "Lawmakers Enact $30.2 Billion Anti-Crime Bill," *CQA* 50 (1994, 273–94): 293.

CHAPTER 2

1. Harry S. Truman, "Statement and Directive by the President on Immigration to the United States of Certain Displaced Persons and Refugees in Europe. December 22, 1945," in *Public Papers of the Presidents of the United States* (Washington, DC: US Government Printing Office, 1955, 168–70), 168. *Public Papers of the Presidents of the United States* hereafter shortened to *PPPUS.*
2. Lyndon B. Johnson, "Remarks upon Signing Order Providing for the Coordination by the Attorney General of Federal Law Enforcement and Crime Prevention Programs. February 7, 1968," in *PPPUS* (Washington, DC: US Government Printing Office, 1969, 179–82), 181.
3. Johnson, "Annual Message to the Congress on the District of Columbia Budget. January 25, 1966," in *PPPUS* (Washington, DC: US Government Printing Office, 1967, 68–77), 73.
4. Johnson, "Special Message to the Congress on Crime and Law Enforcement. March 9, 1966," in *PPPUS* (Washington, DC: US Government Printing Office, 1967, 291–99), 294.
5. Johnson, "Annual Budget Message to the Congress, Fiscal Year 1967. January 24, 1966," in *PPPUS* (Washington, DC: US Government Printing Office, 1967, 47–68), 64.
6. Johnson, "Statement by the President upon Signing the Omnibus Crime Control and Safe Streets Act of 1968. June 19, 1968," in *PPPUS* (Washington, DC: US Government Printing Office, 1969, 725–28), 726.
7. Ibid.
8. Ibid.

9. Johnson, "Special Message to the Congress on Crime and Law Enforcement. March 19, 1966," in *PPPUS* (Washington, DC: US Government Printing Office, 1967, 291–99), 293–94.

10. Johnson, "Special Message to the Congress: The Nation's Capital. February 27, 1967," in *PPPUS* (Washington, DC: US Government Printing Office, 1968, 226–39), 233.

11. Johnson, "Special Message to the Congress on the District of Columbia: The Nation's First City. March 13, 1968," in *PPPUS* (Washington, DC: US Government Printing Office, 1969, 383–94), 384–85.

12. Johnson, "Remarks in Kansas City, Missouri, at the Meeting of the International Association of Chiefs of Police. September 14, 1967," in *PPPUS* (Washington, DC: US Government Printing Office, 1968, 831–36), 832.

13. "Law Enforcement Training," *Congressional Quarterly Almanac* 21 (1965), 634. *Congressional Quarterly Almanac* is hereafter shortened to *CQA*.

14. Richard M. Nixon, "Statement about Assaults on Police Officers and Directive to the Attorney General. November 1, 1970," in *PPPUS* (Washington, DC: US Government Printing Office, 1971, 384–85).

15. Nixon, "Annual Budget Message to the Congress, Fiscal Year 1972. January 29, 1971," in *PPPUS* (Washington, DC: US Government Printing Office, 1973, 80–95), 91.

16. Nixon, "Campaign Statement about Crime and Drug Abuse. October 28, 1972," in *PPPUS* (Washington, DC: US Government Printing Office, 1973, 1058–59), 1058.

17. Nixon, "Remarks about a Special Message to the Congress on Special Revenue Sharing for Law Enforcement. March 2, 1971," in *PPPUS* (Washington, DC: US Government Printing Office, 1972), 374.

18. Nixon, "Radio Address about the State of the Union Message on Law Enforcement and Drug Abuse Prevention. March 10, 1973," in *PPPUS* (Washington, DC: US Government Printing Office, 1974, 180–84), 183.

19. "Crime and Law Enforcement," *CQA* 26 (1970): 77.

20. "Assaults on Police," *CQA* 26 (1970): 568–69.

21. "Police, Firefighters Benefits," *CQA* 32 (1976): 520–21.

22. Ronald R. Reagan, "Message to the Congress Transmitting Proposed Crime Control Legislation. March 16, 1983," in *PPPUS* (Washington, DC: US Government Printing Office, 1984, 401–2), 401.

23. Reagan, "Remarks at the Annual Conference of the National Sheriff's Association in Hartford, Connecticut, June 20, 1984," in *PPPUS* (Washington, DC: US Government Printing Office, 1985, 884–88), 887.

24. Reagan, "Statement on Signing the Bill to Regulate Armor-Piercing Ammunition. August 28, 1986," in *PPPUS* (Washington, DC: US Government Printing Office, 1987), 1131–32.

25. "1990 Crime Control Act: Major Provisions," *CQA* 46 (1990): 499.

26. "Police Brutality," *CQA* 48 (1992): 334.

27. William J. Clinton, "Remarks at the Children's Town Meeting. February 20, 1993," in *PPPUS* (Washington, DC: US Government Printing Office, 1992, 146–65), 151; Clinton, "Remarks to Justice Department Employees. April 29, 1993," in *PPPUS* (Washington, DC: US Government Printing Office, 1994, 534–36), 535.

28. Clinton, "Remarks to Law Enforcement Organizations and an Exchange with Reporters. April 15, 1993," in *PPPUS* (Washington, DC: US Government Printing Office, 1994, 435–37), 436.

29. "Clinton Throws Down the Gauntlet," *CQA* 49 (1993): 85–89.

30. Clinton, "Remarks Announcing the COPS Distressed Neighborhoods Pilot Project. May 29, 1998," in *PPPUS* (Washington, DC: US Government Printing Office, 1999, 851–52), 852.

31. Clinton, "Remarks on Receiving the Abraham Lincoln Courage Award in Chicago. June 30, 1995," in *PPPUS* (Washington, DC: US Government Printing Office, 1996, 1171–75), 1173.

32. Clinton, "Remarks on Signing the Bulletproof Vest Partnership Grant Act and the Care for Police Survivors Act. June 16, 1998," in *PPPUS* (Washington, DC: US Government Printing Office, 1999), 968–70.

33. "Senate OKs Omnibus Anti-Crime Bill," *CQA* 49 (1993, 293–300): 300.

34. "Lawmakers Enact $30.2 Billion Anti-Crime Bill," *CQA* 50 (1994, 273–87): 274.

35. Ibid., 287.

36. "Tough Talk, Little Progress on GOP's Crime Agenda," *CQA* 51 (1995, 6-3–6-8): 6-3.

37. George W. Bush, "Statement on Congressional Action on Counterterrorism Legislation. October 24, 2001," in *PPPUS* (Washington, DC: US Government Printing Office, 2002), 1299.

38. Elizabeth A. Palmer and Keith Perine, "Provisions of the Anti-Terrorism Bill," *Congressional Quarterly Weekly Report*, February 2, 2002, 329.

39. "Remarks by the President at the National Peace Officers' Memorial," Barack Obama, Office of the Press Secretary, the White House, May 15, 2010, http://www.whitehouse.gov/the-press-office/remarks-president-national-peace-officers (site discontinued; accessed December 3, 2010).

40. "Obama: Arizona's New Law is 'Misguided,'" National Public Radio, April 26, 2010, http://www.npr.org/templates/story/story.php?storyId=126285583 (accessed December 3, 2010).

CHAPTER 3

1. Harry S. Truman, "Letter to the Vice President Urging Senate Action to Raise the Salaries of Federal Executives. September 26, 1949," in *Public Papers of the Presidents of the United States* (Washington, DC: US Government Printing Office, 1950), 487–88. *Public Papers of the Presidents of the United States* hereafter shortened to *PPPUS*.
2. "New Federal Judgeships," *Congressional Quarterly Almanac* 5 (1949): 572. *Congressional Quarterly Almanac* hereafter shortened to *CQA*.
3. Truman, "Federal Judges, Judgeships," *CQA* 6 (1950): 407.
4. Ibid.
5. Truman, "Federal Judgeships," *CQA* 8 (1952): 239–40.
6. Dwight D. Eisenhower, "Memorandum Convening the President's Conference on Administrative Procedure. April 29, 1953," in *PPPUS* (Washington, DC: US Government Printing Office, 1954, 219–21), 219.
7. John F. Kennedy, "Annual Budget Message to the Congress, Fiscal Year 1961. January 18, 1960," in *PPPUS* (Washington, DC: US Government Printing Office, 1962, 37–110), 105.
8. Eisenhower, "Special Message to the Congress on the Legislative Program. May 3, 1960," in *PPPUS* (Washington, DC: US Government Printing Office, 1961, 385–94), 389.
9. Eisenhower, "The President's News Conference of March 2. March 2, 1955," in *PPPUS* (Washington, DC: US Government Printing Office, 1956, 302–15), 313–14.
10. "Federal Judgeships," *CQA* 9 (1953): 332–33.
11. "Federal Judgeships," *CQA* 10 (1954): 401–2.
12. "Salaries Commission," *CQA* 10 (1954), 408–9.
13. "Federal Judges," *CQA* 14 (1958): 76.
14. "Judgeships," *CQA* 13 (1957): 689.
15. "Miscellany: Judgeships," *CQA* 15 (1959): 84.
16. "1959 Presidential Nominations," *CQA* 15 (1959, 664–71): 664.
17. Kennedy, "Letter to the President of the Senate and to the Speaker of the House Proposing Creation of Additional Federal Judgeships. February 10, 1961," in *PPPUS* (Washington, DC: US Government Printing Office, 1962, 83–84), 83.
18. Eisenhower, "Statement by the President upon Signing Bill Providing for an Increase in the Federal Judiciary. May 19, 1960," in *PPPUS* (Washington, DC: US Government Printing Office, 1961, 389–90), 389.
19. Kennedy, "Letter to the President of the Senate and to the Speaker of the House on the Need for Improving the Administration of Criminal Justice. March 8, 1963," in *PPPUS* (Washington, DC: US Government Printing Office, 1964, 244–45), 244.
20. Lyndon B. Johnson, "Remarks to the Delegates to the Second National Conference of United States Marshals. September 27, 1966," in *PPPUS* (Washington, DC: US Government Printing Office, 1967, 1081–82), 1081.
21. Kennedy, "Special Message to the Congress on Crime and Law Enforcement. March 9, 1966," in *PPPUS* (Washington, DC: US Government Printing Office, 1967, 291–99), 295.
22. Johnson, "Special Message to the Congress on Crime in America. February 6, 1967," in *PPPUS* (Washington, DC: US Government Printing Office, 1968, 134–45), 143.
23. Johnson, "Special Message to the Congress: The Nation's Capital. February 27, 1967," in *PPPUS* (Washington, DC: US Government Printing Office, 1968, 226–40), 234.
24. Johnson, "Crime and Law Enforcement," 184.
25. Johnson, "Letter to Senator Hart Expressing His Views on Pending Civil Rights Legislation. February 19, 1968," in *PPPUS* (Washington, DC: US Government Printing Office, 1969), 243.
26. Johnson, "Special Message to the Congress on Civil Rights. January 24, 1968," in *PPPUS* (Washington, DC: US Government Printing Office, 1969, 55–62), 61.
27. Johnson, "Special Message to the Congress on Crime and Law Enforcement: To Insure Public Safety. February 7, 1968," in *PPPUS* (Washington, DC: US Government Printing Office, 1969, 183–96), 184.
28. Johnson, "Letter to Senator Hart Expressing His Views on Pending Civil Rights Legislation. February 19, 1968," in *PPPUS* (Washington, DC: US Government Printing Office, 1969), 243.
29. Ibid., 194.
30. Johnson, "Special Message to the Congress on the District of Columbia: The Nation's First City. March 13, 1968," in *PPPUS* (Washington, DC: US Government Printing Office, 1969, 383–94), 386.
31. Ibid.

32. Johnson, "Remarks upon Signing Bills Relating to United States Magistrates and to Judges in the District of Columbia Cases. October 17, 1968," in *PPPUS* (Washington, DC: US Government Printing Office, 1969), 1046–47.
33. "Federal Judgeships," *CQA* 22 (1966): 575.
34. "Congress Reforms Federal Bail Procedures," *CQA* 22 (1966): 572–75.
35. "President's Crime Program," *CQA* 23 (1967): 847.
36. "Evidence Suppression." In *CQ Almanac, 1967*, 23rd ed., 08-873. Washington, DC: Congressional Quarterly, 1968. http://library.cqpress.com/cqalmanac/cqa67-1313057.
37. Richard M. Nixon, "Statement Outlining Actions and Recommendations for the District of Columbia. January 31, 1969," in *PPPUS* (Washington, DC: US Government Printing Office, 1970, 40–48), 42.
38. Nixon, "Statement on Signing Bills Relating to District Judges and Customs Courts. June 3, 1970," in *PPPUS* (Washington, DC: US Government Printing Office, 1971), 476.
39. Nixon, "Statement Outlining Actions and Recommendations," 42.
40. Nixon, "Remarks on Signing the District of Columbia Court Reform and Criminal Procedure Act of 1970. July 29, 1970," in *PPPUS* (Washington, DC: US Government Printing Office, 1971), 625–26.
41. Nixon, "Statement Outlining Actions and Recommendations," 45.
42. Nixon, "Special Message to the Congress Proposing Establishment of a Legal Services Corporation. May 5, 1971," in *PPPUS* (Washington, DC: US Government Printing Office, 1972, 618–22), 619.
43. Nixon, "Special Message to the Congress on the Administration's Legislative Program. September 11, 1970," in *PPPUS* (Washington, DC: US Government Printing Office, 1971, 719–38), 729.
44. Ibid.
45. Nixon, "Remarks in West Palm Beach, Florida. October 27, 1970," in *PPPUS* (Washington, DC: US Government Printing Office, 1971, 950–56), 954.
46. Nixon, "Campaign Statement About Crime and Drug Abuse. October 28, 1972," in *PPPUS* (Washington, DC: US Government Printing Office, 1971, 1058–59), 1058.
47. Nixon, "Remarks at the Opening Session of the National Conference on the Judiciary in Williamsburg, Virginia. March 11, 1971," in *PPPUS* (Washington, DC: US Government Printing Office, 1972, 416–23), 422.
48. "Crime and Law Enforcement," *CQA* 26 (1970): 77; "Circuit Court Executives," *CQA* 26 (1970): 556.
49. "Crime and Law Enforcement," 77.
50. "Public Defender System," *CQA* 26 (1970): 336–38.
51. "Speedy Trials," *CQA* 27 (1971): 792–93.
52. "Three-Judge Courts," *CQA* 29 (1973): 373.
53. "Pre-trial Diversion," *CQA* 29 (1973): 391.
54. "Judicial Disqualification," *CQA* 29 (1973): 391.
55. Gerald R. Ford, "Address at the Yale University Law School Sesquicentennial Convocation Dinner. April 25, 1975," in *PPPUS* (Washington, DC: US Government Printing Office, 1976, 587–94), 592.
56. Ford, "Special Message to the Congress on Crime. June 19, 1975," in *PPPUS* (Washington, DC: US Government Printing Office, 1976, 839–51), 843.
57. Ford, "Remarks at a News Briefing on the Special Message to the Congress on Crime. June 19, 1975," in *PPPUS* (Washington, DC: US Government Printing Office, 1976, 838–39), 838; Ford, "Address Before a Joint Session of the California State Legislature. September 5, 1975," in *PPPUS* (Washington, DC: US Government Printing Office, 1976, 1340–47), 1344; Ford, "Interview with Reporters in Knoxville, Tennessee, October 7, 1975," in *PPPUS* (Washington, DC: US Government Printing Office, 1976, 1609–18), 1617; Ford, "The President's News Conference of October 10, 1975. October 10, 1975," in *PPPUS* (Washington, DC: US Government Printing Office, 1976, 1657–73), 1659; Ford, "Remarks at a Federal Bar Association Dinner in Miami, Florida. February 14, 1976," in *PPPUS* (Washington, DC: US Government Printing Office, 1977, 326–32), 328.
58. Ford, "Remarks at the Sixth Circuit Judicial Conference in Mackinac Island, Michigan. July 13, 1975," in *PPPUS* (Washington, DC: US Government Printing Office, 1976, 984–88), 986.
59. Ford, "Special Message to the Congress on Crime. June 19, 1975," in *PPPUS* (Washington, DC: US Government Printing Office, 1976, 839–51), 846.
60. "Remarks at the Sixth Circuit Judicial Conference in Mackinac Island, Michigan. July 13, 1975," in *PPPUS* (Washington, DC: US Government Printing Office, 1976, 984–88), 985.
61. "Federal District Judgeships," *CQA* 32 (1976, 426–28): 426.
62. "Three Judge Courts," *CQA* 32 (1976): 411.
63. "Crime and Judiciary," *CQA* 31 (1975, 519–21): 520.
64. "Controversial Espionage, Sabotage, Insanity Defense, Death Penalty Provisions Draw Fire from Critics of S 1," *CQA* 31 (1975, 544–45): 544.

65. "Congress Revises Rules of Criminal Procedure." In *CQ Almanac, 1975*, 31st ed., 533–36. Washington, DC: Congressional Quarterly, 1976. http://library.cqpress.com/cqalmanac/cqa75-1215023.

66. Jimmy Carter, "Remarks at the 100th Anniversary Luncheon of the Los Angeles County Bar Association. May 4, 1977," in *PPPUS* (Washington, DC: US Government Printing Office, 1978, 834–41), 838.

67. Carter, "Message to the Congress on Proposed Legislation. February 27, 1979," in *PPPUS* (Washington, DC: US Government Printing Office, 1980, 342–46), 342.

68. Ibid., 343.

69. Ibid., 344.

70. "Law Enforcement/Judiciary," *CQA* 33 (1977, 26–28): 27.

71. Ibid.

72. "Law Enforcement/Judiciary," *CQA* 34 (1978, 23–25): 24.

73. "New Judgeships," *CQA* 34 (1978: 173–77): 173.

74. Ibid.

75. Ibid.

76. "Law Enforcement/Judiciary," *CQA* 33 (1977, 26–28): 27; "Law Enforcement/Judiciary," *CQA* 34 (1978, 23–25): 23.

77. "Law Enforcement/Judiciary," *CQA* 33 (1977, 26–28): 28.

78. "Judicial Tenure," *CQA* 34 (1978): 198.

79. "Law Enforcement/Judiciary," *CQA* 35 (1979, 28–30): 28; "Magistrates' Jurisdiction," *CQA* 35 (1979, 375–76): 375.

80. "Law Enforcement/Judiciary," *CQA* 35 (1979, 28–30): 29.

81. Ibid.; "Law Enforcement/Judiciary," *CQA* 36 (1980, 28–29): 28.

82. Ibid.; "Supreme Court Jurisdiction," *CQA* 35 (1979, 396–98): 396.

83. "Dispute Resolution Act," *CQA* 35 (1979, 394–96): 394.

84. "Prosecution Diversion Bill," *CQA* 35 (1979, 401–2).

85. "Criminal Code Bills Die in Both Chambers," *CQA* 36 (1980, 393–95): 395.

86. "Legal Services Corp.," *CQA* 36 (1980): 399.

87. "Pretrial Bail Program," *CQA* 36 (1980, 406–7): 406.

88. Ibid.

89. Ronald W. Reagan, "Remarks in New Orleans, Louisiana, at the Annual Meeting of the International Association of Chiefs of Police. September 28, 1981," in *PPPUS* (Washington, DC: US Government Printing Office, 1982, 839–46), 841.

90. Reagan, "Message to the Congress Transmitting Proposed Crime Control Legislation. March 16, 1983," in *PPPUS* (Washington, DC: US Government Printing Office, 1984, 401–2), 401.

91. Reagan, "Radio Address to the Nation on Proposed Crime Legislation. February 18, 1984," in *PPPUS* (Washington, DC: US Government Printing Office, 1985), 225–26.

92. Reagan, "Message to the Congress Transmitting Proposed Crime Control Legislation," 401–2; Reagan, "Remarks in New Orleans," 842; Reagan, "Radio Address to the Nation on Crime and Criminal Justice Reform. September 11, 1982," in *PPPUS* (Washington, DC: US Government Printing Office, 1983, 1136–38), 1137; Reagan, "Radio Address to the Nation on Proposed Crime Legislation, February 18, 1984," 225–26; Reagan, "Message to the Congress on America's Agenda for the Future. February 6, 1986," in *PPPUS* (Washington, DC: US Government Printing Office, 1987, 149–63), 155.

93. Reagan, "Radio Address to the Nation on Crime," 1137.

94. Reagan, "Message to the Congress Transmitting Proposed Crime Control Legislation. March 16, 1983," in *PPPUS* (Washington, DC: US Government Printing Office, 1982, 401–2), 402.

95. Reagan, "Radio Address to the Nation on Proposed Crime Legislation," 225–26.

96. Reagan, "Message to the Congress on America's Agenda for the Future. February 6, 1986," in *PPPUS* (Washington, DC: US Government Printing Office, 1987, 149–63), 155.

97. Reagan, "Radio Address to the Nation on Proposed Crime Legislation," 225–26.

98. Reagan, "Remarks in New Orleans," 842.

99. Ibid.

100. Reagan, "1988 Legislative and Administrative Message: A Union of Individuals. January 25, 1988," in *PPPUS* (Washington, DC: US Government Printing Office, 1989, 91–121), 96.

101. "Law Enforcement/Judiciary," *CQA* 37 (1981, 29–30): 30; "State, Justice, Commerce Appropriations," *CQA* 37 (1981, 364–68): 364; Nadine Cohodas, "Law Enforcement/Judiciary," *CQA* 38 (1982, 371–72): 372; "LSC Kept Alive; Reagan Board Unconfirmed," *CQA* 38 (1982, 412–13): 412.

102. Reagan, "Statement on Signing the Sentencing Act of 1987. December 7, 1987," in *PPPUS* (Washington, DC: US Government Printing Office, 1988), 1450.

103. Reagan, "Statement on Signing the Sentencing Guidelines Act of 1986. July 11, 1986," in *PPPUS* (Washington, DC: US Government Printing Office, 1987, 947–48), 947.

104. Reagan, "Remarks at a White House Briefing on Proposed Criminal Justice Reform Legislation. October 16, 1987," in *PPPUS* (Washington, DC: US Government Printing Office, 1988), 1192–94; Reagan, "Message to the Congress Transmitting Proposed Criminal Justice Reform Legislation. October 16, 1987," in *PPPUS* (Washington, DC: US Government Printing Office, 1988), 1195–96.

105. "Pretrial Services Program," *CQA* 37 (1981): 433; "Pretrial Services Program," *CQA* 38 (1982): 383.

106. "Bail Revision Measure," *CQA* 37 (1981, 433–34): 434.

107. "Law Enforcement/Judiciary," *CQA* 38 (1982, 371–72): 372.

108. "Insanity Defense Unchanged," *CQA* 38 (1982, 418–19): 419.

109. Ibid.

110. "New Appeals Court," *CQA* 39 (1983, 311–12): 312.

111. "Insanity Defense Revisions," *CQA* 39 (1983, 314–15): 314.

112. "Anti-Crime Package Stalls in Senate Again," *CQA* 39 (1983, 315–17): 316.

113. Ibid.

114. Ibid.

115. Ibid.

116. "Exclusionary Rule Change," *CQA* 40 (1984): 227–28.

117. "Major Crime Package Cleared by Congress," *CQA* 40 (1984, 215–24): 216.

118. Ibid., 215.

119. "Law/Judiciary," *CQA* 40 (1984, 25–30): 25.

120. Ibid., 216–17.

121. "Easing Court Burdens," *CQA* 44 (1988, 119–20): 120.

122. George H. W. Bush, "White House Fact Sheet on Combating Violent Crime. May 15, 1989," in *PPPUS* (Washington, DC: US Government Printing Office, 1990, 560–65), 563; G. H. W. Bush, "Message to the Congress Transmitting Proposed Legislation to Combat Violent Crime. June 15, 1989," in *PPPUS* (Washington, DC: US Government Printing Office, 1990, 738–41), 740.

123. G. H. W. Bush, "Message to the Congress Transmitting Proposed Crime Control Legislation. March 11, 1991," in *PPPUS* (Washington, DC: US Government Printing Office, 1992, 246–47), 246.

124. G. H. W. Bush, "White House Fact Sheet on Combating Violent Crime. May 15, 1989," in *PPPUS* (Washington, DC: US Government Printing Office, 1990, 560–65), 564; also in G. H. W. Bush, "Message to the Congress Transmitting Proposed Legislation to Combat Violent Crime. June 15, 1989," in *PPPUS* (Washington, DC: US Government Printing Office, 1990, 738–41), 740.

125. G. H. W. Bush, "Message to the Congress Transmitting Proposed Crime Control Legislation. March 11, 1991," in *PPPUS* (Washington, DC: US Government Printing Office, 1992, 246–47), 246.

126. "Bill Creates 85 Judgeships for Bush to Fill," *CQA* 46 (1990, 520–23): 520.

127. G. H. W. Bush, "Remarks at the National Peace Officers' Memorial Day Ceremony. May 15, 1989," in *PPPUS* (Washington, DC: US Government Printing Office, 1990, 557–60), 558; also G. H. W. Bush, "White House Fact Sheet on Combating Violent Crime. May 15, 1989," in *PPPUS* (Washington, DC: US Government Printing Office, 1990, 560–65), 563.

128. "Anti-Crime Bill Falls Victim to Partisanship," *CQA* 47 (1991, 262–70): 262.

129. "Legal Services Corporation," *CQA* 47 (1991, 295–96): 296.

130. "Legal Services Corporation Legislation Stalls," *CQA* 48 (1992, 317–18): 317.

131. "Legal Services Corporation," *CQA* 47 (1991, 295–96): 296.

132. "Remarks to the Law Enforcement Community in London, Ohio. February 15, 1994," in *PPPUS* (Washington, DC: US Government Printing Office, 1995, 257–63), 261.

133. William J. Clinton, "Interview with Larry King. June 5, 1995," in *PPPUS* (Washington, DC: US Government Printing Office, 1996, 808–18), 813.

134. Clinton, "Statement on Signing Legislation on Witness Retaliation, Witness Tampering, and Jury Tampering. October 1, 1996," in *PPPUS* (Washington, DC: US Government Printing Office, 1997), 1735.

135. "Busy Year for Legal, Judicial Issues," *CQA* 50 (1994, 298–300): 298.

136. "Lawmakers Enact $30.2 Billion Anti-Crime Bill," *CQA* 50 (1994, 273–87): 274.

137. "Crime Bill Provisions," *CQA* 50 (1994, 287–94): 290.

138. "Republicans Advance Six Anti-crime Bills," *CQA* 51 (1995): 6-4.

139. "Tough Talk, Little Progress on GOP's Crime Agenda," *CQA* 51 (1995, 6-3–6-8): 6-5.

140. "Backers Save Legal Services Agency," *CQA* 51 (1995, 6-27–6-28): 6-27.

141. "Other Legislation Related to the Legal System," *CQA* 51 (1995, 6-29–6-33): 6-32.

142. Ibid.

143. Ibid.

144. Ibid.

145. "Lawmakers Consider Other Bills Related to Law, Judiciary," *CQA* 52 (1996, 5-42–5-47): 5-46.

146. "Other Legislation Aimed at Crime Prevention," *CQA* 52 (1996, 5-38–5-42): 5-40.

147. "Federal Judicial Circuits to be Examined," *CQA* 53 (1997, 5-18–5-19): 5-18.

148. Elizabeth A. Palmer, "House Votes to Expand Federal Judges' Gun Rights, Use of Cameras in Court," *Congressional Quarterly Weekly Report*, May 27, 2000, 1277. *Congressional Quarterly Weekly Report* is hereafter shortened to *CQWR*.

149. George W. Bush, "Remarks Announcing Nomination for the Federal Judiciary. May 9, 2001," in *PPPUS* (Washington, DC: US Government Printing Office, 2002, 504–5), 504.

150. G. W. Bush, "Remarks in Blountville, Tennessee. November 2, 2002," in *PPPUS* (Washington, DC: US Government Printing Office, 2003, 1969–75), 1972; G. W. Bush, "The President's Radio Address. February 22, 2003," in *PPPUS* (Washington, DC: US Government Printing Office, 2004, 197–98), 197.

151. G. W. Bush, "Remarks on the Judicial Confirmation Process. October 30, 2002," in *PPPUS* (Washington, DC: US Government Printing Office, 2003, 1929–32), 1929–30.

152. G. W. Bush, "Remarks at a Bush-Cheney Reception in St. Louis. January 5, 2004," in *PPPUS* (Washington, DC: US Government Printing Office, 2005, 8–13), 11; G. W. Bush, "Remarks at a Bush-Cheney Reception in Palm Beach Gardens, Florida. January 8, 2004," in *PPPUS* (Washington, DC: US Government Printing Office, 2005), 28–34; G. W. Bush, "Remarks at a Bush-Cheney Reception in Knoxville. January 8, 2004," in *PPPUS* (Washington, DC: US Government Printing Office, 2005), 23–28; G. W. Bush, "Remarks at a Bush-Cheney Reception in Atlanta, Georgia. January 15, 2004," in *PPPUS* (Washington, DC: US Government Printing Office, 2005), 72–77; G. W. Bush, "Remarks at a Bush-Cheney Reception in New Orleans. January 15, 2004," in *PPPUS* (Washington, DC: US Government Printing Office, 2005), 66–71; G. W. Bush, "Remarks at a Bush-Cheney Reception in Old Greenwich, Connecticut. January 29, 2004," in *PPPUS* (Washington, DC: US Government Printing Office, 2005), 159–64.

153. G. W. Bush, "The President's Radio Address. November 2, 2002," in *PPPUS* (Washington, DC: US Government Printing Office, 2003, 1975–76), 1975.

154. G. W. Bush, "Remarks at High Point University in High Point, North Carolina. July 25, 2002," in *PPPUS* (Washington, DC: US Government Printing Office, 2003, 1287–93), 1292.

155. G. W. Bush, "Remarks at Madison Central High School in Madison, Mississippi. August 7, 2002," in *PPPUS* (Washington, DC: US Government Printing Office, 2003, 1357–64), 1361; G. W. Bush, "Remarks in Charlotte, North Carolina. October 24, 2002," in *PPPUS* (Washington, DC: US Government Printing Office, 2003, 1876–83), 1879.

156. G. W. Bush, "Remarks to the United States Attorneys Conference. November 29, 2001," in *PPPUS* (Washington, DC: US Government Printing Office, 2002, 1459–62), 1460.

157. "DNA Testing, Victims' Rights Clear," *CQA* 60 (2004, 12-8–12-10): 12-8.

158. Ibid.

159. Keith Perine, "'Heightened Tensions' Fray Judicial-Legislative Relations" *CQWR*, September 18, 2004, 2148–53.

160. Charlie Savage and Sheryl Gay Stolberg, "Obama Says Liberal Courts May Have Overreached," *New York Times*, April 29, 2010, http://www.nytimes.com/2010/04/30/us/politics/30court.html (accessed January 15, 2011).

161. David G. Savage, "Obama and Supreme Court may be on Collision Course" *Los Angeles Times*, July 6, 2010, http://articles.latimes.com/print/2010/jul/06/nation/la-na-court-roberts-obama (accessed January 15, 2011).

CHAPTER 4

1. Dwight D. Eisenhower, "Annual Budget Message to the Congress for Fiscal Year 1957. January 16, 1957," in *Public Papers of the Presidents of the United States* (Washington, DC: US Government Printing Office, 1958, 12–156), 124. *Public Papers of the Presidents of the United States* is hereafter shortened to *PPPUS*.

2. "Proposals to Set Aside Court Decisions," *Congressional Quarterly Almanac* (1958, 287–88). *Congressional Quarterly Almanac* is hereafter shortened to *CQA*.

3. "Mallory Rule," *CQA* 14 (1958, 295–97): 295.

4. "Congressional View of Supreme Court Improved in 1959," *CQA* 15 (1959, 205–8): 206.

5. Ibid.

6. Lyndon B. Johnson, "Statement by the President on Establishing the President's Commission on Law Enforcement and Administration of Justice. July 26, 1965," in *PPPUS* (Washington, DC: US Government Printing Office, 1966), 785–87.

7. Johnson, "Statement by the President Upon Signing Bills Providing Rehabilitative Techniques for Adult Offenders. September 10, 1965," in *PPPUS* (Washington, DC: US Government Printing Office, 1966), 991.

8. Johnson, "Remarks in Kansas City, Missouri, at the Meeting of the International Association of Chiefs of Police. September 14, 1967," in *PPPUS* (Washington, DC: US Government Printing Office, 1968, 831–36), 832.

9. Johnson, "Special Message to the Congress on Crime and Law Enforcement. March 9, 1966," in *PPPUS* (Washington, DC: US Government Printing Office, 1967, 291–99): 291.

10. Johnson, "Remarks to the Delegates to the Conference of State Committees on Criminal Administration. October 15, 1966," in *PPPUS* (Washington, DC: US Government Printing Office, 1967, 1206–9), 1207.

11. Johnson, "Special Message to the Congress on Crime in America. February 6, 1967," in *PPPUS* (Washington, DC: US Government Printing Office, 1968, 134–45), 137.

12. Johnson, "Special Message to the Congress: The Nation's Capital. February 27, 1967," in *PPPUS* (Washington, DC: US Government Printing Office, 1968, 226–39), 237.

13. Johnson, "Special Message to the Congress on Crime and Law Enforcement," 296.

14. Johnson, "Special Message to the Congress on Crime and Law Enforcement: 'To Insure Public Safety.' February 7, 1968," in *PPPUS* (Washington, DC: US Government Printing Office, 1969, 183–96), 189.

15. "Correctional Training," *CQA* 21 (1965): 631–32; "Prisoner Rehabilitation," *CQA* 21 (1965): 635.

16. "Correctional Training," 631.

17. "Public Health Service," *CQA* 22 (1966): 590.

18. "Manpower Training Act Amendments Passed," *CQA* 22 (1966): 841.

19. "Bail Reform Act of 1966," *CQA* 26 (1970): 212.

20. "Capital Punishment," *CQA* 24 (1968): 693.

21. Richard M. Nixon, "Statement Outlining a 13-Point Program for Reform of the Federal Corrections System. November 13, 1969," in *PPPUS* (Washington, DC: US Government Printing Office, 1970, 924–28), 927.

22. Ibid., 926.

23. Ibid., 924–28.

24. "Congress Enacts No New Programs for Crime Control," *CQA* 25 (1969, 687–88): 688; "Campaign Statement About Crime and Drug Abuse. October 28, 1972," in *PPPUS* (Washington, DC: US Government Printing Office, 1973, 1058–59), 1059.

25. Nixon, "Annual Budget Message to the Congress, Fiscal Year 1972. January 29, 1971," in *PPPUS* (Washington, DC: US Government Printing Office, 1972, 80–95), 91.

26. Nixon, "13-Point Program," 926.

27. Ibid., 927.

28. Ibid.

29. Ibid., 926.

30. Nixon, "Radio Address about the State of the Union Message on Law Enforcement and Drug Abuse Prevention. March 10, 1973," in *PPPUS* (Washington, DC: US Government Printing Office, 1974, 180–84), 181.

31. "Crime and Law Enforcement," *CQA* 26 (1970): 77.

32. "Other Major Bills," *CQA* 26 (1970): 87.

33. "Prison Improvements," *CQA* 27 (1971): 791–92.

34. "Prisoner Rehabilitation," *CQA* 28 (1972): 525.

35. "Habeas Corpus," *CQA* 28 (1972): 258–59.

36. "Parole Practices," *CQA* 28 (1972): 261–62.

37. "Pre-Trial Rehabilitation," *CQA* (1972): 598–99.

38. "Death Penalty," *CQA* 28 (1972, 259–61): 259.

39. "Criminal Law Review," *CQA* (1973): 374–76.

40. Gerald R. Ford, "Remarks to the Annual Convention of the International Association of Chiefs of Police. September 24, 1974," in *PPPUS* (Washington, DC: US Government Printing Office, 1975, 184–88), 186.

41. Ford, "Address at the Yale University Law School Sesquicentennial Convocation Dinner. April 25, 1975," in *PPPUS* (Washington, DC: US Government Printing Office, 1976, 587–94), 592.

42. Ford, "Special Message to the Congress on Crime. June 19, 1975," in *PPPUS* (Washington, DC: US Government Printing Office, 1976, 839–51), 845.

43. Ibid., 846.

44. Ibid., 843.

45. Ford, "Remarks at a Federal Bar Association Dinner in Miami, Florida. February 14, 1976," in *PPPUS* (Washington, DC: US Government Printing Office, 1977, 326–32), 327; Ford, "Remarks and a Question-and-Answer Session in Wilkesboro, North Carolina. March 13, 1976," in *PPPUS* (Washington, DC: US Government Printing Office, 1977, 698–708), 707; Ford, "Remarks in Anaheim at the Annual Convention of the California Peace Officers Association. May 24, 1976," in *PPPUS* (Washington, DC: US Government Printing Office, 1977, 1675–79), 1676.

46. "Parole Reorganization," *CQA* 31 (1975): 540–41.

47. "State-Justice Funds," *CQA* 32 (1976, 717–24): 720.

48. "Controversial Espionage, Sabotage, Insanity, Death Penalty Provisions Draw Fire from Critics of S 1," *CQA* (1975, 544–45): 545.

49. James Carter, "Statement on Signing HR 10 Into Law. May 23, 1980," in *PPPUS* (Washington, DC: US Government Printing Office, 1981, 965–66): 965.

50. "Law Enforcement/Judiciary," *CQA* 34 (1978, 23–25): 24; "Rights of Institutionalized," *CQA* 34 (1978): 206–9.

51. "Senate-Passed Criminal Code Dies in House," *CQA* 34 (1978, 165–73): 172.

52. Ibid.

53. "Labor-HHS-Education Funds," *CQA* 36 (1980, 222–27): 223.

54. "Criminal Code Bill Dies in Both Chambers," *CQA* 36 (1980, 393–95): 395.

55. "Senate Judiciary Reports Criminal Code Bill," *CQA* 35 (1979, 363–69): 368.

56. "Federal Death Penalty," *CQA* 35 (1979): 369.

57. "Federal Death Penalty," *CQA* 37(1981, 419–20): 419.

58. "Rights of Institutionalized," *CQA* 35 (1979, 402–4): 403; "Law Enforcement/Judiciary," *CQA* 36 (1980, 28–29): 29.

59. "Rights of the Institutionalized Bill Cleared," *CQA* 36 (1980): 383–84.

60. Ronald R. Reagan, "Remarks Announcing Federal Initiatives against Drug Trafficking and Organized Crime. October 14, 1982," in *PPPUS* (Washington, DC: US Government Printing Office, 1983, 1313–17), 1316.

61. Reagan, "1988 Legislative and Administrative Message: A Union of Individuals. January 25, 1988," in *PPPUS* (Washington, DC: US Government Printing Office, 1989, 91–121), 98.

62. Reagan, "Message to the Congress on America's Agenda for the Future. February 6, 1986," in *PPPUS* (Washington, DC: US Government Printing Office, 1987, 149–63), 155.

63. Reagan, "1988 Legislative and Administrative Message," 96.

64. "Major Crime Package Cleared by Congress," *CQA* 40 (1984): 215–25.

65. "Anti-Crime Package Stalls in Senate Again," *CQA* 39 (1983, 315–17): 317.

66. "Senate Death Penalty Bill," *CQA* 40 (1984): 227.

67. Ibid.

68. "Abortion Amendments," *CQA* 41 (1985): 248–49.

69. Ibid.

70. Ibid.

71. "Legislative Summary: Law/Judiciary," *CQA* 44 (1988, 25–27): 25.

72. "Crime Bills Move Ahead With Partisan Push," *CQA* 45 (1989, 259–60): 259.

73. "Death Penalty Measures Advance in the Senate," *CQA* (1989, 260–62): 261.

74. Ibid.

75. George H. W. Bush, "Remarks at the National Peace Officers' Memorial Day Ceremony. May 15, 1989," in *PPPUS* (Washington, DC: US Government Printing Office, 1990, 557–60), 558; G. H. W. Bush, "White House Fact Sheet on Combating Violent Crime. May 15, 1989," in *PPPUS* (Washington, DC: US Government Printing Office, 1990, 560–65), 564.

76. Ibid.

77. "Crime Bills Move Ahead with Partisan Push," *CQA* 45 (1989, 259–60).

78. G. H. W. Bush, "Remarks to Drug Enforcement Administration Officers in New York, New York. March 9, 1989," in *PPPUS* (Washington, DC: US Government Printing Office, 1990, 198–201), 199.

79. G. H. W. Bush, "White House Fact Sheet on Combating Violent Crime. May 15, 1989," in *PPPUS* (Washington, DC: US Government Printing Office, 1990, 560–68), 561.

80. G. H. W. Bush, "Message to the Congress Transmitting Proposed Legislation to Combat Violent Crime. June 15, 1989," in *PPPUS* (Washington, DC: US Government Printing Office, 1990, 738–41), 739.

81. G. H. W. Bush, "Remarks at the National Peace Officers' Memorial Day Ceremony. May 15, 1989," in *PPPUS* (Washington, DC: US Government Printing Office, 1990, 557–60), 558.

82. G. H. W. Bush, "Message to the Congress Transmitting Proposed Crime Control Legislation. March 11, 1991," in *PPPUS* (Washington, DC: US Government Printing Office, 1992, 246–47), 246.

83. "1990 Crime Control Act: Major Provisions," *CQA* 46 (1990): 499.

84. "Anti-Crime Bill Falls Victim to Partisanship," *CQA* 47 (1991, 262–65): 262; "No Compromise Forged on Crime Bill," *CQA* 48 (1992, 311–13): 311.

85. "Interview with Larry King. January 20, 1994," in *PPPUS* (Washington, DC: US Government Printing Office, 1995, 106–16), 113.

86. Ibid.

87. William J. Clinton, "Remarks and an Exchange with Reporters on Anticrime Legislation. August 11, 1994," in *PPPUS* (Washington, DC: US Government Printing Office, 1995, 1460–62), 1461.

88. Clinton, "Letter to Members of the Senate on Anticrime Legislation. August 22, 1994," in *PPPUS* (Washington, DC: US Government Printing Office, 1995, 1490–91), 1491.

89. Clinton, "Remarks Accepting the Presidential Nominations at the Democratic National Convention in Chicago. August 29, 1996," in *PPPUS* (Washington, DC: US Government Printing Office, 1997, 1409–17), 1414.

90. Clinton, "The President's Radio Address. March 1, 1997," in *PPPUS* (Washington, DC: US Government Printing Office, 1998), 225–26.

91. Clinton, "Remarks on Ending Drug Use and Availability for Offenders and an Exchange with Reporters, January 12, 1998," in *PPPUS* (Washington, DC: US Government Printing Office, 1999, 38–40), 38.

92. Clinton, "Remarks Announcing the Anticrime Initiative and an Exchange with Reporters. August 11, 1993," in *PPPUS* (Washington, DC: US Government Printing Office, 1994, 1360–63), 1362.

93. Clinton, "Remarks to the Law Enforcement Community in London, Ohio. February 15, 1994," in *PPPUS* (Washington, DC: US Government Printing Office, 1995, 257–63), 260.

94. Clinton, "The President's Radio Address and an Exchange with Reporters. July 27, 1996," in *PPPUS* (Washington, DC: US Government Printing Office, 1997, 1204–6), 1205.

95. "Lawmakers Enact $30.2 Billion Anti-Crime Bill," *CQA* 50 (1994, 273–87): 274.

96. Ibid.

97. "Lawmakers Enact $30.2 Billion Anti-Crime Bill," 274.

98. "House Republicans Advance Six Anti-Crime Bills," *CQA* 51 (1995): 6-4.

99. "Other Legislation Related to the Legal System," *CQA* 51 (1995, 6-29–6-33): 6-31.

100. "Other Legislation Aimed at Crime Prevention," *CQA* 52 (1996, 5-38–5-42): 5-42.

101. "Lawmakers Consider Other Bills Related to Law, Judiciary," *CQA* 52 (1996, 5-42–5-47): 5-45.

102. "Tough Talk, Little Progress on GOP's Crime Agenda," *CQA* 51 (1995: 6-3–6-8): 6-3.

103. "House Key Votes: Death-Row Appeals," *CQA* 52 (1996, C-37).

104. "House Republicans Advance Six Anti-Crime Bills," 6-4.

105. George W. Bush, "Remarks at the White House Conference on Faith-Based and Community Initiatives in Los Angeles, California. March 3, 2004," in *PPPUS* (Washington, DC: US Government Printing Office, 2005), 297–304.

106. G. W. Bush, "Inaugural Address. January 20, 2001," in *PPPUS* (Washington, DC: US Government Printing Office, 2002, 1–3), 2.

107. G. W. Bush, "Remarks at a Bush-Cheney Reception in Knoxville. January 8, 2004," in *PPPUS* (Washington, DC: US Government Printing Office, 2005, 23–28).

108. G. W. Bush, "Remarks on the Anniversary of the USA Freedom Corps. January 30, 2003," in *PPPUS* (Washington, DC: US Government Printing Office, 2004, 102–7), 105.

109. G. W. Bush, "Faith-Based and Community Initiatives," 303.

110. G. W. Bush, "Anniversary of the USA Freedom Corps," 105.

111. G. W. Bush, "Remarks Announcing the Nomination of John P. Walters to be Director of the Office of National Drug Control Policy. May 10, 2001," in *PPPUS* (Washington, DC: US Government Printing Office, 2002, 506–9), 508.

112. G. W. Bush, "Statement on Signing the Prison Rape Elimination Act of 2003. September 4, 2004," in *PPPUS* (Washington, DC: US Government Printing Office, 2005), 1091.

113. "DNA Testing, Victims' Rights Clear," *CQA* 60 (2004, 12-8–12-10): 12-8.

114. "McCain, Obama disagree with Child Rape Ruling," *Associated Press*, June 26, 2008, http://msnbc.msn.com/id/25379989/ns/politics-decision_08 (site discontinued; accessed December 3, 2010); Sara Kugler, "Obama Criticizes Supreme Court Death Penalty Ruling," June 26, 2008, http://www.nyun.com/national/obama-criticizes-supreme-court-death-penalty/80761 (accessed December 3, 2010).

115. Pat Towell, "Defense Bill Wins Solid House Passage: Side Issues Delay Senate Action," *Congressional Quarterly Weekly Report*, September 29, 2001, 2278.

CHAPTER 5

1. Harry S. Truman, "Letter to the Chairman, Senate Committee on Finance, in Support of a Narcotics Control Bill. August 24, 1951," in *Public Papers of the Presidents of the United States* (Washington, DC: US Government Printing Office, 1952), 486. *Public Papers of the Presidents of the United States* is hereafter shortened to *PPPUS*.

2. Dwight D. Eisenhower, "Statement by the President upon Signing Bill Providing for the Treatment of Narcotics Users in the District of Columbia. June 24, 1953," in *PPPUS* (Washington, DC: US Government Printing Office, 1954), 448–49.

3. Eisenhower, "Annual Message to the Congress on the State of the Union. January 6, 1955," in *PPPUS* (Washington, DC: US Government Printing Office, 1956, 7–30), 25.

4. John F. Kennedy, "Statement by the President Announcing a Forthcoming White House Conference on Narcotics. May 29, 1962," in *PPPUS* (Washington, DC: US Government Printing Office, 1963), 443–44.

5. "Narcotic Addict Act Marks Change in Policy," *Congressional Quarterly Almanac* 22 (1966, 317–20). *Congressional Quarterly Almanac* is hereafter shortened to *CQA*.

6. Lyndon B. Johnson, "Special Message to the Congress on Crime in America. February 6, 1967," in *PPPUS* (Washington, DC: US Government Printing Office, 1968), 134–45.

7. Johnson, "Remarks at the Signing of the Drug Abuse Control Amendments Bill. July 15, 1965," in *PPPUS* (Washington, DC: US Government Printing Office, 1966, 754–55), 754.

8. Johnson, "Special Message to the Congress on Law Enforcement and the Administration of Justice. March 8, 1965," in *PPPUS* (Washington, DC: US Government Printing Office, 1966, 263–71), 266.

9. Johnson, "Special Message to the Congress on Crime and Law Enforcement. March 9, 1966," in *PPPUS* (Washington, DC: US Government Printing Office, 1967, 291–99), 296.

10. Johnson, "Statement by the President upon Signing Bill Relating to Traffic in or Possession of Drugs such as LSD. October 25, 1968," in *PPPUS* (Washington, DC: US Government Printing Office, 1969), 1070–71.

11. Johnson, "Special Message to the Congress on Crime and Law Enforcement: "To Insure Public Safety. February 7, 1968," in *PPPUS* (Washington, DC: US Government Printing Office, 1969, 183–96), 190.

12. Ibid., 191.

13. Johnson, "Special Message to the Congress Transmitting Reorganization Plan I of 1968 Relating to Narcotics and Drug Abuse Control. February 7, 1968," in *PPPUS* (Washington, DC: US Government Printing Office, 1969, 197–98), 197.

14. "Major Anticrime Bills Approved as Violence Increases," *CQA* 24 (1968, 116–18): 116.

15. "Budget Fiscal Year 1973, January 24, 1972," in *PPPUS* (Washington, DC: US Government Printing Office, 1974, 78–99), 89.

16. Richard M. Nixon, "Remarks during a Visit to New York City to Review Drug Abuse Law Enforcement Activities. March 20, 1972," in *PPPUS* (Washington, DC: US Government Printing Office, 1973, 449–50), 449.

17. Ibid.

18. Nixon, "Special Message to the Congress on Drug Abuse Prevention and Control. June 17, 1971," in *PPPUS* (Washington, DC: US Government Printing Office, 1972, 739–49), 747.

19. Nixon, "Remarks to Athletes Attending a White House Sponsored Conference on Drug Abuse. February 3, 1972," in *PPPUS* (Washington, DC: US Government Printing Office, 1973, 144–47), 146.

20. Nixon, "Annual Budget Message to the Congress Fiscal Year 1971. February 2, 1970," in *PPPUS* (Washington, DC: US Government Printing Office, 1971, 46–68), 65.

21. Nixon, "Statement Announcing an Expanded Federal Program to Combat Drug Abuse. March 11, 1970," in *PPPUS* (Washington, DC: US Government Printing Office, 1971), 256–57.

22. Nixon, "Special Message to the Congress on Drug Abuse Prevention and Control. June 17, 1971," in *PPPUS* (Washington, DC: US Government Printing Office, 1972, 739–49), 741.

23. Nixon, "Annual Budget Message to the Congress, Fiscal Year 1972. January 29, 1971," in *PPPUS* (Washington, DC: US Government Printing Office, 1972, 80–95), 91.

24. Nixon, "Second Annual Report to the Congress on US Foreign Policy. February 25, 1971," in *PPPUS* (Washington, DC: US Government Printing Office, 1972, 219–345), 335.

25. Nixon, "Drug Abuse Prevention and Control," 747.

26. Nixon, "Campaign Statement about Crime and Drug Abuse. October 28, 1972," in *PPPUS* (Washington, DC: US Government Printing Office, 1973, 1058–59), 1059.

27. Nixon, "Memorandum Establishing the Cabinet Committee on International Narcotics Control. September 7, 1971," in *PPPUS* (Washington, DC: US Government Printing Office, 1972, 937–38), 937.

28. Nixon, "Radio Address about the State of the Union Message on Law Enforcement and Drug Abuse Prevention. March 10, 1973," in *PPPUS* (Washington, DC: US Government Printing Office, 1974, 180–84), 181.

29. Nixon, "Drug Abuse Prevention and Control," 745.

30. Nixon, 743.

31. Nixon, "Campaign Statement about Crime and Drug Abuse. October 28, 1972," in *PPPUS* (Washington, DC: US Government Printing Office, 1973, 1058–59), 1058.

32. Ibid., 1059.

33. Nixon, "Radio Address," 181.

34. Nixon, "The President's News Conference of March 15, 1973. March 13, 1973," in *PPPUS* (Washington, DC: US Government Printing Office, 1974, 202–13), 209.

35. Nixon, "Special Message to the Congress on National Legislative Goals. September 10, 1973," in *PPPUS* (Washington, DC: US Government Printing Office, 1974, 761–86), 781.

36. Gerald R. Ford, "Special Message to the Congress Proposing Legislation to Control Drug Trafficking. February 21, 1974," in *PPPUS* (Washington, DC: US Government Printing Office, 1975, 192–94), 193.

37. Nixon, "Special Message to the Congress on Control of Narcotics and Dangerous Drugs. July 14, 1969," in *PPPUS* (Washington, DC: US Government Printing Office, 1970), 513–18.

38. Nixon, "Drug Abuse Prevention and Control," 743.

39. Ibid., 747.

40. Nixon, "Special Message to the Congress on Legislative Reform. October 13, 1969," in *PPPUS* (Washington, DC: US Government Printing Office, 1970, 788–96), 796.

41. Nixon, "Drug Abuse Prevention and Control," 746.

42. Ibid., 746.

43. Nixon, "Special Message to the Congress on the Administration's Legislative Program. September 11, 1970," in *PPPUS* (Washington, DC: US Government Printing Office, 1971, 719–38), 728.

44. Nixon, "Remarks on Signing the Comprehensive Drug Abuse Prevention and Control Act of 1970. October 27, 1970," in *PPPUS* (Washington, DC: US Government Printing Office, 1971), 948–49.

45. Nixon, "Drug Abuse Prevention and Control," 741–42.

46. Nixon, "Statement on Establishing the Office for Drug Abuse Law Enforcement. January 28, 1972," in *PPPUS* (Washington, DC: US Government Printing Office, 1973, 115–18), 115.

47. Nixon, "Message to the Congress Transmitting Reorganization Plan 2 of 1973 Establishing the Drug Enforcement Administration. March 28, 1973," in *PPPUS* (Washington, DC: US Government Printing Office, 1974, 228–33), 228.

48. Nixon, "Statement about the Drug Abuse Office and Treatment Act of 1972. March 21, 1972," in *PPPUS* (Washington, DC: US Government Printing Office, 1973, 454–57), 454.

49. Nixon, "Drug Abuse Prevention and Control," 746.

50. Nixon, "Proclamation 4080, Drug Abuse Prevention Week, 1971. September 17, 1971," in *PPPUS* (Washington, DC: US Government Printing Office, 1972), 959–60.

51. "Crime and Law Enforcement," *CQA* 25 (1969, 83–84): 83.

52. "Crime and Law Enforcement," *CQA* 26 (1970): 77; "Four Major Crime Bills Cleared 91st Congress," *CQA* 26 (1970): 125–26.

53. "Heroin Addiction," *CQA* 27 (1971): 576.

54. "Alcoholism Programs," *CQA* 29 (1973): 317.

55. "Congress Repeals 'No-Knock' Laws," *CQA* 30 (1974): 273–75.

56. Gerald Ford, "Remarks at the Irving Bar Association Law Day Dinner in Irving, Texas. April 9, 1976," in *PPPUS* (Washington, DC: US Government Printing Office, 1977, 1057–63), 1059.

57. Ford, "Special Message to the Congress on Crime. June 19, 1975," in *PPPUS* (Washington, DC: US Government Printing Office, 1976, 839–51), 849.

58. Ford, "Special Message to the Congress on Drug Abuse. April 27, 1976," in *PPPUS* (Washington, DC: US Government Printing Office, 1977, 1218–24), 1222.

59. Ibid, 1222–23.

60. Ford, "Remarks at a Federal Bar Association Dinner in Miami, Florida. February 14, 1976," in *PPPUS* (Washington, DC: US Government Printing Office, 1977, 326–32), 330; Ford, "Statement on Drug Abuse. February 23, 1976," in *PPPUS* (Washington, DC: US Government Printing Office, 1977), 422.

61. Ford, "On Crime," 850.

62. Ford, "On Drug Abuse," 1220.

63. Ibid., 1220.

64. Ibid., 1221.

65. Ibid.

66. Ford, "Dinner in Miami, Florida," 330.

67. Ford, "On Drug Abuse," 1221.

68. Ford, "Statement on Drug Abuse. February 23, 1976," in *PPPUS* (Washington, DC: US Government Printing Office, 1977), 422; Ibid., "Remarks at the Irving Bar Association Law Day Dinner in Irving, Texas. April 9, 1976," in *PPPUS* (Washington, DC: US Government Printing Office, 1977, 1057–63), 1061.

69. James Carter, "Strategy Council: Remarks to Members of the Council. November 7, 1977," in *PPPUS* (Washington, DC: US Government Printing Office, 1978, 1976–77), 1976.

70. "Senate-Passed Criminal Code Dies in House," *CQA* 34 (1978, 165–73): 171.

71. "Drug Abuse Programs," *CQA* 34 (1978): 209.

72. "Drug Loophole," *CQA* (1979): 401; "Drug Loophole Plugged," *CQA* (1980): 392.

73. Ronald R. Reagan, "Radio Address to the Nation on Federal Drug Policy. October 2, 1982," in *PPPUS* (Washington, DC: US Government Printing Office, 1983, 1252–53), 1253.

74. Reagan, "Remarks Announcing the Campaign Against Drug Abuse and a Question-and-Answer Session with Reporters. August 4, 1986," in *PPPUS* (Washington, DC: US Government Printing Office, 1987, 1045–50), 1046.

75. Reagan, "Campaign Against Drug Abuse," 1047; Ibid., "Address to the Nation on the Campaign Against Drug Abuse. September 1, 1986," in *PPPUS* (Washington, DC: US Government Printing Office, 1987, 1178–82), 1180.

76. Reagan, "1988 Legislative and Administrative Message: A Union of Individuals. January 25, 1988," in *PPPUS* (Washington, DC: US Government Printing Office, 1989, 91–121), 98.

77. Reagan, "Remarks at a White House Briefing for Service Organization Representatives on Drug Abuse. July 10, 1986," in *PPPUS* (Washington, DC: US Government Printing Office, 1987, 1022–24), 1023.

78. Reagan, "Federal Drug Policy," 1253.

79. Reagan, "Question-and-Answer Session Following a White House Luncheon for Editors and Broadcasters from Southeastern States. April 16, 1982," in *PPPUS* (Washington, DC: US Government Printing Office, 1983, 438–86), 484.

80. Reagan, "Federal Drug Policy," 1252.

81. Reagan, "Radio Address to the Nation on Relations with Mexico and Canada. January 4, 1986," in *PPPUS* (Washington, DC: US Government Printing Office, 1987, 9–10), 9.

82. Reagan, "Statement by Principal Deputy Press Secretary Speaks on Illegal Drug Trafficking Between Mexico and the United States. May 30, 1986," in *PPPUS* (Washington, DC: US Government Printing Office, 1987, 696), 696.

83. Reagan, "Radio Address to the Nation on the President's Trip to Indonesia and Japan. April 29, 1986," in *PPPUS* (Washington, DC: US Government Printing Office, 1987, 526–27), 527.

84. Reagan, "Remarks at a White House Briefing for the Public-Private Partnerships Conference. September 11, 1986," in *PPPUS* (Washington, DC: US Government Printing Office, 1987, 1168–69), 1169.

85. Reagan, "Remarks in New Orleans, Louisiana, at the Annual Meeting of the International Association of Chiefs of Police. September 28, 1981," in *PPPUS* (Washington, DC: US Government Printing Office, 1982, 839–46), 842.

86. Reagan, "Federal Drug Policy," 1252.

87. Reagan, "Remarks in New Orleans, Louisiana," 842.

88. Reagan, "Announcement of the Establishment of the National Narcotics Border Interdiction System. March 23, 1983," in *PPPUS* (Washington, DC: US Government Printing Office, 1984), 436.

89. Reagan, "Radio Address to the Nation on Proposed Crime Legislation. February 18, 1984," in *PPPUS* (Washington, DC: US Government Printing Office, 1985, 225–26), 225.

90. Ibid.

91. Reagan, "Radio Address to the Nation on Crime and Criminal Justice Reform. September 11, 1982," in *PPPUS* (Washington, DC: US Government Printing Office, 1983, 1136–38), 1137.

92. Reagan, "Federal Drug Policy," 1252.

93. Reagan, "Message to the Congress Transmitting Proposed Crime Control Legislation. March 16, 1983," in *PPPUS* (Washington, DC: US Government Printing Office, 1984, 401–2), 402.

94. Reagan, "Remarks and a Question-and-Answer Session with Elected Republican Women Officials. January 13, 1984," in *PPPUS* (Washington, DC: US Government Printing Office, 1985, 32–37), 36; Reagan, "Radio Address to the Nation on Proposed Crime Legislation. February 18, 1984," in *PPPUS* (Washington, DC: US Government Printing Office, 1985, 225–26), 225.

95. Reagan, "Remarks and a Question-and-Answer Session with Elected Republican Women Officials. January 13, 1984," in *PPPUS* (Washington, DC: US Government Printing Office, 1985, 32–37), 36.

96. Reagan, "The President's News Conference. March 6, 1981," in *PPPUS* (Washington, DC: US Government Printing Office, 1982, 205–12): 210.

97. Reagan, "Statement by Principal Deputy Press Secretary Speaks on Efforts to Eradicate Drug Abuse. July 20, 1986," in *PPPUS* (Washington, DC: US Government Printing Office, 1987), 1024–25; Ibid., "Interview with Richard M. Smith, Morton M. Kondracke, Margaret Garrard Warner, and Elaine Shannon of *Newsweek* on the Campaign Against Drug Abuse. August 1, 1986," in *PPPUS* (Washington, DC: US Government Printing Office, 1987), 1038–45.

98. Reagan, "Remarks on Signing the National Drug Abuse Education Week Proclamation. November 1, 1983," in *PPPUS* (Washington, DC: US Government Printing Office, 1984, 1526–27), 1527.

99. Reagan, "Remarks on Signing the National Drug Abuse Education and Prevention Week Proclamation. September 21, 1984," in *PPPUS* (Washington, DC: US Government Printing Office, 1985, 1346–47), 1346.

100. Reagan, "Remarks on Signing the Just Say No to Drugs Week Proclamation. May 20, 1986," in *PPPUS* (Washington, DC: US Government Printing Office, 1987), 629–30.

101. Reagan, "Remarks at a White House Briefing for Service Organization Representatives on Drug Abuse. July 10, 1986," in *PPPUS* (Washington, DC: US Government Printing Office, 1987, 1022–24), 1022.

102. Reagan, "Remarks on Signing Executive Order 12368, Concerning Federal Drug Abuse Policy Functions. June 24, 1982," in *PPPUS* (Washington, DC: US Government Printing Office, 1983), 813.

103. Reagan, "Service Organization Representatives," 1022.

104. Reagan, "Remarks Announcing the Campaign Against Drug Abuse and a Question-and-Answer Session with Reporters. August 4, 1986," in *PPPUS* (Washington, DC: US Government Printing Office, 1987, 1045–50), 1046.

105. Reagan, "Statement on Signing the Aviation Drug-Trafficking Control Act. October 19, 1984," in *PPPUS* (Washington, DC: US Government Printing Office, 1985), 1579.

106. Reagan, "Service Organization Representatives," 1023.

107. Reagan, "Remarks on Signing an Executive Order and a Message to Congress Transmitting Proposed Legislation to Combat Drug Abuse and Trafficking. September 15, 1986," in *PPPUS* (Washington, DC: US Government Printing Office, 1987), 1182–83; Reagan, "Executive Order 12564—Drug Free Federal Workplace. September 15, 1986," in *PPPUS* (Washington, DC: US Government Printing Office, 1987), 1183–87.

108. Reagan, "Message to the Congress Transmitting Proposed Legislation to Combat Drug Abuse and Trafficking. September 15, 1986," in *PPPUS* (Washington, DC: US Government Printing Office, 1987), 1187–89.

109. Reagan, "Remarks on Signing the Anti–Drug Abuse Act of 1986. October 27, 1986," in *PPPUS* (Washington, DC: US Government Printing Office, 1987), 1447–48.

110. Reagan, "Executive Order 12590—National Drug Policy Board, March 26, 1987," in *PPPUS* (Washington, DC: US Government Printing Office, 1973), 293–95.

111. Reagan, "Remarks on Signing the Executive Order Establishing the White House Conference for a Drug Free America. May 5, 1987," in *PPPUS* (Washington, DC: US Government Printing Office, 1999, 466–67; Reagan, "Executive Order 12595—White House Conference for a Drug Free America. May 5, 1987," in *PPPUS* (Washington, DC: US Government Printing Office, 1988), 467–69.

112. "Drug Offense Penalties," *CQA* 38 (1982): 420.

113. "Law Enforcement/Judiciary," *CQA* 38 (1982, 21–22): 21.

114. "Drug Treatment Program," *CQA* 39 (1983): 314.

115. "Other Bills," *CQA* 39 (1983): 317.

116. "Law/Judiciary," *CQA* 40 (1984): 25–26.

117. "Major Crime Package Cleared by Congress," *CQA* 41 (1984, 215–24): 215.

118. Ibid.

119. "Aviation Drug Trafficking," *CQA* 41 (1984): 226.

120. "Other Drug Initiatives of the 1980s," *CQA* 45 (1989): 255.

121. "Education Bill Passes Both Chambers," *CQA* 43 (1987): 525.

122. "Law/Judiciary," *CQA* 44 (1988, 25–27): 25.

123. "More Anti-Drug Bills Cleared in 1989," *CQA* 45 (1989: 252–58): 256.

124. Ibid.

125. George H. W. Bush, "Interview with Gerald Boyd of the *New York Times* and Katherine Lewis of the *Houston Post*. January 25, 1989," in *PPPUS* (Washington, DC: US Government Printing Office, 1990, 13–15), 13–14.

126. G. H. W. Bush, "Address on Administration Goals Before a Joint Session of Congress. February 9, 1989," in *PPPUS* (Washington, DC: US Government Printing Office, 1990, 74–78), 77.

127. G. H. W. Bush, "Remarks at the Annual Conference of the Veterans Of Foreign Wars. March 6, 1989," in *PPPUS* (Washington, DC: US Government Printing Office, 1990, 172–76), 175.

128. G. H. W. Bush, "Remarks to Members of the Business and Industry Association of New Hampshire in Manchester. February 13, 1989," in *PPPUS* (Washington, DC: US Government Printing Office, 1990, 84–87), 86.

129. G. H. W. Bush, "Remarks to Members of the National Association of Attorneys General. March 13, 1989," in *PPPUS* (Washington, DC: US Government Printing Office, 1990, 221–23), 222.

130. G. H. W. Bush, "Remarks to the National Legislative Conference of the Independent Insurance Agents of America. March 14, 1989," in *PPPUS* (Washington, DC: US Government Printing Office, 1990, 233–37), 236.

131. G. H. W. Bush, "Address to the Nation on the National Drug Control Strategy. September 5, 1989," in *PPPUS* (Washington, DC: US Government Printing Office, 1990), 1136–40.

132. G. H. W. Bush, "Business and Industry Association," 86.

133. Ibid.

134. G. H. W. Bush, "Remarks at a Luncheon Hosted by the Forum Club in Houston, Texas. March 16, 1989," in *PPPUS* (Washington, DC: US Government Printing Office, 1990, 246–52), 247.

135. G. H. W. Bush, "Remarks on Signing the Executive Order Creating the President's Drug Advisory Council. November 13, 1989," in *PPPUS* (Washington, DC: US Government Printing Office, 1990), 1505.

136. G. H. W. Bush, "Remarks to the Law Enforcement Community in Wilmington, Delaware. March 22, 1989," in *PPPUS* (Washington, DC: US Government Printing Office, 1990, 295–98), 297.

137. G. H. W. Bush, "Remarks to the National Association of Manufacturers. March 23, 1989," in *PPPUS* (Washington, DC: US Government Printing Office, 1990, 301–4), 304.

138. G. H. W. Bush, "Remarks at the Presentation Ceremony for the National Teacher of the Year Award. April 5, 1989," in *PPPUS* (Washington, DC: US Government Printing Office, 1990, 362–64), 363.

139. G. H. W. Bush, "Paris Economic Summit: Economic Declaration. July 16, 1989," in *PPPUS* (Washington, DC: US Government Printing Office, 1990, 961–69), 968.

140. G. H. W. Bush, "The President's News Conference in Paris. July 16, 1989," in *PPPUS* (Washington, DC: US Government Printing Office, 1990, 969–76), 970.

141. G. H. W. Bush, "The President's News Conference. July 28, 1989," in *PPPUS* (Washington, DC: US Government Printing Office, 1990, 1025–31), 1031; also G. H. W. Bush, "The President's News Conference. August 23, 1989," in *PPPUS* (Washington, DC: US Government Printing Office, 1990, 1096–1105), 1100; also G. H. W. Bush, "Statement on United States Emergency Antidrug Assistance for Colombia. August 25, 1989," in *PPPUS* (Washington, DC: US Government Printing Office, 1990), 1109.

142. G. H. W. Bush, "Remarks on Signing the National POW/MIA Recognition Day Proclamation. July 28, 1989," in *PPPUS* (Washington, DC: US Government Printing Office, 1990, 1032–34), 1033.

143. G. H. W. Bush, "Statement by Press Secretary Fitzwater on President Bush's Meeting with President Carlos Saul Menem of Argentina. September 27, 1989," in *PPPUS* (Washington, DC: US Government Printing Office, 1990), 1267.

144. G. H. W. Bush, "Toasts at the State Dinner for President Carlos Salinas de Gortari of Mexico. October 3, 1989," in *PPPUS* (Washington, DC: US Government Printing Office, 1990, 1302–4), 1303.

145. G. H. W. Bush, "Remarks Following Discussions with Prime Minister Felipe Gonzalez Marquez of Spain. October 19, 1989," in *PPPUS* (Washington, DC: US Government Printing Office, 1990, 1362–64), 1363.

146. G. H. W. Bush, "Remarks and a Question-and-Answer Session with Students at Pickard Elementary School in Chicago, Illinois. November 20, 1989," in *PPPUS* (Washington, DC: US Government Printing Office, 1990, 1549–53), 1550.

147. G. H. W. Bush, "Letter to the Speaker of the House of Representatives and the President of the Senate Transmitting a Report on the Denial of Federal Benefits for Certain Drug Offenders. August 30, 1989," in *PPPUS* (Washington, DC: US Government Printing Office, 1990, 1119–20), 1119.

148. "More Anti-Drug Bills Cleared in 1989," *CQA* 45 (1989, 252–58): 257.

149. Ibid.

150. "Bush Signs Stripped-Down Crime Bill," *CQA* 46 (1990, 486–99): 499.

151. "Andean Initiative," *CQA* 47 (1991): 127.

152. "Drug Abuse Education," *CQA* 47 (1991): 387.

153. "Program Reauthorization," *CQA* 47 (1991): 389.

154. "Drug, Mental Health Programs Revamped," *CQA* 48 (1992): 422–26.

155. William J. Clinton, "The President's Radio Address. February 11, 1995," in *PPPUS* (Washington, DC: US Government Printing Office, 1996, 231–32), 231.

156. Clinton, "Remarks Announcing the 1997 National Drug Control Strategy and an Exchange with Reporters. February 25, 1997," in *PPPUS* (Washington, DC: US Government Printing Office, 1998), 199–203.

157. Clinton, "Remarks to the Law Enforcement Community in London, Ohio. February 15, 1994," in *PPPUS* (Washington, DC: US Government Printing Office, 1995, 257–63), 259.

158. Clinton, "The President's Radio Address. March 1, 1997," in *PPPUS* (Washington, DC: US Government Printing Office, 1998), 225–26.

159. Clinton, "The President's Radio Address. February 14, 1998," in *PPPUS* (Washington, DC: US Government Printing Office, 1999, 230–31), 231.

160. Clinton, "Remarks at Prince Georges County Correctional Center in Upper Marlboro, Maryland. February 9, 1994," in *PPPUS* (Washington, DC: US Government Printing Office, 1995, 210–14), 212.

161. Clinton, "Interview with Larry King. January 20, 1994," in *PPPUS* (Washington, DC: US Government Printing Office, 1995, 106–16), 113.

162. Clinton, "Remarks at a Town Meeting in Detroit. February 10, 1993," in *PPPUS* (Washington, DC: US Government Printing Office, 1994, 73–85): 84.

163. Clinton, "Remarks and a Question and Answer Session with High School Students in Bensonville, Illinois. May 11, 19993," in *PPPUS* (Washington, DC: US Government Printing Office, 1994, 614–24), 619.

164. Clinton, "Law Enforcement Community in London, Ohio," 259.

165. Clinton, "Remarks to the American Federation of Teachers. July 28, 1995," in *PPPUS* (Washington, DC: US Government Printing Office, 1996, 1321–27), 1326.

166. Clinton, "The President's Radio Address. March 1, 1997," in *PPPUS* (Washington, DC: US Government Printing Office, 1998), 225–26.

167. Clinton, "Statement on Senate Action on Narcotics Certification for Mexico. March 29, 1997," in *PPPUS* (Washington, DC: US Government Printing Office, 1998), 329; Clinton, "Interview with the *San Antonio Express News*, the *Los Angeles Times*, and the *Dallas Morning News*. May 1, 1997," in *PPPUS* (Washington, DC: US Government Printing Office, 1998, 518–21), 519; Clinton, "Interview with Jacob Goldstein of CNN Radio Noticias. May 1, 1997," in *PPPUS* (Washington, DC: US Government Printing Office, 1998), 521–25.

168. Clinton, "The President's News Conference with Prime Minister Jean Chretien of Canada. April 8, 1997," in *PPPUS* (Washington, DC: US Government Printing Office, 1998, 405–11), 411.

169. Miles A. Pomper, "Foreign Affairs: Colombian President Pastrana Has No Trouble Selling Hill on Need for Anti-Drug Aid," *Congressional Quarterly Weekly Report*, January 29, 2000, 198. *Congressional Quarterly Weekly Report* is hereafter shortened to *CQWR*. Peter W. Cohn, "Congress Casts Hopeful Eye on Mexico's Transition," *CQWR*, November 18, 2000, 2729.

170. Clinton, "The President's Radio Address. February 14, 1998," in *PPPUS* (Washington, DC: US Government Printing Office, 1999, 230–31), 231.

171. Clinton, "Remarks on Signing the Comprehensive Methamphetamine Control Act of 1996. October 3, 1996," in *PPPUS* (Washington, DC: US Government Printing Office, 1997, 1745–47), 1746.

172. Clinton, "Remarks on Advertising of Distilled Liquor and an Exchange with Reporters. April 1, 1997," in *PPPUS* (Washington, DC: US Government Printing Office, 1998), 368–70.

173. Clinton, "Statement on U.S. Sentencing Commission Action on Penalties for Drug Offenses. April 29, 1997," in *PPPUS* (Washington, DC: US Government Printing Office, 1998), 512.

174. "Other Legislation Aimed at Crime Prevention," *CQA* 52 (1996, 5-38–5-42): 5-39–5-40.

175. Charles R. Wolfpoff, "Lawmakers Seek to Increase Methamphetamine Penalties," *CQWR*, September 21, 1996, 2677.

176. Lori Nitschke, "Panel Rejects Plan for Sentences," *CQWR*, September 9, 1995, 2723.

177. "Other Legislation Aimed at Crime Prevention," *CQA* 53 (1997, 5-15–5-18): 5-15.

178. Carroll J. Doherty, "Bills Would Strike Symbolic Blow at Mexico Over Drug Trade," *CQA* (1997): 596–97.

179. "Senate Sidesteps Decertification of Mexico's Anti-Drug Effort," *CQA* 53 (1997): 8-44–8-45.

180. "Last-Minute Spending Signals Shift in Drug War," *CQA* 54 (1998): 2-118.

181. "House Backs Hyde's Effort, Passing Bill to Curb Abuse in Federal Property Seizures," *CQA* 55 (1999, 18-44–18-46): 18-44.

182. "Bill Requires Government to Show Seized Property Was Used in Crime," *CQA* 56 (2000): 15-38.

183. "Both Chambers Take Action to Criminalize Possession, Sales of 'Date Rape' Drugs," *CQA* 55 (1999): 18-48.

184. "Colombia Drug-Fighting Aid," *CQA* 56 (2000): C-6.

185. George W. Bush, "Joint Statement by President George Bush and President Vicente Fox, Towards a Partnership for Prosperity: The Guanajuato Proposal. February 16, 2001," in *PPPUS* (Washington, DC: US Government Printing Office, 2002, 97–98), 98.

186. G. W. Bush, "The President's News Conference with President Vicente Fox of Mexico in San Cristobal, Mexico. February 16, 2001," in *PPPUS* (Washington, DC: US Government Printing Office, 2002, 91–97), 94.

187. G. W. Bush, "Remarks Announcing the Nomination of John P. Walters to be Director of the Office of National Drug Control Policy. May 10, 2001," in *PPPUS* (Washington, DC: US Government Printing Office, 2002, 506–9), 508.

188. G. W. Bush, "Remarks to Faith-based and Community Leaders in New Orleans, Louisiana. January 15, 2004," in *PPPUS* (Washington, DC: US Government Printing Office, 2005, 60–66), 65.

189. G. W. Bush, "Nomination of John P. Walters," 508.

190. Ibid.

191. G. W. Bush, "Statement on Signing the Departments of Commerce, Justice, and State, the Judiciary, and Related Agencies Appropriations Act, 2002, November 28, 2001," in *PPPUS* (Washington, DC: US Government Printing Office, 2003, 1458–59), 1458.

192. Ibid.

193. Seth Stern, "Echoes of Colombia Haunt Mexico Plan," *CQWR*, December 3, 2007, 3594–95.

194. Miles A. Pomper, "Bush Recertifies 20 Nations as Lawmakers Re-Examine Drug War Cooperation Law," *CQWR*, March 3, 2001, 492.

195. "Annual Abortion Fight Delayed," *CQA* 58 (2002, 2–18–2–20): 2–18.

196. Elizabeth A. Palmer, "Senate CJS Bill Takes Contentious Stands on Immigration Law, Peacekeeping Funds," *CQWR*, July 21, 2001, 1776.

197. Seth Stern, "Moving Against the Meth Labs," *CQWR*, March 6, 2006, 602.

198. "Obama Seeks Crack Cocaine Sentence Changes," *Associated Press*, April 29, 2009, http://www.msnbc.msn.com/cleanprint/CleanPrintProxy.aspx?1291385686328 (site discontinued; accessed December 2, 2010).

199. "Barack Obama on Drugs," OnTheIssues. http://www.ontheissues.org/2008/Barack_Obama_Drugs.htm (accessed November 24, 2008).

200. Larry Margasak, "Judge Urges Changes in Cocaine Sentences," *The Akron Beacon Journal*, April 30, 2009, A4.

201. Shawn Zellker, "Obama Takes a Second Look at Drug Enforcement," *CQWR*, June 15, 2009, 1352.

202. Jerry Seper, "Obama Faces Mexican Drug War," *The Washington Times*, January 2, 2009, http://www.washingtontimes.com/news/2009/jan/2/obama-faces-mexican-drug-war (accessed December 3, 2010).

203. Barack Obama, "Proclamation 8494 of April 8, 2010: National D.A.R.E. Day, 2010" April 8, 2010, *The Federal Register*, April 13, 2010, vol. 75, No. 70, 18749–50.

CHAPTER 6

1. Harry S. Truman, "Statement by the President on Driving Safety. June 18, 1945," in *Public Papers of the Presidents of the United States* (Washington, DC: US Government Printing Office, 1946), 128. *Public Papers of the Presidents of the United States* is hereafter shortened to *PPPUS*.

2. Ronald R. Reagan, "Statement on Signing a Bill Concerning the Establishment of Alcohol Traffic Safety Programs. October 25, 1982," in *PPPUS* (Washington, DC: US Government Printing Office, 1983), 1378.

3. Reagan, "Remarks on Signing the National Drunk and Drugged Driving Awareness Week Proclamation. December 13, 1982," in *PPPUS* (Washington, DC: US Government Printing Office, 1983), 1599–1600.

4. Reagan, "Remarks at a White House Ceremony Marking Progress Made in the Campaign Against Drunk Driving. May 14, 1984," in *PPPUS* (Washington, DC: US Government Printing Office, 1985, 692–93), 692.

5. Reagan, "Remarks at River Dell High School in Oradell, New Jersey. June 20, 1984," in *PPPUS* (Washington, DC: US Government Printing Office, 1985, 881–84), 882.

6. George H. W. Bush, "Remarks on Signing the National Drunk and Drugged Driving Awareness Week Proclamation. December 11, 1989," in *PPPUS* (Washington, DC: US Government Printing Office, 1990, 1679–80), 1680.

7. William J. Clinton, "Remarks in Marrero, LA. October 24, 1996," in *PPPUS* (Washington, DC: US Government Printing Office, 1997, 1919–23), 1922.

8. Clinton, "The President's Radio Address. October 19, 1996," in *PPPUS* (Washington, DC: US Government Printing Office, 1997, 1867–68), 1867; ibid., "Memorandum on Reducing Teenage Driving Under the Influence of Illicit Drugs. October 19, 1996," in *PPPUS* (Washington, DC: US Government Printing Office, 1997, 1868–69), 1868.

9. Clinton, "Remarks on Signing a Memorandum on Standards to Prevent Drinking and Driving. March 3, 1998," in *PPPUS* (Washington, DC: US Government Printing Office, 1999), 316–17; ibid., "Memorandum on Standards to Prevent Drinking and Driving. March 3, 1998," in *PPPUS* (Washington, DC: US Government Printing Office, 1999), 318.

10. "Drunken Driving," *Congressional Quarterly Almanac* 49 (1993): 316–17. *Congressional Quarterly Almanac* hereafter shortened to *CQA*.

11. "Other Legislation Related to Transportation," *CQA* 50 (1994, 171–74): 174.

12. "Lawmakers Enact $30.2 Billion Anti-Crime Bill," *CQA* 50 (1994, 273–95): 293.

13. Isaiah J. Poole, "Transportation Money Comes with Strings," *Congressional Quarterly Weekly Report*, April 10, 2004, 851.

CHAPTER 7

1. "Conservatives Kill Domestic Violence Bill," *Congressional Quarterly Almanac* 36 (1980): 443–45. *Congressional Quarterly Almanac* hereafter shortened to *CQA*.

2. Ibid.

3. George H. W. Bush, "Remarks at the Annual Meeting of the American Association of University Women. June 26, 1989," in *Public Papers of the Presidents of the United States* (Washington, DC: US Government Printing Office, 1990, 797–800), 799. *Public Papers of the Presidents of the United States* hereafter shortened to *PPPUS*.

4. "Bill to Deter Sex Violence," *CQA* 46 (1990): 507.

5. "Bills Introduced to Stop Violence Against Women," *CQA* 42 (1991): 294.

6. "Battered Women," *CQA* 48 (1992): 335.

7. William J. Clinton, "Remarks to the Law Enforcement Community in London, Ohio. February 15, 1994," in *PPPUS* (Washington, DC: US Government Printing Office, 1995, 257–63), 262.

8. Clinton, "Remarks on Observance of National Domestic Violence Awareness Month. October 2, 1995," in *PPPUS* (Washington, DC: US Government Printing Office, 1996, 1750–53), 1752.

9. Clinton, "Remarks in Columbus, Ohio. August 26, 1996," in *PPPUS* (Washington, DC: US Government Printing Office, 1997, 1355–60), 1358.

10. Clinton, "Statement on Signing the National Defense Authorization Act for Fiscal Year 1997. September 23, 1996," in *PPPUS* (Washington, DC: US Government Printing Office, 1998), 1645–47.

11. Clinton, "Remarks on Signing the National Defense Authorization Act for Fiscal Year 1997 and an Exchange with Reporters. September 23, 1996," in *PPPUS* (Washington, DC: US Government Printing Office, 1997, 1643–45), 1644.

12. "Senate OKs Omnibus Anti-Crime Bill," *CQA* 49 (1993, 293–300): 299.

13. "Lawmakers Enact $30.2 Billion Anti-Crime Bill," *CQA* 50 (1994, 273–95): 274.

14. "Other Legislation Aimed at Crime Prevention," *CQA* 52 (1996, 5-38–5-42): 5-39.

15. Clinton, "Statement on the Supreme Court Decision Striking Down a Provision of the Violence Against Women Act. May 15, 2000," in *PPPUS* (Washington, DC: US Government Printing Office, 2001), 934.

16. George W. Bush, "Remarks on Domestic Violence Prevention. October 8, 2003," in *PPPUS* (Washington, DC: US Government Printing Office, 2004, 1265–69), 1265.

17. Jill Barshay, "Men on the Verge of Domestic Abuse Protection" *Congressional Quarterly Weekly Report*, September 5, 2005, 2276.

18. Nia-Malika Henderson, "Obama Launches Initiatives to Fight Domestic Violence," *The Washington Post*, October 27, 2010, http://www.washingtonpost.com/wp-dyn/content/article/2010/10/27/AR201010270530 (site discontinued; accessed December 3, 2010).

19. Barack Obama, "Presidential Proclamation—National Domestic Violence Awareness Month," October 1, 2010, http://www.whitehouse.gov/the-press-office/2010/10/01/presidential-proclamation (site discontinued; accessed December 3, 2010).

20. Bonnie Erbe, "Obama's Endless Czar List Now Includes a Domestic Violence Aide," *US News*, CBS News, June 29, 2009, http://www.cbsnews.com/stories/2009/06/30/usnews/whispers/main5125627.shtml (accessed December 3, 2010).

CHAPTER 8

1. "Religious Violence," *Congressional Quarterly Almanac* 44 (1988): 121. *Congressional Quarterly Almanac* hereafter shortened to *CQA*.
2. "Hate Crime Statistics to be Published," *CQA* 46 (1990): 506–7.
3. "Hate Crimes," *CQA* 48 (1992): 333.
4. William J. Clinton, "Opening Remarks at the White House Conference on Hate Crimes. November 10, 1997," in *Public Papers of the Presidents of the United States* (Washington, DC: US Government Printing Office, 1998, 1533–35), 1533. *Public Papers of the Presidents of the United States* hereafter shortened to *PPPUS*. Clinton, "Remarks on Proposed Hate Crimes Prevention Legislation. April 6, 1999," in *PPPUS* (Washington, DC: US Government Printing Office, 2000), 503–5; Clinton, "Memorandum on Hate Crimes in Schools and College Campuses. April 6, 1999," in *PPPUS* (Washington, DC: US Government Printing Office, 2000), 505–6.
5. "Lawmakers Enact $30.2 Billion Anti-Crime Bill," *CQA* 50 (1994, 273–95): 274.
6. "Elementary, Secondary Education Provisions," *CQA* 50 (1994, 392–95): 394.
7. "After Standoff, Conferees Cut Hate Crimes Provisions from Defense Authorization," *CQA* 56 (2000): 15-27–15-29; "Hate Crimes," *CQA* 56 (2000): C-5.
8. "Republicans Block Efforts to Expand Hate Crimes Ban," *CQA* 58 (2002): 13-11–13-12.
9. Barack Obama, "Proclamation 8387—Lesbian, Gay, Bisexual and Transgender Pride Month, 2009. June 1, 2009," *The Federal Register*, June 4, 2009.
10. Ibid.
11. Obama, "Proclamation 8529—Lesbian, Gay, Bisexual and Transgender Pride Month, 2010. May 28, 2010," *The Federal Register*, June 7, 2010.

CHAPTER 9

1. "Crime Victims," *Congressional Quarterly Almanac* 28 (1972): 259. *Congressional Quarterly Almanac* hereafter shortened to *CQA*.
2. "Crime and Law Enforcement," *CQA* 28 (1972): 15.
3. "Crime Control Amendments," *CQA* 29 (1973): 370–71.
4. Gerald R. Ford, "Remarks at a News Briefing on the Special Message to the Congress on Crime. June 19, 1975," in *Public Papers of the Presidents of the United States* (Washington, DC: US Government Printing Office, 1976, 838–39), 838. *Public Papers of the Presidents of the United States* hereafter shortened to *PPPUS*.
5. Ford, "Special Message to the Congress on Crime. June 19, 1975," in *PPPUS* (Washington, DC: US Government Printing Office, 1976, 839–51), 840.
6. Ford, "Address Before a Joint Session of the California State Legislature. September 5, 1975," in *PPPUS* (Washington, DC: US Government Printing Office, 1976, 1340–47), 1343.
7. Ford, "Remarks in Anaheim at the Annual Convention of the California Peace Officers Association. May 24, 1976," in *PPPUS* (Washington, DC: US Government Printing Office, 1977, 1675–79), 1676.
8. Ford, "Special Message to the Congress on Crime," 847.
9. "Law Enforcement/Judiciary," *CQA* 33 (1977, 26–28): 28.
10. "Law Enforcement/Judiciary," *CQA* 34 (1978, 23–25): 24.
11. "Crime Victims Aid," *CQA* 34 (1978): 196.
12. "Senate Judiciary Reports Criminal Code Bill," *CQA* 35 (1979, 363–69): 368.
13. "Victims of Crime," *CQA* 36 (1980): 398–99.
14. Ibid.
15. Ronald R. Reagan, "Remarks in New Orleans, Louisiana, at the Annual Meeting of the International Association of Chiefs of Police. September 28, 1981," in *PPPUS* (Washington, DC: US Government Printing Office, 1982, 839–46), 841; Reagan, "Proclamation 4929—Crime Victims Week, 1982. April 14, 1982," in *PPPUS* (Washington, DC: US Government Printing Office, 1983, 464–65), 464; Reagan, "Remarks on Signing Executive Order 12360 Establishing the President's Task Force on Victims of Crime. April 23, 1982," in *PPPUS* (Washington, DC: US Government Printing Office, 1983), 507–8; Reagan, "Executive Order 12360—President's Task Force On Victims of Crime. April 23, 1982," in *PPPUS* (Washington, DC: US Government Printing Office, 1983), 508–9.
16. Reagan, "Proclamation 4929—Crime Victims Week, 1982. April 14, 1982," in *PPPUS* (Washington, DC: US Government Printing Office, 1983, 464–65), 465.

17. Reagan, "Proclamation 5044—Crime Victims Week, 1983. April 7, 1983," in *PPPUS* (Washington, DC: US Government Printing Office, 1984), 513–14; Reagan, "Proclamation 5182—Crime Victims Week, 1984. April 13, 1984," in *PPPUS* (Washington, DC: US Government Printing Office, 1985, 529); Reagan, "Remarks on Signing the Victims of Crime Week Proclamation. April 19, 1985," in *PPPUS* (Washington, DC: US Government Printing Office, 1986), 463–65.

18. Reagan, "Remarks on Signing the Missing Children Act and the Victim and Witness Protection Act of 1982. October 12, 1982," in *PPPUS* (Washington, DC: US Government Printing Office, 1983, 1290–99), 1299.

19. "Victims, Witnesses of Crime," *CQA* 38 (1982): 382–83.

20. "Major Crime Package Cleared by Congress," *CQA* 40 (1984, 215–24): 220.

21. Ibid.

22. George H. W. Bush, "Remarks at a Campaign Rally for Gubernatorial Candidate John Engler in Grand Rapids, Michigan. October 16, 1990," in *PPPUS* (Washington, DC: US Government Printing Office, 1991, 1422–24), 1423; G. H. W. Bush, "Remarks to a Reception for Congressional Candidate Genevieve Atwood in Salt Lake City, Utah. November 4, 1990," in *PPPUS* (Washington, DC: US Government Printing Office, 1991, 1543–44), 1544; G. H. W. Bush, "Remarks at a Republican Campaign Rally in Tyler, Texas. November 5, 1990," in *PPPUS* (Washington, DC: US Government Printing Office, 1991, 1547–49), 1548.

23. G. H. W. Bush, "Remarks at a White House Ceremony for the Observance of National Crime Victims' Rights Week. April 25, 1989," in *PPPUS* (Washington, DC: US Government Printing Office, 1990), 564–65.

24. G. H. W. Bush, "Remarks at a White House Ceremony for the Observance of National Crime Victims' Rights Week. April 22, 1991," in *PPPUS* (Washington, DC: US Government Printing Office, 1992), 411–13.

25. "Pornography Victims' Compensation Act," *CQA* 48 (1992): 331–32.

26. William J. Clinton, "Remarks Accepting the Presidential Nominations at the Democratic National Convention in Chicago. August 29, 1996," in *PPPUS* (Washington, DC: US Government Printing Office, 1997, 1409–17), 1413.

27. Clinton, "Statement on Signing the Victim Rights Clarification Act of 1997. March 19, 1997," in *PPPUS* (Washington, DC: US Government Printing Office, 1998), 328.

28. "Crime Bill Provisions," *CQA* 50 (1994, 287–94): 293.

29. Ibid.

30. "Tough Talk, Little Progress on GOP's Crime Agenda," *CQA* 51 (1995, 6-3–6-8): 6-3.

31. Ibid., 6-4–6-5.

32. "Other Legislation Aimed at Crime Prevention," *CQA* 52 (1996): 5-38–5-42.

33. "Other Legislation Aimed at Crime Prevention," *CQA* 53 (1997): 5-16.

34. "Senate Panel Endorses Amending Constitution to Ensure Victims' Rights," *CQA* 55 (1999): 18-38–18-39.

35. "Sponsors of Victims' Rights Amendment Pull Bill in Face of Senate Opposition," *CQA* 56 (2000): 15-46–15-47.

36. "Bush Calls Upon Americans to Unite in 'Monumental Struggle of Good vs. Evil' After Terrorist Attacks," *CQ Weekly* Online, September 15, 2001, 2159–61.

37. Adriel Bettelheim, "Senators Want to Extend Sept. 11 Fund to Victims of Past Terrorism," *Congressional Quarterly Weekly Report*, May 25, 2002, 1401. *Congressional Quarterly Weekly Report* hereafter shortened to *CQWR*.

38. "DNA Testing, Victims' Rights Clear," *CQA* 60 (2004): 12-8–12-10.

39. Jennifer Dlouhy, "Victims' Rights Proponents Postpone Amendment Push, Settle for Senate-Passed Bill," *CQWR*, April 24, 2004, 967.

40. Barack Obama, "Presidential Proclamation—National Crime Victims Week," April 16, 2010, http://www.whitehouse.gov/the-press-office/presidential-proclamation-national-crime (accessed December 3, 2010). Also available in *The Federal Register*, April 21, 2010, 20889–890.

41. Obama, "Proclamation 8492: National Sexual Assault Awareness Month," *The Federal Register*, April 7, 2010, 17845–846.

CHAPTER 10

1. Harry S. Truman, "Address in Columbus at a Conference of the Federal Council of Churches. March 6, 1946," in *Public Papers of the Presidents of the United States* (Washington, DC: US Government Printing

Office, 1947, 141–44), 142. *Public Papers of the Presidents of the United States* hereafter shortened to *PPPUS*.

2. "Juvenile Delinquency," *Congressional Quarterly Almanac* 9 (1953): 201–2. *Congressional Quarterly Almanac* hereafter shortened to *CQA*.

3. Ibid.

4. Dwight D. Eisenhower, "Address at the Opening Session of the White House Conference on Children and Youth, College Park, Maryland. March 27, 1960," in *PPPUS* (Washington, DC: US Government Printing Office, 1961, 313–17), 316.

5. Eisenhower, "Remarks to the 44th National Council of the Boy Scouts of America. May 29, 1954," in *PPPUS* (Washington, DC: US Government Printing Office, 1955, 515–17), 515–16.

6. Eisenhower, "Annual Message to the Congress on the State of the Union. January 6, 1955," in *PPPUS* (Washington, DC: US Government Printing Office, 1956, 7–30), 25.

7. Eisenhower, "Special Message to the Congress Recommending a Health Program. January 31, 1955," in *PPPUS* (Washington, DC: US Government Printing Office, 1956, 216–23), 222.

8. John F. Kennedy, "Special Message to the Congress on the Nation's Youth. February 14, 1963," in *PPPUS* (Washington, DC: US Government Printing Office, 1964), 164–72.

9. Ibid.

10. Kennedy, "Letter to the Speaker of the House of Representatives Concerning Measures to Combat Juvenile Delinquency. May 11, 1961," in *PPPUS* (Washington, DC: US Government Printing Office, 1962, 373–74), 373.

11. Eisenhower, "Remarks Upon Signing the Juvenile Delinquency and Youth Offenses Control Act. September 22, 1961," in *PPPUS* (Washington, DC: US Government Printing Office, 1962), 616.

12. Eisenhower, "On the Nation's Youth," 164–72.

13. "Crime Bills," *CQA* 17 (1961): 82.

14. Lyndon B. Johnson, "Letter to the Attorney General on a Program to Combat Juvenile Delinquency in the District of Columbia. August 22, 1964," in *PPPUS* (Washington, DC: US Government Printing Office, 1965), 1005.

15. Johnson, "Special Message to the Congress Recommending a 12-Point Program for America's Children and Youth. February 8, 1967" in *PPPUS* (Washington, DC: US Government Printing Office, 1968, 156–60), 158.

16. Johnson, "Special Message to the Congress on Crime and Law Enforcement: 'To Insure Public Safety.' February 7, 1968," in *PPPUS* (Washington, DC: US Government Printing Office, 1969, 183–96), 187–88.

17. Johnson, "Remarks Upon Signing the Juvenile Delinquency Prevention and Control Act of 1968. July 31, 1968," in *PPPUS* (Washington, DC: US Government Printing Office, 1969), 855.

18. Johnson, "Special Message to the Congress: The Nation's Capital. February 27, 1967," in *PPPUS* (Washington, DC: US Government Printing Office, 1968, 226–39), 236.

19. "No Action Taken to Regulate Firearms Shipments," *CQA* 20 (1964, 270–73): 270.

20. "Juvenile Delinquency Act," *CQA* 21 (1965): 632–33.

21. "1968 Legislative Action," *CQA* 24 (1968): 117–18.

22. Richard M. Nixon, "Statement Outlining a 13-Point Program for Reform of the Federal Corrections System. November 13, 1969," in *PPPUS* (Washington, DC: US Government Printing Office, 1970, 924–28), 925.

23. Nixon, "Annual Budget Message to the Congress Fiscal Year 1971. February 2, 1970," in *PPPUS* (Washington, DC: US Government Printing Office, 1971, 46–68), 66.

24. "Juvenile Justice Institute," *CQA* 28 (1972): 526–27.

25. "Runaway Youth Act," *CQA* 28 (1972): 526.

26. "Prison Grants," *CQA* 28 (1972): 543.

27. "Juvenile Delinquency," *CQA* 28 (1974): 278–82.

28. Gerald R. Ford, "Special Message to the Congress on Crime. June 19, 1975," in *PPPUS* (Washington, DC: US Government Printing Office, 1976, 839–51), 847.

29. "Law Enforcement/Judiciary," *CQA* 33 (1977, 26–28): 26.

30. "Juvenile Justice Extension," *CQA* 33 (1977): 569–70.

31. "Juvenile Justice Programs," *CQA* 36 (1980): 402–3.

32. "Major Crime Package Cleared by Congress," *CQA* 40 (1984, 215–24): 218.

33. Ronald R. Reagan, "Message to the Congress Reporting on Federal Juvenile Delinquency Programs. February 25, 1987," in *PPPUS* (Washington, DC: US Government Printing Office, 1988), 175–76.

34. "Juvenile Justice Bill," *CQA* 44 (1988): 119.

35. William J. Clinton, "Remarks Announcing the Anticrime Initiative and an Exchange with Reporters. August 11, 1993," in *PPPUS* (Washington, DC: US Government Printing Office, 1994, 1360–63), 1362.
36. Clinton, "Remarks on the Youth Crime Gun Interdiction Initiative. July 8, 1996," in *PPPUS* (Washington, DC: US Government Printing Office, 1997, 1082–84), 1083.
37. Ibid.
38. Clinton, "Remarks at the University of Massachusetts in Boston. February 19, 1997," in *PPPUS* (Washington, DC: US Government Printing Office, 1998, 174–79), 177.
39. Clinton, "Statement on Juvenile Crime Legislation. May 8, 1997," in *PPPUS* (Washington, DC: US Government Printing Office, 1998), 577.
40. Clinton, "Interview on MTV's 'Enough is Enough' Forum. April 19, 1994," in *PPPUS* (Washington, DC: US Government Printing Office, 1995, 714–26), 719.
41. Clinton, "Interview with Larry King. June 5, 1995," in *PPPUS-Online* (Washington, DC: US Government Printing Office, 1996, 808–14), 814.
42. Clinton, "Remarks to the American Federation of Teachers. July 28, 1995," in *PPPUS-Online* (Washington, DC: US Government Printing Office, 1996, 1165–71), 1165.
43. Clinton, "Remarks Accepting the Presidential Nominations at the Democratic National Convention in Chicago. August 29, 1996," in *PPPUS* (Washington, DC: US Government Printing Office, 1997, 1409–17), 1413.
44. "Other Judiciary Measures Considered in 1992," *CQA* 48 (1992, 332–35): 334.
45. "Senate OKs Omnibus Anti-Crime Bill," *CQA* 49 (1993, 293–300): 299.
46. "Lawmakers Enact $30.2 Billion Anti-Crime Bill," *CQA* 50 (1994, 273–95): 274.
47. "Panel Seeks to Curb Juvenile Crime," *CQA* 52 (1996): 5-29–5-30.
48. "Other Measures Related to Juvenile Justice," *CQA* 52 (1996): 5-30–5-31.
49. Ibid.
50. "Myriad Disputes Slow Progress of GOP Juvenile Crime Bills," *CQA* 53 (1997): 5-3–5-7.
51. Ibid.
52. "Juvenile Crime Bills Stall in Senate," *CQA* 57 (2001): 14-17–14-18.

CHAPTER 11

1. Alan K. Ota, "Senators Pan Entertainment Industry's Plan to Shield Children From Violence, but Legislation in Doubt This Year," *Congressional Quarterly Weekly Report*, September 30, 2000, 2272–73. *Congressional Quarterly Weekly Report* hereafter shortened to *CQWR*.
2. "Child Abuse: $85 million for Prevention and Treatment" CQ Press Electronic Library, CQ Almanac Online Edition, cqal73–1228583. Originally published in *Congressional Quarterly Almanac 1973* (Washington, DC: Congressional Quarterly, 1974), http://www.cqpress.com/cqal73–1228583 (site discontinued; accessed November 24, 2010).
3. Ronald R. Reagan, "Remarks at a White House Ceremony Marking the Opening of the National Center for Missing and Exploited Children. June 13, 1984," in *Public Papers of the Presidents of the United States* (Washington, DC: US Government Printing Office, 1985), 844–46. *Public Papers of the Presidents of the United States* hereafter shortened to *PPPUS*.
4. Reagan, "Remarks on Signing the Missing Children Act and the Victim and Witness Protection Act of 1982. October 12, 1982," in *PPPUS* (Washington, DC: US Government Printing Office, 1983, 1290–99), 1298.
5. Reagan, "Remarks on Signing the Child Protection Act of 1984. May 21, 1984," in *PPPUS* (Washington, DC: US Government Printing Office, 1985, 721–22), 722.
6. Reagan, "Message to the Congress Transmitting Proposed Legislation on Child Protection and Obscenity Enforcement. November 9, 1987," in *PPPUS* (Washington, DC: US Government Printing Office, 1988), 1313–15.
7. Reagan, "Child Protection Act of 1984," 722.
8. Reagan, "Radio Address to the Nation on School Violence and Discipline. January 7, 1984," in *PPPUS* (Washington, DC: US Government Printing Office, 1985, 18–19), 18.
9. Ibid.
10. "Major Crime Package Cleared by Congress," *Congressional Quarterly Almanac* 40 (1984, 215–24): 218. *Congressional Quarterly Almanac* hereafter shortened to *CQA*.
11. "Child Pornography Bill," *CQA* 40 (1984): 225.
12. "Child Abuse Bill Cleared," *CQA* 42 (1986): 88.
13. "New Child Pornography Law," *CQA* 42 (1986): 88.

14. "Bush Signs Stripped-Down Crime Bill," *CQA* 46 (1990, 486–99): 493.

15. Ibid., 499.

16. "Other Children's Aid Bills Considered in 1991," *CQA* 47 (1991, 386–87): 387.

17. "Other Judiciary Measures Considered in 1992," *CQA* 48 (1992, 332–35): 334.

18. William J. Clinton, "Remarks to Justice Department Employees. April 29, 1993," in *PPPUS* (Washington, DC: US Government Printing Office, 1994, 534–36), 535.

19. Clinton, "Remarks on Signing the Executive Order to Facilitate Payment of Child Support and an Exchange with Reporters. February 27, 1995," in *PPPUS* (Washington, DC: US Government Printing Office, 1996, 319–21), 320.

20. Clinton, "Remarks to the American Federation of Teachers. July 28, 1995," in *PPPUS* (Washington, DC: US Government Printing Office, 1996, 1321–25), 1325.

21. Clinton, "Statement on Signing the International Parental Kidnapping Crime Act of 1993. December 2, 1993," in *PPPUS* (Washington, DC: US Government Printing Office, 1994), 2093.

22. Clinton, "Remarks on Signing the National Child Protection Act of 1993. December 20, 1993," in *PPPUS* (Washington, DC: US Government Printing Office, 1994, 2192–93), 2192.

23. Clinton, "Remarks at the Children's Town Meeting. February 20, 1993," in *PPPUS* (Washington, DC: US Government Printing Office, 1994, 146–65), 151.

24. Clinton, "Remarks at the National Education Association School Safety Summit in Los Angeles, California. April 8, 1995," in *PPPUS-Online* (Washington, DC: US Government Printing Office, 1996, 504–8), 506; also Clinton, "The President's Radio Address. December 6, 1997," in *PPPUS* (Washington, DC: US Government Printing Office, 1998), 1723–34.

25. Clinton, "Message to the Congress Transmitting the Gun-Free School Zones Amendments Act of 1995. May 10, 1995," in *PPPUS* (Washington, DC: US Government Printing Office, 1996, 809–10), 809; Clinton, "Remarks in Columbus, Ohio. August 26, 1996," in *PPPUS* (Washington, DC: US Government Printing Office, 1997, 1355–60), 1359.

26. Clinton, "Remarks and a Question-and-Answer Session with the National PTA Legislative Conference. March 14, 1995," in *PPPUS-Online* (Washington, DC: US Government Printing Office, 1996, 343–49), 348–49.

27. Clinton, "Remarks to Justice Department Employees. April 29, 1993," in *PPPUS* (Washington, DC: US Government Printing Office, 1994, 534–36), 535; Clinton, "Remarks to the Law Enforcement Community in London, Ohio. February 15, 1994," in *PPPUS* (Washington, DC: US Government Printing Office, 1995, 257–63), 261.

28. Clinton, "Remarks in Monrovia, California. July 22, 1996," in *PPPUS* (Washington, DC: US Government Printing Office, 1997, 1177–79), 1178.

29. Clinton, "Letter to Members of the Senate on Anticrime Legislation. August 22, 1994," in *PPPUS* (Washington, DC: US Government Printing Office, 1995, 1490–91), 1491.

30. Clinton, "The President's Radio Address. August 24, 1996," in *PPPUS* (Washington, DC: US Government Printing Office, 1997, 1334–35), 1335; Clinton, "Remarks to the U.S. Conference of Mayors in Cleveland, Ohio. June 22, 1996," in *PPPUS* (Washington, DC: US Government Printing Office, 1997, 1112–19), 1118.

31. "Senate OKs Omnibus Anti-Crime Bill," *CQA* 49 (1993, 293–300): 294.

32. Ibid.

33. "Several Education Bills See Action in Congress," *CQA* 49 (1993): 413–14.

34. "Elementary, Secondary Education Provisions," *CQA* 50 (1994, 392–96): 394.

35. "Other Legislation Aimed at Crime Prevention," *CQA* 52 (1996, 5-38–5-42): 5-38.

36. "Other Legislation Related to the Legal System," *CQA* 51 (1995, 6-29–6-33): 6-30.

37. "Aimed at Crime Prevention," 5-42.

38. Ibid., 5-42.

39. "Lawmakers Consider Other Bills Related to Law, Judiciary," *CQA* 52 (1996, 5-42–5-47): 5-46.

40. Ibid.

41. "Broadcasters Agree to Rate Television Programs," *CQA* 53 (1997): 3-39–3-40.

42. "Anti-Crime Package Seeks to Protect Women and Children from Violence," CQ Press Electronic Library, *CQA* Online Edition, cqal00–834–24302–1082251, http://www.library.cqpress.com/cqalmanac/cqa00–834–24302–1082251 (accessed November 24, 2010). Originally published in *CQ Almanac 2000* (Washington: Congressional Quarterly, 2001).

43. George H. W. Bush, "Remarks at the White House Conference on Faith-Based and Community Initiatives in Los Angeles, California. March 3, 2004," in *PPPUS* (Washington, DC: US Government Printing Office, 2005, 297–304), 303.

44. G. H. W. Bush, "Remarks Prior to a Cabinet Meeting and an Exchange with Reporters. April 9, 2001," in *PPPUS* (Washington, DC: US Government Printing Office, 2002, 379–80), 379.
45. G. H. W. Bush, "Remarks at the White House Conference on Missing, Exploited, and Runaway Children. October 2, 2002," in *PPPUS* (Washington, DC: US Government Printing Office, 2003, 1702–6), 1704.
46. Ibid., 1705.
47. G. H. W. Bush, "Remarks on Children's Online Safety. October 23, 2002," in *PPPUS* (Washington, DC: US Government Printing Office, 2003, 1872–75), 1874.
48. Ibid., 1873.
49. G. H. W. Bush, "Statement on Signing the Prosecutorial Remedies and Other Tools to End the Exploitation of Children Today Act of 2003. April 30, 2003," in *PPPUS* (Washington, DC: US Government Printing Office, 2004, 400–401), 400.
50. Ibid.
51. G. H. W. Bush, "Statement on Congressional Action on the Keeping Children and Families Safe Act of 2003. June 25, 2003," in *PPPUS* (Washington, DC: US Government Printing Office, 2004), 696.
52. G. H. W. Bush, "Remarks and a Question-and-Answer Session in Niles, Michigan. May 3, 2004," in *PPPUS* (Washington, DC: US Government Printing Office, 2005, 699–714), 711.
53. "House Targets Crimes Against Kids," *CQA* 58 (2002): 13-5–13-6.
54. Ibid.
55. "Court Ruling Holds on 'Virtual' Child Porn," *CQA* 58 (2002): 13-10–13-11.
56. "New Era of Oversight for Justice," *CQA* 59 (2003): 13-3–13-4.
57. Keith Perine, "Children's Online Safety is Aim of House-Passed Package of Bills," *CQWR*, November 19, 2007, 3491.
58. Barack Obama, "Proclamation 8355—National Child Abuser Prevention Month, 2009," April 1, 2009; Barack Obama, "Proclamation 8490—National Child Abuse Prevention Month, 2010," April 1, 2010. *The Federal Register*, April 7, 2010, 17841–842.
59. Barack Obama, "Proclamation 8570—Family Day 2010," September 27, 2010. *The Federal Register*, September 30, 2010, 60563–566.

CHAPTER 12

1. "No Action Taken to Regulate Firearms Shipments," *Congressional Quarterly Almanac* 20 (1964): 270–73. *Congressional Quarterly Almanac* hereafter shortened to *CQA*.
2. Lyndon B. Johnson, "Special Message to the Congress on Law Enforcement and the Administration of Justice. March 8, 1965," in *Public Papers of the Presidents of the United States* (Washington, DC: US Government Printing Office, 1966, 263–71), 267. *Public Papers of the Presidents of the United States* hereafter shortened to *PPPUS*.
3. Johnson, "Special Message to the Congress on Crime and Law Enforcement. March 9, 1966," in *PPPUS* (Washington, DC: US Government Printing Office, 1967, 291–99), 294.
4. Johnson, "Statement by the President on His Gun Control Proposals. June 24, 1968," in *PPPUS* (Washington, DC: US Government Printing Office, 1969, 738–39), 739; Johnson, "Special Message to the Congress: 'The People's Right to Protection.' June 24, 1968," in *PPPUS* (Washington, DC: US Government Printing Office, 1969), 740–42.
5. Johnson, "Special Message to the Congress on Crime in America. February 6, 1967," in *PPPUS* (Washington, DC: US Government Printing Office, 1968, 134–45), 142.
6. Johnson, "Special Message to the Congress: The Nation's Capital. February 27, 1967," in *PPPUS* (Washington, DC: US Government Printing Office, 1968, 226–39), 233.
7. Johnson, "Special Message to the Congress on Crime and Law Enforcement: To Insure Public Safety. February 7, 1968," in *PPPUS* (Washington, DC: US Government Printing Office, 1969, 183–96), 184, 193.
8. Johnson, "Special Message to the Congress on the District of Columbia: 'The Nation's First City.' March 13, 1968," in *PPPUS* (Washington, DC: US Government Printing Office, 1969, 383–94), 385–86.
9. Johnson, "Remarks Upon Signing the Gun Control Act of 1968. October 22, 1968," in *PPPUS* (Washington, DC: US Government Printing Office, 1969, 1059–60), 1059.
10. "Review of the Session," *CQA* 21 (1965, 79–83): 80; "Anticrime Program Presented to Congress," *CQA* 21 (1965, 628–31): 630.
11. "Gun Control Legislation," *CQA* 37 (1981): 420.
12. "The President's News Conference of June 29, 1972. June 29, 1972," in *PPPUS* (Washington, DC: US Government Printing Office, 1972, 705–18), 715.

13. "Gun, Ammunition Control," *CQA* 25 (1969): 705–6.

14. "Crime and Law Enforcement," *CQA* 26 (1970): 77; "Gun Control Act Amendment," *CQA* 26 (1970): 555–56.

15. "Crime and Law Enforcement," *CQA* 28 (1972): 15.

16. Gerald R. Ford, "Remarks and a Question-and-Answer Session at a Public Forum in Indianapolis. April 22, 1976," in *PPPUS* (Washington, DC: US Government Printing Office, 1977, 1148–59), 1153.

17. Ford, "Interview with Television Reporters in San Francisco. September 22, 1975," in *PPPUS* (Washington, DC: US Government Printing Office, 1976, 1509–18), 1510; Ford, "The President's News Conference of October 10, 1975. October 10, 1975," in *PPPUS* (Washington, DC: US Government Printing Office, 1976, 1657–73), 1660; Ford, "Remarks and Question-and-Answer Session at the University of New Hampshire in Durham. February 8, 1976," in *PPPUS* (Washington, DC: US Government Printing Office, 1977, 215–33), 218; Ford, "Remarks and a Question-and-Answer Session at a Public Forum in Indianapolis. April 22, 1976," in *PPPUS* (Washington, DC: US Government Printing Office, 1977, 1148–69), 1153.

18. Ford, "Remarks at a News Briefing on the Special Message to the Congress on Crime. June 19, 1975," in *PPPUS* (Washington, DC: US Government Printing Office, 1976, 838–39), 839; Ford, "University of New Hampshire," 218; Ford, "Public Forum in Indianapolis," 1153; "Crime and Judiciary," *CQA* 31 (1975): 1148–59.

19. Ford, "Special Message to the Congress on Crime. June 19, 1975," in *PPPUS* (Washington, DC: US Government Printing Office, 1976, 839–51), 848.

20. Ibid.

21. Ibid.; Ford, "Public Forum in Indianapolis," 1153.

22. "Law Enforcement and Judiciary," *CQA* 32 (1976, 17–18): 18.

23. "Senate-Passed Criminal Code Dies in House," *CQA* 34 (1978, 165–73): 171.

24. Richard M. Nixon, "Statement on Amendments to the Gun Control Act of 1968. January 27, 1969," in *PPPUS* (Washington, DC: US Government Printing Office, 1969), 126.

25. "Law Enforcement/Judiciary," *CQA* 38 (1982, 20–21): 21.

26. "Threats to Public Officials," *CQA* 38 (1982): 382.

27. "Bill Easing Gun Law Dies," *CQA* 38 (1982): 415.

28. "Anti-Crime Package Stalls in Senate Again," *CQA* 39 (1983, 315–17): 316.

29. "Major Crime Package Cleared by Congress," *CQA* 29 (1984, 215–24): 218.

30. "Law/Judiciary," *CQA* 41(1985, 23–25): 24.

31. "Armor-Piercing Bullets," *CQA* 41 (1985): 232–33; "Armor-Piercing Bullet Ban," *CQA* 42 (1986): 85–86.

32. "Law/Judiciary," 24; "Federal Gun Law," *CQA* 41 (1985, 228–30): 229; "Congress Relaxes Federal Gun Control Laws," *CQA* 42 (1986): 82–85.

33. "Law/Judiciary," *CQA* 44 (1988, 25–27): 26.

34. "Gun Curb Stall on Hill; Some Imports Banned," *CQA* 45 (1989, 262–65): 262.

35. George H. W. Bush, "Remarks on Afghanistan and a Question-and-Answer Session with Reporters. February 16, 1989," in *PPPUS* (Washington, DC: US Government Printing Office, 1990, 100–106), 105; G. H. W. Bush, "Remarks at a Luncheon Hosted by the Forum Club in Houston, Texas. March 16, 1989," in *PPPUS* (Washington, DC: US Government Printing Office, 1990, 246–52), 247.

36. G. H. W. Bush, "Statement by Press Secretary Fitzwater on the Suspension of Semiautomatic Weapons Imports. April 5, 1989," in *PPPUS* (Washington, DC: US Government Printing Office, 1990), 373–74.

37. "Gun Curbs Stall on Hill: Some Imports Banned," *CQA* 45 (1989): 262–65.

38. G. H. W. Bush, "Question-and-Answer Session with Reporters," 105.

39. G. H. W. Bush, "Remarks at the National Peace Officers' Memorial Day Ceremony. May 15, 1989," in *PPPUS* (Washington, DC: US Government Printing Office, 1990, 557–60), 558.

40. G. H. W. Bush, "White House Fact Sheet on Combating Violent Crime. May 15, 1989," in *PPPUS* (Washington, DC: US Government Printing Office, 1990, 560–65), 561; also G. H. W. Bush, "Message to the Congress Transmitting Proposed Crime Control Legislation. March 11, 1991," in *PPPUS* (Washington, DC: US Government Printing Office, 1992), 246–47.

41. G. H. W. Bush, "White House Fact Sheet on Combating Violent Crime. May 15, 1989," in *PPPUS* (Washington, DC: US Government Printing Office, 1990, 560–65), 562; G. H. W. Bush, "Message to the Congress Transmitting Proposed Crime Control Legislation. March 11, 1991," in *PPPUS* (Washington, DC: US Government Printing Office, 1992), 246–47.

42. "Crime Bills Move Ahead with Partisan Push," *CQA* 45 (1989, 259–60): 259.

43. "Assault Weapons Ban Is Dropped; Waiting Period on Handguns Blocked; *CQA* 46 (1990): 500–501.

44. Ibid.

45. "Gun Curbs Stall on Hill; Some Imports Banned," *CQA* 45 (1989): 262–65; "Assault Weapons Ban Is Dropped," 500–501.
46. "Anti-Crime Bill Falls Victim to Partisanship," *CQA* 47 (1991, 262–70): 262; "No Compromise Forged on Crime Bill," *CQA* 48 (1992, 311–13): 311.
47. "Brady Bill Part of Stalled Crime Package," *CQA* 47 (1991, 271–73): 271.
48. "Other Judiciary Measures Considered in 1992," *CQA* 48 (1992, 332–35): 335.
49. William J. Clinton, "Remarks in Columbus, Ohio. August 26, 1996," in *PPPUS* (Washington, DC: US Government Printing Office, 1997, 1355–60), 1358.
50. Clinton, "Letter to Hunters and Sportsmen. April 29, 1994," in *PPPUS* (Washington, DC: US Government Printing Office, 1995), 804.
51. Clinton, "Remarks in Columbus, Ohio," 1358.
52. "Remarks to the NAACP Convention in Charlotte, North Carolina. July 10, 1996," in *PPPUS* (Washington, DC: US Government Printing Office, 1997, 1101–9), 1105.
53. Clinton, "Remarks Announcing the Anticrime Initiative and an Exchange with Reporters. August 11, 1993," in *PPPUS* (Washington, DC: US Government Printing Office, 1994, 1360–63), 1362.
54. Clinton, "Memorandum on Importation of Modified Semiautomatic Assault-Type Rifles. November 14, 1997," in *PPPUS* (Washington, DC: US Government Printing Office, 1998, 1575–76), 1576.
55. Clinton, "Anticrime Initiative," 1362.
56. Clinton, "Remarks to the NAACP Convention," 1105.
57. Clinton, "The President's Radio Address. February 6, 1999," in *PPPUS* (Washington, DC: US Government Printing Office, 2000), 177.
58. "Armored Car Guards," *CQA* 49 (1993): 225.
59. "President Signs 'Brady' Gun Control Law," *CQA* 49 (1993): 300–303.
60. "'Brady 2' Never Makes it Out of Starting Gate," *CQA* 50 (1994): 284.
61. "Lawmakers Enact $30.2 Billion Anti-Crime Bill," *CQA* 50 (1994, 273–95): 274.
62. "Tough Talk, Little Progress on GOP's Crime Agenda," *CQA* 51 (1995, 6-3-6-8): 6-3.
63. "House Votes to Repeal Assault Weapons Ban," *CQA* 52 (1996): 5–32.
64. "Armored Car Guards," *CQA* 53 (1997): 3–17.
65. "Juvenile Justice Bill Gets Hung Up on Dispute Over Gun Control," *CQA* 56 (2000): 15-15-15-18.
66. "Juvenile Crime Bill Heads Straight To Senate Floor," *CQA* 55 (1999): 18-4-18-5.
67. George W. Bush, "Remarks Announcing the Project Safe Neighborhoods Initiative in Philadelphia, Pennsylvania. May 14, 2001," in *PPPUS* (Washington, DC: US Government Printing Office, 2002, 525–27), 526.
68. G. W. Bush, "Remarks at the National Peace Officers' Memorial Day Ceremony. May 15, 1989," in *PPPUS* (Washington, DC: US Government Printing Office, 1990, 557–60), 558.
69. Shawn Zeller, "Gun Lobby Fires Back at Press Coverage," *Congressional Quarterly Weekly Report*, June 25, 2007, 1893. *Congressional Quarterly Weekly Report* hereafter shortened to *CQWR*.
70. "House Hands Firearms Lobby a Win," *CQA* 59 (2003): 13-14-13-15.
71. "Senate Defeats Gun Liability Bill," *CQA* 60 (2004): 12-13-12-14.
72. "Republicans Victorious on Gun Liability," *CQA* 61 (2005): 14-13-14-14.
73. Ibid.
74. Ibid.
75. John McCormick, "Obama puts Gun-Control issue on Back Burner," *Chicago Tribune*, April 27, 2009, http://www.chicagotribune.com/news/nationworld/chi-obama-gunsapr27,0,4100539 (site discontinued; accessed December 2, 2010).
76. From the 2008 Philadelphia primary debate, on the even of the Pennsylvania Primary, April 16, 2008.
77. Shawn Zeller, "NRA Sees Anti-Gun Agenda in Ban on Surplus M11-s," *CQWR*, September 20, 2010, 2126.
78. Jason Ryan, "Obama to Seek New Assault Weapons Ban," ABC News, February 25, 2009, http://www.abcnews.go.com/Politics/story/?id=6960824&page=1 (site discontinued; accessed December 2, 2010).

CHAPTER 13

1. Harry S. Truman, "Address Before the Attorney General's Conference on Law Enforcement Problems. February 15, 1950," in *Public Papers of the Presidents of the United States* (Washington, DC: US Government Printing Office, 1951), 156–58. *Public Papers of the Presidents of the United States* hereafter shortened to *PPPUS*.

2. Truman, "Memorandum to Department and Agency Heads Requesting Their Cooperation with the Senate Special Crime Investigating Committee. June 17, 1950," in *PPPUS* (Washington, DC: US Government Printing Office, 1951), 484; Truman, "The President's News Conference of March 29, 1951. March 29, 1951," in *PPPUS* (Washington, DC: US Government Printing Office, 1952), 201–3.

3. "Survey of Interstate Crime," *Congressional Quarterly Almanac* 7 (1951, 341–52): 346. *Congressional Quarterly Almanac* hereafter shortened to *CQA*.

4. Ibid., 347.

5. Ibid., 341, 345.

6. "Survey of Interstate Crime," *CQA* 6 (1950, 437–43): 437.

7. Ibid., 439.

8. Ibid., 441.

9. Dwight D. Eisenhower, "Annual Budget Message to the Congress, FY 1961, January 14, 1960," in *PPPUS* (Washington, DC: US Government Printing Office, 1960, 37–110), 105.

10. "Labor Investigations," *CQA* 14 (1958): 674–75.

11. "Coin Machines, Gambling," *CQA* (1959): 738–40.

12. Ibid.

13. "Select Labor Committee Issues Final Report," *CQA* (1960, 699–703): 702.

14. Ibid., 703.

15. Ibid., 701.

16. John F. Kennedy, "Remarks Upon Signing Bills to Combat Organized Crime and Racketeering. September 13, 1961," in *PPPUS* (Washington, DC: US Government Printing Office, 1962), 600.

17. "Crime Bills," *CQA* 17 (1961): 82; "Bills Enacted," *CQA* 17 (1961): 382–84.

18. "Bills Enacted," *CQA* 17 (1961, 382–84): 383.

19. "Crime Bills," 82.

20. Lyndon B. Johnson, "Remarks to the United States Marshals. August 18, 1964," in *PPPUS* (Washington, DC: US Government Printing Office, 1965, 981–92), 982.

21. Johnson, "Special Message to the Congress on Law Enforcement and the Administration of Justice. March 8, 1965," in *PPPUS* (Washington, DC: US Government Printing Office, 1966, 263–71), 266; Johnson, "Remarks at a Meeting With Federal Enforcement Officials to Deal with the Problem of Organized Crime. May 5, 1966," in *PPPUS* (Washington, DC: US Government Printing Office, 1967, 483–84), 483.

22. Johnson, "Special Message to the Congress on Crime and Law Enforcement. March 9, 1966," in *PPPUS* (Washington, DC: US Government Printing Office, 1967, 291–99), 294.

23. Ibid.

24. Johnson, "Special Message to the Congress on Crime in America. February 6, 1967," in *PPPUS* (Washington, DC: US Government Printing Office, 1968, 134–45), 144.

25. Johnson, "Special Message to the Congress: The Nation's Capital. February 27, 1967," in *PPPUS* (Washington, DC: US Government Printing Office, 1968, 226–39), 233.

26. Ibid.

27. Johnson, "Special Message to the Congress on Crime and Law Enforcement: 'To Insure Public Safety.' February 7, 1968," in *PPPUS* (Washington, DC: US Government Printing Office, 1969, 183–96), 183–84, 192.

28. Johnson, "Special Message to the Congress on Crime and Law Enforcement: 'To Insure Public Safety.' February 7, 1968," in *PPPUS* (Washington, DC: US Government Printing Office, 1969, 183–96), 192.

29. "Crime Hearings Told of 'Cosa Nostra' Syndicate," *CQA* 19 (1963): 1101–2.

30. "Anticrime Program Presented to Congress," *CQA* 21 (1965, 628–31): 629.

31. Richard M. Nixon, "Special Message to the Congress on Legislative Reform. October 13, 1969," in *PPPUS* (Washington, DC: US Government Printing Office, 1970, 788–96), 795.

32. Ibid.

33. Nixon, "Special Message to the Congress on a Program to Combat Organized Crime in America. April 23, 1969," in *PPPUS* (Washington, DC: US Government Printing Office, 1970), 315–21.

34. Nixon, "Annual Budget Message to the Congress Fiscal Year 1971. February 2, 1970," in *PPPUS* (Washington, DC: US Government Printing Office, 1971, 46–68), 65.

35. Nixon, "Statement on Signing Executive Order Establishing the National Council on Organized Crime. June 4, 1970," in *PPPUS* (Washington, DC: US Government Printing Office, 1971), 483–84.

36. Nixon, "Special Message to the Congress on the Administration's Legislative Program. September 11, 1970," in *PPPUS* (Washington, DC: US Government Printing Office, 1971, 719–38), 729.

37. Nixon, "Special Message to the Congress on the Administration's Legislative Program. September 11, 1970," in *PPPUS* (Washington, DC: US Government Printing Office, 1971, 719–38), 729.

38. Nixon, "Special Message to the Congress Resubmitting Legislative Proposals. January 26, 1971," in *PPPUS* (Washington, DC: US Government Printing Office, 1972, 61–73), 65.
39. "Crime and Law Enforcement," *CQA* 26 (1970): 77.
40. "Four Major Crime Bills Cleared 91st Congress," *CQA* 26 (1970): 125–26.
41. Nancy E. Marion, *Government Versus Organized Crime* (Upper Saddle River, NJ: Prentice Hall, 2008), 222.
42. "Four Major Crime Bills," 125–26.
43. Ibid.
44. James Jacobs, *Busting the Mob: United States v. Cosa Nostra* (New York: New York University Press, 1994).
45. Gerald R. Ford, "Address Before a Joint Session of the California State Legislature. September 5, 1975," in *PPPUS* (Washington, DC: US Government Printing Office, 1976, 1340–47), 1346.
46. Ford, "Special Message to the Congress on Crime. June 19, 1975," in *PPPUS* (Washington, DC: US Government Printing Office, 1976, 839–51), 849.
47. Jimmy Carter, "The President's News Conference of March 24, 1977. March 24, 1977," in *PPPUS* (Washington, DC: US Government Printing Office, 1978, 496–504), 504.
48. "Horse Race Betting," *CQA* 32 (1976): 427–28.
49. "Senate-Passed Criminal Code Dies in House," *CQA* 34 (1978, 165–73): 171.
50. "Illegal Cigarette Sales," *CQA* 34 (1978): 177–78.
51. "Senate Judiciary Reports Criminal Code Bill," *CQA* 35 (1979, 363–69): 367.
52. Ibid.
53. Ibid., 368.
54. "Lottery Materials Shipments," *CQA* 35 (1979): 383.
55. Ronald R. Reagan, "Remarks Announcing Federal Initiatives Against Drug Trafficking and Organized Crime. October 14, 1982," in *PPPUS* (Washington, DC: US Government Printing Office, 1983, 1313–17), 1315.
56. Reagan, "Remarks in Miami, Florida, to Members of the South Florida Task Force and Members of Miami Citizens Against Crime. November 17, 1982," in *PPPUS* (Washington, DC: US Government Printing Office, 1983, 1488–91), 1490.
57. Reagan, "Remarks at an Event Sponsored by the American Legion Auxiliary. March 1, 1984," in *PPPUS* (Washington, DC: US Government Printing Office, 1985, 277–81), 279.
58. Reagan, "Message to the Congress on America's Agenda for the Future. February 6, 1986," in *PPPUS* (Washington, DC: US Government Printing Office, 1987, 149–63), 156.
59. Reagan, "Remarks in Miami, Florida," 1489.
60. Reagan, "Federal Initiatives Against Drug Trafficking," 1316.
61. Reagan, "Remarks in New Orleans, Louisiana, at the Annual Meeting of the International Association of Chiefs of Police. September 28, 1981," in *PPPUS* (Washington, DC: US Government Printing Office, 1982, 839–46), 842.
62. Reagan, "Radio Address to the Nation on Crime and Criminal Justice Reform. September 11, 1982," in *PPPUS* (Washington, DC: US Government Printing Office, 1983, 1136–38), 1137.
63. Reagan, "Federal Initiatives Against Drug Trafficking," 1315.
64. Ibid., 1315–16; Reagan, "Remarks on Establishing the President's Commission on Organized Crime. July 28, 1983," in *PPPUS* (Washington, DC: US Government Printing Office, 1984, 1092–94), 1093; Reagan, "Executive Order 12435: President's Commission on Organized Crime. July 28, 1983," in *PPPUS* (Washington, DC: US Government Printing Office, 1984), 1094–95.
65. Reagan, "Federal Initiatives Against Drug Trafficking," 1316; "Remarks in Miami, Florida," 1490.
66. "Panel OKs RICO Revision," *CQA* 44 (1988): 82–83.
67. "Indian Gambling," *CQA* 44 (1988): 622.
68. "Attempts to Limit RICO Fail Again," *CQA* 46 (1990): 536–38.
69. "Bill to Limit RICO Fails to Reach Floor," *CQA* 47 (1991): 292–93.
70. "Money-Laundering Bill Finally Gets Home," *CQA* 48 (1992): 121.
71. "Congress Puts a Limit on Sports-Based Lotteries," *CQA* 48 (1992): 219–20.
72. William J. Clinton, "Statement on Organized Crime in the United States and Italy. December 12, 1993" in *PPPUS* (Washington, DC: US Government Printing Office, 1994, 2155–56), 2155
73. Ibid.
74. Clinton, "Remarks on International Crime Control Strategy. May 12, 1998," in *PPPUS* (Washington, DC: US Government Printing Office, 1998), 741.
75. "Bill Facilitates Police Wiretapping." In *CQ Almanac, 1994*, 50th ed., 215–16. Washington, DC: Congressional Quarterly, 1995. http://library.cqpress.com/cqalmanac/cqa94-1103249.
76. "Other Legislation Related to the Legal System," *CQA* 51 (1995, 6-29–6-33): 6-31.

77. "Bills Affecting American Indians Taken Up by Lawmakers," *CQA* 51(1995): 7-55–7-66.
78. "Lawmakers Consider Other Bills Related to Law, Judiciary," *CQA* 52 (1996, 5-42–5-47): 5-44.
79. "Internet Gambling," *CQA* 53 (1997): 3-43.
80. "House Votes to Limit Online Gaming," *CQA* 59 (2003): 18-5–18-6.
81. "Internet Gambling Curbs Enacted," *CQA* 62 (2006): 16-16–16-17.

CHAPTER 14

1. "Bills to Restrict Obscene Matter," *Congressional Quarterly Almanac* 9 (1953): 324. *Congressional Quarterly Almanac* hereafter shortened to *CQA*.
2. "Juvenile Delinquency," *CQA* 9 (1953): 201–2.
3. "Bills to Restrict Obscene Matter," *CQA* 9 (1953): 324.
4. Richard M. Nixon, "Special Message to the Congress on Legislative Reform. October 13, 1969," in *Public Papers of the Presidents of the United States* (Washington, DC: US Government Printing Office, 1970, 788–96), 796. *Public Papers of the Presidents of the United States* hereafter shortened to *PPPUS*.
5. Nixon, "Special Message to the Congress on the Administration's Legislative Program. September 11, 1970," in *PPPUS* (Washington, DC: US Government Printing Office, 1971, 719–38), 729.
6. Nixon, "Special Message to the Congress Resubmitting Legislative Proposals. January 26, 1971," in *PPPUS* (Washington, DC: US Government Printing Office, 1972, 61–73), 65.
7. "Crime and Law Enforcement," *CQA* 25 (1969): 83–84.
8. "Crime and Law Enforcement," *CQA* 26 (1970): 77.
9. Ibid.
10. "Senate-Passed Criminal Code Dies in House," *CQA* 34 (1978, 165–75): 171.
11. "Child Pornography," *CQA* 33 (1977): 520–23.
12. "Senate Judiciary Reports Criminal Code Bill," *CQA* 35 (1979, 363–69): 368.
13. Ronald R. Reagan, "Remarks at the Annual Convention of the National Religious Broadcasters. January 30, 1984," in *PPPUS* (Washington, DC: US Government Printing Office, 1985, 117–21), 120.
14. "Child Pornography Bill," *CQA* 39 (1983): 318.
15. Jennifer A. Dlouhy, "Hatch Substitute Amendment to 'Virtual' Pornography Bill Pushes Constitutional Envelope," *Congressional Quarterly Weekly Report*, October 26, 2002, 2816. *Congressional Quarterly Weekly Report* hereafter shortened to *CQWR*.
16. Keith Perine, "AMBER Child Crimes Bill Clears, Propelled by News and Strategy," *CQWR*, April 12, 2003, 879–81.
17. Perine, "Bill Would Simplify Child Pornography Prosecutions," *CQWR*, September 29, 2008, 2613.

CHAPTER 15

1. "Wiretapping," *Congressional Quarterly Almanac* 17 (1961): 385–87. *Congressional Quarterly Almanac* shortened to *CQA*.
2. Ibid.
3. "Wiretapping," *CQA* 9 (1953): 309.
4. "Wiretapping," *CQA* 17 (1961): 385.
5. "Congress Enacts Five Anti-Crime Bills," *CQA* 17 (1961, 381–85): 368.
6. "Review of the Session," *CQA* 20 (1964, 76–78): 77.
7. "Major Anti-Crime Bills Approved as Violence Increases," *CQA* 24 (1968, 116–237): 118.
8. Ibid.
9. Ronald R. Reagan, "The President's News Conference of June 19. June 19, 1969," in *Public Papers of the Presidents of the United States* (Washington, DC: US Government Printing Office, 1970, 470–80), 475. *Public Papers of the Presidents of the United States* hereafter shortened to *PPPUS*.
10. "Electronic Eavesdropping," *CQA* 28 (1972, 241–42).
11. "Law Enforcement and Judiciary," *CQA* 32 (1976, 17–18): 18.
12. "Law Enforcement and Judiciary," *CQA* 32 (1976): 395–96.
13. Jimmy Carter, "Message to the Congress Reporting on Recommendations of the National Commission for the Review of Federal and State Laws. April 2, 1979," in *PPPUS* (Washington, DC: US Government Printing Office, 1980), 587–90.
14. "Law Enforcement/Judiciary," *CQA* 33 (1977, 26–28): 28; "Wiretapping Limits," *CQA* 33 (1977): 596–97.
15. Adam Berlow, "Law Enforcement/Judiciary," *CQA* 34 (1978): 163–64.

16. "Controls Tightened on Use of Wiretaps," *CQA* 34 (1978): 186–87.
17. "Senate-Passed Criminal Code Dies in House," *CQA* 34 (1978, 165–73): 172.
18. "House Bars Most Polygraph Tests for Workers," *CQA* 43 (1987): 675–76.
19. "Labor," *CQA* 44 (1988): 23–24.

CHAPTER 16

1. William J. Clinton, "Statement on Signing the Economic Espionage Act of 1996. October 11, 1996," in *Public Papers of the Presidents of the United States* (Washington, DC: US Government Printing Office, 1997, 1814–15), 1814. *Public Papers of the Presidents of the United States* hereafter shortened to *PPPUS*.
2. Clinton, "Remarks Announcing Steps to Make the Internet Family-Friendly. July 16, 1997," in *PPPUS* (Washington, DC: US Government Printing Office, 1998, 960–61), 960.
3. "Computer Fraud," *Congressional Quarterly Almanac* 35 (1979): 384. *Congressional Quarterly Almanac* hereafter shortened to *CQA*.
4. "Major Crime Package Cleared by Congress," *CQA* 40 (1984, 215–24): 215.
5. Ibid., 221.
6. "Computer Tampering," *CQA* 40 (1984): 498.
7. "Record Rentals/Copyrights," *CQA* 39 (1983): 313.
8. "Record Rentals Ban," *CQA* 44 (1988): 85.
9. "Copyright System Gets Overhaul," *CQA* 48 (1992): 227.
10. "Other Judiciary Measures Considered in 1992," *CQA* 48 (1992, 332–35): 333.
11. "Crime Bill Provisions," *CQA* 50 (1994, 287–94): 293.
12. "FOIA Enters the Electronic Age," *CQA* 52 (1996): 5-33–5-34.
13. "Other Legislation Aimed at Crime Prevention," *CQA* 52 (1996, 5-38–5-42): 5-42.
14. Ibid., 5–42.
15. "Patent Overhaul Sparks Lively Debate," *CQA* 53 (1997, 3-15–3-16): 3-15.
16. "Congress Clears Bill to Punish ID Theft," *CQA* 54 (1998): 17-16–17-17.
17. "Anti-Crime Package Seeks to Protect Women and Children from Violence," *CQA* 56 (2000): 15–19.
18. "Lawmakers Compromise on Sentencing Guidelines for Intellectual Property Theft," *CQA* 55 (1999): 18-59–18-60.
19. "Broadband Deregulation Blocked," *CQA* 58 (2002): 17-3–17-4.
20. "Congress Restricts Junk E-Mail," *CQA* 59 (2003): 18-6–18-8.
21. "Lawmakers Take Aim at ID Theft," *CQA* 60 (2004): 12-11–12-12.
22. "Bills to Halt Online Piracy Scrapped," *CQA* 69 (2004): 14-6–14-7.
23. "Electronic Privacy vs. 'Spyware,'" *CQA* 60 (2004): 14-9–14-10.
24. "'Spyware' Legislation Falters Again," *CQA* 61 (2005): 16-4–16-5.

INDEX

Abolishing Child Pornography Act, 181
Act for Better Child Care Services, 130
Administration for Children, Youth and Families, 131
Administrative Office of the U.S. Courts, 19
Adoption Opportunities Program, 130
After School Crime Prevention Program Grants, 123
Aimee's Law, 91, 123
aircraft hijacking, 42
air piracy, 155
Alcohol, Drug Abuse, and Mental Health Reorganization Act, 74
Alien Smuggling Prosecution Act, 175
Alternative Juvenile Justice Incarceration Act, 120
AMBER Alert plan, 135, 136, 137, 181
America After School Act, 123
American Bar Association (ABA), 21, 26
American Civil Liberties Union (ACLU), 29
American Indian reservations, 172, 173, 175
Amtrak, 16
Andean Counterdrug Initiative, 78
Anslinger, Harry, 164
Anti–Car Theft Act of 1992, 5
Anti–Drug Abuse Act of 1986, 67
Anti-Drug Enforcement Act of 1986, 67
Anti-Terrorism Act of 1974, 51
Appalachian, New York, 164
Arming Pilots Against Terrorism Act, 155
armored car guards, 151
Armored Car Industry Reciprocity Act, 153
arrest warrants, 24
Ashcroft v. The Free Speech Coalition, 137
Aviation Drug Trafficking Control Act, 67

bail, 19, 27, 30, 64, 104
Bailey v. United States, 153
Bail Reform Act Amendments, 21
Bail Reform Act of 1966, 20, 39

Balanced Juvenile Justice and Crime Prevention Act of 1997, 122
Ballistic Imaging Evaluation and Study Act, 156
barbituates, 65
Belk, George, 164
Bell, Griffin (attorney general), 25
Bennett, William J. (drug czar), 71, 72
boot camps, 47, 119, 121
Boy Scouts, 134
Brady, James, 150
Brady Bill II, 151
Brady Handgun Violence Prevention Act, 120, 124, 150, 151, 153, 155, 156
bribery, 165
Broadcast Decency Enforcement Act, 182
Brown Commission, 42
Bureau of Alcohol, Tobacco, Firearms and Explosives (BATF), 146, 154, 157
Bureau of Health Service (PHS), 39
Bureau of Justice Statistics, 139
Bureau of Narcotics. See U.S. Bureau of Narcotics
Bureau of Prisons (BOP). See U.S. Bureau of Prisons
Burger, Warren E. (chief justice), 22, 29
Bush, George H. W. (president), 31, 46, 47, 71–72, 73, 82, 87, 88, 93, 105, 150
Bush, George W. (president), 1, 14, 35, 36, 49, 78, 87, 91, 97, 108, 135–36, 138, 149–50, 155
Byrd, James, Jr., 98

California v. Cabazon Band of Mission Indians, 172
Campus Law Enforcement Emergency Response Act of 2007, 15
CAN-SPAM Act, 195
capital punishment, 7, 28, 32, 37–53, 40, 42, 43, 44, 45, 47, 48, 50, 52, 70, 75, 106, 147, 154
Capital Punishment Procedures Act, 47
Capitol police, 14, 15
Career Criminal Impact Program, 42

carjacking, 5
Carter, Jimmy (president), 43, 64, 65, 87, 147, 170, 178, 185
Child Abduction Prevention Act, 181
child abuse, 111, 129
Child Abuse Prevention and Treatment Act of 1973, 127
Child Abuse Prevention and Treatment Act of 1974, 130
Child and Family Development Act, 130
Child and Family Services and Improvement Act, 79
Child Obscenity and Pornography Prevention Act, 181
Child Pornography Prevention Act, 181
Child Protection Act of 1984, 128, 130
Child Protection and Obscenity Enforcement Act of 1987, 128, 130, 186
Children's Internet Protection Act, 194
Children's Safety Act, 97
Child Safety and Youth Violence Prevention Act, 123
child support, 131, 135
child victims, 127–40
Child Welfare Services Program, 79
cigarette bootlegging, 170–71
Citizens' Self-Defense Act, 159
Civil Remedies for Victims of Racketeering Activity and Theft Act, 169
Civil Rights of Institutionalized Persons Act, 43
Civil Service Commission, 38
Cleveland Local 555, 165
Clinton, William Jefferson (president), 1, 12–13, 32, 34, 47, 74–75, 82, 87, 88, 96, 106, 108, 119–20, 131–32, 134, 150–51, 153, 174, 191
cocaine, 52, 70, 75, 76, 79, 80
Colombia, 63, 77, 78
Columbine High School, 143, 154
Combat Meth Act of 2005, 79
Commission on Marijuana and Drug Abuse, 63
Commission on Violent Crime Against Women, 88
Committee on Juvenile Delinquency and Youth Crime, 115
Committee on Youth Employment, 114
Communications Act, 183
Communications Decency Act, 191, 194
Community Oriented Policing Services (COPS), 1, 2, 15
Comprehensive Crime Control Act of 1983, 27
Comprehensive Crime Control Act of 1989, 46, 149
Comprehensive Drug Abuse Prevention and Control Act of 1970, 61, 62, 63

Comprehensive Methamphetamine Control Act of 1996, 75
Comprehensive Omnibus Crime Bill, 73
Conference on Children and Youth, 139
Controlled Dangerous Substances Act, 61, 62
Controlled Substance Imports and Export Act, 70
Controlled Substances Act, 76
cop-killer bullets, 11, 12, 148, 156, 157
Cops on the Beat program, 12
Copyright Act of 1976, 192
Correctional Rehabilitation Study Act, 39
Court of Judicial Conduct and Disability, 26
courts, 17–36
Crime Control and Community Protection Act, 123
Crimes Against Minors Act, 132
Crime Victims' Fund, 104, 106, 129
Crime Victims' Week, 103, 105
Criminal Code Revision Act, 30
criminal forfeiture, 28, 64, 68, 77, 128, 179
Criminal Justice Act Amendments, 21
Criminal Justice Act of 1964, 22
Criminal Justice Reform Act, 28
Cyber Security Act, 197
Cyber Security Enhancement Act, 195

David Ray Ritcheson Hate Crimes Prevention Act, 98, 99
Deadly Driver Reduction and Buron H. Greene Memorial Act, 83
Death In Custody Reporting Act of 2009, 52
death penalty. *See* capital punishment
Defense Authorization Law of 2001, 78
Defense of Marriage Act, 36
Detectives Nemorin and Andrews Anti–Gun Trafficking Act, 156
Dial-a-Porn Prevention and Corrections Act, 180
Dispute Resolution Resource Center, 26
District of Columbia Court Reform and Criminal Procedure Act of 1970, 21
District of Columbia Gun Control Act, 144
District of Columbia v. H. Shawn Zeller, 157
District Youth Services Office, 115
DNA testing, 13, 51, 52, 138
Domestic Council, 64
domestic crime, 85, 87–93
domestic violence, 129, 130
drug abuse, 55, 57–84
Drug Abuse Control Amendments Bill, 58
Drug Abuse Monitoring Program, 69
Drug Abuse Office and Treatment Act of 1972, 61
Drug Abuse Prevention and Control Act of 1970
Drug Abuse Prevention Week, 62
Drug Abuse Resistance Education Act (DARE), 1
drug courts, 57

Drug Enforcement Agency (DEA), 11, 61, 63, 65, 66, 68, 75
Drug-Free America Act, 67, 69
Drug-Free Schools and Communities Act Amendments of 1989, 72
Drug Interdiction and International Cooperation Act of 1986, 67
Drug Kingpin Death Penalty Act, 75
Drug Sentencing Reform and Cocaine Kingpin Trafficking Act, 80
drunk driving, 5, 55, 81–84
Drunk Driving Repeat Offender Prevention Act, 84

Economic Espionage Act of 1996, 191
Effective Antiterrorism Tools for Law Enforcement Act, 187
Effective Child Pornography Prosecution Act, 138, 182
Eisenhower, Dwight (president), 18, 37, 57, 114, 164
Elder Abuse Victims Act, 109
Elderly Victims of Crime Act, 105
Elementary and Secondary Education Act Reauthorization, 96, 133
Emergency Detention Act of 1950, 41
Empowering Our Local Communities Act of 2007, 84
Enhanced Violent Crime Community Policing Act of 2009, 16
espionage, 43, 44, 45, 48, 184
exclusionary rule, 27, 28, 30, 31, 46
extortion, 165

Fair Sentencing Act of 2010, 80
Faith-Based Charities Bill, 124
faith-based initiatives, 50, 78, 135
Family-Friendly Internet Access Act, 194
Family Viewing Cable Television Act, 180, 181
Family Violence Prevention and Services Act, 91, 130
Federal Bail Reform Act, 19
Federal Bureau of Investigation (FBI), 3, 10, 11, 13, 20, 106, 128, 134, 154, 159, 164, 183, 186
Federal Communications Commission (FCC), 52, 135
Federal Courts Improvement Act, 34
Federal Courts Study Committee, 31
Federal Criminal Code, 23, 25, 27, 30, 42, 43, 102, 104, 105, 168, 170, 171, 178, 186, 195
Federal Diversion Act of 1979, 27
Federal Drug Treatment Bill, 76
Federal Firearms Act, 143, 144, 145, 166
Federal Indian Gaming Regulatory Commission, 175

federalization of crime, 2–6, 199
    implications of, 4–6
Federal Judicial Center, 19, 20, 31
Federal Prison Bureau Nonviolent Offender Relief Act, 2
Federal Prison Industries, 38, 51, 52, 147
Federal Trade Commission, 197
Federal Waging Statute, 167
Financial Crimes Prosecution and Recovery Act, 186
Firearm Commerce Modernization Act, 157
Firearms Corrections and Improvements Act, 157
Firearms Safety and Violence Prevention Act, 153
Firearms Violence Information Clearinghouse, 153
Fiscal 1985 Continuing Appropriations Resolution, 5
Foley, Edward, 164
Ford, Gerald (president), 23, 42, 63–64, 102, 103, 117, 146, 170
Foreign Intelligence Surveillance Act, 185
Freedom and Child Protection Act, 194
Freedom from Sexual Trafficking Act, 135
Freedom of Information Act (FOIA), 193
Fugitive Felon Act, 166
Furman v. Georgia, 43, 44

Gambino Crime Family, 167
gambling, 164, 165, 166, 167, 168, 169, 170, 172, 173, 174, 175, 195, 197
Gang Deterrence and Community Protection Act, 124
Gang Prevention, Intervention and Suppression Act, 125
Gang Prevention and Effective Deterrence Act, 124
genocide, 48
Goldwater, Barry, 4
good faith exception, 28, 31, 33
Gore, Al (senator), 127
Gore, Tipper, 127
grand jury, 26, 169
Graphic Postcard Act, 180, 181
Grokster, 196
Gun Buy Back Partnership Grant Act, 155
Gun Control Act of 1968, 144, 145, 147, 148
Gun Crime Reporting Act, 124
Gun-Free School Zones Amendments Act of 1995, 131
Gun Owners of America, 122

habeas corpus, 22, 28, 31, 32, 38, 41, 44, 45, 46, 47, 49
Hagerman, Amber, 136
halfway houses, 115

handguns, 46, 141, 143–59
Harris, Eric, 154
hate crimes, 85, 95–99, 124
Hate Crimes Against the Homeless Enforcement
 Act, 98
Hate Crimes Prevention Act, 97
Hate Crimes Prevention Week, 96
Hate Crimes Statistics Improvement Act, 97, 99
heroin, 60, 63, 64
Higher Education Act of 1965, 15
Hinckley, John, 29
Hoffa, Jimmy, 41, 165
Hoover, J. Edgar, 164
House Economic and Educational Opportunities
 Committee, 122
House Education and Labor Committee, 73
House Judiciary Committee, 29, 30, 32, 39, 103,
 113, 121, 122, 146, 150, 153, 174
House Judiciary Crime Subcommittee, 12
House Judiciary Subcommittee No. 3, 41
House Judiciary Subcommittee No. 5, 41
House Judiciary Subcommittee on Commercial
 and Administrative Law, 34
House Judiciary Subcommittee on Crime, 146
House Judiciary Subcommittee on Crime and
 Criminal Justice, 150
House Select Committee on Crime, 41, 63
human trafficking, 90, 135, 187
Hutcheson, Maurice, 165

identity theft, 196, 197
Identity Theft and Assumption Deterrence Act,
 194
immigration, 15
Immigration and Naturalization Service, 72
Incorporation Transparency and Law Enforcement
 Assistance Act, 15
Infant Abandonment Prevention Act, 139
insanity defense, 24, 28, 29, 30, 31
Institute for the Continuing Studies of Juvenile
 Justice, 116
Intercept Child Predators Act of 2007, 187
Interdepartmental Council on Juvenile
 Delinquency, 116
International Brotherhood of Teamsters Union,
 41, 65
International Development and Humanitarian
 Assistance Act of 1971, 60
International Megan's Law, 139
International Narcotics Control Board, 60
International Parental Kidnapping Crime Act of
 1993, 131
International Relations Committee, 77
International Security Assistance Act of 1971, 60
Internet, 135, 136, 154, 175, 177, 181, 188

Internet Crimes Against Children Task Forces, 135
Internet Equalization Bill, 145
Internet Gambling Regulation, Consumer
 Protection, and Enforcement Act, 197
Interstate Wire Act, 175
i-SAFE, 139

Jacob Wetterling, Megan Kanka, and Pam Lychner
 Sex Offender Registration and Notification
 Act, 138
Johnson, Lyndon B. (president), 4, 9–10, 19–20,
 21, 38–39, 58–59, 95, 115, 143, 144, 145,
 166–67
Judicial Conference of the United States, 18, 22,
 24, 27
judicial council, 18
Judicial Improvements Act of 1990, 32
jury tampering, 32
Juvenile Crime Control Act, 120
Juvenile Crime Control and Delinquency
 Prevention Act, 123
Juvenile Crime Reduction Act, 125
Juvenile Delinquency and Youth Offenses Control
 Act of 1961, 114, 115, 116
Juvenile Delinquency Prevention Act, 115
Juvenile Delinquency Prevention and Control Act
 Amendments of 1972, 117
Juvenile Delinquency Prevention and Control Act
 of 1967, 116
Juvenile Delinquency Prevention and Control Act
 of 1968, 116, 117
Juvenile Delinquency Prevention Block Grant
 Program, 123
Juvenile Justice and Delinquency Prevention Act
 of 1974, 117, 118
Juvenile Justice and Delinquency Prevention Act
 of 1988, 119
juvenile offenders, 6, 111, 113–25, 144, 155
 and guns, 151, 154

Kagan, Elena (Supreme Court justice), 36
Kanka, Megan, 134
Keeping Children and Families Safe Act of 2003,
 91, 136, 138
Keeping the Internet Devoid of Sexual Predators
 Act, 139, 197
Kefauver, Estes (senator), 163, 164
Kefauver hearings, 163
Kennedy, John F. (president), 19, 58, 114, 143–
 44, 165
 assassination of, 143
Kennedy, Robert, 165, 184
Kenya, 108
kidnapping, 42, 44, 48, 169, 184
 of children, 132

King, Rodney, 12
Klebold, Dylan, 154
Knowland, William (senator), 17

Laci and Conner's Law, 91
Law Enforcement, 9–16
Law Enforcement Assistance Administration
    (LEAA), 4, 9, 10, 11, 41
Law Enforcement Officer's Procedural Bill of
    Rights Act of 2009, 16
Law Enforcement Officer's Safety Improvement
    Act, 16, 155
Leach-LaFalce Internet Gambling Enforcement
    Act, 195
Legal Aid Agency, 21
Legal Services Corporation (LSC), 21, 25, 28,
    32, 34
Legislative Branch Appropriations Bill, 14
Lesbian, Gay, Bisexual, and Transgender Pride
    Month, 98
Lewisburg Federal Penitentiary, 41
Library of Congress police, 15
Licavoli, Peter, 165
loan-sharking, 170
Local Government Law Enforcement Block
    Grants Act, 14
Local Law Enforcement Enhancement Act of
    2005, 15
Local Law Enforcement Hate Crimes Prevention
    Act, 97
LSD, 58

Malaysia, 66
Mallory, Andrew, 37
Mallory Rule, 37
Mallory v. United States, 37, 38
mandatory sentences, 23, 33, 60, 61, 64, 70, 79,
    95, 121, 124, 138, 148, 149, 151, 153, 154,
    157
Mann Act, 199
Manpower Training Act, 39
marijuana, 65
Marion Malley Walsh Drunk Driving Act, 83
Matsch, Richard (U.S. district judge), 107
Matthew Shepard Local Law Enforcement Hate
    Crimes Prevention Act, 97, 98
McCarthy, Carolyn (representative), 155
McClellan, John (senator), 164
McClellan Committee, 164
McVeigh, Timothy, 50
media and violence, 120, 127, 154
Megan's Law, 85, 134
Mental Health and Substance Abuse Juvenile
    Services Improvement Act of 2007, 125
merit selection of judges, 25

methamphetamines, 51, 76, 77, 79
Mexico, 63, 66, 74, 77, 78, 80
Military Domestic and Sexual Violence Response
    Act, 92
Missing Alzheimer's Disease Alert Program, 106
missing children, 128, 129
Missing Children's Act, 128
Missing Children's Assistance Act, 119
money laundering, 33, 77, 170, 173, 174
Mothers Against Drunk Driving (MADD), 81, 82
motor vehicle theft, 5

Narcotic Addict Rehabilitation Act of 1966, 58,
    60
National Academy of Sciences, 156
National Academy of the FBI, 10
National Center for Missing and Exploited
    Children, 132–33
National Center for the State Courts, 22
National Child Abuse Prevention Month, 139
National Child Protection Act of 1993, 131
National Clearinghouse for Drug Abuse
    Information and Education, 59
National Commission on Reform of Federal
    Criminal Laws, 168
National Commission on Violent Crime, 88
National Council on Organized Crime, 168
National Court of Appeals, 24
National Crime Commission, 165
National Crime Victims Week, 109
National DARE Day, 80
National Defense Education Act, 10
National Diffusion Network, 73
National Domestic Violence Awareness Month,
    92
National Driver Registry, 83
National Drug Abuse Education Proclamation, 67
National Drug Abuse Training Center, 61
National Drug Control Strategy of 1989, 71
National Drug Policy Board, 67
National Drunk and Drugged Driving Awareness
    Week, 81
National Drunk Driving Standard Legislation, 82
National Firearms Act, 143
National Gambling Impact and Policy
    Commission, 174
National Highway Traffic Safety Administration,
    84
National Instant Criminal Background Check
    System, 158
National Institute for Juvenile Justice and
    Delinquency, 122
National Institute on Drug Abuse (NIDA), 61,
    64, 65, 78
National Minimum Drinking Age Bill, 81

National Narcotics Border Interdiction System, 66
National Organization for the Reform of Marijuana Laws (NORML), 65
National Pornography Victims Awareness Week, 180
National Prison Rape Reduction Commission, 50
National Research Council, 156
National Rifle Association (NRA), 152, 156
National Right-to-Carry Reciprocity Act, 159
National School Safety Center, 128
National Sex Offender Registry, 138
National Sexual Assault Awareness Month, 109
National Wiretap Commission, 185
National Youth Antidrug Media Campaign, 75
Nationwide Gun Buyback Act, 156
neglected children, 127
New York City Youth Board, 113
Ninth Circuit Court of Appeals, 35
Nixon, Richard M. (president), 10–11, 21–22, 40, 59–62, 65, 101, 116, 145, 146, 167–68, 177–78, 184
No Frills Prison Act, 49
No Guns for Violent Perpetrators Act, 155
no-knock searches, 63
Noose Hate Crime Act of 2009, 99

Obama, Barack (president), 2, 15–16, 36, 52, 79–80, 92, 98, 109, 139
Office for Drug Abuse Law Enforcement, 61
Office for the Protection of Victims of Trafficking, 135
Office of Cyberspace Policy, 198
Office of Justice Assistance, Research, and Statistics (OJARS), 118
Office of Juvenile Justice and Delinquency Prevention (OJJDP), 118, 119, 120, 122, 123, 125
Office of Management and Budget, 69
Office of National Drug Control Policy, 76, 77
Office of United States Magistrates, 20
Office of Victims' Advocate, 92
off-track betting, 170, 174
Ohio Conference of Teamsters, 165
Oklahoma City bombing, 50, 107, 108
Older Americans Act, 124
Olmstead v. United States, 183
Omnibus 1994 Crime Bill, 106, 121
Omnibus Anti-Drug Bill, 45, 119
Omnibus Appropriations Bill of 1996, 13
Omnibus Budget Reconciliation Act of 1990, 130
Omnibus Crime Control and Safe Streets Act of 1968, 41, 82, 145
Omnibus Trade and Competitiveness Act, 179
Online Personal Privacy Act, 195

organized crime, 2, 6, 19, 66, 128, 143, 161, 163–76
Organized Crime Control Act, 168
Organized Retail Crime Act, 176

Parental Choice in Television Act, 180
Peace Officers' Memorial, 15
Pell Grants, 48
Plastic Gun Law, 156
plea bargaining, 23, 24, 155
police brutality, 7, 10
Police Cadet Corps, 10, 12
pornography, 6, 161, 163–76, 177–82
    involving children, 28, 111, 128, 129, 130, 132, 133, 135, 136, 137, 138, 181, 187
Pornography Forfeiture Proceedings Venue Act, 179
Pornography Victims' Compensation Act, 105, 180
Pornography Victims Protection Act, 179, 180
Postal Reorganization Act, 178
Powder-Crack Cocaine Penalty Equalization Act of 2009, 80
Powell, Lewis, Jr. (Supreme Court justice), 45
predatory crimes, 23
Pregnant Women Support Act, 92
Presidential Commission on Drunk Driving, 81
President's Advisory Commission on Narcotic and Drug Abuse, 58
President's Crime Commission, 168
President's Drug Advisory Council, 72
Presser, William, 165
pretrial discovery, 24
pretrial release, 25
pretrial services, 29
Prevent All Cigarette Trafficking Act (PACT Act), 176
Prisoner Rehabilitation Act, 38
prison industries. See Federal Prison Industries
Prison Industries Improvement Act, 45
Prison Rape Elimination Act, 50
prison riots, 41
prisons, 37–53
Prohibition of Transportation of Salacious Advertising Act, 177
Project Child Safe, 135
Project Exile Safe Streets and Neighborhoods Act, 124, 154
Project Safe Neighborhoods, 155
Promoting Safe and Stable Families Program, 79
Prosecutorial Remedies and Other Tools to End the Exploitation of Children Today Act of 2003 (PROTECT Act), 136
prostitution, 165
Protection Act, 15

Protection Against Scams on Seniors Act, 195
Protection of Lawful Commerce in Arms Act,
    156, 157
Protection of Minors from Obscenity Act, 177
PROTECT Our Children Act, 139
Providing Reliable Officers, Technology,
    Education, Community Prosecutors, and
    Training in Our Neighborhoods Act, 15
Public Awareness and Private Sector Initiatives Act
    of 1986, 67
Public Corruption Prosecution Improvements
    Act, 188
Public Health Service, 39

Quality Child Care Demonstration Act, 131

Racial Profiling Prohibition Act, 14
Racketeer Influenced and Corrupt Organizations
    Act (RICO), 130, 168–69, 172, 173, 174,
    175
racketeering, 45
Reagan, Ronald W. (president), 11, 27–28, 29,
    31, 44, 45, 65–68, 72, 81, 103, 105, 127,
    128, 147, 148, 171–72, 179, 186
    assassination attempt, 150
Remove Intoxicated Drivers (RID), 82
Research of Alcohol Detection Systems for
    Stopping Alcohol-Related Fatalities
    Everywhere Act (ROADS SAFE Act), 84
Respecting States Rights and Concealed Carry
    Reciprocity Act, 159
Restitution Amendments Act, 104
Roberts, John (chief justice), 36
Role Models Academy, 122
Rosenthal, Lynn, 92
Runaway and Homeless Youth Act of 1974, 118,
    119
Runaway Youth Act, 117

Safe and Secure America Act, 188
Safe and Sober Streets Act, 83
Safe Housing Identity Exception for the Lives of
    Domestic Violence Victims Act, 91–92
Safe Prisons Communications Act, 52
safe schools initiative, 131
Safe Streets Act, 9, 184
Saturday Night Specials, 146, 147, 149, 155
Save the Children Act, 131
school violence, 133
Scott Campbell, Stephanie Roper, Wendy Preston,
    Louarna Gillis, and Nila Lynn Crime
    Victims' Rights Act, 109
Second Amendment Enforcement Act, 157
Second Amendment Protection Act of 1997, 153,
    155, 156

Security and Freedom Ensured Act (SAFE Act),
    187
Select Committee to Study Current Pornographic
    Materials, 177
Senate Criminal Justice Subcommittee, 191
Senate Judiciary Committee, 17, 24, 29, 35, 44,
    45, 49, 88, 102, 103, 107, 108, 122, 138,
    147, 164, 172, 175, 184, 193
Senate Judiciary Committee on Constitutional
    Rights, 22
Senate Judiciary Courts Subcommittee, 29
Senate Judiciary Juvenile Delinquency
    Subcommittee, 116
Senate Judiciary Subcommittee on Administrative
    Practice and Procedure, 185
Senate Judiciary Subcommittee on Criminal Laws
    and Procedures, 40
Senate Judiciary Subcommittee on Internal
    Security, 11
Senate Judiciary Subcommittee on National
    Penitentiaries, 41, 117
Senate Judiciary Subcommittee on Penitentiaries,
    41
Senate Judiciary Subcommittee to Investigate
    Juvenile Delinquency, 113
Senate Labor and Human Resources Committee,
    133
Senate Operations Permanent Investigations
    Subcommittee, 167
Senate Select Committee on Improper Activities
    in the Labor or Management Field, 164
Senate Select Committee on Intelligence
    Operations, 185
Senate Special Committee to Investigate
    Organized Crime in Interstate Commerce,
    164
Senate Special Crime Investigating Committee,
    163
sentencing, 23, 28, 30
Sentencing Act of 1987, 28
sentencing guidelines, 33
Sentencing Guidelines Act of 1986, 28
Sentencing Reform Act of 1984, 28
Sex Offender Registry, 138
sex tourism, 137
Sex Trafficking Act, 90
sexual predators, 91, 132, 136
Single Convention on Narcotic Drugs, 60
Siragusa, Charles, 164
Sjodin, Dru, 138
Social Security Administration, 49
Sotomayor, Sonia (Supreme Court justice), 36
Special Action Office of Drug Abuse Prevention,
    61
Special Council on Narcotics Control, 66

Speedy Trial Act of 1971, 22
Speedy Trial Act of 1974, 29
sports bribery/betting, 169, 174
stalking, 90
State Justice Institute, 31, 130
Stockton, California, 149
Stop AIDS in Prison Act, 53
Stop Material Unsuitable for Teens Act, 181
Stop Trafficking of Pornography in Prisons Act, 181
Streamcast Networks Inc., 196
Study of the Effect of Marijuana on Human Sexual Response, 64
Substance Abuse Services Amendments of 1986, 67

Taking Back Our Streets Act, 107
Tanzania, 108
Task Force on the Victims of Crime, 103
Tax Reform Act, 172
Teen Dating Violence Prevention Act, 92
telemarketing fraud, 106
television ratings, 134, 180
Thailand, 66
three-strikes provision, 32, 33, 48
treason, 43, 44, 48, 184
Truman, Harry S. (president), 9, 17, 57, 81, 113, 163
Turkey, 63

Unborn Victims of Violence Act, 91
underworld crime. *See* organized crime
Uniform Crime Reports, 2
United Brotherhood of Carpenters and Jointers of America, 165
United States v. Morrisson, 90
United States v. Shaefer, 182
Urban Terrorism Prevention Act, 11
USA Patriot Act, 14, 187, 188
U.S. Board of Parole, 42
U.S. Border Patrol, 75
U.S. Bureau of Drug Abuse Control
U.S. Bureau of Narcotics, 59, 164
U.S. Bureau of Narcotics and Dangerous Drugs, 59, 61
U.S. Bureau of Prisons, 39, 42, 46, 49, 52, 53, 65
U.S. Coast Guard, 65, 68, 72
U.S. Customs Service, 72
U.S. Department of Agriculture, 62
U.S. Department of Commerce, 113
U.S. Department of Defense, 52, 71, 72, 92, 186
U.S. Department of Energy, 186
U.S. Department of Health, Education, and Welfare, 39, 59, 60, 61, 114, 117

U.S. Department of Health and Human Services, 72, 131
U.S. Department of Justice, 1, 5, 12, 21, 26, 36, 38, 40, 42, 48, 58, 59, 61, 66, 68, 70, 75, 79, 92, 95, 106, 108, 117, 119, 120, 128, 135, 147, 157, 165, 166, 167, 168, 174, 176, 179
U.S. Department of Transportation, 5, 14, 82
U.S. Department of Treasury, 59, 61, 68, 104, 119, 144, 147, 149, 151, 197
U.S. Parole Commission, 42
U.S. Probation Service, 65
U.S. Sentencing Commission, 27, 33, 75, 76, 80, 96, 97, 106, 107, 132, 133

Valachi, Joseph, 167
V-chip, 191
Victim and Witness Protection Act of 1982, 103
Victims Justice Act, 107
victims of crime, 85, 101–9
Victims of Crime Act of 1977, 102
Victims of Crime Amendments Act, 105
Victims of Handgun Crimes Compensation Tax Act, 104, 105
Victims of Handgun Crimes Trust Fund, 104, 105
Victims' Rights Clarification Act of 1997, 106
Victims' Rights Constitutional Amendment, 106
Violence Against Women Act, 88, 89, 90, 92, 135
Violent Crime Control and Law Enforcement Act of 1994, 1
Vocational Rehabilitation Act, 39

Wagering Tax Act, 168
Wagering Tax Amendment, 168
Web Video Violence Act, 197
White House Conference for a Drug Free America, 68
White House Conference on Narcotics, 58
wiretaps, 6, 129, 137, 161, 165, 167, 174, 175, 181, 183–88
witness immunity, 167, 168, 169, 184
Witness Security and Protection Grant Program, 176
witness tampering, 32

Youth Conservation Corps, 114
Youth Crime Deterrence Act of 2007, 125
Youth Handgun Ban, 151
youth rehabilitation centers, 115

Zero Tolerance, 72